THE X FILES™

LITTLE GREEN MEN - MONSTERS AND VILLAINS VOLUME 2

WWW.TITAN-COMICS.COM

THE X FILES

INTRODUCTION

MULDER: "WHEN CONVENTION AND SCIENCE OFFER US NO ANSWERS, MIGHT WE NOT FINALLY TURN TO THE FANTASTIC AS A PLAUSIBILITY?"

SCULLY: "WHAT I FIND FANTASTIC IS THAT THERE ARE ANY ANSWERS BEYOND THE REALM OF SCIENCE. THE ANSWERS ARE THERE. YOU JUST HAVE TO KNOW WHERE TO LOOK."

Although mythology-rich and steeped in the idea of conspiracy, The X-Files was always about the unexplained - and the pursuit of the truth to make the unexplainable, well... explainable. While extraterrestrials and conspiracy remained the backbone of the show, some of the most memorable episodes centered around the paranormal, unexplained phenomena, and monsters - both human and non-human. Mulder and Scully's investigations shone a light into the terrifying and the macabre, from the darkest reaches of human depravity to genetic mutations, from the fantastical to the brutally believable.

Over the course of their investigations, the two agents encountered a horde of ghouls, from vampires and ghosts to death fetishists; the psychically-gifted to time-travelers; AI gone wrong to real-life monsters and, of course, the extraterrestrial, to name just a few.

In this special collection, The Official X-Files Magazine pays homage to the monsters (both human or otherwise), villains and theories that kept fans entertained over the years. From the bizarre to the creepy, the kooky to the down-right chilling, it's time to come out from behind the sofa and step into the world of the unexplained once again...

The X-Files
The Official Collection
Volume Two
ISBN: 9781782763727

Published by Titan
A division of Titan Publishing Group Ltd.,
144 Southwark Street,
London SE1 0UP.

Collecting material previously published in the Official X-Files Magazine 1993-2002.

A CIP catalogue record for this title is available from the British Library.

First Edition March 2016
10 9 8 7 6 5 4 3 2 1

Printed in China.
Titan.

Editor
Natalie Clubb

Senior Designers
Rob Farmer, Andrew Leung

Senior Executive Editor
Divinia Fleary

Contributing Editor
Martin Eden

Art Director
Oz Browne

Acting Studio Manager
Selina Juneja

Publishing Manager
Darryl Tothill

Publishing Director
Chris Teather

Operations Director
Leigh Baulch

Executive Director
Vivian Cheung

Publisher
Nick Landau

ACKNOWLEDGMENTS

Titan Would Like to Thank...

The cast and crew of *The X-Files* for giving up their time to be interviewed, and Josh Izzo and Nicole Spiegel at Fox for all their help in putting this volume together.

CONTENTS

MONSTERS & VILLAINS

CONT

24

86

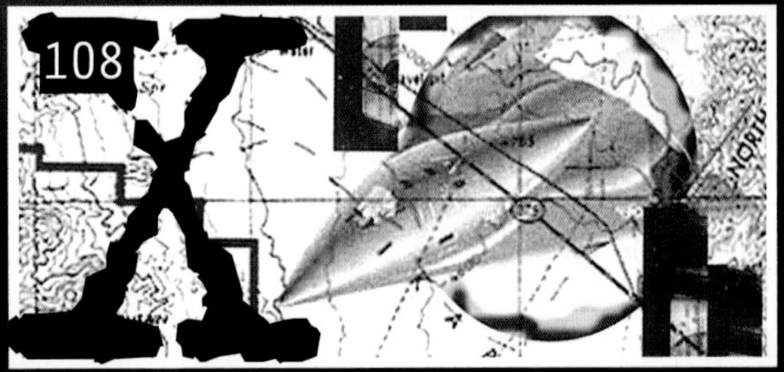

108

ENTS

112

169

THE X FILES

BAD

BLOOD

Who'd be an FBI agent? If you're not trying to uncover government conspiracies or chasing UFOs, you're being faced with some of the world's deadliest, most powerful villains. **Werewolves, vampires, mutant sewer monsters...** even **evil tattoos Mulder, Scully, Doggett and Reyes** have had their fair share of nasty foes. Kate Anderson has taken a look back over the past eight and a half years of the show to pick out the very worst of the worst. Prepare yourselves, readers, for...

THE X-FILES' TOP 20 VILLAINS!

20 THE "EVE" GIRLS

FIRST APPEARANCE: "Eve"
BACKGROUND: Identical eight-year-old girls, Teena Simmons and Cindy Reardon, were born as a result of a top secret program – once run by the government – in which a group of genetically-controlled children were raised and monitored. But they are far from being as sweet and innocent as they look.
MOST DASTARDLY DEED: Murdering both their fathers.
OTHER DASTARDLY DEEDS: Poisoning an adult Eve and trying to do the same to Mulder and Scully, by spiking their drinks.
SOUNDBITE: "We didn't do anything wrong. We're just little girls."
Where are they now? In a mental institution. Hopefully.

ANALYSIS
POWERFULNESS: 5
RUTHLESSNESS: 6
SCARINESS: 3
CRAFTINESS: 8
OVERALL VILLAIN RATING: 5

19 GERRY SCHNAUZ

FIRST APPEARANCE: "Unruhe"
BACKGROUND: A formerly institutionalized paranoid schizophrenic, Gerry Schnauz is a psychotic killer. He kidnaps young women and leaves them for dead by giving them a primitive botched lobotomy with an ice pick inserted through their eyes! He claims to be trying to rid his victims of the unrest he believes torments them.
MOST DASTARDLY DEED: Lobotomizing his victims!
OTHER DASTARDLY DEEDS: Murdering a prison guard; attacking his father, (leaving him wheelchair-bound); trying to lobotomize Scully.
SOUNDBITE: "It was the howlers."
Where is he now? Deceased – shot dead by Agent Mulder.

ANALYSIS
POWERFULNESS: 6
RUTHLESSNESS: 6
SCARINESS: 6
CRAFTINESS: 6
OVERALL VILLAIN RATING: 6

18 THE PEACOCK BROTHERS

FIRST APPEARANCE: "Home"
BACKGROUND: The ultra-creepy Peacock brothers live in a rundown property in the rural community of Home, Pennsylvania. But this freakish family has a gruesome secret – they've been breeding their own stock – and we're not talking farmyard animals either.
MOST DASTARDLY DEED: In-breeding with their own mother!
OTHER DASTARDLY DEEDS: Brutally murdering the local sheriff and his wife; burying a new-born baby alive.
SOUNDBITE: "Mother!"
Where are they now? Two brothers, deceased. The whereabouts of the eldest brother is unknown. He was last seen fleeing with their mother in the family's huge white Cadillac.

ANALYSIS
POWERFULNESS: 7
RUTHLESSNESS: 7
SCARINESS: 9
CRAFTINESS: 7
OVERALL VILLAIN RATING: 7

EACH VILLAIN GETS HIS/HER/ITS OWN EVIL-RATING, COMPRISING OF FOUR GENERAL CATEGORIES (POWERFULNESS, RUTHLESSNESS, SCARINESS AND CRAFTINESS) AS WELL AS A FINAL OVERALL RATING WHICH TAKES THESE FACTORS INTO ACCOUNT AND ALSO CONSIDERS THEIR IMPACT ON THE SHOW AND THE VIEWERS.

17 DR FRANKLYN

FIRST APPEARANCE: "Sanguinarium"
BACKGROUND: Dr Franklyn is a successful and respected plastic surgeon whose clinic is plagued by a series of mysterious deaths during routine surgery. But it's not human error - more like human sacrifice. Franklyn is a black magician; cursed with the sin of vanity, he uses human sacrifice and sorcery in order to transform his looks beyond the limits of surgery.
MOST DASTARDLY DEED:
Killing patients for the sake of his own vanity!
OTHER DASTARDLY DEEDS:
Murdering Nurse Waite by putting a hex curse on her.
Where are they now? Probably practising at another unsuspecting cosmetic surgery clinic, albeit with a completely new face.

ANALYSIS
POWERFULNESS: 7
RUTHLESSNESS: 8
SCARINESS: 6
CRAFTINESS: 7
OVERALL VILLAIN RATING: 7

Not that bad...?

The X-Files is littered with characters whose motives are anything but clear. And they don't come any more ambiguous than...

Marita Covarrubias

Marita initially proved to be a valuable ally to Mulder. However, her motives became dubious when she was revealed to be in league with Alex Krycek. She was infected with the black oil as part of the Syndicate's project to develop an alien vaccine. But she gets her revenge on the Cigarette-Smoking Man, assisting Krycek to push him down a flight of stairs.

Diana Fowley

Mulder's founding partner on *The X-Files*, and a former flame. Diana tried to worm her way back into Mulder's confidence – and his affections. But he eventually discovered that she had her own agenda – working for the Cigarette-Smoking Man. However, she did give her life to save Mulder's.

The Well-Manicured Man

Even more powerful than the Cigarette-Smoking Man, the Well-Manicured man will stop at nothing to protect his secrets. Ruthless, manipulative but also charming, he fears nothing or no one – only the truth. But in the end he sacrificed his own life to provide Mulder with the vaccine against the alien virus to save Scully.

Deputy Director Alvin Kersh

Always a thorn in Mulder and Scully's side, Kersh is the newly appointed Deputy Director of the FBI. He will do anything to save face for the bureau. Where his true motives lie – and who's pulling his strings – only time will tell. But he may have allegiances to those who want to hide the truth – at any cost.

Shannon McMahon

There's more to the mysterious Justice Department employee than meets the eye – much, much more. An invincible 'super soldier' engineered by the government, McMahon clams to want to expose the men who created her. A trained killer, and clearly extremely dangerous, it remains unclear as to whether she can be trusted. Though she did save Agent Doggett's life when Knowle Rohrer – another super soldier – tried to kill him.

16 THE TATTOO

FIRST APPEARANCE: **"Never Again"**
BACKGROUND: A Betty Page-like tattoo with a mind of its own! But divorcee Ed Jerse soon begins to regret getting the tattoo when it starts taunting him and trying to control him, slowly driving him insane.
MOST DASTARDLY DEED: Causing Ed to murder his neighbor in a fit of rage.
OTHER DASTARDLY DEEDS: Drives Ed to attack Scully.
SOUNDBITE: "You'd break my heart over a cheap redhead?"
Where is it now? Burnt off when Ed plunged his arm into an incinerator.

ANALYSIS
POWERFULNESS: 7
RUTHLESSNESS: 9
SCARINESS: 3
CRAFTINESS: 8
OVERALL VILLAIN RATING: 7

15 LUTHER LEE BOGGS

FIRST APPEARANCE: **"Beyond the Sea"**
BACKGROUND: A death row inmate, Boggs claims he is capable of channeling with the spirit world. He tries to use his psychic ability to get a reprieve from death row by helping Mulder and Scully find a serial killer.
MOST DASTARDLY DEED: Strangled five members of his family during Thanksgiving dinner.
OTHER DASTARDLY DEEDS: Slaughtering pet animals and manipulating an already vulnerable Agent Scully by claiming that he has a message for her from her recently deceased father.
SOUNDBITE: (singing) "Somewhere... beyond the sea..."
Where is he now? Deceased. Needless to say Boggs didn't get his reprieve.

ANALYSIS
POWERFULNESS: 6
RUTHLESSNESS: 7
SCARINESS: 8
CRAFTINESS: 7
OVERALL VILLAIN RATING: 7

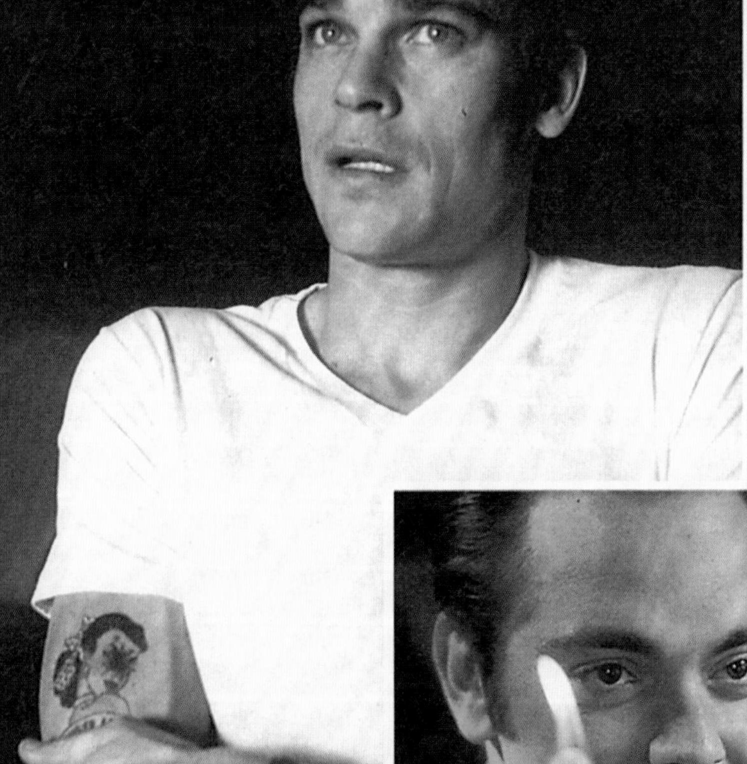

14 CECIL L'IVELY

FIRST APPEARANCE: **"Fire"**
BACKGROUND: Cecil L'ively uses his pyrokinetic powers – the ability to conduct and control fire – to kill a number of British aristocrats. When his latest victim flees to America, he relentlessly pursues him, resuming the role of the family's caretaker in order to get closer and finish the job.
MOST DASTARDLY DEED: Murdering members of the British aristocracy by causing them to burst into flames.
OTHER DASTARDLY DEEDS: Killing the caretaker.
SOUNDBITE: "Care for a light?"
Where is he now? Behind bars, following his close encounter with accelerant, which prevented his escape by causing him to burst into flames.

ANALYSIS
POWERFULNESS: 8
RUTHLESSNESS: 8
SCARINESS: 8
CRAFTINESS: 8
OVERALL VILLAIN RATING: 8

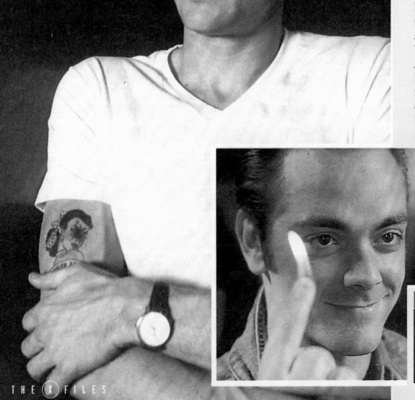

13 BILLY MILES

FIRST APPEARANCE: **Pilot**
BACKGROUND: Alien abductee Billy Miles, missing and presumed dead, suddenly reappears. But he's now an alien, with super strength, capable of slicing people's heads off and penetrating metal with his bare hands! Billy is a human replacement – a new kind of alien created to repopulate the earth. And he's unstoppable.
MOST DASTARDLY DEED: Beheading Dr Parenti and putting his head into a specimen jar!
OTHER DASTARDLY DEEDS: More beheadings; slicing into Skinner's head and ruthlessly pursuing Scully and her unborn baby.
Where is he now? Unknown.

ANALYSIS
POWERFULNESS: 9
RUTHLESSNESS: 8
SCARINESS: 8
CRAFTINESS: 8
OVERALL VILLAIN RATING: 8

KILLER BILL

When actor Zachary Ansley reprised his X-Files role of Billy Miles in Season Seven, it soon became an altogether different, deadlier kind of role. Ian Spelling caught up with the actor.

THE X-FILES MAGAZINE: After so many years, how did "Requiem" come about?
ANSLEY: At the end of Season Seven they were bringing David Duchovny's stories full-circle. Since I was the first case that Mulder and Scully ever worked on together, Chris Carter and the writers thought it was a good idea to bring the Billy Miles character back and open up that storyline again. It was really cool. This business is so crazy. You face rejection all the time and you feel really fortunate whenever you get a chance to work. You never expect someone to call years later and ask you to come back and play a small role you'd played years earlier. I was delighted to get the call.

What do you remember about being on an *X-Files* set again for "Requiem"?
Well, first the show was now being shot in Los Angeles and not Vancouver. Also, my first day was in Big Bear, up in the mountains about two hours outside Los Angeles. We shot my scenes for the pilot on location, too. A few of the same people – David, Gillian, Chris and, I think, a makeup person – were still with the production. They welcomed me back and it really didn't seem that strange after that first day. By day two I was right back into it again. And, actually, there were a couple of other actors there who were in the pilot. Sarah (Koskoff) was back as Theresa and Leon Russom played my dad (Detective Miles) again. Leon had played my camp counselor in an episode of *21 Jump Street* about a year before we did *The X-Files* pilot. It was great to see him and make that connection again.

How did your other subsequent appearances come about?
There was talk after "Requiem" that maybe Billy Miles might make another appearance. I got a call that summer saying they might want me, but he didn't show up until later in the season. That's when I did "DeadAlive." Billy had been a longtime abductee again and was coming back, and the story unfolded from there. The storyline kept evolving.

Do you think you've played Billy Miles for the last time?
I don't know. They've really given me no hints. There was talk that he'd come back during the ninth season, but Chris hasn't tipped his hand. If I get back, I'll be delighted and if I don't, I had a great time on the show, was proud to be a part of it, and the character was much fuller than I'd ever expected. No complaints. If I do any more it would just be another bonus.

What else have you been up to lately?
My episode of *UC: Undercover* aired in October. I just played Mercutio in a production of *Romeo & Juliet*. I got a few days in a TV movie called *Dead in a Heartbeat*, which just aired (on TNT). I'm still in Canada. As an actor here I'm more of a bigger fish in a smaller pond, which I like. It all works out in the end. It goes in streaks. You can't get too excited by the great things or too defeated by the bad things. I'm just trying to keep a healthy balance about it all.

Not 2shy

Joe Nazzaro chews the fat with actor Timothy Carhart, the man who portrayed the deadly Virgil Incanto in "2Shy".

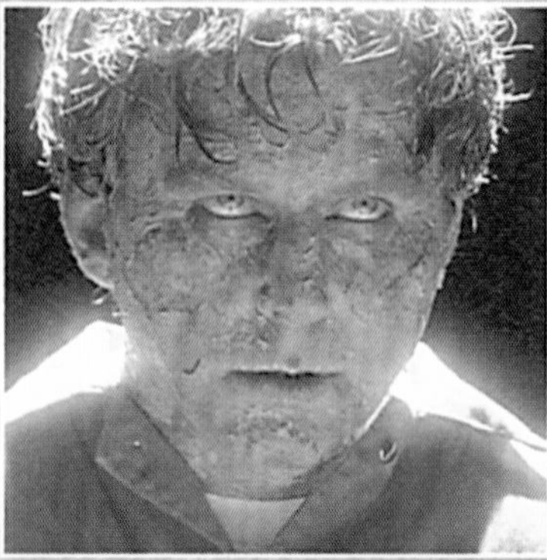

The *X-Files* has had its share of unforgettable monsters, but one of the more notorious creations has got to be Virgil Incanto. Incanto was played by actor Timothy Carhart, whose villainous credentials had been established after playing Harlan the rapist in *Thelma and Louise.* "From that point onwards," Carhart recalls, "I was offered a lot of very dark characters, and I guess *The X-Files* was just an extension of that."

Unlike many larger-than-life *X-Files* villains, Incanto remains a mystery. Much of the character's mystique is due to the fact that little is revealed about him during the episode. "He's a loner," claims Carhart, "and you only see about five percent of what's going on with him. He doesn't give much away, and that's how it came off the page when I read it. A great acting teacher once said, 'Leave something back. Don't give the audience 100 percent. Let them guess a little bit,' because it adds a bit of mystery and pulls them in and makes them look a little closer, so I deliberately held back with that character. I have to say that [director] David Nutter was right there saying, 'That's the direction, Tim: less, less, less!' It was a good acting lesson for me."

"2Shy" is still regarded as one of the more visceral *X-Files* episodes due to the copious amounts of slime used in scenes between Incanto and his victims. "It *was* pretty slimy," the actor chuckles, "especially that shot where I'm over that woman, and there's all this goo pouring out of my mouth. I remember doing that and thinking, 'I hope my mother doesn't see this!' That wasn't much fun, and not very flattering either. It wasn't exactly the romantic vampire that they portray in Broadway plays. But it was fun. I was hoping for a while that they were going to have Virgil escape from prison and come back and terrorize the neighborhood, but I guess they've moved on."

To date, it's Carhart's roles in *The X-Files* and *Star Trek: The Next Generation* (in *Redemption, Part 2*) that he gets recognized for the most. "I was in the airport at Atlanta, and this big beefy biker guy in full colors came up to me and I thought he was going to beat the hell out of me. He said, 'I didn't like the way you treated Data!' I thought, 'What the hell is he talking about?' until I realized he was talking about *Star Trek*. He then broke into a big grin and shook my hand, but it scared the hell out of me."

And how does Timothy Carhart feel about that kind of recognition? "It's kind of wonderful, and it's kind of frustrating. I'm fine with *The X-Files*, because the show has a lot of integrity. I think it's amusing that people are still interested, and that it affected them so much. I'm kind of thrilled about that."

12 VIRGIL INCANTO

FIRST APPEARANCE: **"2Shy"**
BACKGROUND: A college professor or translator, Virgil Incanto used the Internet to attract his female victims. He preyed on lonely, overweight women and killed them by sucking their body fat. Incanto used his victims' bodies to replenish a chemical deficiency in his own in order to survive.
MOST DASTARDLY DEED: Killing his dates!
OTHER DASTARDLY DEEDS: Murders a prostitute, a local detective and his kindly landlady. And he also tries to add Scully to his list of victims.
SOUNDBITE: "I was just feeding the hunger."
Where is he now? In prison.

ANALYSIS

POWERFULNESS: 7
RUTHLESSNESS: 9
SCARINESS: 7
CRAFTINESS: 9
OVERALL VILLAIN RATING: 8

11 JOHN LEE ROCHE

FIRST APPEARANCE: "Paper Hearts"
BACKGROUND: One of the first criminals Mulder ever profiled, Roche was a prolific serial killer, abducting and killing young girls. He cut out heart-shaped pieces of fabric from their clothes as a trophy.
MOST DASTARDLY DEED: Murdering approximately 16 young girls.
OTHER DASTARDLY DEEDS: Manipulating Mulder's emotions; making the vulnerable agent believe that his sister was amongst Roche's victims.
SOUNDBITE: "I took your sister away from all this. To a happier place."
Where is he now? Deceased, shot by Mulder when he abducted another little girl.

ANALYSIS
POWERFULNESS: 7
RUTHLESSNESS: 8
SCARINESS: 10
CRAFTINESS: 9
OVERALL VILLAIN RATING: 8

10 LEONARD BETTS

FIRST APPEARANCE: "Leonard Betts"
BACKGROUND: A freak of nature turned Leonard Betts into a cancer-eating fiend. Riddled with cancer, Leonard needed to ingest live human cancerous tissue in order to survive. Capable of regenerating himself, all his victims were also dying from the disease.
MOST DASTARDLY DEED: Brutally attacking Agent Scully.
OTHER DASTARDLY DEEDS: Attacks and kills a man dying from lung cancer; also murders his EMT partner.
SOUNDBITE: "I'm sorry, but you have something I need."
Where are they now? Deceased, killed by Agent Scully with defibrillation pads.

ANALYSIS
POWERFULNESS: 9
RUTHLESSNESS: 8
SCARINESS: 9
CRAFTINESS: 8
OVERALL VILLAIN RATING: 9

9 CHINGA

FIRST APPEARANCE: "Chinga"
BACKGROUND: Spooky-looking-doll belonging to an equally spooky looking little girl, Polly Turner. Found by Polly's father, a lobster fisherman, shortly before he met a horrific death. Chinga somehow has the ability to cause people to harm themselves – often fatally – in the most gruesome ways.
MOST DASTARDLY DEED: Forcing Dave the butcher to thrust a large carving knife into his eye.
OTHER DASTARDLY DEEDS: Making Jane Froelich kill herself with a broken phonograph record; and causing Polly's mum Melissa to repeatedly hit herself in the head with a hammer.
SOUNDBITE: "I want to play."
Where is it now? Probably playing happy families with some other poor, unsuspecting family.

ANALYSIS
POWERFULNESS: 8
RUTHLESSNESS: 9
SCARINESS: 9
CRAFTINESS: 8
OVERALL VILLAIN RATING: 9

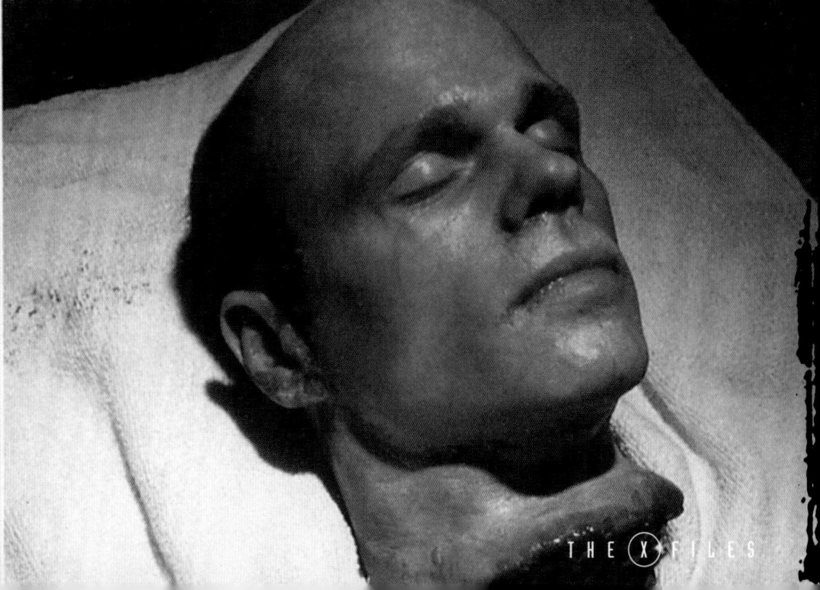

8 ROBERT 'PUSHER' MODELL

FIRST APPEARANCE: **"Pusher"**
BACKGROUND: A highly intelligent sociopath with the ability to control people's minds. Robert Patrick Modell served in the army and applied to join the FBI, but was rejected. So he became a contract killer instead.
MOST DASTARDLY DEED: Forcing Mulder to play a deadly game of Russian Roulette – with his life, and Scully's.
OTHER DASTARDLY DEEDS: He caused Agent Frank Burst to suffer a fatal heart attack and willed Agent Collins to set himself on fire.
SOUNDBITE: "Biology tells us we're all dying... and original sin tells me ain't nobody innocent."
Where is he now? Deceased. Modell was dying of a fatal brain tumor, but was ultimately murdered by his fraternal twin sister.

ANALYSIS

POWERFULNESS: 9
RUTHLESSNESS: 9
SCARINESS: 8
CRAFTINESS: 9
OVERALL VILLAIN RATING: 9

Memories of Modell

Robert Wisden recalls his work as Pusher
By Joe Nazzaro

For Robert Wisden, *The X-Files* audition was no big deal. After all, he'd auditioned for the series on half a dozen other occasions, but this time, he walked away with the role of Robert Modell, the self-styled samurai warrior with the power to control men's minds in "Pusher."

"I was told to get on it quickly," remembers the Vancouver actor, "because some casting situations had fallen through in Los Angeles, so I ran downtown and did the audition. It was one of those actor's dreams where the casting people chase you out and say, 'You've got it, come back in!' so it was on the spot, and I was speaking to the producer and director in the same half hour that I auditioned."

"I can't imagine anyone else playing that part but him," declares Vince Gilligan, who wrote "Pusher" as well as the follow-up episode "Kitsunegari" two seasons later. "We were so lucky he walked in. We had looked at so many people, and then he walked in literally the day before shooting started and just nailed it, and we said, 'Oh man, somebody sent us this guy from heaven!'"

Although "Pusher" soon became one of the highlights of *The X-Files* third season, Wisden wasn't very happy with his performance at the time. "I actually came home quite despondent after my week-and-a-half shooting, because I was nervous that the choice I'd made to not overact and to not put anything into the character was the wrong one. I hadn't seen any dailies, and no one was telling me anything. Then I got a phone call from Rob Bowman the director, who left me a message telling me what an extraordinary performance he thought it was. Until then, I didn't even realize that they were pleased with it, but when it did make a splash within *X-Files* circles, I was surprised to say the least."

Because his character was left near death as the episode ended, Wisden never thought Modell would be making another appearance in the series. "Like everyone else, I thought the character was dead, so when I got the phone call saying they'd brought me back, I was as surprised as the viewers were." He returned, however, for "Kitsunegari," where Modell is actually the red herring – it turns out that the Pusher-like crimes have been committed by his fraternal twin sister (played by Diana Scarwid). "I've only seen that episode once," Wisden comments. "It was good."

In recent months, Wisden has largely left his villainous roles behind, playing more upstanding characters in such projects as *Jeremiah, Smallville, Final Destination*, and the upcoming mini-series *The Snow Queen*. "Recently it seems like I've been playing a lot of teenagers' fathers. The villain thing comes along periodically, less now that I'm out of my thirties."

And while the actor is still a bit surprised that his *X-Files* character was so well received, he's still pleased to have been part of the experience. "I did get [trading] cards in the mail and people asked me to sign them, that sort of thing. But when I went online to look up what these people were talking about, the amount of stuff on there really blew my mind. It's one of those shows that captures people's imaginations. The Mulder/Scully relationship was so strong, and the occult factor was so well realized, and I have to say that Vancouver's rainy, gloomy quality in the seasons it was shot here was really mesmerizing. To steal one of their phrases, I can see why people were totally abducted by it."

7 MR PEATTIE

FIRST APPEARANCE: "Theef"
BACKGROUND: Peattie uses folk magic to inflict harm onto the family of the doctor he believes responsible for killing his daughter. He blames modern medicine for her death and says he could have saved her. Seeking revenge, he uses hexcraft to kill the doctor's family, one by one, in the most heinous ways.
MOST DASTARDLY DEED: Causing the doctor's wife's body to burn to a charred black whilst undergoing an MRI exam by microwaving her hex doll.
OTHER DASTARDLY DEEDS: Using a hex doll to make Scully go blind and cursing his victims with rare, fatal diseases.
SOUNDBITE: "An eye for an eye."
Where is he now? Presumably still lying in a comatose state in hospital.

ANALYSIS
POWERFULNESS: 9
RUTHLESSNESS: 9
SCARINESS: 9
CRAFTINESS: 8
OVERALL VILLAIN RATING: 9

6 DONNIE PFASTER

FIRST APPEARANCE: "Irresistible"
BACKGROUND: As a death fetishist, Donnie Pfaster derives extreme pleasure from items belonging to dead people. His obsession has escalated to the point of murder – and mutilation. After serving a five year-year prison sentence, he escapes to carry on his work.
MOST DASTARDLY DEED: Abducting Scully – twice!
OTHER DASTARDLY DEEDS: Murdered five women; killed Reverend Orison and mutilated buried corpses in a graveyard.
SOUNDBITE: "Is your hair normal or dry?"
Where is he now? Deceased, shot by Agent Scully.

ANALYSIS
POWERFULNESS: 8
RUTHLESSNESS: 9
SCARINESS: 9
CRAFTINESS: 9
OVERALL VILLAIN RATING: 9

5 EUGENE VICTOR TOOMS

FIRST APPEARANCE: "Squeeze"
BACKGROUND: A liver-eating genetic mutation, capable of elongating his body, babyfaced Eugene Tooms is over 100 years old. His murder spree reoccurs every thirty years, when he comes out of hibernation looking for sustenance – five human livers. The former Animal Control Officer is eventually captured and placed into a sanatorium, only to be subsequently released by a Parole Board.
MOST DASTARDLY DEED: Five victims every thirty years since 1903, including businessman George Usher and his own doctor.
OTHER DASTARDLY DEEDS: Viciously attacking Scully and trying to frame Mulder, alleging that the FBI agent beat him up.
SOUNDBITE: "Grrrr."
Where is he now? Deceased, crushed to death by an escalator! Surely even Tooms couldn't have survived that?!

ANALYSIS
POWERFULNESS: 9
RUTHLESSNESS: 9
SCARINESS: 10
CRAFTINESS: 9
OVERALL VILLAIN RATING: 9

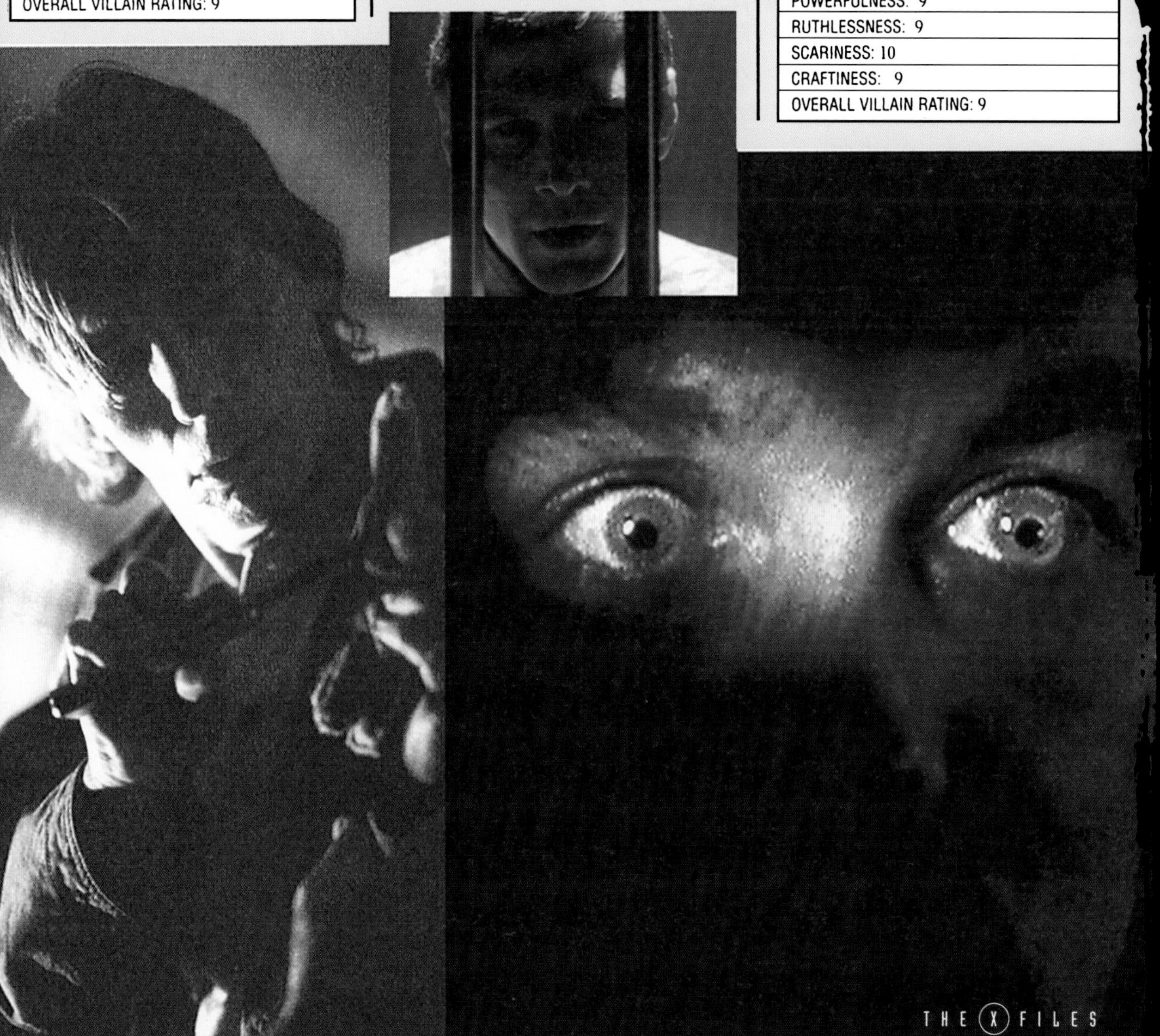

4 THE ALIEN BOUNTY HUNTER

Brian Thompson is a big, imposing guy and a pretty good actor, too. So it made perfect sense that the producers of *The X-Files* turned to him to portray the mysterious Alien Bounty Hunter, a character that's turned up in numerous mythology episodes over the years, beginning with "Colony" and "End Game" back in Season Two. The actor's other genre credits include *Star Trek: The Next Generation*, *Buffy the Vampire Slayer*, *Charmed* and *Mortal Kombat: Annihilation*, while non-genre credits include the TV series *Key West* and the big screen comedy *Joe Dirt*. Ian Spelling recently caught up with Thompson at his home in L.A.

THE X-FILES MAGAZINE: When you first arrived on *The X-Files* set, how familiar were you with the show and/or the mythology?
THOMPSON: I didn't know the show at all. I'd spent the previous five months in Europe filming *Dragonheart*. I knew the director Rob Bowman and casting director Rick Millikan, and I knew that they did quality shows, so I went in for an interview and met with Chris Carter, and they offered me the job.

Did anyone tell you that your first appearance could evolve into a recurring role? And did they give you much background about the character?
There was almost no background on the character, and I wasn't told it would reoccur. They told me not to judge the character by the first script because he would be much more developed in the second script. Chris (Carter) wrote the scene that took place on the sub in which I uttered the line about Mulder's sister: "She's alive." That tied me to the mythology and then months later, out of the blue, they asked me to come back and do a couple more shows. And then the next season, then the next, and here we are today.

How hard/easy was it to craft a performance for such an enigmatic character?
At first I wasn't sure what to do, but once I made the decisions about his purpose, his behavior was clear. He comes from a place of efficiency. He is precise and purposeful, not emotionless, just very controlled.

How was working with David and Gillian Anderson?
I love them both. David is a wonderful wit and gentlemen with great insights and humor. Gillian has this infectious laugh and giggle that is heartwarming, as well as a serious side, which is (that of) a great actress and insightful person.

Which of your *X-Files* episodes were you most pleased with?
I really liked the first two, because they were so well produced. The two episodes together are a movie. I also loved "The Unnatural" because it brought a very American theme into *The X-Files* with a lot of heart that you don't get to visit in many episodes because of the dark nature of conspiracy theory stories.

This issue is devoted to the show's Top 20 villains and you came in at number four. How do you feel about that?
I'm number four, hmm. I was unaware of that. I say I demand a recount! And I say we conduct the poll in a state where my brother is governor. Let me know when the vote is being held and I will run some ads beforehand. I find fourth very disappointing. They only give trophies for the top three spots. What do I even get, a certificate or something?

Um, moving on... What reaction do you get from people? Do you get wary glances, instant recognition, both?
Both. What I find the funniest is when people are wary of me. They are suspicious but don't know why.

What else have you been up to?
Epoch just aired on the Sci Fi Channel. It also stars David Keith. *The Order* is due out soon. I play a terrorist who wants to blow up the temple in Jerusalem. And I'm presently working on an action-adventure/thriller called *The First Thing We Do*.

Lastly, what do you get up to when you're not working?
I've got two children and two pet squirrels named April and Mr. Squirrel. I kite surf for recreation and exercise. And it's true I got two holes in one in the same year. I'd have rather have won the lottery!

BOUNTY HUNTER profile

FIRST APPEARANCE: **"Colony"/ "End Game"**
BACKGROUND: The Alien Bounty Hunter first appeared on the scene when his craft crashes in the Arctic and he's been a menace ever since. Seemingly invincible, he has the ability to heal the sick and to shapeshift; to morph his appearance and take on anyone's identity. And there are many more like him.
MOST DASTARDLY DEED: 'Abducting' Mulder.
OTHER DASTARDLY DEEDS: Beating Mulder up – on more than one occasion; killing doctors at abortion clinics; destroying the Samantha clones and generally disposing of anyone who gets in his way.
Where is he now? Your guess is as good as ours!

ANALYSIS

POWERFULNESS:	10
RUTHLESSNESS:	9
SCARINESS:	9
CRAFTINESS:	9
OVERALL VILLAIN RATING:	9

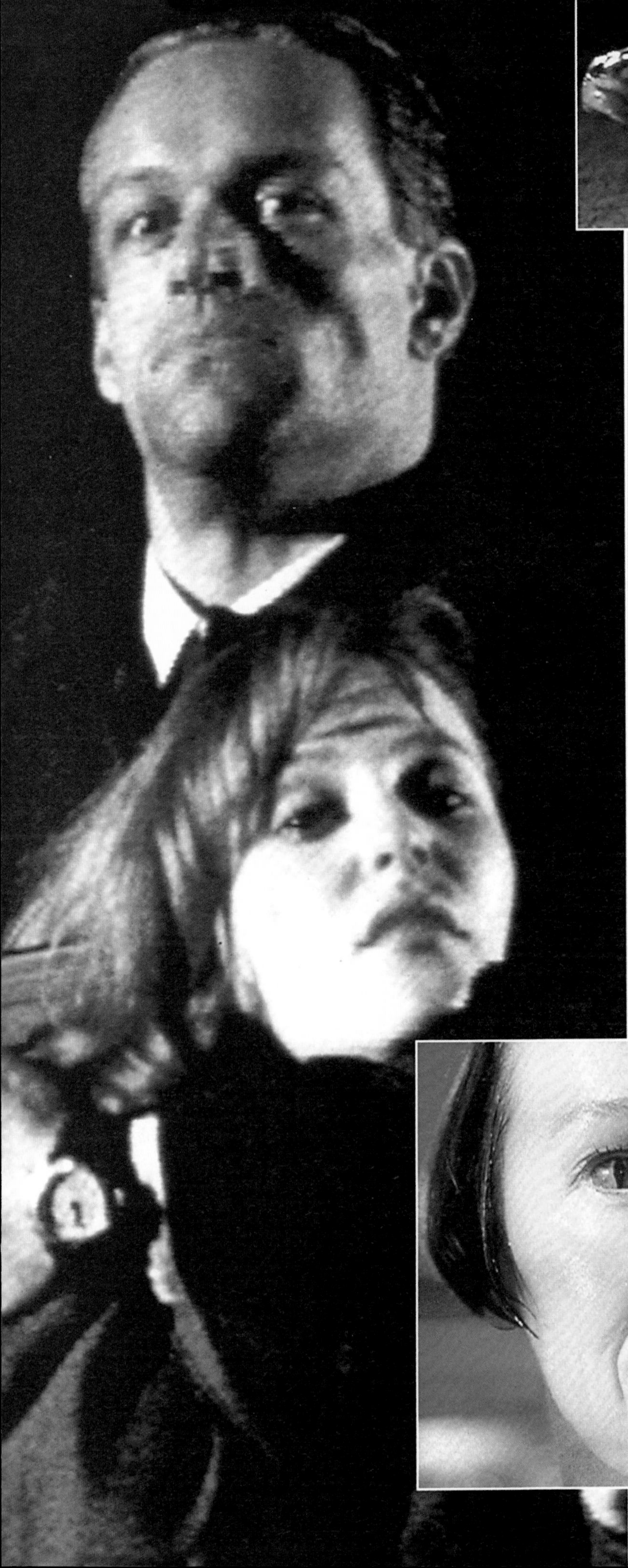

3 MRS PADDOCK

FIRST APPEARANCE: "Die Hand Die Verletzt"
BACKGROUND: Supremely scary substitute teacher and devil worshipper. Mrs Paddock used Black Magic to prevent the town's grisly secret – their involvement in satanic rituals – from being exposed.
MOST DASTARDLY DEED: Placing a spell on student Shannon Ausbury, making her slash her wrists.
OTHER DASTARDLY DEEDS: Somehow causing Jim Ausbury to be attacked and swallowed by a large snake; removing the heart and eyes from another student.
SOUNDBITE: "I'm old-fashioned, Agent Scully, I can't bring myself to believe children are capable of such things as they are these days."
Where is she now? Disappeared; so hopefully not teaching at a school near you!

ANALYSIS
POWERFULNESS: 10
RUTHLESSNESS: 9
SCARINESS: 10
CRAFTINESS: 8
OVERALL VILLAIN RATING: 9

2 ALEX KRYCEK

FIRST APPEARANCE: **"Sleepless"**
BACKGROUND: The treacherous Alex Krycek first appeared on the scene as Mulder's eager, wet-behind-the-ears new partner. He tried to worm his way into Mulder's confidence, but he was in fact working for the Cigarette-Smoking Man. However, he was forced to flee and go underground when his treachery was exposed. Often the Cigarette-Smoking Man's chief henchman, if there's dirty work to be done, Krycek's the man to get the job done.
MOST DASTARDLY DEED: Murdering Mulder's father in cold blood.
OTHER DASTARDLY DEEDS: He was involved in the murder of Scully's sister, Melissa; silenced Duane Barry before Mulder had a chance to question him about Scully's abduction; and injected Skinner with nanotechnology atoms programmed to kill him.
Where is he now? Deceased, shot in the head by AD Skinner.

ANALYSIS
POWERFULNESS: 9
RUTHLESSNESS: 10
SCARINESS: 9
CRAFTINESS: 10
OVERALL VILLAIN RATING: 9

Mysterious and deadly – after eight years on the show, those are the only two facts we can confirm about the Cigarette-Smoking Man. In a special profile, K. Stoddard Hayes provides a perspective on *The X-Files'* official number one villain.

Musings on a Cigarette-Smoking Man

"He's the most dangerous man alive, not so much because he believes in his actions, but because he believes these actions are all which life allows him."

Frohike, "Musings of a Cigarette-Smoking Man"

A shadowy silhouette blowing smoke. An ashtray full of crushed cigarette butts. A red and white packet of Morley's. The Cigarette-Smoking Man has been here.

The X-Files' most mysterious figure prefers to remain in the shadows. In his first few appearances, he doesn't even speak. We see him sitting silent in the background of FBI meetings, chain-smoking and watching. We see him walking through a vast storage warehouse in the Pentagon to file away critical bits of evidence like the chip taken from an abductee, or the alien contents of the Erlenmeyer flask. When he does come out in the open, to give orders, make deals, or even to confront Mulder, Scully or Skinner, then we know that something important is at stake.

Sometimes 'Cancer Man,' as Mulder calls him, acts with direct and brutal force. He brings troops to capture or kill Mulder, and to beat up Albert Hosteen and his young relatives ("Anasazi"); he forces Mulder and Scully out of a missile silo and locks Krycek inside ("Apocrypha"); he even murders his own son, Agent Spender, when Spender lets him down ("One Son"). These actions and others are clear evidence that he's not afraid to use any means necessary to achieve his ends. However, he prefers to keep his power quiet, subtle, unseen. Private conversations in offices, hospitals, or remote places; secret assassinations; the complete disappearance of bodies, documents, and any evidence of his activities.

His role in the Consortium is clearly one of great power, but not of absolute power. He speaks among his colleagues as an equal, but often has to persuade them to move in the direction he thinks necessary. And sometimes he has to account for a serious problem. He's no more truthful with his Consortium colleagues than he is with the rest of the world. On several occasions, we see him tell them that a situation is 'handled,' when it is not. In "Anasazi," the Smoking Man tells the others that he has already recovered the data tape, when we know it is still in Skinner's pocket. But even the Smoking Man's schemes and lies can't fool the Consortium all the time. When Mulder proves to be alive after his apparent suicide, the Smoking Man visits the Elder, boasting about Mulder's usefulness, despite his threat to their mole in the FBI. As soon as he leaves, the Elder orders his assassin to proceed – with the Smoking Man's murder. ("Redux II")

The Cigarette-Smoking Man seems to be the Consortium's enforcer, the one who orders the most drastic actions, and sees them carried out. When Krycek first reports to the Smoking Man and his FBI associates that Scully is a problem, it's Smoking Man who replies, "Every problem has a solution." ("Sleepless") The sequel to this implied order to make Scully disappear, is Scully's abduction by Duane Barry. The Smoking Man even admits to Mulder, by implication, that he orchestrated Scully's abduction and return. When Mulder bursts into his apartment, puts a gun to his head, and demands, "Why her? Why her, and not me?" the Smoking Man replies, "I like you. I like her, too. That's why I returned her to you." ("One Breath").

The scariest thing about the Cigarette-Smoking Man is that he believes, always, that what he is doing is right. No matter how criminal or violent or amoral his actions appear, in his own mind they are always justified by his

(continues overleaf...)

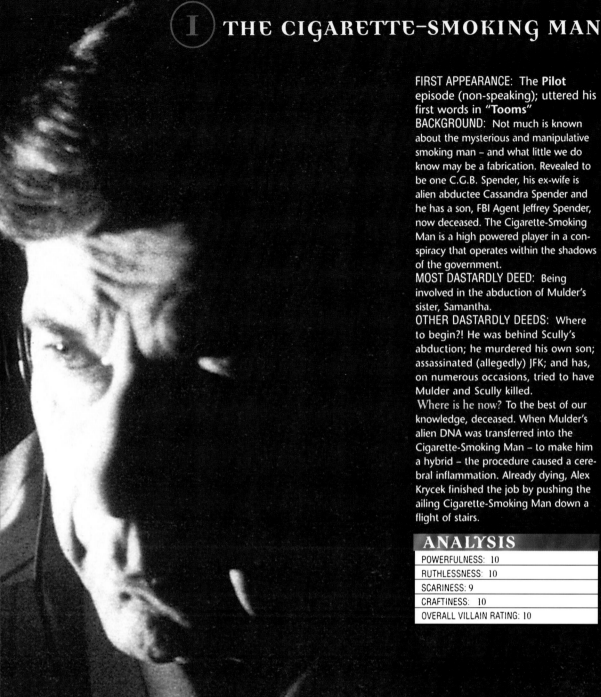

I THE CIGARETTE-SMOKING MAN

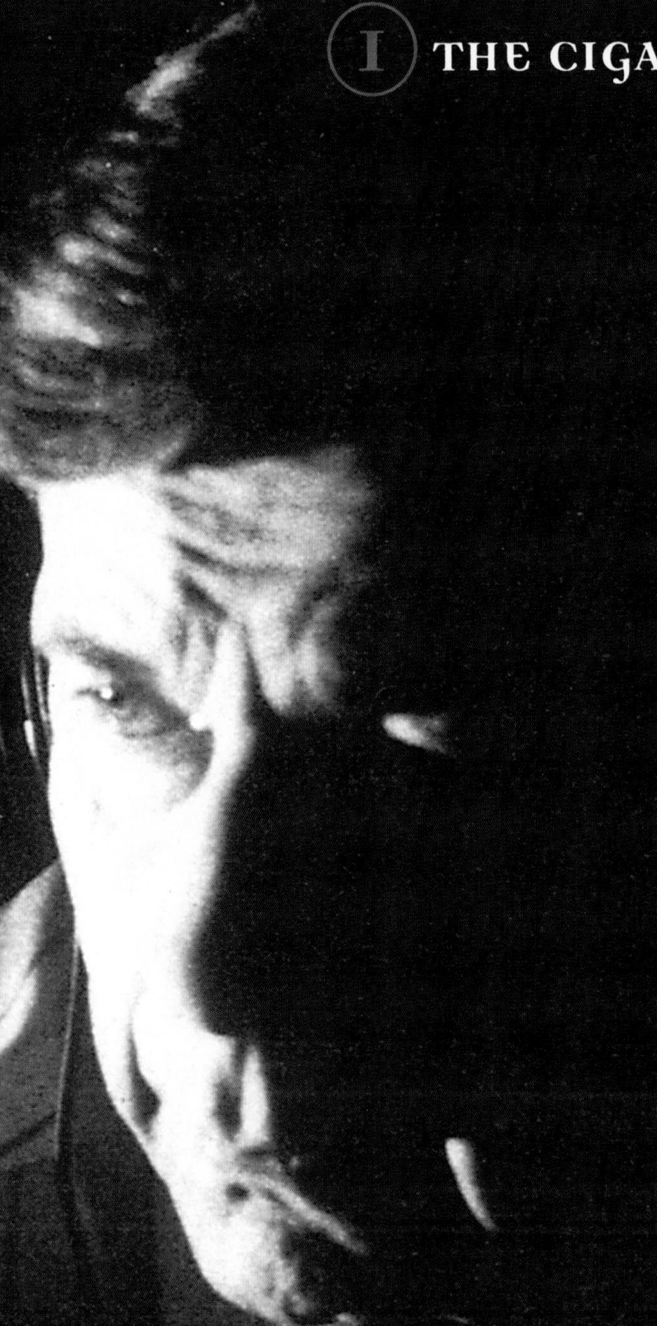

FIRST APPEARANCE: The **Pilot** episode (non-speaking); uttered his first words in "**Tooms**"
BACKGROUND: Not much is known about the mysterious and manipulative smoking man – and what little we do know may be a fabrication. Revealed to be one C.G.B. Spender, his ex-wife is alien abductee Cassandra Spender and he has a son, FBI Agent Jeffrey Spender, now deceased. The Cigarette-Smoking Man is a high powered player in a conspiracy that operates within the shadows of the government.
MOST DASTARDLY DEED: Being involved in the abduction of Mulder's sister, Samantha.
OTHER DASTARDLY DEEDS: Where to begin?! He was behind Scully's abduction; he murdered his own son; assassinated (allegedly) JFK; and has, on numerous occasions, tried to have Mulder and Scully killed.
Where is he now? To the best of our knowledge, deceased. When Mulder's alien DNA was transferred into the Cigarette-Smoking Man – to make him a hybrid – the procedure caused a cerebral inflammation. Already dying, Alex Krycek finished the job by pushing the ailing Cigarette-Smoking Man down a flight of stairs.

ANALYSIS
POWERFULNESS: 10
RUTHLESSNESS: 10
SCARINESS: 9
CRAFTINESS: 10
OVERALL VILLAIN RATING: 10

"Don't try to threaten me, Mulder, I've watched presidents die." *CSM, "One Breath"*

goals. Again and again, he tells Mulder, Scully, or anyone else who will listen, that what he's doing is necessary for the greater good, to save Earth from alien invasion. His interrogation of Jeremiah Smith may be one of the few times that he speaks absolutely honestly about his beliefs and intentions:

"Who are you to give them hope? We give them happiness, and they give us authority... Men can never be free, because they're weak, corrupt, worthless and restless. The people believe in authority. They've grown tired of waiting for miracle and mystery. Science is their religion. No greater explanation exists for them. They must never believe any differently if the project is to go forward." ("Talitha Cumi")

Just when scenes like this convince us that the Cigarette-Smoking Man is no more than a ruthless killer and cynical manipulator, he does something helpful and incalculable, like shooting his own assassin before the man can kill Scully ("En Ami"), or producing a chip that will cure Scully's cancer, or ordering the Alien Bounty Hunter to heal Mrs. Mulder. He even tells Scully that he spent decades concealing from Mulder his knowledge that Samantha was dead, "Out of kindness... Allow him his ignorance. It's what gives him hope." ("Closure")

Nowhere is his ambivalence more evident than in his attitudes toward Mulder and Scully. Though he has conspired in repeated attempts to murder, abduct, or professionally ruin them, he still seems to regard them with both affection and admiration. He has often used Scully as a tool to get at Mulder, as in her abductions. Yet when he spends several days with her in "En Ami," he tells her that she is special to him because he had the power to cure her cancer:

"I held your life in my hands. Your cancer was terminal. I had a cure. Can you imagine what that's like, to have the power to extinguish a life, or to save it and let it flourish?"

This could be just trying to get under her guard, but Scully herself doesn't think so. She tells Mulder, "For a moment I saw something more in him. A longing for something more than power, maybe something he could never have."

As for Mulder, it's impossible to count all the times the Smoking Man has praised Mulder's abilities and determination, usually in the context of warning his Consortium colleagues not to underestimate him. In "Redux II" he seems pleased and hopeful at the prospect of recruiting Mulder to work with him instead of against him. His affection for Mulder arises initially from his long association with the Mulder family and especially his relationship

"You murdered my father. You killed Scully's sister, and if Scully dies, I will kill you. I don't care whose father you are, I will put you down." *Mulder, "Redux"*

The Smoky Episodes:

Season One
"Pilot"
"Young at Heart"
"Tooms"
"The Erlenmeyer Flask"

Season Two
"Little Green Men"
"Sleepless"
"Duane Barry"
"Ascension"
"One Breath"
"F. Emasculata"
"Anasazi"

Season Three
"The Blessing Way"
"Paper Clip"
"731"
"Apocrypha"
"Avatar"
"Wetwired"
"Talitha Cumi"

Season Four
"Herrenvolk"
"Musings of a Cigarette Smoking Man"
"Tunguska"
"Terma"
"Memento Mori"
"Zero Sum"
"Demons"

Season Five
"Redux"
"Redux II"
"The Red and the Black"
"The End"

The X-File movie

Season Six
"The Beginning"
"Triangle"
"Two Fathers"
"One Son"

Season Seven
"The Sixth Extinction II: Amor Fati"
"Closure"
"En Ami"
"Requiem"

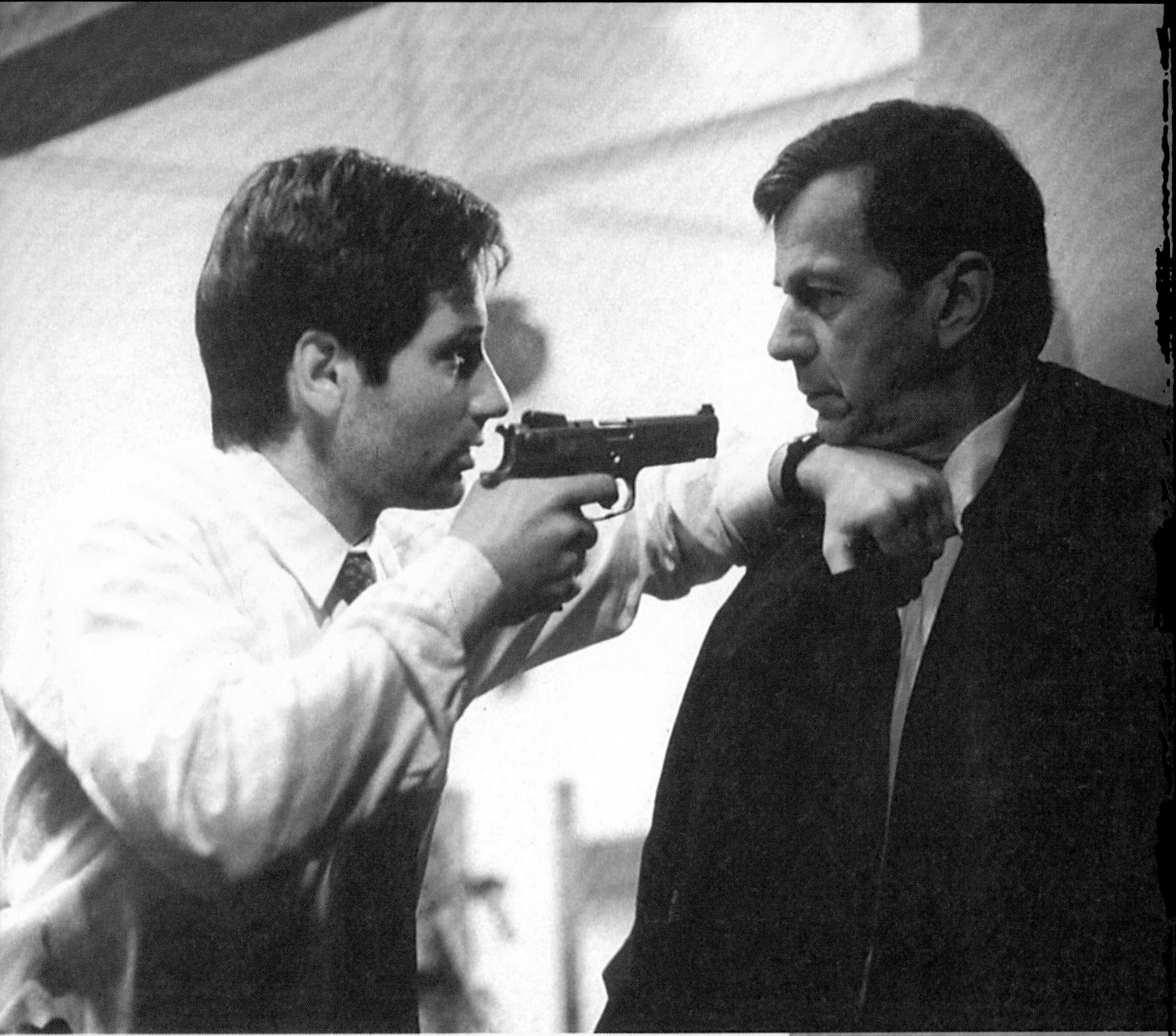

"You deal with this man, you offer him anything, he will own you forever. You can't ask the truth of a man who trades in lies. I won't let you. Find another way."

Skinner to Mulder, "Memento Mori"

with Mulder's mother. He likes to think of Mulder as his son, and even lets both Mulder and Diana Fowley believe that this is the truth. His role in Samantha Mulder's disappearance will never be fully clear, but it surely pleases him to play the part of adopted father to one of Bill Mulder's children.

The importance that the Cigarette-Smoking Man places on his relationship to Mulder may be the final proof that he really is dead. The first time we saw him assassinated, Skinner declared him presumed dead ("Redux II"), but he turned up alive in Canada before that season ended. Now, however, more than a year has gone, without any trace of a man who reported himself terminally ill the last time we saw him. More significantly, we've seen all the permutations of Mulder's abduction and return, the alien replicants, and the birth of Scully's baby, without seeing so much as a wisp of smoke or a single crushed cigarette butt. Surely the Cigarette-Smoking Man would have taken a hand in those important events, if he were still around. By now, it's safe to conclude that he, like Krycek and the rest of the Consortium, is genuinely, finally dead. Does anyone miss the smoke? ●

STRETCHING AS AN ACTOR

*With "Squeeze" and "Tooms" both released on video this month, Paula J Vitaris talks to their stretchy star, actor **Doug Hutchison***

NAME: DOUG HUTCHISON
KNOWN ALIAS/ALIASES: "EUGENE TOOMS"

Panic struck America's Fox Network when heavy-weight boxing champion Mike Tyson broke his thumb and cancelled a match scheduled for last November 4th. What could be substituted for the highly-publicized fight?

Eugene Victor Tooms to the rescue! A liver-gobbling genetic mutant even Tyson would be loathe to face, he remains, two years after his appearance in **The X-Files** episodes "Squeeze" and "Tooms", one of the show's most popular monsters. With a two-hour hole in the schedule, the network reached into its storage cabinet and offered up a 'Tooms Night', to the surprise and delight of the audience – including Tooms himself, actor Doug Hutchison.

"It's a trip!" exclaims the vegetarian Hutchison, still amazed that an acting job has linked him forever with raw human livers. Tooms was spawned in Baltimore, but Hutchison's own breeding ground is Detroit, where he grew up intending to become a rock musican. When a teacher convinced him to try acting, he moved to New York to study at the Juilliard school. But the free-spirited actor soon realized he wasn't cut out for formal study, and dropped out of school, becoming active in New York and regional theatre. A disastrous musical, "Shout and Twist", brought him back to L.A., and he decided to remain there after that "nightmarish" experience to pursue film work. He soon landed roles in episodic television and in the feature films *Fresh Horses* and *The Chocolate War*.

Hutchison became Tooms when his agent sent him to read for the role in "Squeeze". "I went into the room, and Harry Longstreet, the director, and the producers were there," he recalls. "We started to plunge into this interrogation scene, and Harry said, 'I'd like you to do this without any emotion.' So I'm thinking, 'Oh great, I'm just going to sit here and say yes, no, and be emotionless.' So I did it. And afterwards he said, 'Okay, that's very good, and now I'd like you to show me that you can be this serial killer. Pretend that you're stalking your victims. I just want to see your potential for evil.' And I'm thinking, 'What is this? This is ridiculous! What does he want me to do? Make a face, or what?' So I sat and I pondered his direction, and as I was thinking about it, he [must have] thought that I mis-understood, and he said, 'Do you understand what I'm saying?' And it just jumped out of me before I knew it came out, but I said, '*Yeah, I got it - you want me to stalk you, you m*****- ****er!?*" The director may have been taken aback, but producer/ writers Glen Morgan and James Wong loved Hutchison's repressed intensity.

Hutchison came to fall in love with the character. "It was a very sweet challenge for me," he says. "I'm a very animated person, and I tend to bring a lot of animation to my roles. This was a particularly good challenge because I felt there was a stillness to this character. I had been intrigued by stillness for quite a while since seeing Anthony Hopkins [as Hannibal Lecter]" - another fan of raw human livers - "in *The Silence of the Lambs*. He captured the art of stillness so well, and I was inspired by his performance."

In fact, Hutchison so enjoyed playing Tooms that he was determined to reprise the role. A writer and filmmaker as well an actor (a documentary Hutchison and his brother Eric made about their grandfather won second prize at a Seattle independent film festival), he wrote a sequel script entitled "Dark He Was and Golden-Eyed" and sent it to executive producer Chris Carter. "I was adamant about coming back on the show," Hutchison declares. In return, he received a phone call from one of the network lawyers, informing him that legal ramifications prevented his script from even being read. By then it was moot anyway; shortly after he sent his script to Carter, his agent called with the news that **The X-Files** wanted him back for "Tooms", an eponymous sequel written by Morgan and Wong.

Hutchison's ideas differed quite a bit from Morgan and Wong's script. "The fly in the ointment for me was how Tooms hibernates for 30 years if he gets five livers," he says. "I wanted to figure out a way to have him around *forever*. [So, in my script, Tooms] was in an experiment to find out how I could remain so young and immortal; he was infused with a drug that backfired and ended up escaping the asylum. [So now, he's] eating livers like M&Ms - he's on a rampage. I also dealt with where Tooms might have come from" - Hutchison's script suggests he is an incarnation of a ravenous, liver-eating Central American Indian god - "so it had a lot of flashbacks. And Tooms talked a lot at the end, because Scully and I had a confrontation."

Hutchison has kept busy since his time on **The X-Files**. He has appeared in guest spots on several television shows and made a pilot for Fox, though sadly not one that was picked up for a full series. He also has two feature film roles in the can: he plays a child rapist in Warner Brothers' upcoming *A Time to Kill*, based on the popular novel by John Grisham, and a drugged-up robber in the independent film *All Points Between*. More importantly for ***X-Files*** fans, he also has a recurring role in Morgan and Wong's new science fiction war series on Sky, *Space: Above And Beyond*.

A third episode featuring Eugene Victor Tooms has been suggested, but Hutchison feels that, no matter what, the character will always be a part of him. The fan mail keeps flowing in, and Hutchison has been a guest at **X-Files** conventions across the USA. "I was aware of the *Star Trek* conventions," he notes, "but I had no concept of what they were really about and how many people actually show up. My first **X-Files** convention was in San Diego. There were over *2,000* people - I signed autographs for five and a half hours!" His insistence on greeting each autograph seeker personally resulted in the convention personnel finally giving up and leaving him to find his own way home.

Hutchison says he loves mingling with the crowd; his current "long-haired and scruffy" appearance is a disguise that permits him to talk to fans without their knowing who he is. "I'm having a riot being this anonymous dude," he laughs. "I'll talk with people and jam with them, and then go up on stage, and they'll come up to me afterwards and go, 'I didn't know you were Tooms, man! I talked to you for twenty minutes!' That's been a real thrill."

Paula J Vitaris writes about The X-Files *for* Cinefantastique

THE Passion OF DARK NOONAN

In another exclusive interview, Dave Hughes talks to actor Tom Noonan, whose serial killer John Lee Roche confirmed the fourth season story "Paper Hearts" as an *X-Files* classic.

Actor Tom Noonan frightens people on the street. It isn't that he means to. It's just that after an acting career in which his highest-profile roles have been serial killers – both sociopathic (*Manhunter*) and psychopathic (*Last Action Hero*), villainous materminds (*Heat*) and power-crazed drug dealers (*RoboCop 2*) – the public at large tend to regard the family man whom *X-Files* writer/producer Vince Gilligan describes as "a deadpan, wry, quiet actor" with a degree of suspicion. Such was Gilligan's admiration for Noonan that he created the character of child killer John Lee Roche, the black hole at the centre of the breathtaking fourth season story "Paper Hearts", specifically with the actor in mind. The upside of this is that Noonan's perfect performance may well be rewarded this summer with an Emmy award for Best Guest Actor in a Series, the same honour awarded to Peter Boyle last year for "Clyde Bruckman's Final Repose". The downside? More fearful looks from frightened passers-by.

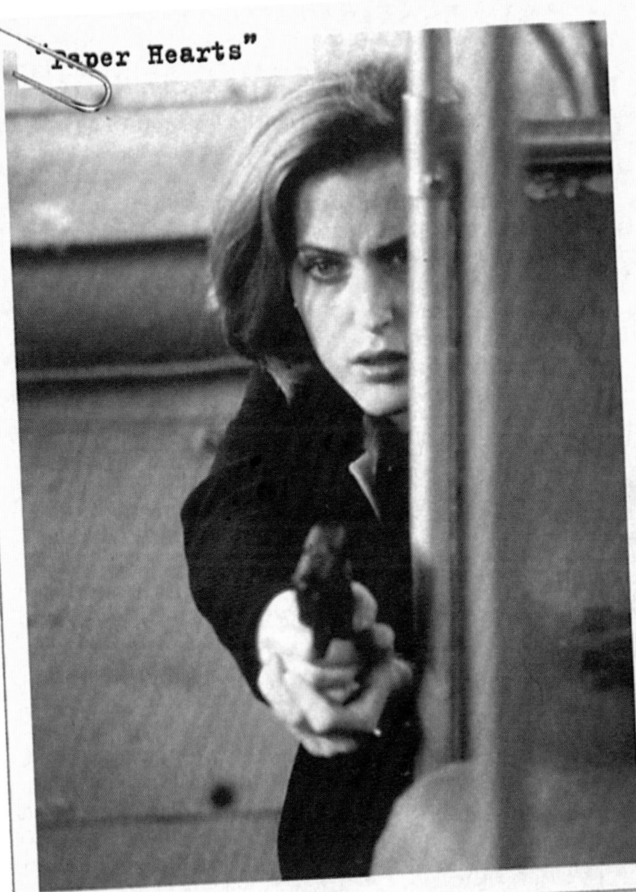
"Paper Hearts"

My own apprehension at interviewing Noonan had less to do with any subconscious fears that he might turn out to be as scary and unbalanced as his most famous screen creations, and more to do with the fact that Noonan is almost as challenging a personality to profile as his most famous creation, Francis Dollarhyde, the character Noonan played in Michael Mann's masterpiece *Manhunter*, arguably the most finely-crafted, visually stunning and psychologically complex thriller of the '80s. For far from being the actor with a unparralleled line in serial killers many may perceive him to be, Tom Noonan is an uncommonly versatile performer who writes (films, plays, novels, short stories and even songs), directs (for film, television and the stage), produces (through his company, Genre Pictures), composes (under the *nom de plume* Ludovico Sorret), edits (under another pseudonym, Richmond Arrley), and still finds time to run the New York-based theatre company he founded in 1982. After weeks of painstaking research, Noonan proved no more fathomable an interview subject than Francis Dollarhyde was to journalist Freddy Lounds (Stephen Lang) when the 'Red Dragon' revealed himself in *Manhunter* with the chilling words, "Well, here... I... am!"

Noonan began his prolific career on the New York stage, appearing in such productions as "Five of Us", "Farmyard", Harvey Fierstein's "Spookhouse", Sam Shepard's "Buried Child" and Lanford Wilson's "Poster of the Cosmos", before moving into film with a minor role in *Willie and Phil*, Paul Mazursky's oddball take on Francois Truffaut's *Jules et Jim*. Since then, he has appeared in more than twenty feature films, from Eddie Murphy's *Best Defense* to *Eddie Macon's Run*, supplementing his acting in the areas outlined above, marking out his territory as one of the industry's most remarkable hyphenates. Two days before he was due to leave for Los Angeles to act in yet another feature film, I put aside my reservations and spoke to Tom Noonan in New York, where he lives with his wife and two daughters.

Noonan says that he was not initially aware that Vince Gilligan wrote the character of John Lee Roche, the serial killer who torments Mulder by making him believe that his sister Samantha was one of his own murder victims, with Noonan in mind, adding that such knowledge would not have influenced his decision to take the role. "If a script's good, it's good, you know?" he says. "It doesn't have to be written for you. I read it first, and then the director called me up, and the writer got on the phone and told me it was written for me, but I didn't know when I read it."

Interestingly, in the hit-and-miss post-modern blockbuster *Last Action Hero*, in which Noonan appears both as himself and his on-screen counterpart, a serial killer named 'The Ripper', there is a scene in which the killer breaks through into the real world and turns up at the première of his own film, at which point his agent screams at him, "Do you want to play serial killers for the rest of your life?". Noonan may well have had these deliberately ironic words ringing in his ears as he read Gilligan's script for "Paper Hearts", but says that those fears were quickly dispelled by the quality of the writing. "I guess I do worry about that a little bit," he admits, "because I think that if you put that out in the world too much, it tends to come back on you a little. You know, it's strange to be walking around and have people frightened or weirded out by you, and not even know why. I mean, most of them don't remember you were the person in the show. So, I have mixed feelings sometimes about doing [characters] like that, but it was so well written, I didn't really think twice about it.

"I really liked the part," he adds, "but I also liked the show. I'd never really seen *The X-Files* much before, because I'm not a big TV viewer. But when they offered me the part, I started watching it, and I actually really liked the show. I liked the humour in it." Nevertheless, there was precious little humour in "Paper Hearts", in which Noonan plays a character whom is possibly the most monstrous creation to have appeared on *The X-Files* to date, notwithstanding such supernatural horrors as vampires, werewolves, zombies, and flukeworm-hybrid horrors that live in the wastepipe of the water closet. "When you play a part like that, you try not to think about that aspect of it," Noonan responds to this observation. "You just try to make him human and normal, and you try to love the guy, and have some good feeling toward him, you know?" Nevertheless, it could not have been easy to love someone like Roche, who murders sixteen young girls, and then seemingly takes great pleasure in vicariously reliving one of those murders through Mulder. "I had a very positive kind of motivation for that character, [in that] he thinks he's sent them to a better place," says Noonan. "The major thing I try to do is connect with [Mulder]," he explains, "and when I say things that are exceedingly horrific, that upset him, I really don't know why he's upset. I mean, we've shared this wonderful thing, you know? That's how I saw it – that we were connected in a way that we couldn't deny, and I really tried to feel that for him. What's nice is that David's character in the show is someone who does really want to get to the bottom of things," he continues. "And to really push him in that way was fun to play. I mean, I really care about him, and I felt very connected to him, [because] I think you are often more connected with someone you hate or are angry with than you are with someone you like. Hate is a great connector, as is anger."

Ever since Thomas Harris' *Red Dragon* (the novel on which *Manhunter* was based) and its sequel, *The Silence of the Lambs*, popularised the FBI practice of preparing psychological profiles in order to trap wanted men, film and television have been replete with detectives and agents trying to get under the skin of their quarry. Perhaps Noonan, as an actor, undertakes a similar endeavour in order to play serial killer characters such as Roche and *Manhunter's* Francis Dollarhyde. "It's not that I'm trying to get under their skin," he demurs. "It's more, for me, that when I play a part, [I feel] that this is the only chance this character is ever going to get to live [so] I feel a great obligation to give this person a chance to exist."

Noonan also believes that many actors attempt to deal with the monstrous nature of such characters by portraying them as so far removed from normal humanity that they are very difficult to relate to, a technique which he believes is unrealistic. "I don't think that the people who do *those things*," he says, deliberately avoiding any specific reference to what '*those things*' might be, "are that far removed from people who don't. They are human beings, and they do those things for reasons that are very understandable to them, and once you treat them as real people, they don't come across as two-dimensional. And that's when it really bothers people," he adds, "because they don't really want to deal with the fact that these are really somewhat normal people. I mean, ninety nine per cent of the time, most people who do this kind of thing function normally – it's just this... *wrinkle* that sets them apart. They don't sit around salivating and drooling. Most serial killers are family men with wives and children and jobs, and most of the time they're relatively normal." Indeed, the first thing you tend to hear after a serial killer is captured is his neighbours saying what a nice guy he was! "Yeah," Noonan laughs. "'He took care of my kids when I went out!'" In the same way, it's almost more comforting to see a picture of a Charles Manson – someone who's clearly 'helter skelter' – rather than the butter-wouldn't-melt all-American boys many convicted killers resemble. Noonan concurs. "I tend not to read about these people when I'm doing these parts, but I have read about them, and they all tend to be bright, imaginative, driven people."

Certainly, there is no question that Noonan's *Manhunter* character, Francis Dollarhyde, is a bright, warm, intelligent and affectionate person whose perverse and divergent desire to become the 'Red Dragon' of William Blake's famous painting 'The Great Red Dragon and the Woman Clothed in the Rays of the Sun' drives him to murder families – or 'change' them, as he euphemistically, and chillingly, refers to his killings. Indeed, it is almost as though Dollarhyde is an artist, and retired detective Will Graham (William Petersen) is the art critic trying to understand the man and the motivation for the work. Unfortunately, much of Dollarhyde's motivation in Thomas Harris' novel was excised before and during the shooting of the film, something which director Michael Mann attempted to rectify for a 'director's cut' prepared a few years ago for a US cable network. "They actually did a full body tattoo on me, but [even though] we shot it both ways" – ie, with the 'red dragon' tattoo and without – "we never saw that in the finished film because Michael thought that it trivialised my performance in some way. For instance, I did the scene with Stephen [Lang] both with my shirt on and with my shirt off. And in the scene with the blind girl [Joan Allen] where I take her hand and put it on my

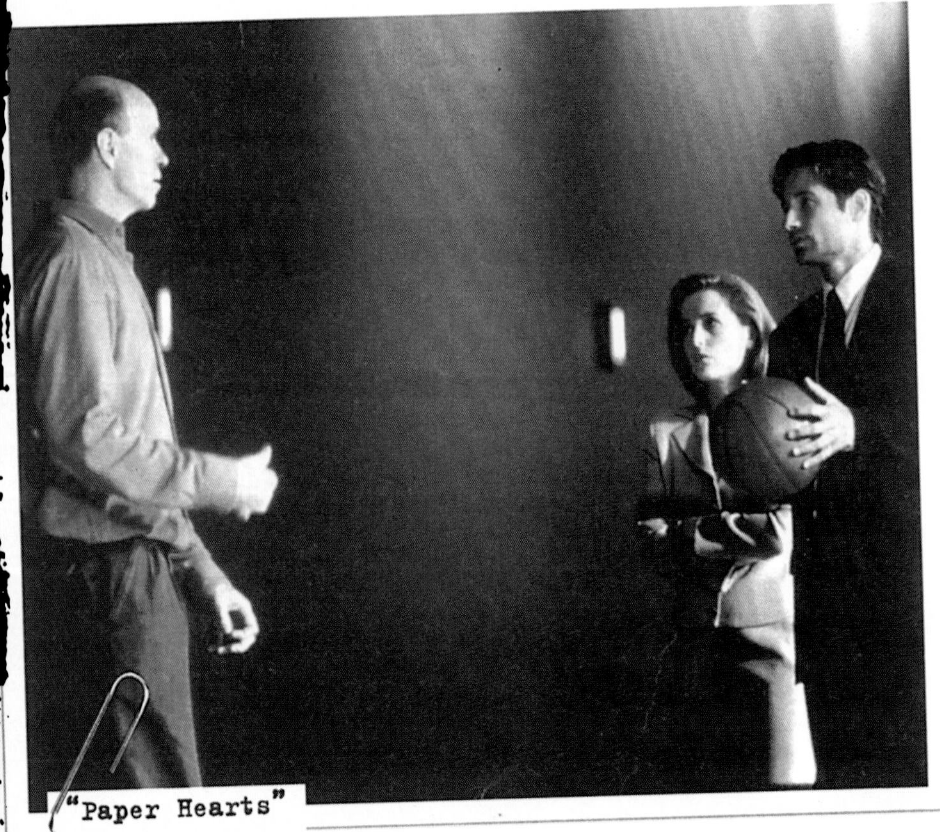

"Paper Hearts"

chest, originally I'm putting her hand both on my heart *and* on the image of the red dragon, the tattoo of who I was." Noonan also recalls another scene which was cut because Mann felt that it might make Dollarhyde's character too sympathetic. "There's a scene where [the blind girl] and I are out driving, and we go into a gas station, and I imagine that the service station attendant has hurt her," he explains. "I pick him up and throw him through a plate glass window, but I think Michael felt that that was too much, that it made me too noble and too sympathetic."

Oddly enough, both writer Vince Gilligan and director Rob Bowman had similar fears during the filming of "Paper Hearts". In his interview with this magazine in Issue 25, Gilligan remembers feeling that, "in some of the [rushes], I was a little afraid we'd gone too far, and I thought, 'Gee, maybe he's too matter-of-fact and this isn't going to work'."

"I had no idea," laughs Noonan. "I was doing it the way I thought it should be done, which was sort of low-key and normal, and they just kept saying, 'Oh this is great! It's great!' But, apparently, the director said that they were a little frightened I was doing it too 'normal,' and it was only later, when they put it together and realised it was really scary, they were happy."

Gilligan agrees, admitting that his doubts about Noonan's chillingly low-key delivery were unfounded. "I was wrong," he says, "because when that episode was cut together, it worked better than I hoped it would. Tom did a fantastic job, without any emotion." For his part, Noonan says that rather than attempting to over-analyse his character, get inside his head or under his skin, "I just kind of do what I do, you know? To me, it's just acting. And the more *me* that it feels, the better I think it is. I'm not the kind of actor that plays characters, really. I just try to believe what's happening, and just be present. That's not the only way to act, but it's the way I prefer."

This could hardly have been the approach Noonan took for the part of 'The Ripper' in *Last Action Hero*, in which he appeared opposite Arnold Schwarzenegger, Charles Dance, Academy Award winner F Murray Abraham and newcomer Austin O'Brien. Indeed, one of the principal reasons why a sequel was never made may have been that Noonan had eaten all of the scenery! "That was the intention," he laughs. "I tend to go over the top on that one because it was meant to be a fictional character; not a stereotype, exactly, but a cartoon of sorts. And in some ways it's easier playing a character like that, than somebody like Francis Dollarhyde, [because] it takes less..." He trails off, seemingly about to say that it take less of himself to play a role like 'The Ripper'. "I really had fun doing that part," he adds, "and I really liked that movie. The problem is they rushed it out – they should have spent a year post-producing that movie, because it takes time to figure out what makes a movie work."

Noonan says that he had an equally enjoyable time working on *The X-Files*, and with a far more satisfying end result. How did he find the experience? "What's great about *The X-Files* is that the people who run the show are the creators," he says. "You watch the beginning of the show, and you see that most of those producers mentioned are actually the writers and directors. I've not done a lot of TV," he goes on, "but the show doesn't have the feel of a TV show – it feels like a feature. It feels like everyobody who is there really wants to be there and really loves the show; they're all huge fans. They would sit around during breaks talking about an episode they had seen the week before. They're also very young: most people on the show are young and Canadian, and there is this great feeling of excitement on set which you almost never find in TV. Which is not the fault of anybody in TV, it's just difficult to get that feeling in the way that most shows are set up. It was certainly better than most features I've worked on. It was just really fun. I was like, do you have to kill me? Can't I come back?"

TOM NOONAN AT THE MOVIES

Heat (actor)
Last Action Hero (actor)
Robocop 2 (actor)
Collision Course (actor)
Mystery Train (actor)
The Man With One Red Shoe (actor)
Doris and Inez (actor)
Monster Squad (actor)
Manhunter (actor)
F/X: Murder by Illusion (actor)
Tom Goes to the Bar (actor)
Best Defense (actor)
Easy Money (actor)
Eddie Macon's Run (actor)
Wolfen (actor)
Heaven's Gate (actor)
Gloria (actor)
Willie and Phil (actor)
The Wife (actor, writer, director, producer, composer*, editor†)
The Pesky Suitor (producer, editor†)
What Happened Was... (actor, writer, director, producer, composer*, editor†)
BoneDaddy (actor, writer, director, composer*, editor†)
Romance (composer)
The Chauffeur (writer)
Zing! (writer)
Dam (writer)
Dead and Dumb (writer)
The Psychic Dentist (writer)
The Dark (writer)
P.A.N.I.C. (writer)
Bagdad (writer)
Fast and Loose (writer)

TOM NOONAN ON TELEVISION

The X-Files (actor)
Early Edition (actor)
Heaven and Hell (actor)
Monsters (actor)
The Equalizer (actor)
The $10,000,000 Getaway (actor)
Midtown (actor)
Tales from the Darkside (actor)
Rage (actor)
Malcolm (writer, director, composer*, editor†)
The Bargain (writer, director, composer*, editor†)
The Eternal Sideman (writer, director, producer, editor†)
What Alice Knew (composer*)
The Odds (composer*)
Red Wind (writer, producer)

TOM NOONAN AT THE THEATRE

Wifey (actor, writer, director, producer, composer*)
What Happened Was... (actor, writer, director, producer, composer*)
The Breakers (actor, composer*)
A Poster of the Cosmos (actor)
Spookhouse (actor)
Farmyard (actor)
Buried Child (actor)
Split (actor)
Swallow (writer)
Starring Beck Falcone (writer)
Queer and Alone (producer)
Hitting Town (producer)
Xmas Concert '92 (producer)
Two by Bose (producer)
Hoover (producer)
Goodbye and Keep Cold (composer*)
Flow My Tears (composer*)
My Hollywood Uncle (composer*)

**aka 'Ludovico Sorret'*
†aka 'Richmond Arrley'

EPISODE GUIDE

4.10: "PAPER HEARTS" Episode #4X08

Original US tx 15 December 96 Original UK tx 16 March 97

MARTHA'S VINEYARD

Mulder has a dream in which he 'sees' the final resting place of a murdered young girl. Upon awakening, he visits the area and is shocked to find the bones of a dead girl; the hallmarks of the crime indicate that the murderer may have been John Lee Roche, a serial killer whom Mulder helped to convict many years earlier.

Roche was given multiple life sentences in 1990, having confessed to the murder of thirteen young girls aged between eight and 10, abducted from their homes since 1979. In each case, Roche – a vacuum cleaner salesman – cut a heart-shaped piece from the dresses of his young victims as a morbid keepsake. The discovery of these 'souvenirs' – sixteen in all – leads to the realisation that Roche has yet more victims unaccounted for, stretching back to 1975 and possibly further.

Mulder and Scully question Roche in jail, but with no hope of ever seeing freedom, the man has little to gain by assisting with their enquiries. Instead, he goads Mulder by making a cryptic comment about him "taking this case personally". Mulder's next dream makes chilling sense of the comment, as he recalls the night in 1973 when his own sister, Samantha, was abducted. But this time, the bright lights that fill the room of his parents' summer home as his sister is taken are not from a spaceship, but from the headlights of the evil Roche's car.

Could Roche be responsible for Samantha's abduction? Could the memories he has of that night have been a psychological smokescreen for something far worse than alien abduction? Could Mulder's entire obsessive quest to find the truth of his sister's disappearance end with an interview in a jail cell?

Principal Credits

Created by	Chris Carter
Produced by	Ten Thirteen Productions for Twentieth Century Fox TV
Executive Producers	Chris Carter, Howard Gordon, RW Goodwin
Producers	Joseph Patrick Finn, Kim Manners, Rob Bowman
Co-Producers	Vince Gilligan, Frank Spotnitz, Paul Rabwin
Consulting Producers	Ken Horton, James Wong & Glen Morgan
Music	Mark Snow

Episode Credits

Written by Vince Gilligan
Directed by Rob Bowman

Special Agent Fox Mulder	David Duchovny
Special Agent Dr Dana Scully	Gillian Anderson
John Lee Roche	Tom Noonan
Assistant Director Walter S Skinner	Mitch Pileggi
Frank Sparks	Byrne Piven
Mrs Mulder	Rebecca Toolan
Day Care Operator	Jane Perry
Samantha Mulder	Vanessa Morley
El Camino Owner	Edward Diaz
Local Cop	Paul Bittante
Caitlin	Carly McKillip

F.Y.I.

"Paper Hearts" is perhaps writer/producer Vince Gilligan's finest work to date, and an episode which must surely reward him with a Prime Time Emmy Award when the honours are announced next month. According to Gilligan, interviewed about the episode last issue, the inspiration for the heart-breaking, breathtaking story came from the idea that Mulder's sister, Samantha, had been abducted and murdered by an all-too-earthly serial killer, rather than abducted and cloned by extra-terrestrials. "Samantha's abduction has always been a bedrock of the show," he explains. "If I turned it on its ear, there'd be no end to the interesting moments I could cobble out of that, because what you're saying is 'all bets are off'."

Gilligan was understandably delighted with the chilling portrayal of John Lee Roche by Tom Noonan [*see exclusive interview on page 44 - Ed*], whom the writer says did "a fantastic job, without any emotion. This is a weird thing to say," he adds, "[but] sometimes, when a character is torturing someone because of some deep felt feeling on his part, it's almost easier to take than someone who's doing it in such a lackadasical, blasé way. It's more monstrously evil when they're idly watching someone in pain."

Actress Vanessa Morley was once again called upon to play the young Samantha Mulder, just as she had in the first season episode "Conduit" and the second season's "Little Green Men", despite the fact that she had aged four years in the intervening period!

On its initial US broadcast, "Paper Hearts" scored a Nielsen rating of 10.7/16, equating approximately fifteen million viewers in ten million homes, while its Sky premiere drew 1.16 million viewers, the show's highest rating for more than a month.

Noteworthy Dialogue Transcript

MULDER: "Where were you in 1973?"
ROCHE: "What, the whole year?"
MULDER: "November. 27th of November. Do you know what I'm getting at?"
ROCHE: "I was selling vacuum cleaners in 1973. I made a sales trip to Martha's Vineyard in that year. I sold a vacuum cleaner to your father..."

Scream on

HE SCARIEST *X-FILES* EPISODES... EVER!

by KATE ANDERSON

So where do you prefer watching The X-Files? laybe you like sprawling yourself on your favorite couch...)r perhaps you like to get a bowl of popcorn and chill out n your lovely fold-out chair. But sometimes you don't have nuch of an option. Y'see, certain episodes can only be watched rom one position: behind the couch. Yep, you know the ones. o TV show does horror like The X-Files. So to celebrate this, e've decided to select what we think are 10 of the creepiest X-iles episodes ever, and we'll be meeting some of the scariest tars along the way. So, sit down; dim the lights; close the urtains... and get behind that couch!

DUE TO GRAPHIC AND MATURE CONTENT, READER DISCRETION IS ADVISED...

"Home"

Season Four, Episode Three

The story: The gruesome discovery of a dead and horribly deformed newborn baby leads Mulder and Scully to investigate their prime suspects – the freakish Peacock brothers. In doing so, the agents stumble upon the family's shocking secret; a secret the brothers tried to bury when they disposed of the infant.
The scary bits: The deformed and violent Peacock boys; the horrific murder of Sheriff Taylor and his wife; the body under the bed; and the underlying incest theme. Imagery doesn't get much more gruesome and shocking than this. This is definitely not one to watch before bedtime!
X-tra: "Home" was the first (although most certainly not the last) episode to be preceded by a warning about its mature and graphic content. Incidentally, science fiction fans may recognise the ill-fated Deputy Paster; Sebastian Spence played Cade Foster in *First Wave*.
Deathcount: 6 (newborn baby – buried alive; Sheriff Taylor and wife – clubbed to death; Deputy Paster – decapitated; Sherman Peacock – booby trapped; George Peacock – shot)

our town

"Our Town"

Season Two, Episode 24

The story: The owner of a meat processing plant in a small town comes under investigation after people start to mysteriously disappear.
The scary bits: Cannibalism! One thing's for certain, watching this episode will make you think twice about eating a certain type of fast food – for a while, anyway!
Deathcount: 6 (George Kearns – beheaded; Paula Gray – shot; Doris Kearns – death by axe; Walter Chaco – beheaded; Sheriff Arens – shot; Truck driver – presumably killed when his truck crashed and plunged into river; a lot of chickens)

grotesque

"Grotesque"

Season Three, Episode 14

The story: An imprisoned serial killer claims he is possessed by an evil spirit. Mulder becomes obsessed with the case, causing him to clash with the agent in charge, who just so happens to be his former mentor.
The scary bits: An over-the-edge Mulder on a path of self-destruction; the killer's victims made into gargoyles – eek! Overall, a psychologically scary episode that makes the real world as it were seem a very, very frightening place indeed.
Deathcount: 3+ (Artist's model – slashed and mutilated; Another male victim – same facial mutilations; Agent Nemhauser – presumably slashed to death, body encased in clay; A roomful of killer's victims made into gargoyles – presumably all met a similar death)

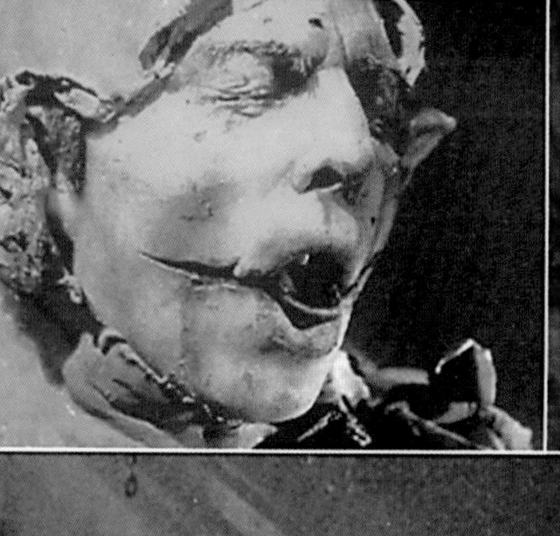

"IRRESISTIBLE"

Season Two, Episode 13

The story: Death fetishist Donnie Pfaster turns to murder in order to satisfy his cravings. Whilst investigating the murder of one of Pfaster's victims, a prostitute, Scully unwittingly becomes Pfaster's next target.
The scary bits: From his ultra creepy voice to his strange obsession with hair, Donnie Pfaster sends shivers down the spine. As Scully points out at the end of the episode, the seemingly normal boy-next-door types like Pfaster are the most frightening kinds of monsters. The mere thought that the boy next door in the button-down shirt could be the devil in disguise doesn't bear thinking about.
X-tra: Donnie Pfaster returned for a final confrontation with Scully in Season Seven's "Orison" – Scully put an end to his killing spree once and for all.
Deathcount: 1 (prostitute – murdered by Pfaster)

"CHINGA"

Season Five, Episode 10

The story: On vacation in Maine, Scully stumbles across a supermarket where shoppers have inexplicably mutilated themselves, and the butcher has apparently committed suicide. Prime suspect is Melissa Turner and her eerie-looking young daughter.
The scary bits: From the *Child's Play*-like doll to the shoppers clawing at their eyes, this episode is littered with nasty, creepy imagery. Polly and Chinga make for one scary double act.
X-tra: "Chinga" was co-written by horror supremo Stephen King (with Chris Carter). The episode is also known as "Bunghoney" due to the original title being a rather vulgar Spanish colloquialism!
Deathcount: 3 (Dave the butcher – large knife in eye (self-inflicted); Jane Froelich – broken record in throat (self-inflicted); Deputy Riggs – beaten with own nightstick (self-inflicted))

fresh bones

"FRESH BONES"

SEASON TWO, EPISODE 15

The story: Mulder and Scully find themselves battling the dark forces of voodoo whilst investigating a series of unusual deaths involving US soldiers assigned to oversee the incarceration of Haitian refugees.
The scary bits: Lots of ooze and yucky stuff. Most notably, the closing scene at the cemetery. Scully's hallucination is hair-raising stuff. Not one for the faint hearted. You just might want to keep your remote control in er, hand...
X-tra: *Due South*'s Callum Keith Rennie appears as the groundskeeper. "Fresh Bones" was the highest rated episode of the first two seasons.
Deathcount: 3 (Private Dunham – stabbed; Pierre Bauvais – unknown, although likely beaten to death (by Colonel Wharton); Colonel Wharton – buried alive, trapped in coffin)

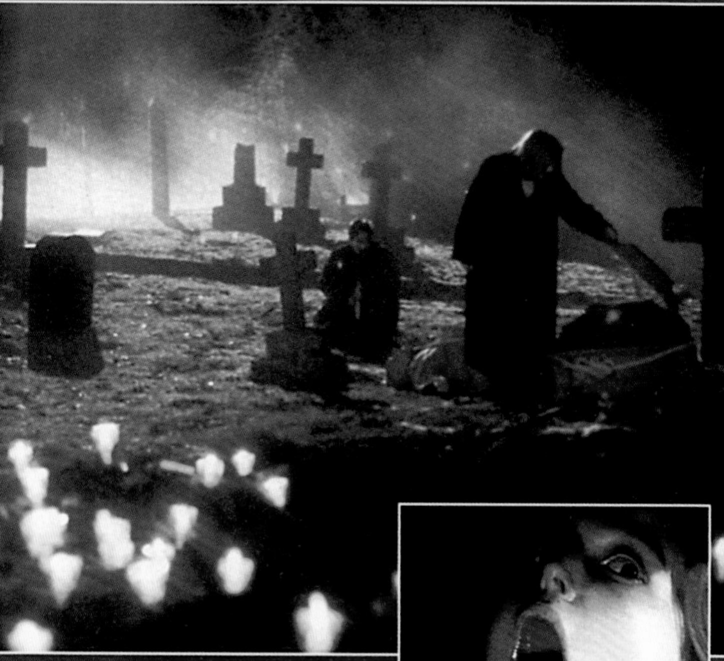

"DIE HAND DIE VERLETZT"

SEASON TWO, EPISODE 14

die hand die verletzt

The story: Mulder and Scully investigate the grisly murder of a teenager in a small town populated by devil worshippers.
The scary bits: The entire episode is chock full of dark themes (repressed memories, ritual abuse) and scary moments. Oh, and one ultra creepy character – Mrs Paddock! Not to mention the pig embryo hallucination scene – yuck! Memories of dissection classes at school have never been so horrifying!
X-tra: The title is German for "The Hand That Wounds".
Deathcount: 6 (Jerry Stevens – choked to death by evil supernatural force, his eyes and heart were removed; Shannon Ausbury – under a spell, slashed her wrists; Jim Ausbury – crushed to death and devoured by huge snake; 3 school teachers/occultists – shot)

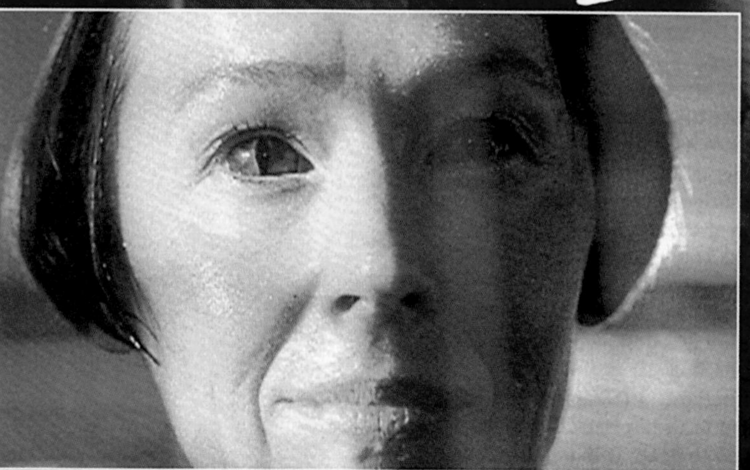

"Via Negativa"

Season Eight, Episode Seven

The story: When two F.B.I. Agents on routine surveillance of a religious cult die mysteriously, Doggett and Skinner must investigate a killer who leaves no trace of his crimes.

The scary bits: While the whole episode gets increasingly creepy, the visceral impact of one scene really stands out: Doggett holding a bloody severed head – Scully's! 'Nuff said!

X-tra: Yet another episode that earned itself a viewer discretion warning for its violent and graphic content.

Deathcount: 25! (2 F.B.I. agents, 1 homeless man and 20 cult members – all head trauma; Andre Bormanis – eaten by rats; Anthony Tippet – self-inflicted head injury from table saw)

via negativa

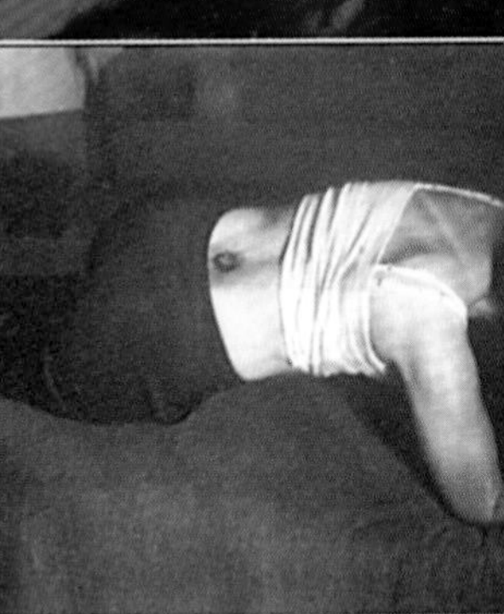

"Roadrunners"

Season Eight, Episode Four

The story: Agent Scully goes solo to consult on a murder case involving the mysterious death of a traveler beaten to death. She finds herself stuck in a remote town with a bunch of truly creepy townsfolk, who are part of a cult who worship a giant, slug-like creature.

The scary bits: Where to begin?! This episode has probably the most violent teaser in *X-Files* history; the brutal murder of a disabled man who has his skull viciously bashed in is distressing to say the least.

X-tra: This episode was partly inspired by the 1955 movie *Bad Day at Black Rock*, starring Spencer Tracy. The creature was designed to resemble a banana slug.

Deathcount: 3 (Disabled man – stoned to death; Hank Gulatarski – bashed to death with hammer; slug creature – shot 3 times)

"The Calusari"

Season Two, Episode 21

The story: The mysterious death of a toddler at an amusement park and the subsequent deaths of two other members of the same family leads Mulder and Scully to an unlikely suspect. But it turns out their young suspect is in fact possessed by an evil force – the spirit of his stillborn twin brother.

The scary bits: From the deeply disturbing – and controversial – teaser sequence to the exorcism scene, this is one frighteningly creepy episode, made all the more so because it involves the death of a young child. Although the denouement may be nothing new, it's nevertheless riveting.

X-tra: Upon its original UK terrestrial transmission, a BBC announcer warned viewers about the program's content; specifically that it contained scenes that some viewers could find upsetting.

Deathcount: 3 (Teddy Holvey – run over by a miniature fairground train; Steve Holvey – chokes to death when his tie gets entangled in a garage door opener; Golda – attacked and killed by roosters)

the calusari

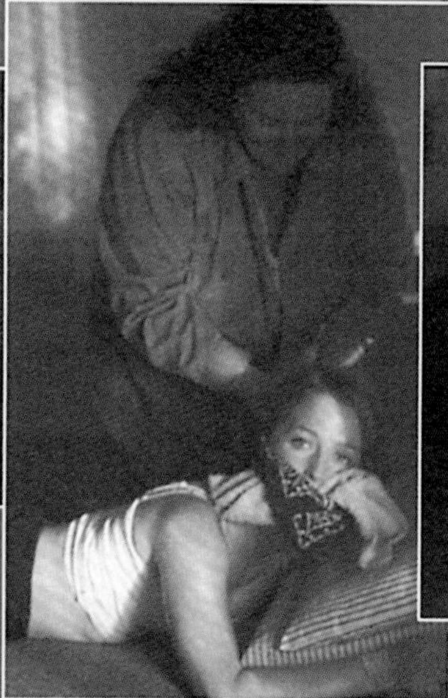

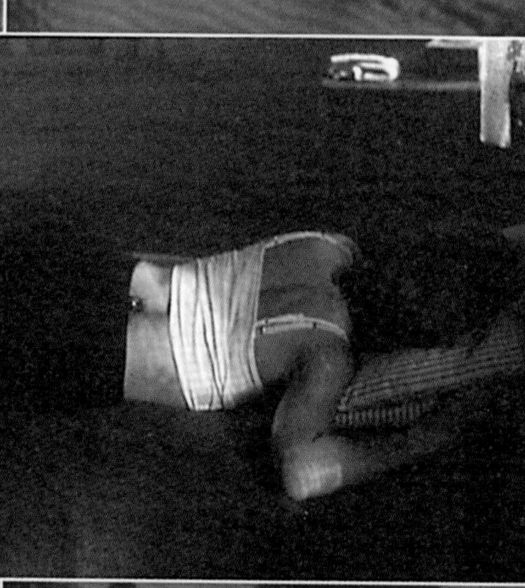

ners

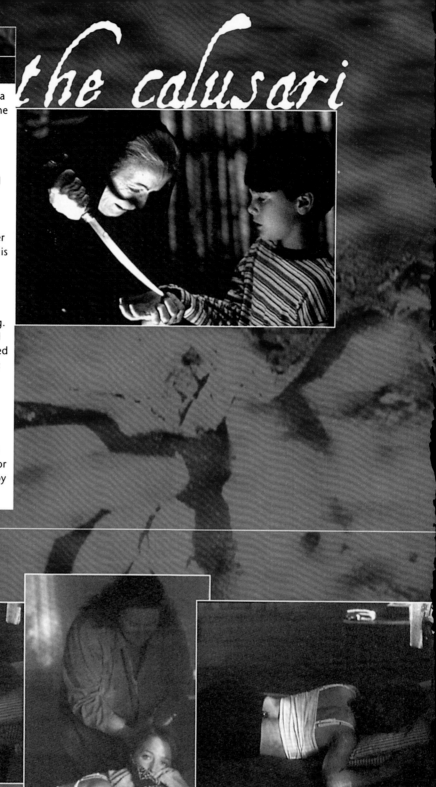

He played one of the most horrifying characters in one of the most controversial X-Files episodes ever. **John Trottier** – George Peacock from "Home" – met up with **Ian Spelling** for a revealing, rare interview

JOHN!

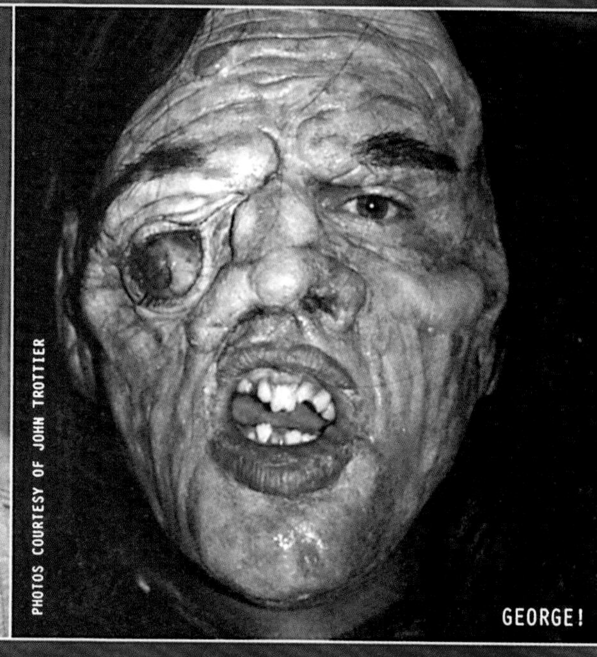

PHOTOS COURTESY OF JOHN TROTTIER

GEORGE!

"The funny thing about 'Home' is that while we were doing it, I don't remember it being controversial," actor John Trottier recalls. In the fourth-season hour, directed by Kim Manners and written by Glen Morgan and James Wong, F.B.I. Special Agents Mulder and Scully encounter the Peacocks. Their meeting with the in-bred brothers George (Trottier), Sherman (Adrian Hughes) and Edmund (Chris Norris), and their adoring multiple amputee mom (Karin Konoval) – proves one of their strangest cases ever.

"[My mother] said, '['Home'] was horrible. It was **disgusting**. And I've never been so **proud** of you!'"

"It was an incredibly intense experience," says Trottier. "If I recall, it took about three weeks to film. We were on set for two full weeks and then a bit of another week, and we were doing 16-hour days. You forgot that what you were doing was more intense than your usual show or, from what they told me, a regular episode of *The X-Files*. When the episode actually came on I was working as an acting teacher for a university, and I brought a bunch of my students over to my house to watch it. They all just stared at the screen with their jaws wide open, wondering what the hell kind of double life I was leading. But while we were on the set shooting 'Home' I didn't get the feeling that it was potentially so dark and controversial."

Trottier almost didn't get his chance to shine in the classic *X-Files* episode. The Canadian actor had actually been cast for an earlier Season Four episode, "Herrenvolk," in which he would have been called upon to climb up a telephone pole, endure a bee sting and then fall to the ground. As shooting approached, however, the production couldn't find a convincing body double for Trottier, who stands six-foot-five and tips the scale at 300 pounds. So the casting director called Trottier's agent and apologetically explained that another actor would have to play the role. During that very same call the casting director asked if Trottier might be interested in reading for a larger part, but one with no dialogue. That other part, of course, was George Peacock in "Home."

"I got the script and read it, and the story was obviously unique," Trottier says. "You don't see too many shows dealing with infanticide and incest. Looking back on it, that's pretty harsh material. But as the actor, that's not my jurisdiction. I'm going in and spending hours and hours and hours in make-up, and being exhausted by that. I haven't even gone in front of a camera yet. I'm thinking only about how am I going to help this makeup work into my character. So I never put a lot of thought into the story, other than how I'd fit into it.

"After I watched it, that's when I kind of realized that the story was pretty controversial and that we'd done something very unusual. The reaction of my students was pretty funny, but what my mother said to me that night I'll never forget. She said, 'It was horrible. It was disgusting. And I've never been so proud of you!'

"The controversy surprised me, I guess. It was so much fun to film that I think most cast were surprised that it came out as dark as it did. The scene when we killed the sheriff (Tucker Smallwood), that's when it actually became real to me. We had these clubs and we were beating on a sleeping bag. But there was so much fake blood that they had to take about 45 minutes between each shot to hose down the set and clean everything up. After one of the shots they forgot to clean off our boots, so they had to go back and clean the set again because we'd walked in with bloody boots.

John with Mitch Pileggi and a Peacock brother

After that it was like, 'Oh, this is a little more violent than I thought.' The scene in which we were burying the baby I actually got in trouble with my fellow actors. I was singing 'I've Been Working on the Railroad' as I buried the baby, and they were like, 'John, what are you doing? This is serious. Get into this!' I was thinking that the camera was about 85 miles away, over there in a field, and that we were acting through make-up. So I thought, 'Let's have fun with it.' But they didn't see it that way.

"Another scene that was disturbing to viewers was the baby scene at the beginning of the episode. It was the last shot we did. We probably shot that at six in the morning. That was pretty crazy. It was six in the morning and we'd been under rain machines all night. We were all so tired. But there was a sense of camaraderie and I know I keep saying this, but it was fun. We just had no sense that it was going to be anything more than what it was. I have to say that Kim Manners probably had a sense. He'd get this sly smile and just laugh. I kind of recall him saying, 'I can't believe we're doing this. I can't believe we're doing this.

Trottier likes to think of himself as a "working actor." He turned up, again under layers of makeup, in the fantasy miniseries *Voyage of the Unicorn*, and he pops up frequently in television commercials, including recent spots for the St. Louis Cardinals baseball franchise and the antacid *Beano*, in which he was cast as a monk. Trottier was "short-listed" several times for *Millennium*, but never actually appeared on the show. Later, he landed a small role as a gunfighter in a *Harsh Realm* episode. He also returned to *The X-Files* about a year after "Home."

"I'd been under so much makeup doing 'Home' that no one who watched the show would recognize m if I came back as a different character," Trottier notes. "So I playe a psychologist in 'The End,' which wa the last episode of *The X-Files* shot up here in Vancouver. It was a speaking role I was the first psychologist who talks to the little boy chess champion. It was pretty cool to go back. Everyone remembered me and welcomed me back, which was a lot of fun. But the set was a bit melancholy because we shot my scenes on one of the production's la days in Vancouver."

When he's not on a set acting, Trottier can usually be found teaching As noted, he was working at a university when "Home" first aired. These days he teaches high school drama classes. And just as Trottier screened "Home" for his university students he does likewise for his high schoolers. "Every Halloween I show that episode to my grade eights," Trottier explains. "I have to get little permission slips signed by their parents. But it's pretty cool. I'm known as 'That *X-Files* Guy' at the school, and that's fine by me."●

On the set of "Home"

"You don't see too many shows dealing with infanticide and incest. Looking back on it, that's pretty harsh material."

EPISODE GUIDE

4.2: "HOME" Episode #4X03

Original US tx 11 October 96 Original UK tx scheduled for spring 97

HOME, PENNSYLVANIA

In the sleepy town of Home, an inhuman creature is born at the old Peackocks' property and subsequently buried in the dead of night, amid a raging lightning storm. Later, some kids playing baseball in sight of the Peacock family's shunned house discover a shallow grave containing the corpse of a grossly malformed baby.

The local sheriff agrees to an autopsy, but will only allow it to be conducted in the police station's restroom. On inspection of the body, Scully instantly knows that the creature was afflicted with "every birth defect known to man," but also discovers that the baby was alive when it was buried. Scully and Mulder immediately suspect the suspicious-looking Peacock family – a group of redneck throwbacks whom the local sheriff says "breed their own stock, if you know what I mean." However, the family has no surviving female members. Mulder is eager to leave the case to the local authorities, but Scully is deeply affected by the autopsy she had to perform. "I never saw you as a mother before," Mulder tells her.

At the Peacock place, the agents soon discover enough evidence to make the family the prime suspects. Before the sheriff can have them arrested, however, the Peacocks load up their old Cadillac and pay a visit to his house, brutally clubbing him and his wife to death to the tune of a classic '50s song. Once again, the trail leads to the Peacock family. Do they, as Scully believes, have a woman captive at the house who is the unwilling mother of the dead child? And now that the sheriff is dead, are the agents and his deputy enough of a force to bring the family in?

Principal Credits

Produced by	Ten-Thirteen Productions for 20th Century-Fox TV
Executive Producer	Chris Carter
Co-Executive Producers	Howard Gordon, R W Goodwin
Producers	Joseph Patrick Finn, Kim Manners, Rob Bowman
Consulting Producers	Ken Horton, James Wong and Glen Morgan
Co-Producers	Vince Gilligan, Frank Spotnitz, Paul Rabwin
Music	Mark Snow

Episode Credits

Written by	Glen Morgan and James Wong
Directed by	Kim Manners
Special Agent Fox Mulder	David Duchovny
Special Agent Dr Dana Scully	Gillian Anderson
Sheriff Andy Taylor	Tucker Smallwood
Deputy Barney Pastor	Chris Nelson Norris
Sherman Peacock	Adrian Hughes
George Peacock	John Trotter
Mrs Peacock	Karin Konoval
Deputy Barney Paster	Sebastian Spence
Barbara Taylor	Judith Maxie
Radio Singer	Kenny James
Right Fielder	Lachlain Murdoch
Catcher	Neil Dennis
Batter	Cory Fry
Pitcher	Douglas Smith

F.Y.I.

The award-winning writer/producer combo of Glen Morgan and James Wong made a triumphant return to the show with this extraordinary episode about the most dysfunctional family in America which polarised X-Philes with its strong visceral content. "They came back with a blast," says Gillian Anderson. "[It's] probably one of the most bizarre episodes we've had. It's about a strange family [who] have been breeding their own cattle, pigs, chickens – even their own... family." There's no place like Home, all right.

"Home" was the first *X-Files* episode to include a warning of the graphic nature of the show, which read as follows: 'DUE TO SOME GRAPHIC AND MATURE CONTENT, PARENTAL DISCRETION IS ADVISED.' Yet despite its graphic content, there is still room for a few classic Morgan/Wong in-jokes, such as the one where Scully attempts to move a herd of pigs by repeating the words "Baa-ram-ewe", the old sheep's secret message from the movie, *Babe*. Although the third episode of the fourth season to be filmed (hence the designation 4X03), "Home," was actually the second to be shown, scoring a Nielsen rating of 11.9 (approximately 21 million homes.)

Noteworthy Dialogue Transcript

SCULLY: "What about your family?"

MULDER: "Well, aside from the need for corrective lenses and a tendency to be abducted by extra-terrestrials involved in an international government conspiracy, the Mulder family passes genetic muster."

Unexplained Plot Discrepancies

Mulder and Scully are trespassing when they first enter the Peacock property without warrants – the 'evidence' they have is too flimsy to give them Probable Cause. Thus, the incriminating evidence they find at the scene would have been inadmissable. And did the agents really believe that Deputy Pastor was enough of a force to take in the three dangerous and deranged adult male members of the Peacock family?

WHAT A WAY TO GO!

You can't have a decent horror episode without plenty of **blood, guts and death**. And not just any old death either: we're talkin' **gory** beheadings, **bloody** shootings, and that old favorite, death by **flukeworm-regurgitation**.

Martin Eden and Kate Anderson reminisce about some of the most memorable X-Files deaths ever.

DEATH BY: FATAL BOOBY TRAP

Victim: Deputy Barney Paster
When: "Home"
Witness report: Killed when trying to enter the rigged-up Peacock property.

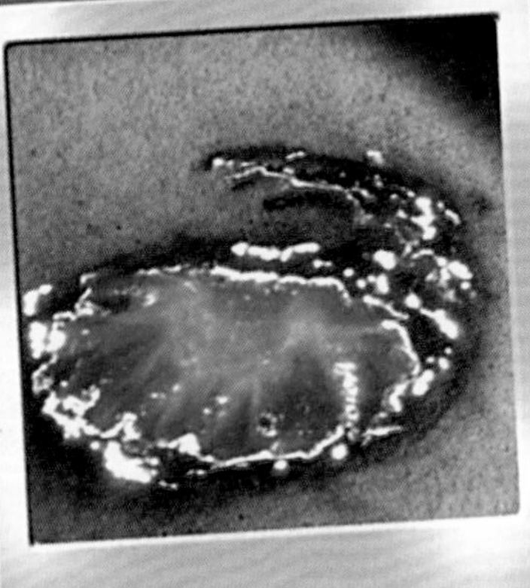

DEATH BY: DISINTEGRATION

Victim: Detective Kelly Ryan
When: "Soft Light"
Witness report: A student of Scully's, Kelly Ryan, is reduced to a pile of carbon when she attempts to apprehend Dr Chester Banton (whose shadow has turned into a deadly dark matter).

DEATH BY: PARASITIC FLUKEWORM

Victim: Unnamed sanitation worker.
When: "The Host"
Witness report: After recovering from an attack by an unknown creature in the New Jersey sewerage system, a workman coughs up a parasitic worm.

DEATH BY: BEING SKINNED ALIVE

Victims: Reincarnated murderers.
When: "Hellbound"
Witness report: A reincarnated murder victim seeks revenge on his reincarnated killers by skinning them alive. Yes, skinning them alive.

DEATH BY: FOLDING BLEACHERS

Victim: Student 'Eric'.
When: "Syzygy"
Witness report: Having accidentally soaked Terri Roberts and Margi Kleinjan with lemonade, the cosmic powered girls decide to crush him to death behind electric motor-powered bleacher seats.

DEATH BY: EXPLODING THROAT

Victims: A team of scientists working at a volcanic research base at Mount Avalon.
When: "Firewalker"
Witness report: The research team are infected by a fungus which causes a spike-shaped protusion to burst through the throat.

Death by: Blue paint

Victim: Nathan Bowman.
When: "Kitsunegari"
Witness report: Robert 'Pusher' Modell's fraternal twin, Linda, decides to take revenge on the prosecutor who helped put him in prison – by covering his entire body in paint.

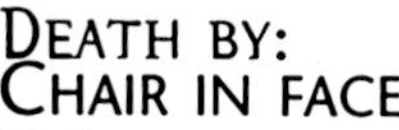

Death by: Chair in face

Victim: Mr Babbitt.
When: "Rush"
Witness report: Speedy teen killer, Max Harden, decides to take revenge on a teacher – by throwing a chair at his face. At top speed.

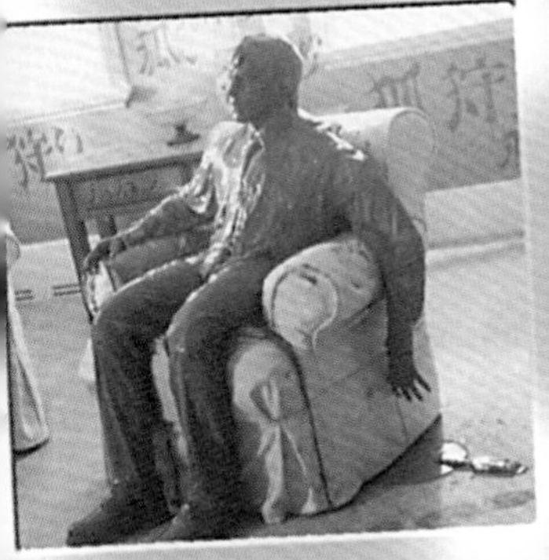

Death by: Exploding spots

Victims: Prisoners at the Cumberland State Correctional Facility.
When: "F. Emasculata"
Witness report: The prisoners are exposed to an organism that causes huge boils to emerge – and erupt – on the victims' faces.

Death by: Microwave

Victim: Nan Weider.
When: "Theef"
Witness report: Having already caused Nan to contract a rare disease, powerful Mr. Peattie places a hex doll in a microwave – while Nan burns to death in a radiology tube. "All done," says Peattie.

Death by: Exploding head

Victims: Patrick and Vicky Crump
When: "Drive"
Witness Report: A local surge in E.L.F. waves has had a devastating effect on the Crumps – they need to travel West to avoid pressure rising in the inner ear.

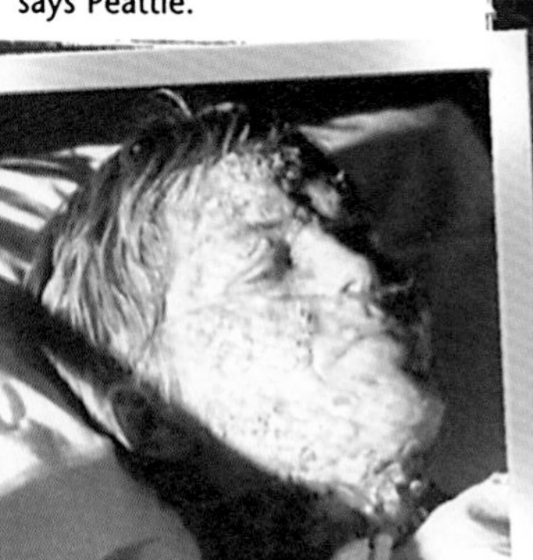

Death by: Electric shock to the face

Victim: Leonard Betts
When: "Leonard Betts"
Witness report: Cancer-eating killer Leonard Betts finally meets his match in Agent Scully. He attacks her but she manages to defend herself using hospital defibrillation pads. On his face.

Death by: Alligator

Victim: Queequeg
When: "Quagmire"
Witness report: Scully's adopted dog is suddenly snatched by something in the bushes; the poor Pomeranian becomes a light snack for a rather large alligator.

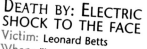

EPISODES: 2X13/7X07

DONNIE PFASTER

"Irresistible" / "Orison"

If there's one thing you can say about *The X-Files*, the series affords actors opportunities no other television show can. In the case of Nick Chinlund, who plays Donnie Pfaster in Season Two's "Irresistible" and Season Seven's "Orison," the thespian got the chance to bring to the screen a man whose sexual fixation with death endangers the lives of the women whom he encounters, including Agent Scully. Not exactly your run-of-the-mill bad guy.

But Pfaster's depravity is precisely what drew Chinlund to the role. After all, anyone can play a stereotypical thug, but it takes something special to portray an eerie death fetishist. "I don't have murderous images running through my

NICK CHINLUND

mind," Chinlund says, reassuringly. "The stillness of the character is what makes it so scary, I think. I try and do as little as possible so people can put their own imagination on it."

His approach works. Five years after his first appearance on the series, Pfaster remains in league with the show's greatest villains, and Chinlund was happy to return for a follow-up episode. "I agreed to do it before I read the script," he explains. "I think it's brilliant and funny actually in a few spots. It was interesting to play the sort of heightened aspect of Donnie's malevolence. He's been in prison for five years, so everything has been percolating while he's in jail. That was interesting to push it up a notch—if you can do that with him."

The actor was also pleased to again work with David Duchovny and Gillian Anderson. Chinlund, it seems, has much in common with *The X-Files* leading man. Both hail from New York and attended Ivy League schools (Chinlund attended Brown University). Both appeared on the Showtime series *Red Shoe Diaries*. And both have a deep-seated affection for basketball. Chinlund, who once aspired to a career in the NBA, says he's one of the few people who can match Duchovny shot for shot. "He's scared of me," Chinlund boasts. "I'll whip his butt."—*Gina McIntyre*

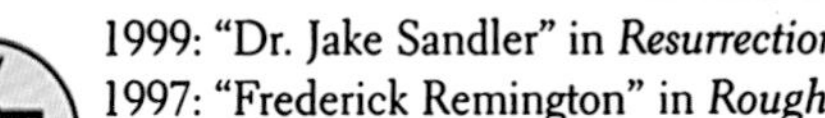

ALSO KNOWN AS:

1999: "Dr. Jake Sandler" in *Resurrection*
1997: "Frederick Remington" in *Rough Riders*
1995: "Nick Parma" in *Letter to My Killer*
1993: "Weldon Small" in *NYPD Blue*

1999: "Mitch" in *Chutney Popcorn*
1999: "Joseph Parker" in *Goodnight, Joseph Parker*
1997: "Bob Morgan" in *Mr. Magoo*
1997: "William 'Billy Bedlam' Bedford" in *Con Air*
1996: "Calderon" in *Eraser*
1992: "Hatchett" in *Lethal Weapon 3*

Phamous Philes

Want to know how best-selling horror-master Stephen King came to write "Chinga," one of Season Five's creepiest outings? Don't give credit to King or Chris Carter for the inspired King/*X-Files* pairing. Thank David Duchovny...and Alex Trebek.

"I met David Duchovny while I was taping a *Jeopardy* show, and he asked if I would like to write an *X-Files* episode," King recalls. "At that time I didn't watch the show, but I discovered that my kids, my older son in particular, were junkies. [Carter] sent me tapes of the first season and pretty soon I, too, became a junkie."

STEPHEN KING

PHOTO BY JAMES LEONARD

Soon afterward, King began working on the script. As is frequently the case in television writing, his original concept for the show was considerably different from the end product.

"The episode began as something that was closer to *Firestarter* than to *Pet Sematary*," King explains. "In the first draft, Mulder and Scully were in a battle with one of those unnamed organisations who wanted to take Polly [the little autistic girl in the story] away and study her. In that first version, most of the bad things were done by a doppelgånger—a projection which was, essentially, Polly's evil twin."

King ran the draft before Carter, who turned the story in different directions.

"Chris liked the doll, and I think he liked the doll's name," says King. "He asked me if I would do a complete rewrite substituting the doll for the twin and making this a Scully solo episode. I agreed."

Carter must have reconsidered the latter idea to some extent, since Mulder does appear briefly throughout "Chinga," bringing some comic relief to an episode heavy on macabre mayhem.

"'Chinga' is quite a bit gorier than the usual *X-Files* episode, but both my first draft and second draft were pretty restrained," says King. "A lot of the gore, particularly in the teaser, was Chris' idea."

The episode's title, apparently, carried its own brand of controversy. A *TV Guide* writer told King that the word "chinga" is a Spanish vulgarity for sex, while another source said it was interpreted to mean "excrement." "So far as I know, I picked the name out of thin air," King insists. "But there is a vibe out there about names, and I have tapped into it before. I don't think anything is really by accident."

Though "Chinga" was heavily rewritten by Carter (who is credited as a cowriter on the episode), King apparently didn't mind the process. Originally, King says, Carter didn't want to take the co-byline. "I thought it was important to give credit where credit was due, and I'm very happy with the final result. Taking all elements of screenplay writing into consideration, from original idea to final execution, I would say it was about a 50/50 split."

If King were king for a day in *The X-Files* script department, his ideal episode "would either be one in which one of the main characters dies, or, much better, one in which Mulder and Scully finally go to bed together."

The best-selling scribe enjoyed his foray into the world of *The X-Files*, and hopes to repeat the experience. "I would like to write another episode for the show," says King, who adds that he's concocted an incomplete idea for a future plot, which he won't reveal. "Working with Chris was a real pleasure. Whether or not it actually happens depends on my schedule."

Don't look for King to pen an *X-Files* novel anytime soon, however. "I don't think I would do a novelization," he says. "Unless, of course, I could write a book in which Mulder and Scully go to bed together."—*Tyson Blue*

Creature Feature

Ian Spelling catches up with actor Jordan Marder, who played one of the most horrifying X-Files creations ever in Season Eight's "The Gift"

Jordan Marder thinks of his *X-Files* episode and the first thing that springs to mind is... "The hours of makeup!" Nevertheless, the actor, has fond memories of his *X-Files* experience. Marder guest-starred as the deformed, long-suffering and illness-eating character referred to as the Creature in "The Gift" during Season Eight of *The X-Files*. You remember the episode: Mulder shot at him (in a flashback sequence) and, near the end of the hour he regurgitated Doggett, who seemed beyond help after taking a bullet from an angry sheriff (played by Michael McGrady) and being buried deep in the ground by over-zealous townsfolk who wanted the Creature to keep healing its sick, even if it prolonged the Creature's torment indefinitely.

"I lost count of how many hours I sat in the chair. It must have been 20, 30, 40, 50 hours, maybe 100 hours. We shot the episode over 14 or 15 days and we also had some test makeups that were 10 to 15 hours each. And those were botched. I also had some days where I did makeup but didn't work. It was an amazing experience, though. They did full body casts over at the special effects department. They molded me into a special gel where I couldn't move and only had a little tube to breathe through for 20 or 30 seconds. Then they'd peel it off you. Between all of that it was 50 to 100 hours."

All of which makes one wonder: what made Marder say yes to the gig and what made *The X-Files* casting department think of Marder? "I have no idea what made them think of me," the actor replies. "The part called for a 300-year-old shaman, a Native American priest. I guess I was called in because of my facial bone structure, but I'm a young man. I'm 28 years old. I went in and they were looking for an actor who, I believe, could convey a lot just with his presence, through his eyes and his face, in his composure. Like most directors and casting directors, they were looking for an answer, for someone to bring something to the table. Usually an actor comes in with a little of what they're after, they hire him and work on it together. That's kind of what happened here. Kim Manners said, 'We need someone who can show a lot of expression in his

"I lost count of how many hours I sat in the chair. It must have been 20, 30, 40, 50 hours, maybe 100 hours."

eyes,' and I just felt that was interesting. It wasn't a tremendous challenge because I think you have to show a lot through the eyes with any character. But this guy was trapped in his own disease, his own illness or, if you want to use a more practical term, he was trapped behind makeup. I thought it was interesting to try to break through that any way possible."

Some actors love the makeup process, arguing that it helps them create a character and that it aids in escaping into the fantasy element of the story at hand. Other actors consider sitting in the makeup chair a huge bore and find that the prosthetics distract them too much to deliver the performance they hope to put across. "I understand both points of view," says Marder. "When you wear makeup, it has to work for you. It'll only work if you allow it to work for you, and you should because as an actor, you're someone playing pretend. That's your job as an actor, your only job, to play the character. I think using the makeup and playing pretend feeds you. If you look at yourself in the mirror after putting on a costume and makeup that's been crafted by masters in their art, it changes you and your decisions and ideas about who you are as a character. You have to be malleable."

Marder reports that he "enjoyed" working on "The Gift", describes the cast and crew as "hard-working" and "like a well-oiled machine," and says he was "very pleased" with the finished episode. "The Gift", of course, is just one of the up and coming young actor's credits. Born in upstate New York, in Croton on the Hudson, Marder started acting professionally at age 10, appearing on Broadway in the show *Strange Interlude* with Glenda Jackson. He received acclaim and an Emmy Award nomination for his performance opposite Lynn Redgrave in *Walking on Air*, PBS Wonderworks' special based on a story of the same name by legendary sci-fi author Ray Bradbury. Later, Marder appeared in such films as Clive Barker's *Lord of Illusions*, *Virtuosity*, *L.A. Confidential* and *American History X*, and he guest-starred on several TV series, including *The Equalizer*, *Spenser for Hire*, *JAG*, *Seven Days*, and *Nash Bridges*. Most recently, he shot another episode of *JAG* in which he played an entirely different character than he did several years ago.

"Right now I'm auditioning, and things seem to be picking up," Marder says. "Hopefully I'll get a dramatic series or a good part in a feature." And if his phone ever rings and it was an *X-Files* casting director inviting Marder back for the next *X-Files* movie? "I'd say yes, absolutely," the actor concludes. "I liked the people. I would even do the makeup again."●

THE X-FILES' VISUAL EFFECTS GUR

lords of Il

BY RON MAGID

PHOTO BY KHAREN HILL

s Pick Their Greatest Triumphs

lusion

At least once a week, they face the darkness inside themselves to bring our worst nightmares to life. The men and women who create *The X Files'* terrifying imagery forever walk that fine line between showing too much or too little, traversing that twilight zone where a little bit will kill but a lot will just make you sick. These guys go for the jugular, and they usually find it.

It's a helluva way to make a living—but also one of the most rewarding. We asked three of *The X-Files'* star effects artists—former visual effects producer Mat Beck (currently overseeing the *X-Files* movie), current visual effects supervisor Laurie Kallsen-George and practical effects maestro David Gauthier—to name their favorite effects from the series. Like the show itself, their choices were never obvious and always surprising.

MAT BECK

Before leaving *The X-Files* to pursue a career creating cool imagery for the big screen (such as torching L.A.'s Wilshire Boulevard for *Volcano*), visual effects supervisor Mat Beck made audiences' skins collectively creep for three terrifying seasons. That's probably why one of Beck's favorite episodes was the uncharacteristically hilarious "Jose Chung's 'From Outer Space.'"

"One of the challenges was that, like *Mars Attacks!*, the effort was made to make it look cheesy," Beck explains. Although camp isn't Beck's strong suit, he nevertheless rose to the challenge of making a sleazy stop-motion monster minus the stop-motion. "I tried to use stop-motion," Beck protests. "A friend of mine was doing a movie that was an homage to Ray Harryhausen and he had a stop-motion puppet that would've been perfect, but I couldn't talk him into [lending] it. So instead, [special effects make-up artist] Toby [Lindala] made this great cyclops suit and we put this stunt guy in it. I shot him against bluescreen at very high speed, so he'd look big.

"It was funny," Beck continues. "I was trying to get a performance out of this stunt guy who was living inside this extremely uncomfortable suit. I'm going, 'Now turn this way, now turn that way', trying to get his actions to match up with these little aliens in the plates we shot earlier. Then, when we were editing, we took out frames so the cyclops appeared to move jerkily. We pixilated him intentionally to make it look like bad stop-motion."

Since the cyclops was only supposed to be about 8 feet tall, the actor in the suit could conceivably have been shot in-camera with the two small actors portraying garden-variety gray aliens. Unfortunately, there were some typical X factors. "First of all, I don't think the suit was ready, which is the typical scheduling," Beck grins. "But don't forget that it was supposed to look like a composite—it was supposed to look as though the little aliens were moving normally and the cyclops was skip-framing."

Beck also shot the suit against bluescreen for the sequence where the cyclops descends from a spaceship to the road on a beam of light. The two aliens were shot reacting to some decidedly non-special effects, which Beck later enhanced.

"We're [panning] over the two gray aliens when one turns to the other and asks, 'What the hell is that?'" Beck

smirks. "The Grays were played by very small actors who had masks on and were literally wearing underwear with a bunch of gray paint on them. They were looking down the street and we did the classic thing where they see this great big light in the sky shining down, but of course the light shining down on the street was a 10K on a Condor crane, so we had to paint all that out, then put in two spaceships. The spaceships were CG [computer generated]. We've never done a miniature spaceship for the show."

Beck did shoot some scenes with the Grays and the cyclops together. But although the characters were all shot in-camera, Beck would later split the cyclops out of the plate, remove some frames to make his movements appropriately jerky, then put him back into the shot.

"It's a subtle thing," Beck says. "He was supposed to look wacky. It was a challenge to get the performance we wanted but at the same time make it look just compelling enough and just cheesy enough. Ironically, because it's a

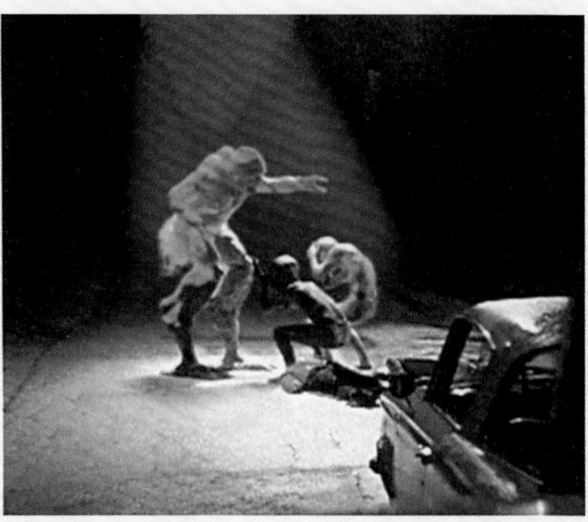

"It was a challenge to make it just compelling enough and just cheesy enough."

Mat Beck on "Jose Chung's 'From Outer Space'"

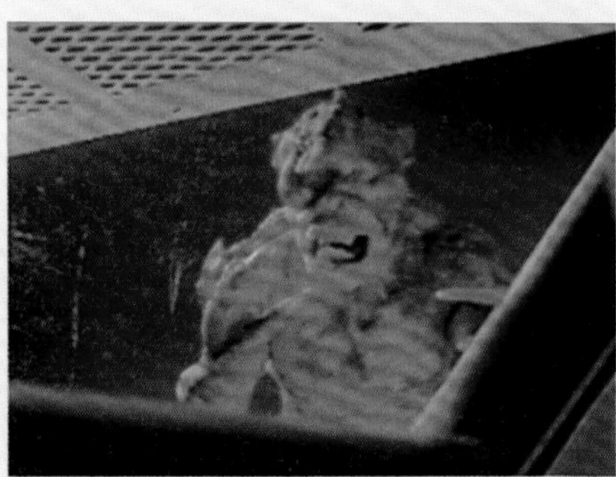

EXTRA CHEESE: MAT BECK [ABOVE RIGHT] AND HIS "CHUNG" ALIENS

comedy, the timings became even more critical. That was a fun one to do."

But while Beck enjoyed the opportunity to do some outrageous, less-than-realistic effects for the usually perfectionistic *X-Files*, he didn't relish the trip down memory lane to his funky low-tech roots: "I have shot stop-motion and I know everybody loves it, but I'll tell you the truth, I honestly was never a huge fan of it," he says. "The reason is that the very stop-motionishness of it was like a screen through which you looked at the stuff and the stuff didn't look that good. For the '50s, it looked real, but it always had that very characteristic look which stood between me and reality.

"Also, if you've ever shot stop-motion, it'll try the patience of Job," he continues. "I did a couple of stop-motion shots on *The Abyss* at Dream Quest, shooting this claw reaching in and trying to unhook something, and that pretty much concluded my career as somebody who shoots stop motion. Until you've spent 12 hours on a dark, smoky set and then had the stop-motion animator say to you, 'You know, I'm not sure if on the last frame I left the clamp in-camera or not when we shot,' you haven't really experienced the joys of stop-motion," he adds sardonically. "But doing this great big cyclops monster who was supposed to look like he was done stop-motion was an adventure."

DAVID GAUTHIER

Of all the effects disciplines, practical effects are often the most difficult and the least appreciated. Unlike visual effects, which are largely created in post-production, practical effects happen on the spot and on-set with the clock ticking; frequently, actors are in close proximity to lethal amounts of water, fire and explosives. They may be tough to pull off, but as far as David Gauthier's concerned, they're the most rewarding. He's the man who's defied odds to create a catalog of practical effects for every *X-Files* episode except the pilot.

The trick to practical effects is that what you see is what you get. It all happens in-camera, or it doesn't happen at all. Gauthier landed on *The X-Files* after handling his particular brand of effects for five years on *MacGyver* and Wes Craven's short-lived foray into television, *Nightmare Café*. But practical effects experience is hard to attain—how to handle the demanding effects can only be learned by doing them, with the special wisdom of the field getting passed down from generation to generation by old masters.

"I started off with John Thomas, the greatest effects guy here in Vancouver, who's since passed away," says Gauthier. "And I also got a chance to apprentice with Henry Mullar, an effects guy from Los Angeles who did a couple of Bond pictures. His dad was an effects guy a long

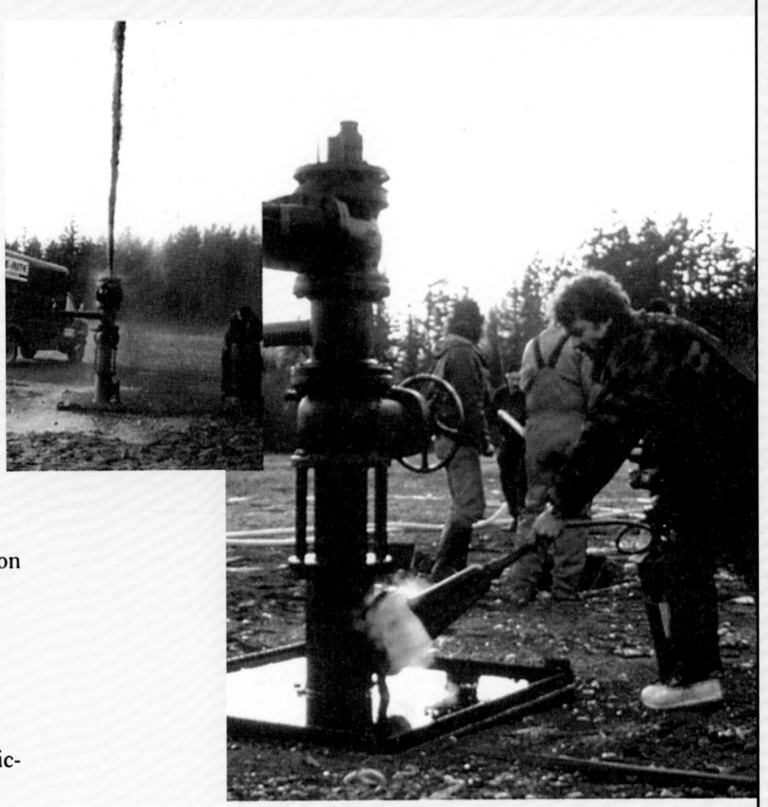

"There wasn't any visual trickery there. We really did light an oil well on fire."

-David Gauthier on "Terma"

time ago, so he comes by his work honestly. I was very privileged to have that kind of tutelage."

Now Chris Carter and company put Gauthier through his paces week after week, and he loves it. "Chris doesn't accept anything less than perfection, so it's really a treat," he says. "The only thing that stops us on this show is the amount of time we've got to do [the effects]. And there's not too many backups. You do it right or you're down the road!"

Gauthier's favorite episodes generally are those that made him sweat. For "Terma," he blew up a van and set an oil well aflame in broad daylight, an effect too close for comfort to David Duchovny. But that's how director Rob Bowman wanted it. The scene called for an alien rock being jammed into an oil well and blowing up the well with a nearby van.

"Rob Bowman wanted David Duchovny

PHOTO BY KHAREN HILL

HOT STUFF: DAVID GAUTHIER [ABOVE] ADDED FIREPOWER TO "TERMA"

to do his own stunt in very close proximity to the van, running toward camera and falling into a closeup," Gauthier says. "There wasn't any visual trickery there. We really did have to light an oil well on fire."

Of course, it wasn't a real oil well, but rather one Gauthier's team fabricated on location using surprisingly low-tech stuff. But low-tech is the name of the game in practical effects.

"The first gag in the sequence was to shoot the oil 175 feet in the air," Gauthier recalls, "so we built an oil well head coming out of a piece of ground we had chosen in a big enough clearing. Then we had a high-pressure pump deliver the oil to the well through 200 feet of eight-inch line and shoot it up in the air."

Only it wasn't oil that was ignited—it was a lot of cleverly disguised water. "We had no water source on location, so we had to store 40,000 gallons of water, which we turned black with 5,000 pounds of tempera paint with a bit of cellulite material added to make it a little thicker, but not too thick. Water goes further than something thicker, and I wanted to get the 'oil' up as high as I could."

The "oil" then drenched David Duchovny's clothes, building tension—Mulder could be incinerated if his oily clothes caught fire when the van blew. Of greater concern to Gauthier was the fact that Duchovny really could be blown to smithereens, or that the crew could be injured by shrapnel flying from the explosives in the van's cargo bay.

"Everyone had to be aware that there could be pieces coming their way, but I had to plan carefully so any projectiles were small enough not to harm anyone," he explains. "I had about 500 feet of hundred grain det[onation] cord, 200 feet of 200 grain det cord and about 55 gallons of gas in an 8-1/2-inch-wide wooden box that I designed and the construction department built inside the van. The biggest explosion was taken by the box, which we laced with enough primercord to break it into small pieces for safety. We couldn't really blow it out the back because then the explosion wouldn't look any good, so it went mostly out the sides and straight up."

To make the explosion safer and more spectacular, Gauthier pre-scored the van so it ripped apart very easily. "The important thing is you don't use explosive force to blow anything apart," he says. "Therefore, it doesn't require a big explosive hit. It was strictly for effect. All I needed to do was provide a small amount of force in order to explode it, and completely set it on fire."

Meanwhile, back at the oil well, Gauthier's team was doing some fancy footwork to set the oil on fire. Since the oil was actually made of water, which doesn't burn, Gauthier used the truck explosion to cover a quick sleight of hand, turning off the black water and replacing it with streams of propane.

"Inside the oil well, I had two 1-1/2" lines that were tied into a 2,000-gallon tank of liquid propane which we pumped out at over 100 [pounds per square inch]," Gauthier recalls. "So keeping in mind David's proximity, I had to design the explosion in the van so it was big enough to disguise the switch. We designed a remote control valve to shut the black water off and turn the propane on."

But switching from water to propane wasn't quite as simple as flicking a switch. "We couldn't just shut the water off because it would back up against the pump, and the pump would explode," he says. "So we built a Y-off section that allowed the water to keep flowing [past the propane ignition point] so it would not go up into the head of the oil well and blow up the pump."

The gag was ready, but Gauthier's crew and Duchovny didn't get any actual rehearsals in because once the van blew, that was it—you don't get any backup trucks on a TV series budget.

"The trick part was to blow up the van with David nearby," Gauthier says. "He ran through it a couple of times. I think David was a bit tense, but anybody stepping within 10 feet of a van that's going to be completely annihilated has got to be a little bit nervous! David has always been really good in terms of listening to what I've got to say and doing exactly what we talked about.

"When we were ready to shoot, my best

boy, Andrew Sculthorp, was behind the scenes with the remote control valve on the propane pumps, and I was by camera with the ignition switch for the van explosion," he continues. "As soon as David was far enough away from the van, I started the whole thing rolling by blowing up the van. Everything was keyed to the sound of the van exploding. Andrew took his own cue and switched from water to propane on the well and the timing ended up perfect."

As with most practical gags, there were several cameras running at different speeds to capture the action from various vantage points. "There were seven cameras running," Gauthier remembers. "We had one camera dug into the ground only a few feet away from the van, and another one up in a crane shooting at 48 frames per second for a slow motion running-away-from-the-explosion shot. This show is not a fan of real slow motion. Chris is a reality man and he wants it to be as it is. That's why we did the whole gag in one shot."

The result was one mother of an explosion, with Duchovny—only 150 feet away from ground zero—leaping into close-up. "As the flames came up, they masked the oil well from camera, and then once they dissipated, we had already ignited the propane and we had 100 foot flames coming out of the oil well head," Gauthier says admiringly. "We could see the van behind him filling the back of his close-up with fire from the explosion. This is one of my favorite effects because it worked flawlessly the first time. It was a lot more complex than what you read on the screen. I'm not sure I counted on all the technical difficulties to make it all work in one [shot], but we were able to give Rob his wish of having David in the shot as the oil well exploded. It actually worked quite well."

LAURIE KALLSEN-GEORGE

It's amazing what ends up airing on *The X-Files*—ideas and images you wouldn't believe any sane television censor would allow. Take for example current *X-Files* visual effects supervisor Laurie Kallsen-George's favorite image: the carcinogenic Leonard Betts vomiting up a new body. The episode, also entitled "Leonard Betts," not only was one of last season's more dripping displays, but it also happened to be Kallsen-George's initial foray into X effects.

Her previous career highlights included adding glows to Tinker Bell at Industrial Light and Magic for Steven Spielberg's saccharine *Hook*. She was there when effects guru Dennis Muren pronounced computer-generated effects to be the wave of the future, but Kallsen-George didn't realize how important those black boxes would personally become until she took over *The X-Files* effects early last season from Area 51, who had their hands full creating imagery for Chris Carter's *Millennium*.

"It was absolutely
was so grotes
the room when

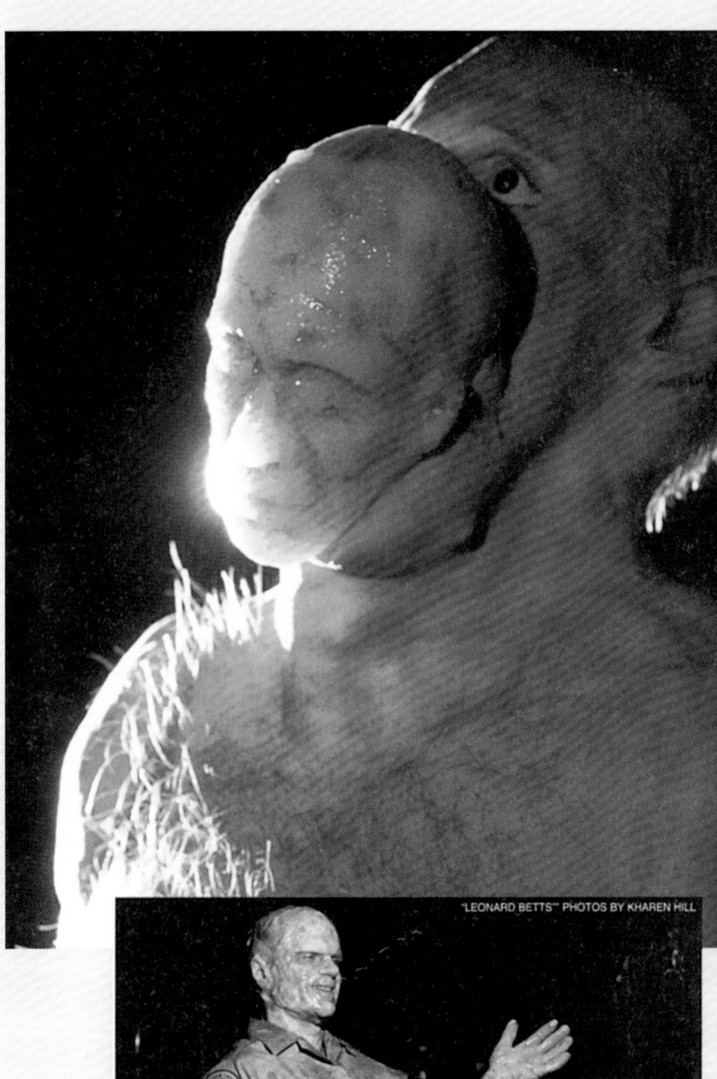
"LEONARD BETTS" PHOTOS BY KHAREN HILL

"I use digital to combine the pictures that exist, or if they don't exist, then I sort of invent them," Kallsen-

flawless and it
que I had to leave
first saw it."

-Laurie Kallsen-George on "Leonard Betts"

George says with a smile. "I use practical stuff constantly because what's real is inevitably better than anything you can make up, but sometimes what you want just doesn't exist at all and then we have to get into the art of illusion. Sometimes the practical stuff is too much there and we only want a suggestion. *The X-Files* has to always ride the fence of what's real and what's not real and how we perceive the things that Scully and Mulder see. We want to keep things just a little less visible than most, to keep them in that gray area."

"Leonard Betts" needed a lot of both practical and digital effects magic, as Kallsen-George raced to meet a near-impossible deadline: "I jumped in halfway through [principal photography] and I sent up little piece of paper diagrams that said 'visual effect as understood by me,'" she says. "The shoot was already 10 days late and then we learned that the airdate was being moved up two weeks. It was going to be the Super Bowl show. That meant we basically had six days to put the whole thing together.

"One of the reasons I absolutely cherish that episode is that when I was told I'd just sort of take over the post on it, I had Toby [Lindala] e-mail me a little image of what he was working on that would be this torso and head for Leonard Betts," she continues. "When I sat down at my computer and opened my e-mail, I saw something that looked very much like a store mannequin, just partial, no features, no nothing. This was on a Tuesday, and we were shooting [the effects plates] on Friday, so I thought, 'Okay, this is going to be a little difficult.'"

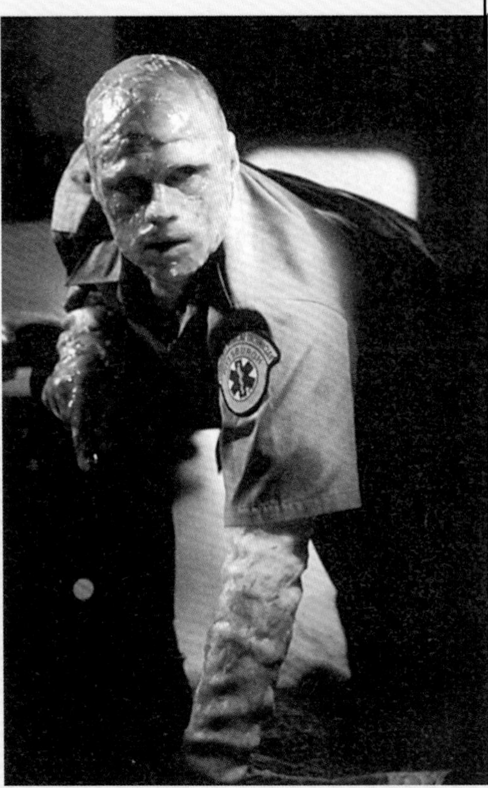

LEONARD'S BEST: LAURIE KALLSEN-GEORGE [ABOVE RIGHT] AND BETTS

Fortunately, Lindala's Betts was a work in progress. "When I got the footage from Toby, which came down after Friday's shoot, it was the most stunning footage I had ever seen," Kallsen-George insists. "It was so life-like. The body he had built sweated and had hair on it, and they ran a close-up camera up its chest that showed a six-square-inch area and it looked real. It was absolutely flawless and it was so grotesque I had to leave the room when I first saw it."

It also caused Kallsen-George and her crew to wonder how they were going to get such graphic images on the air following the Super Bowl at seven o'clock: "The premise is that Leonard Betts is a mutant made of cancer who has to eat cancer to survive and who grows new parts after he feeds," Kallsen-George says. "He gets decapitated and he grows a head, and then he gets killed and he barfs up a whole new body! When we saw the footage, we were all thinking, 'Well, this is going to be an interesting one to put past Standards & Practices at 7 p.m.!'"

But that wasn't Kallsen-George's primary concern: "One of the things that made it absolutely hilarious was the combination of the shoot being delayed and the airdate being moved up so it was one step to the left and we were on the air! We only got this footage on Friday at 8 p.m., after trying to get it through customs and getting it on the wrong flight, and then we had to run it in overtime over the weekend at [an L.A. post house] with an operator working around the clock to put this [episode] together."

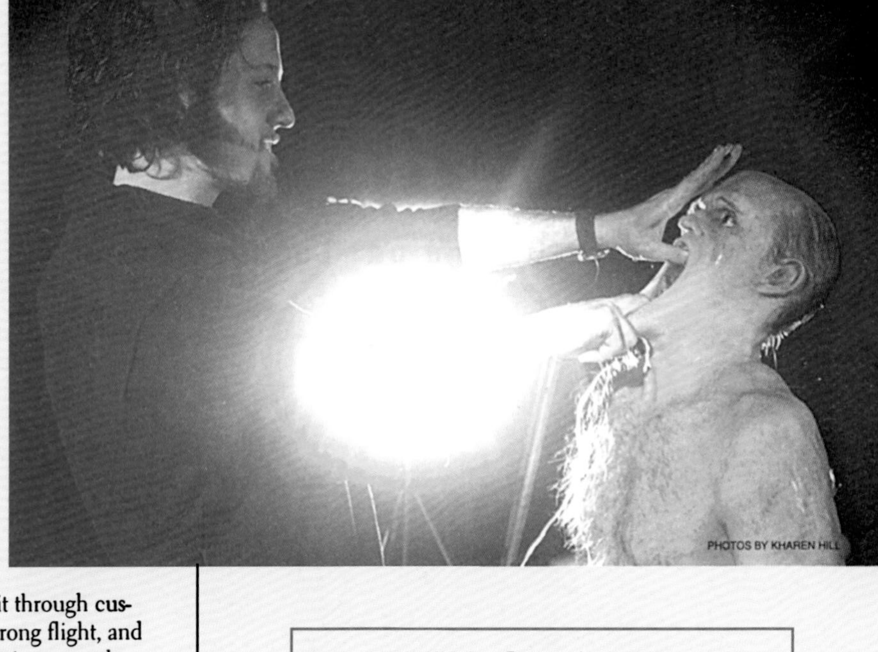

SAY "AHHHH!": TOBY LINDALA GETS BETTS TO OPEN WIDE [ABOVE]

After consulting with Toby Lindala, Kallsen-George planned to use the puppet torso for the last gasp of the former Leonard Betts. "Toby's three-dimensional prosthetic torso was really nice, but we couldn't get a real head up through it, so he designed it so a balloon came up

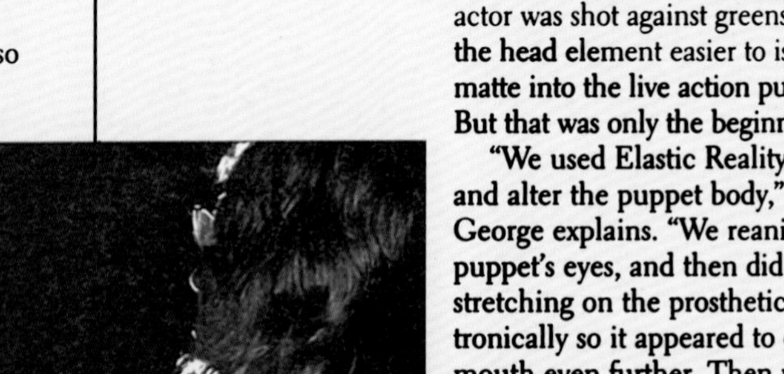

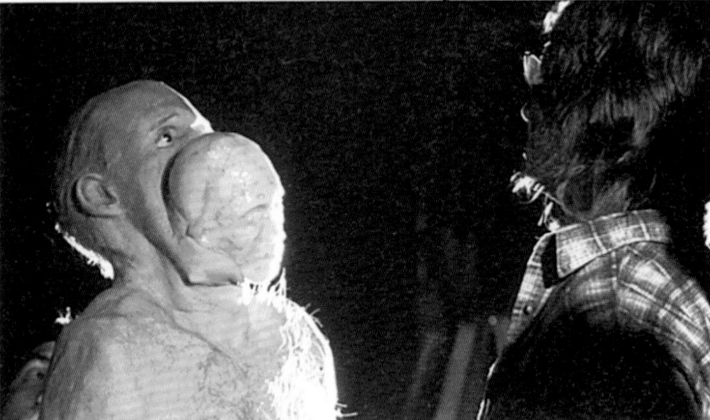

through the mouth," she says. "That was just for timing purposes so we could see when the head would come out. So in the [effect plate], the beautifully animated puppet torso leaned its head back, with its eyes rolling and shaking, opened its mouth and barfed up a balloon head."

The on-set balloon was used to track the motion of Betts' new head as it appeared to emerge from the puppet's mouth. The balloon was eventually removed and digitally replaced with the head of the actual actor in full prosthetic makeup, portraying the new Leonard Betts being vomited. The actor was shot against greenscreen to make the head element easier to isolate and matte into the live action puppet plate. But that was only the beginning.

"We used Elastic Reality to stretch and alter the puppet body," Kallsen-George explains. "We reanimated the puppet's eyes, and then did additional stretching on the prosthetic head electronically so it appeared to open its mouth even further. Then we removed the balloon and put the real actor's head in makeup out through the top. When we brought the new character through, we did additional stretching so as his nose pokes out of the mouth, the lower lip of the old Leonard Betts snaps back so that it looks like the new head is really emerging. We also used Elastic Reality to stretch and distort the new character so he appeared to snap out of his own body and scream. It was pretty grotesque."

Grotesque enough to burn itself into X-Philes' memories, making the scene a favorite of macabre-minded fans. But with the series continuing to push the boundaries of TV FX each week, it's a sure bet that *The X-Files'* visual wizards will top themselves by conjuring up even more amazing images in Season Five and beyond. ●

Beast Master

The X-Files has grown and changed and morphed over the last four years, and Toby Lindala has grown and changed and morphed right along with it. The 27-year-old Vancouverite has worked on the series since the pilot, creating many of the literally eye-popping creatures that have become one of the show's trademarks. In the process, he has evolved from a basement-dwelling, monster-obsessed makeup artist into one of the hottest names in the makeup effects field.

"The first season, I basically did a prosthetic for every second or third episode," Lindala says. "They were done all by myself in a little one-room basement shop."

As *The X-Files'* demand for creatures—and Lindala's talents—grew, he found himself getting more and more work from the show.

"The second season I had four guys working with me. Then the third season I had eight guys. And at the end of the fourth season I had 15," he says.

Now, with Season Five chugging along (and steady work coming in from *Millennium*, *Sleepwalkers* and *Stargate*), Lindala is up to 16 employees. Oh, and he left that basement behind a long time ago. Not too shabby for a young man who got his start cleaning out buckets for the FX crew on *Xtro 2*.

"I worked for virtually nothing for a month, helping all those local [Vancouver] guys," recalls Lindala, a life-long lover of all things horrific. "It was kind of neat, kind of a full circle experience for me to work on a sequel to a picture that really inspired me. But it was a pretty hokey, low-budget movie."

Of course, bigger and better things were in Lindala's future. Bigger and *slimier*, too.

"I'm still hung up on Flukeman," says Lindala, who considers the sewer-dwelling monster to be his coolest creation. "We produced him in 10 days. It was a big challenge because of the space we were working out of. That was one of the first full-body suits we had ever done. We could do it now a lot easier."

Other sentimental favorites include Lord Kinbote (the arm-swinging alien from "Jose Chung's 'From Outer Space'") and Leonard Betts (from, of course, "Leonard Betts"). So far this season on *The X-Files*, Lindala's crew has created malevolent, bark-encrusted tree-men (for "Detour") and misshapen mutants (for "The Post-Modern Prometheus").

But as much as he enjoys breathing life into new menaces for Scully and Mulder, Lindala admits that he'd like to move on to big-screen monsters one of these days.

"We've had a few features approach us," he says. "I'd love to get into some more feature work, just for the schedules. I can't wait until I can have a month to prep a creature!"—*Steve Hockensmith*

PHOTO BY KHAREN HILL

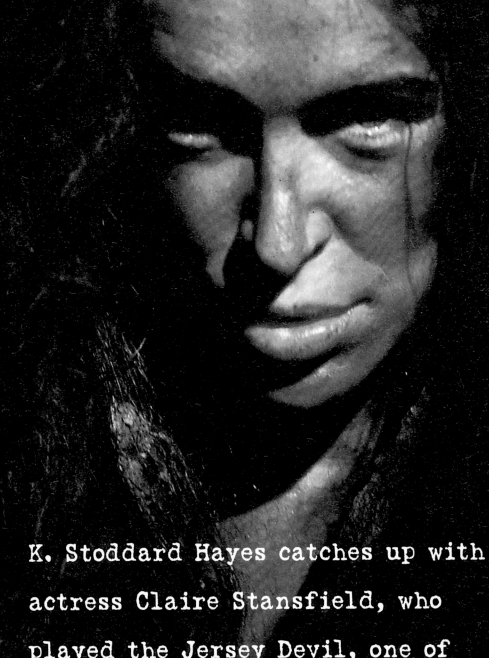

K. Stoddard Hayes catches up with actress Claire Stansfield, who played the Jersey Devil, one of *The X-Files*' very first monsters

DEVIL WOMAN

It's been almost 10 years since Claire Stansfield played the elusive and feral Jersey Devil in the first season *X-Files* episode of the same name. Reminded of how much time has passed, Stansfield has an immediate reaction: "Wow! I hope I still look the same in a thong!"

Stansfield's appearance as the beast woman was partly the result of her friendship with David Duchovny, who she'd met while shooting a commercial. After Duchovny was cast as Mulder in *The X-Files*, he recommended her to Chris Carter for the role of the Jersey Devil. No one had heard of *The X-Files* when Stansfield went to Vancouver to film the episode, which was only the fourth to be produced. For her and for the cast and crew, it was just another job.

"We had no idea it was going to be as huge as it was," she remembers. "For me it was really just a great vacation and getting to hang out with David. So I said, 'Sure!' Then I saw my thong!"

Stansfield's entire wardrobe consisted of the thong, a long wig ("They taped it all on to my breasts, which is rather goopy at the end of the day," recalls Stansfield), and make-up dirt.

It's not the kind of outfit a girl wants to wear in front of her mother. However, Stansfield had to do just that, since her mother lived in Vancouver and was a guest on the set every day. She recalls her mother's reaction to the small crowd of curious onlookers who gathered on the days they were shooting in Vancouver's streets: "Oh, honey, can't they brush your hair a little?"

Another daily presence on the set in those early days was Chris Carter, who had written the episode. Stansfield recalls that Carter and Duchovny had already become good friends. As Duchovny's friend, she got to know Carter as well.

"He's just the coolest guy!" she reports. "As a woman you couldn't be more in heaven than sitting on a set with Chris to your left and David to your right, with your mom behind you giving you the big thumbs up."

However, the Jersey Devil herself looms largest in Stansfield's memory. "I've never played any character like that before or since. To become feral like that, your sense of smell and sound and hearing becomes heightened. I got to be instinctually based as opposed to intellectually or emotionally based. I remember loving it, because it was something so different as an actor."

Stansfield's stunt double was also a bit unusual. Finding a double for the six-foot-one Stansfield is often challenging. Finding a tall professional stunt woman in Vancouver, who would wear the Jersey Devil's nearly non-existent wardrobe, proved impossible.

"They got a stripper," says Stansfield, adding, with mock chagrin: "That's the one who didn't want to wear her robe at all, ever, on the set. So here's me thinking, 'I've got the damn job. Tell that woman to get off the set, go and wait in the trailer and put her robe on!'"

The double ended up doing only one of Stansfield's stunts, a climb over a fence. "Not that I couldn't do it, and I begged them to let me," says Stansfield, "But it was at the beginning of the shoot, and had I hurt myself... She could have been replaced, but I couldn't."

Among the stunts that Stansfield did herself was the Devil's tussle with Mulder. Considering her costume, she was especially glad to have a good friend playing opposite her for that scene.

"It was so much easier for me to straddle him in a thong because he was

"I've been so lucky. I have always worked, and I've had a very interesting career and can't complain."

my buddy, he made me laugh. I wasn't uncomfortable. That's such a gift as an actor… to not even have to think about it. Because that character certainly is not aware of, 'I'm a woman, I'm naked, I'm straddling you.'" She adds, with a laugh, "And this is pre-David being the sexiest man on the planet. He's my buddy. I still laugh when I see him, because I can't believe he's turned into this icon!"

Stansfield has been far from idle since her Jersey Devil days. Because of her appearances as the evil shamaness Alti on *Xena: Warrior Princess*, she has become a name in science fiction fandom. She has made many appearances at sci-fi conventions, where she has been producing and performing in the evening cabaret shows with her fellow actors. One of her specialties in these convention cabarets is performing fan fiction with her fellow actors. Naturally, these performances never fail to delight the all-fan audiences.

She explains her continued interest in the convention circuit: "I said, 'If you want me to do shows, I have to perform. Then I at least feel as though I'm being an actor.' I love to give the fans what they want, but I also need some kind of creative outlet or I start to feel like it's a factory. They keep booking me, and it's not because I'm popular, it's because I put on these shows. For me as a producer-director, I get paid and then I have a thousand people who love whatever you're doing. You couldn't put on a play here and get that many people and raise that much money for charity."

The Jersey Devil is not forgotten, though. Stansfield still gets requests, through the mail or at conventions, for her to autograph her Jersey Devil trading card. And of course, there are the residuals for every "Jersey Devil" rerun, video or DVD, and even tie-ins like an *X-Files* trivia game. "You're like, 'Oh thanks, Chris!' There's no trivia game for [most] shows I've done. *X-Files* just keeps on giving."

Even more rewarding than the conventions has been Stansfield's expanding career as a director. She recently directed a GMC commercial, as well as music videos for Claudia Christian (*Babylon 5*), Sparkle Horse, and Telepopmusik. She even has a digital studio in her California home, where she can edit and produce as well as direct.

"I now have a pretty good little career going from my home," she says, "where I can choose on what level I want to do it and still make money; where as an actor you have no control."

The directing is going so well that a few months ago, Stansfield was ready to turn her back on the financial risks and frustrations of acting.

"I've been so lucky. I have always worked, and I've had a very interesting career and can't complain, but at 36 years old and nearly six foot two, as a woman the odds are just so stacked against you," she says. "I had just lost my passion for it. I know so many talented actors who don't even have agents."

But then she began to get casting calls again, on projects that especially interested her. At the time of this interview, she had just gotten a callback on a project that she hints is a fairly big deal. She can't give any details, of course, but she is excited again about her acting prospects.

"What am I doing now?" she jokes. "Trying to still look good in a thong!" ●

EPISODE GUIDE

3.22: "QUAGMIRE" Episode #3X22
Original US tx 3 May 96 Original UK tx 30 July 96

HEUVELMAN'S LAKE, MILLIKAN, BLUE RIDGE MOUNTAINS, GEORGIA

Two scientists studying an apparent case of frog depopulation in the area of Georgia's Heuvelman's Lake disagree over the cause of the local species' extinction. Later, one of them, Dr Bailey, is dragged screaming into the lake – a death Mulder believes to be caused by 'Big Blue', the local legendary sea serpent. "Oh, tell me you're not serious," groans Scully, her pet dog in tow, as her partner gets a familiar glint in his eye.

The agents meet the surviving scientist, Dr Farraday, who runs a local store selling bait, tackle and tourist-friendly sea serpent merchandise. They question him about the death of Dr Bailey and a missing scout leader, who subsequently turns up, half-eaten, in another fisherman's catch. Later, Farraday himself is attacked as he tramples the woods in fake dinosaur 'boots' in an effort to add realism to his tales of Big Blue. When two teenagers witness a brutal attack on a diver, and a photographer obsessed with capturing a picture of the mythical creature is swept away, Mulder implores the local sheriff to close the lake. He refuses – until he falls into the lake and feels "something big" brush past him underwater.

When Scully's dog, Queequeg, becomes the latest apparent victim of the lake monster, she and Mulder head out onto the water at night, hoping to solve Millikan's mystery once and for all. However, their boat is attacked, leaving them stranded together on a rock to ponder their predicament. Luckily, they are 'rescued' – as it turns out, they were only a few yards from the shore – by Farraday, who convinces Mulder that the serpent, having depleted the lake's supply of frogs, had turned to humans as an alternative food source. Scully, naturally, remains unconvinced by Farraday's stories – swallowed whole by Mulder – of an aquatic dinosaur throwback living in the lake, and yet there is clearly *some* sort of monster on the loose...

Principal Credits

Created by	Chris Carter
Produced by	Ten Thirteen Productions for Twentieth Century Fox TV
Executive Producer	Chris Carter
Co-Executive Producers	Howard Gordon, RW Goodwin
Producers	Joseph Patrick Finn, Kim Manners, Rob Bowman
Co-Producer	Paul Rabwin
Music	Mark Snow

Episode Credits

Written by	Kim Newton
Directed by	Kim Manners
Special Agent Fox Mulder	David Duchovny
Special Agent Dr Dana Scully	Gillian Anderson
Dr Paul Farraday	Timothy Webber
Sheriff Lance Hindt	Chris Ellis
Ted Bertram	Mark Acheson
Ansel Bray	R Nelson Brown
Dr William Bailey	Peter Hanlon
Fisherman	Murray Lowry
Stoner	Tyler Labine
Chick	Nicole Parker
Snorkel Dude	Terrance Leigh

F.Y.I.

One of the Loch Ness monster's (fictional) American equivalents rears its head in the Blue Ridge Mountains of Georgia as Kim Newton, the show's sole female writer at this point, delivers a richly drawn and well-characterised episode, with David Duchovny and Gillian Anderson given a full ten pages of dialogue for a single scene – the notorious 'Converstaion on the Rock' as internet-based X-philes refer to it. In fact, it was story editor Darin Morgan who wrote their dialogue – having already delivered his last full script for the show – and, indeed, it is not the only place in "Quagmire" where his influence is felt. Not only do Nicole Parker and Tyler Labine from Morgan's "War of the Coprophages" make a return appearance – with a new 'Dude' in tow – but the episode marks the final resting place of Scully's dog, Queequeg, inherited from the late Mrs Love in Morgan's "Clyde Bruckman's Final Repose" and subsequently seen in "War of the Coprophages". "We brought it back just to kill it," Co-Executive Producer Frank Spotnitz has admitted, while Supervising Producer Vince Gilligan remarked of the fans' reaction to Queequeg's passing, "You can kill a legion of men and women, but no dogs. People go nuts!"

On its initial US broadcast, "Quagmire" scored a Nielsen rating of 10.2/18, equating approximately 16 million viewers in around ten million homes. Here in the UK, its debut on Sky One drew the season's lowest audience, 0.89 million viewers, while its subsequent BBC airing drew an above average 8.3 million.

Noteworthy Dialogue Transcript

SCULLY: "You're so consumed by your personal vengeance against life, whether it be its inherent cruelties or its mysteries, that everything takes on a warped significance in your megalomaniacal cosmology!"

Fire, Talk With Me

Mark Sheppard, who portrayed villainous Cecil L'Ively way back in Season One's "Fire," rekindles a few memories. Interview by Paul Simpson and Ruth Thomas

"I'll tell you what's weird about my job," Mark Sheppard says, as he casts his mind back almost ten years to his appearance as Cecil L'Ively on the first season *X-Files* episode "Fire." "We all take it very seriously. We're all in this trying to make a world, and adhere to a set of rules that don't really exist. They only exist in the minds of the writers, the creators and the actors – and the fans. We're trying to make this as real as possible. I think that's why *The X-Files* works, because of how much everybody puts into it. Everybody wants it to be good!"

Sheppard followed his role as Paddy Armstrong in the controversial drama *In the Name of the Father,* with an audition for *The X-Files.* "I still have the appointment slip," he recalls. "They wanted to know if I could do an American accent – that was very important. They found actors who could do the American or the English, but not both. They wanted it to be realistic."

Sheppard also demonstrated the sleight of hand that Cecil L'Ively uses to impress the two young boys – a trick that he actually did on camera. "I learned the magic trick for palming the cigarette," he says. "I actually did that at the audition. In the episode, I actually did it in one take, but for some reason they ended up editing it so it looked weird. I knew how to do a 'French drop' with a coin, so on the first day I arrived in Vancouver, I had my wardrobe fitting then went back to the hotel. I took a stick of chewing gum, folded it in half lengthways, and worked out how to palm it for six hours!"

Sheppard quit smoking six years before filming "Fire," so he smoked Honey Rose herbal cigarettes all the time. "It was weird to have to fake it!" he comments. Of course, Cecil L'Ively didn't bother with anything so mundane as a lighter – he was able to light his own cigarettes simply by thinking about it. Sheppard, however, needed assistance from the special effects department.

"There were only three of those cigarettes made," he points out. "This was the early days of *The X-Files* when they didn't have a fortune, and on that episode the stunts were pretty big! The cigarette was the first stunt we did. There were three of them with an incendiary device in the end of the cigarette, and a copper wire that ran out into the side of my mouth. We could then hide it down one side of my face. I asked the special effects guys to show me how the cigarette worked. They said that they only had three, but I insisted, and they finally agreed. One of them put one in his mouth, lit it – and it blew up! They were very embarrassed, and fixed them all, taking the magnesium charge out to make it lighter."

If the episode was being made today, a lot of the fire would probably be created with computer graphics, making it much safer for the actors on the set. In

"There was something special about the first season. They were new, **and they didn't really have their audience."**

1993, that wasn't an option. "It was all real fire on the episode," Sheppard says proudly. "It's not computer fire. There are real flames everywhere. That's me in the hotel corridor – and I got a nice tan on the top of my head! If you watch the episode really closely, you can see me drop. As the stuntman playing Mulder dives out of the way, I'm at the end of the hallway. The camera's on me, and they've only got the one hallway, which they have to blow up at the end. We get there, they blow it up, and suddenly it gets amazingly hot. You see me drop to my knees as Mulder dives to the right, because I'm afraid that my hair is catching fire. *Entertainment Tonight* was filming us, and all you can hear after the stunt finishes is 'Cut – did we get the take?' I was going, 'You bastards, you burned my head!' It was very real fire, and very frightening."

One fire stunt that didn't make it as far as the studio floor was a further display by L'Ively of his powers. "There was a quarter mile of white picket fences catching fire," Sheppard remembers, "and other stuff got taken out. It kept getting pared down before we shot it."

Sheppard was keen to do as much of his own stuntwork as he could. "When I showed up for the audition, the guy from Stunts Canada showed me a video of his arm on fire outside his garage, and asked if I would be willing to do this stunt. I said, 'If I don't get to do this stunt, I'm not going to do this thing!' He was like, 'Oh great!' When I was being lit up and prepped, there were guys three feet away from me who would put me out in a second. But it was still scary. Fire's a very powerful thing. My arm is on fire in the bar. I light the bar on fire with my arm, and all the rest of that stuff."

The only stunt that was not performed by Sheppard was the full body burn, which was carried out by stuntman J.J. "He's actually done full body burns for me three times now, on three different shows," Sheppard comments. "He's a great guy. He has a lot thinner eyebrows than he should! He's a superb stuntman. He did the body burn for me for 'Fire' for 28 seconds, lit up on top of a propane tank. He spent 20 minutes with me beforehand working out what my actions would be so he could match it, then I had to match the screen mask – the copy of my face that he's wearing – in the close-up, which was also done live, not with CGI. They let me do everything else, but they wouldn't let me do that. They lit him up with rubber cement, which is the hottest burning explosive, and exploded him with propane. He went for 28 seconds on this burn, and they shot it with three or four cameras. When they got to the end and put him out, they found out that he didn't have any oxygen – and he'd gone for 28 seconds like that!"

A loss to the episode was the thematic link of *Mendelssohn's Wedding March* which L'Ively was humming as he went about his business. Sheppard found that that proved his bona fides to on-line *X-Files* fans when he first went into an AOL chat room shortly after the second season began. "What was the song, they were asking me," he recalls, "and I realized that they knew more about the show than I did!"

As is often the way with television production, the first scenes of the episode were actually recorded last. "We shot that teaser at the weekend, on the sixth day of a five-day shoot," Sheppard says. "We ran out of time, and because I'd done so much overtime already, I was feeling very generous. So we went off to this house and shot it at the weekend. They slapped the beard on me, and we filmed it with a minimal crew. It was the only way that we could finish the episode!"

The actor is proud of his association with the series, as well as appearing at number 14 in the recent *X-Files Magazine* Top 20 Villains. "Think about how many villains there have been," he says. "There was something special about that first season. They were new, and they didn't really have their audience. They made their audience on the back of that first season, and it was really exciting to be part of that." ●

EPISODE GUIDE

4.3: "TELIKO" Episode #4X04

Original US tx 18 October 96 Original UK tx scheduled for 26 January 96

PHILADELPHIA, PA

On a charter flight from Burkino Faso, West Africa, a French-speaking black man is attacked in the lavatory cubicle by an unseen assailant. He is later found dead by a stewardess, yet he is no longer black...

Soon after, Scully is summoned to Skinner's office to meet with Dr Simon Broom about a series of disappearances of African-American men in Philadelphia. The previous night, the body of Owen Sanders, one of the missing men, was found near a construction site, with no evidence that foul play was involved in his death. However, Sanders appears to have been bleached of all pigment in his skin, hair or eyes, leading Dr Broom to suspect that he is the victim of a rare disease. Mulder, visiting Scully during her early-morning autopsy, senses a conspiracy, especially when Agent Pendrell finds a rare West African passion flower seed in Sanders' body. In addition, Scully finds that the victim's pituitary gland, which regulates skin and hair pigmentation, to be "necrotised" – ie. dead.

Mulder takes this flimsy evidence to his New York-based 'friend at the UN', Marita Covarrubias, for some help with the case. By the time he joins Scully back in Philadelphia, where another black youth has gone missing, he has learned of the discovery of the body on the plane from Africa. The Philadelphia office of the naturalisation department leads the agents to the home of Samuel Aboah, who flees when approached, only to be cornered, Tooms-style, in a drainpipe! Later, doctors Scully and Broom examine Aboah for evidence of skin pigmentation disorders, but find only one anomaly – his pituitary gland is missing. Before they have a chance to question him, however, Aboah himself goes missing. The agents begin a race to catch and question him before they have an epidemic on their hands...

F.Y.I.

"Teliko" is the first script in some time from four-season veteran Howard Gordon, newly promoted to Executive Producer. With "Teliko", Gordon borrows from Morgan and Wong's Eugene Tooms, as Samuel Aboah squeezes in and out of drainpipes, steals vital organs from his victims and continually widens his unnaturally toned eyes at the camera; in the process, he creates an almost equally memorable 'monster'.

Although it was actually the fourth episode of the fourth season to be filmed (hence the designation 4X04), "Teliko," was the second to be shown, scoring a Nielsen rating of 11.8/20 (approximately 12 million homes). At press time, it was unclear whether Sky One, due to transmit the episode on 26 January, would follow broadcast or production order.

The episode's altered opening credo – 'DECEIVE, INVEIGLE, OBFUSCATE' is a reference to a remark made by Scully with regard to Mulder's paranoia, quoted back to her by Mulder, and finally entered in Scully's 'Field Report #74', explained thus: "To obscure the truth, not only from others, but from ourselves."

Zakes Mokae is probably the best known of the episode's fine guest actors, having appeared in such genre films as Wes Craven's *The Serpent and the Rainbow* (which influenced Gordon's earlier *X-Files* script, "Fresh Bones") and Richard Stanley's *Dust Devil*. Conspiracy theorists note: Laurie Holden previously appeared in *Expect No Mercy*, co-starring with Wolf Larson, who plays Steven 'X' Williams' partner in *LA Heat*...

cipal Credits

Produced by	Ten-Thirteen Productions for 20th Century-Fox TV
Executive Producers	Chris Carter, Howard Gordon, R W Goodwin
Producers	Joseph Patrick Finn, Kim Manners, Rob Bowman
Co-Producers	Vince Gilligan, Frank Spotnitz, Paul Rabwin
Consulting Producers	Ken Horton, James Wong & Glen Morgan
Music	Mark Snow

Episode Credits

Written by	Howard Gordon
Directed by	James Charleston
Special Agent Fox Mulder	David Duchovny
Special Agent Dr Dana Scully	Gillian Anderson
Assistant Director Walter S Skinner	Mitch Pileggi
Marcus Duff	Carl Lumbly
Samuel Aboah	Willie Amakye
Marita Covarrubias	Laurie Holden
Agent Pendrell	Brendan Beiser
Burkino Faso Embassy Minister	Zakes Mokae

Noteworthy Dialogue Transcript

MULDER: "I heard you were down here slicing and dicing. Who's the lucky stiff?"

SCULLY: "His name is Owen Sanders. He was reported as the fourth kidnap victim in Philadelphia until his body turned up last night looking like this [indicates black man drained of colour]..."

MULDER: "There's a Michael Jackson joke here, but I just can't find it."

CREATURE FEATURE

by Chandra Palermo

They have skin the texture of day-old pizza, the social skills of sewer rats and an overwhelming desire to gorge themselves on cancer and bile. But—horrific appearances and revolting appetites notwithstanding—*The X-Files*' pantheon of creatures boasts some of the most captivating and popular characters of the show's history. By turns frightening, disgusting and intriguing, the monsters of the week fulfill an all-important function: They give Mulder and Scully cases to investigate. Without them, the agents might be forced to return to tedious background checks or time-consuming budget hearings.

While the variety of mutants who comprise the X-files caseload seems endless, they do share at least one commonality. Beneath the layers of make-up and uncomfortable prosthetic appliances are hardworking actors, struggling to perform under sometimes the most exacting conditions. "It is strange. I don't really recognize myself in there much," says Chris Owens, the actor disguised as Mutato, the double-headed genetic experiment gone awry in Season

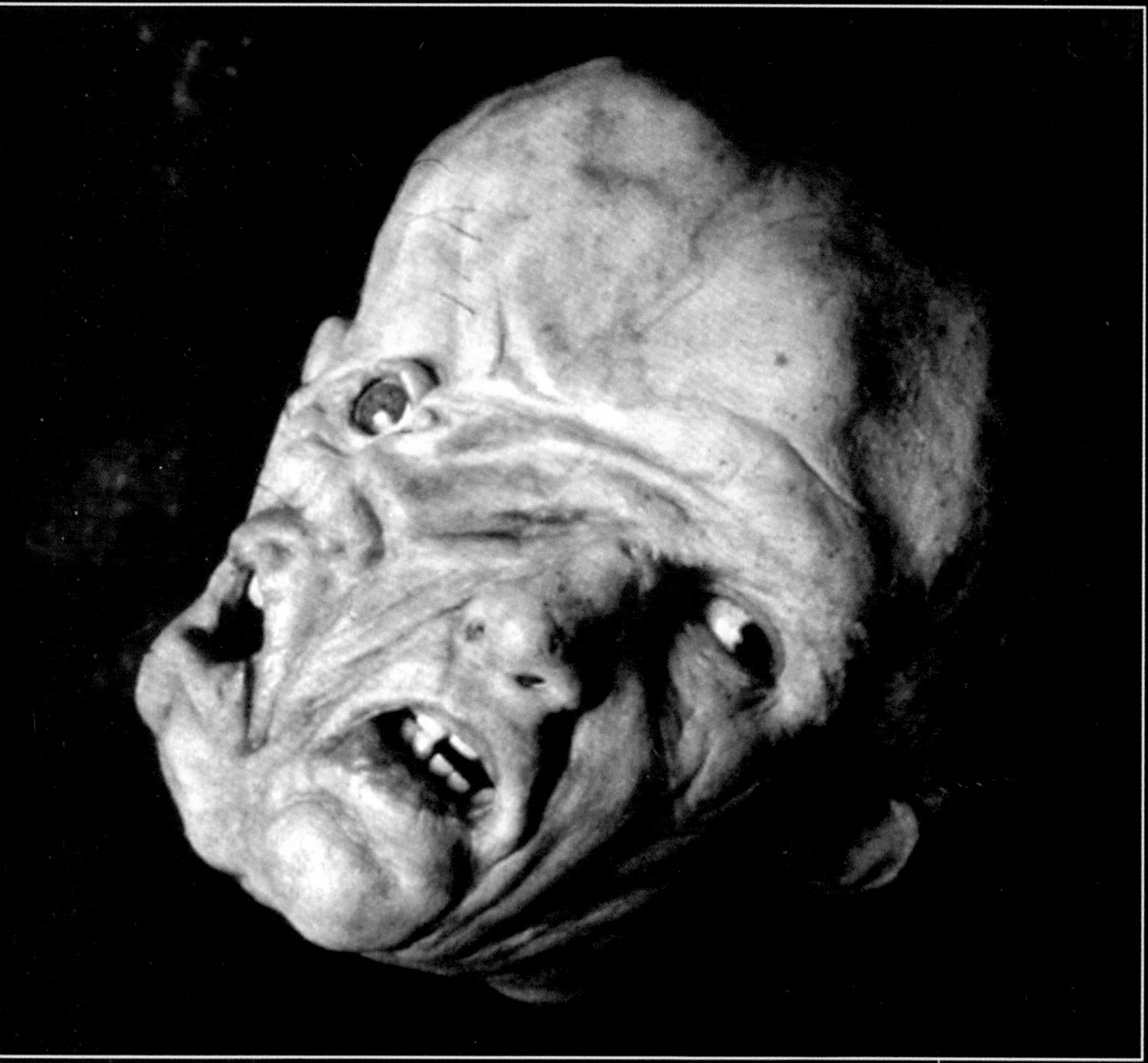

Meet the actors behind The X-Files' most memorable monstrosities, mutants and villainous creeps

DOUBLE AGENT: Before he was Spender, Chris Owens was The Great Mutato (top)

Five's "The Post-Modern Prometheus." "Maybe just a hint in the eyes at the very end—I should say 'the eye.'"

Although becoming a monster is something of a once-in-a-lifetime opportunity, it still takes a special quality to enter the warped psyche of an inhuman creature and brave the pounds of latex necessary to bring the being to life for the camera. Generally, actors are unable to draw on personal experience for these kinds of parts, and just landing these roles can try the stamina of even the most seasoned performer. Imagine preparing to audition for the character of bile-sucking contortionist Eugene Victor Tooms, as Doug Hutchison did for Season One's "Squeeze."

"I didn't have the script, I didn't have any scenes. I had no idea what I was doing or what direction they were going," Hutchison remembers. "I showed up at Fox and Rick Millikan, the casting director, meets me at the trailer and says, 'So, you ready to do this?' And I'm like, 'I guess so. Can you tell me a little bit about this?' He said, 'Yeah. You're playing a character, nobody knows what he is. He's kind of a mutant serial killer. He eats the livers of his victims and he hibernates in a nest for 30 years. Are you ready to go?'"

Admirably, Hutchison assented, despite some understandable trepidation and a raging migraine. When the pain from the headache and the pressure of the situation became too much to handle, Hutchison snapped at director Harry Longstreet. Luckily, the angry outburst came after Longstreet asked the actor to demonstrate his capacity for evil. Rather than take offense, Longstreet cast Hutchison for the part.

> "...The minute they yelled 'Cut,' and I realized I was standing on the streets of Vancouver in a G-string, it was like, ooh, back to reality. 'Can I have a robe?'"
>
> —Claire Stansfield

The experience is different for every actor, however. Claire Stansfield, who also appeared in Season One as the scantily clad Jersey Devil, was spared the audition process. The towering Stansfield was cast on the recommendation of David Duchovny, who mentioned her to Chris Carter because he thought she'd be perfect for the part—a dubious compliment. "I was like, 'Oh, great, you see me as the beast woman,'" she remembers with a laugh.

A huge fan of François Truffaut's *The Wild Child*, a film about a boy raised by wolves, Stansfield jumped at the chance to try her hand at a similarly primal character. She went to the zoo and studied animal behavior, trying her best to mimic their reliance on instinct and acute senses of hearing and smell. Watching the movie again, she realized much of its power stemmed from young actor Jean-Pierre Cargol's ability to frighten the audience yet still evoke pity from them. She tried to bring the same duality to her murderous evolutionary anomaly.

"[The Jersey Devil] wasn't just a scary monster. It was a being you could sympathize with because she was protecting her children and just going on instinct," Stansfield explains. "So then the question comes up [whether] it's murder when you're an animal and it's to protect and it's instinctual. That was the conflict in that episode. And so I tried to make the audience sympathize by completely inhabiting her."

Surprisingly, much of her footage fell to the proverbial cutting room floor, but Stansfield took the cuts in stride. "We shot a ton more stuff, but I thought the way that it was edited and put together made it a lot more believable," she continues. "I think if you had seen more of me, it might have become more like She-Ra of the jungle. I think I'm only in it for about 10 seconds. When I'd sit around and watch it with friends, I'd be like, 'That's me! That was my head! Did you see? That was my hair!'"

Even though she might not have found the same kind of screen time as Mutato or Tooms, Stansfield was also spared the rigorous make-up application most *X-Files* creatures have to endure. Her costume consisted solely of some strategically placed dirt and a G-string. "Anything I was uncomfortable showing, we just made dirty. 'Just put some dirt on that back area,'" she says. "I was in a robe most of the time, and then when I was running around I just sort of became her, so I didn't worry. But the minute they yelled, 'Cut,' I realized I was standing on the streets of Vancouver in a G-string. It was like, ooh, back to reality. 'Can I have a robe?'"

Despite the various hardships of the series' shooting schedule—long hours, night shoots, unconventional wardrobe—the actors behind the characters belonging to the series' creature canon all seem to reflect on their experiences with great fondness. Masochism aside, the performers take pride in the work that won them recognition for achieving the unconventional.

"How many actors do you know that have the opportunity to grow a new head and then give birth to themselves through their mouth?" asks Paul McCrane, the actor who played the titular cancer-consuming mutant Leonard Betts in Season Four's memorable episode. "Those were the kinds of things that are really fun to have done," McCrane says of his character. "But doing them is not always a lot of fun in terms of sitting in the cold make-up chair for a couple of hours in the morning, especially when we're doing exteriors and it was literally in a trailer. But the make-up guys were all great, nothing against them."

McCrane says he even kept a souvenir from the experience. "It's funny because I was then just dating my now wife, and I sent her home a package that had some of the glop that was used for the make-up," he says. "She had it posted on her board at

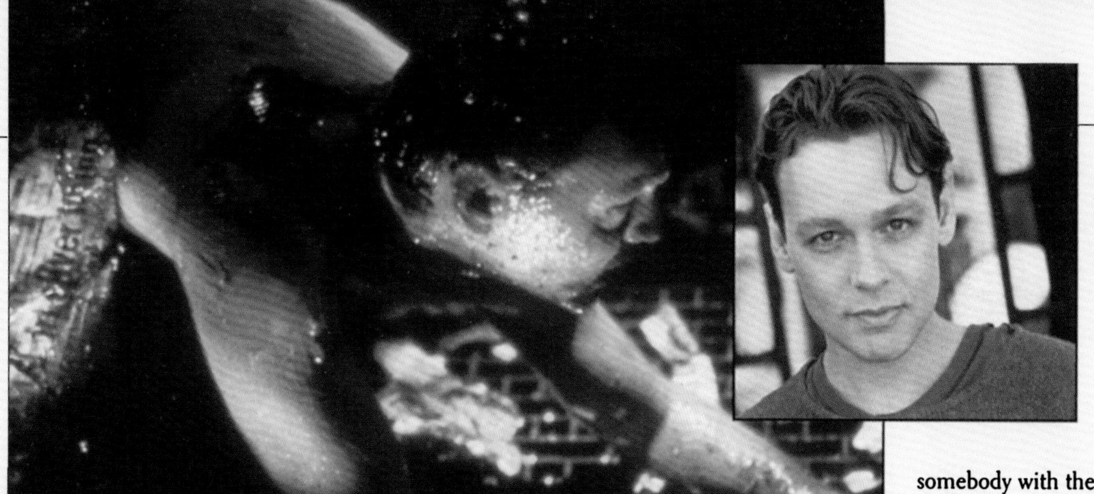

MONSTER MEN: [clockwise from left] Eugene Tooms and his alter ego Doug Hutchison; Leonard Betts and Paul McCrane in *ER*; the Jersey Devil, the Devil and David Duchovny, Claire Stansfield

work for quite a while. She was just grossed out by the whole thing. I think it was harder for her than it was for me."

Few, however, have had to undergo as extensive a transformation as Owens, who spent five hours in preparation every morning before cameras rolled. Given *The X-Files'* tendency for 12-hour-plus workdays, the discomfort level was substantial. "The first day I was in the chair for almost seven [hours]," says the actor, who also played the ill-fated Agent Spender and the young Cigarette-Smoking Man in Season Four's "Musings of a Cigarette-Smoking Man." "We'd put some music on and we'd get some coffee or some soup I could drink through a straw, and then we would go to work. Sometimes we were there an hour before the crew, so we'd be there at like four o'clock in the morning in the dark, starting to put this stuff on. After they put it on, they glued it down, then they'd paint it and that takes quite a while. And then about 45 minutes to get it off, which was, I've got to tell you, the greatest experience. The greatest feeling of my life was getting that thing off every single night."

In addition to having layers of latex glued onto his skin, Owens had to carry the extra weight of an unwieldy, mechanical head, listen to the gear boxes that controlled the movement of the prosthetic appliance and wear a disorienting contact in the eye not obscured by the complicated make-up. And he could only eat food small enough to fit through his tightened mouth.

"It's a pretty compelling look. Very sexy," Owens jokes. "Oh, I tell you, when I got to play Spender, 10 minutes in make-up—I'll take it," he says. "It was so much fun to be able to slap on a suit and say, 'Yeah, I'm ready, let's go. How's the hair?'"

No matter what projects the actors moved on to after their work on the series—McCrane can be seen as arrogant surgeon Dr. Romano on award-winning drama *ER* and Hutchison again shows his nasty side in the critically acclaimed film *The Green Mile*—they will be forever remembered in many hearts as their creature counterparts. McCrane says he's stopped constantly by fans who recognize him as Leonard Betts, and Hutchison insists he paid his rent for a year doing conventions in honor of Tooms.

"[*X-Files* fans] are the best. They're really loyal," says Stansfield, who recently starred in *Xena: Warrior Princess* as malevolent shaman Alti. "In fact, at all the *Xena* conventions that I do, there's always somebody with the little [*X-Files*] collector card for me to sign. And then I get groups of people who will come and pay to watch all the *Xena* craziness just so they can meet the Jersey Devil."

While Owens is remembered for all his contributions to the series, Mutato stands as a singular achievement. "The Post-Modern Prometheus" not only garnered more than a dozen Emmy Award nominations but is also cited as a fan favorite year after year.

"I think after all the hard work from the make-up department and sitting around for hours on end and whatnot, when I saw the finished product, I was really happy with it," Owens says. "It's worth all the sweat and toil and patience. I mean, when I watch the show, there's a few shots of me just kind of running through a frame, and I thought, 'Wow, I spent hours getting ready for this 10-second shot.' But I highly recommend it. Once.

"I wonder about those actors who do this all the time, those people on *Star Trek*, like those Ferengis," he continues. "Those guys are in that all the time. I can't imagine going to work everyday doing that. I mean, it was a wonderful experience, and I'm glad to be a part of that story, but that was more than enough for me. Oh god, give me a suit any day." ●

EPISODE: 6X06

WAYNE WEINSIDER

"Terms of Endearment"

Of all the guest stars to appear on *The X-Files* this season, Bruce Campbell is the only one who can claim a sizeable and devoted cult following. His turns as chainsaw-wielding demon dispatcher Ash in director Sam Raimi's *Evil Dead* films and charming thief Autolycus in *Hercules: The Legendary Journeys* and *Xena: Warrior Princess* have made him a favorite among genre devotees. While famous for his fast-talking, over-the-top style, Campbell was able to display a more dramatic persona as demonic father-to-be Wayne Weinsider in the chilling "Terms of Endearment."

BRUCE CAMPBELL

"I actually agreed to the deal before I even read the script," Campbell explains. "So I went, 'Wah, ooh boy, this is serious!' All I heard was it's this guy who's a demon with a heart of gold. I thought it was a good, fat-ass role. I can't deny that. As a guest star, that's what you look for. You look for the big roles where you can actually cut the stars some slack. I think they like that."

While the actor's frequent excursions to New Zealand to direct and star in episodes of *Hercules* and *Xena* leave him little time to watch television, Campbell is no stranger to *The X-Files* or its remarkable team. His own show, *The Adventures of Brisco County Jr.*, introduced Chris Carter's brainchild in its fledgling days, and Rob Bowman, who directed "Terms of Endearment," also helmed episodes of *Brisco*. Still, Campbell hadn't expected the overwhelming response his *X-Files* appearance generated.

"I'm very active online," he says. "I have a Web site. I have a published e-mail address that people can send stuff to me and it doubled after the airing. My e-mail just flat out doubled. It shows you just how popular the show is, and that's when I went, 'Oh, geez Louise!'"
—Gina McIntyre

© RENAISSANCE PICTURES

ALSO KNOWN AS:

1997: "Hank Cooper" in *The Love Bug*
1995-'99: "Autolycus" in *Hercules: The Legendary Journeys* and *Xena: Warrior Princess*
1995: "Ed Billik" in *Ellen*
1993-'94: "Brisco County Jr." in *The Adventures of Brisco County Jr.*

1997: "Virgil" in *McHale's Navy*
1995: "Charles Travis" in *Congo*
1994: "Smitty" in *The Hudsucker Proxy*
1993: "Ash" in *Army of Darkness*
1987: "Ash" in *Evil Dead II* (above)
1982: "Ashley J. 'Ash' Williams" in *The Evil Dead*

EPISODE: 2x04

AUGUSTUS COLE

"Sleepless"

Tony Todd didn't need any research or make-up to prepare for his *X-Files* role as Augustus Cole, a Vietnam vet surgically altered to eradicate his need for sleep. While shooting Season Two's "Sleepless," sleep deprivation was something with which he could easily identify.

"We only had three days to shoot it because I was in between doing *Homicide* and *Candyman 2*," the accomplished genre actor explains. "They were able to work out that schedule and shoot it at night, so I was already working on half a cup of coffee. I spent most of my time in the air during that period, flying from Baltimore to Vancouver to New Orleans. It was quite an exciting time, and I think I was able to use that

TONY TODD

energy, or lack of energy, with Augustus Cole."

Familiarity with the character was not the only benefit. "I loved [the script]," Todd says. "I thought it was an interesting, compelling take on the Vietnam experience. I believe this is something that could have happened."

Like most guest actors, Todd was impressed with the amount of time and attention the crew devoted to perfecting every detail. And he says he appreciated the chance to be part of the successful show during its infancy. "Sleepless" was an episode of many firsts: Rob Bowman tackled his first *X-Files* directing task, Nicholas Lea made his first appearance as Krycek and X dropped his first clue to Mulder. "I'm proud to be a part of [*The X-Files*'] impressive legacy," he reports.

These days, Todd isn't having much luck catching up on his downtime. Aside from numerous film and television roles, he is starring in August Wilson's new play *King Hedley II*, a project as exciting as it is exhausting. But he's managed to keep a sense of humor about his tiring lifestyle. "Since I did ['Sleepless'], it's been a life of no sleep that's haunted me until this moment."—*Chandra Palermo*

ALSO KNOWN AS:

1998: "King Gilgamesh" in *Hercules: The Legendary Journeys*
1997: "Cecrops" in *Xena: Warrior Princess*
1997: "Det. Eddie Hazell" in *NYPD Blue*
1996: "Dr. Julius Tate" in *Beverly Hills, 90210*
1994: "Matt Rhodes" in *Homicide: Life on the Street*
1990-'91: "Commander Kurn" in *Star Trek: The Next Generation*

1996: "Captain Darrow" in *The Rock*
1994: "Grange" in *The Crow*
1992: "Candyman" in *Candyman*
1990: "Ben" in *Night of the Living Dead*
1989: "Mr. Wright" in *Lean on Me*
1986: "Warren" in *Platoon*

X-Files director Kim Manners has

Scare Tactics

mastered the fine art of spine-tingling

BY STEVE HOCKENSMITH

X-Philes have Jeff Bridges to thank for some of their favourite show's best moments. No, Bridges has never appeared on *The X-Files.* And he's never written or directed an episode, either. But if it wasn't for him, Kim Manners might have never become a director—and *The X-Files* would have lost one of its most consistently compelling talents.

"Humbug," "Grotesque," "Quagmire," "Home," "Max," and "Emily" are just a few of the *X-Files* episodes Manners has directed. He's helmed 21 in all, many of them fan favourites. Yet directing wasn't Manners' first show-business gig. He started off as a busy child actor, winning guest-starring roles on such beloved '50s fare as *Leave it to Beaver.*

When Manners started going for adult leading roles in the late '60s, he found himself competing with Hollywood's hottest young up-and-comers...including Bridges. After Bridges beat him out for the lead roles in two movies in a row—one of which was Peter Bogdanovich's classic *The Last Picture Show*—he threw in the acting towel and set his sights on a behind-the-scenes career.

It wasn't a difficult transition. Before long, he was directing second-unit car chases for TV kingpin Aaron Spelling. Directing gigs on other TV shows followed, eventually leading to a crack at *The X-Files*.

Manners' *X-Files* debut, "Die Hand Die Verletzt," was a creepy classic, quickly establishing him as a master of the macabre. We asked him what bone-chilling surprises he has up his sleeve for his latest episode.

Q: What are you working on right now?

A: We're shooting out in the boondocks for an episode called "Chinga" written by Stephen King. It's pretty exciting. I've always wanted to be able to say one day that I directed some Stephen King, and here I'm finally getting the chance. I heard [a rumour] last season that he might come in and write one, and at the start of this year they confirmed that for me. I campaigned a little bit to direct it. I told Chris [Carter] I wanted to do it.

What's "Chinga" going to be like?

I think it's pretty much classic King. It's about a demonic doll and it takes place in a little lobster town in Maine. It's got a *Fargo*-esque flavor to it. It's going to be a little bit gory and very funny at the same time. I think it's going to be a classic *X-Files*.

It sounds like your kind of episode. You've done some of the spookier shows.

Well, I'm glad you said spookier and not gorier. I think I'm well-suited for the genre. I like spooky and I like scary. It seems to work for me; I seem to work for it. Take an episode like "Home" or "Grotesque." I really like [that kind of thing]. "Chinga" is guaranteed to be spooky and scary. It will scare the [daylights] out of people, I'm sure.

Is it possible to be too spooky? Some people thought "Home" went too far.

You know what I would say to those people? You're not paying attention to the classic fear in life. I think the people who didn't like "Home" didn't know what they were disturbed by. I think they were disturbed by every child's first fear in life, which is that there's something under the bed. And the fact that mom [Mrs. Peacock] was under that bed was what disturbed people most.

I don't think "Home" was distasteful at all. I thought it was a classic hour of horror, as classic as any Frankenstein or Dracula or werewolf [story].

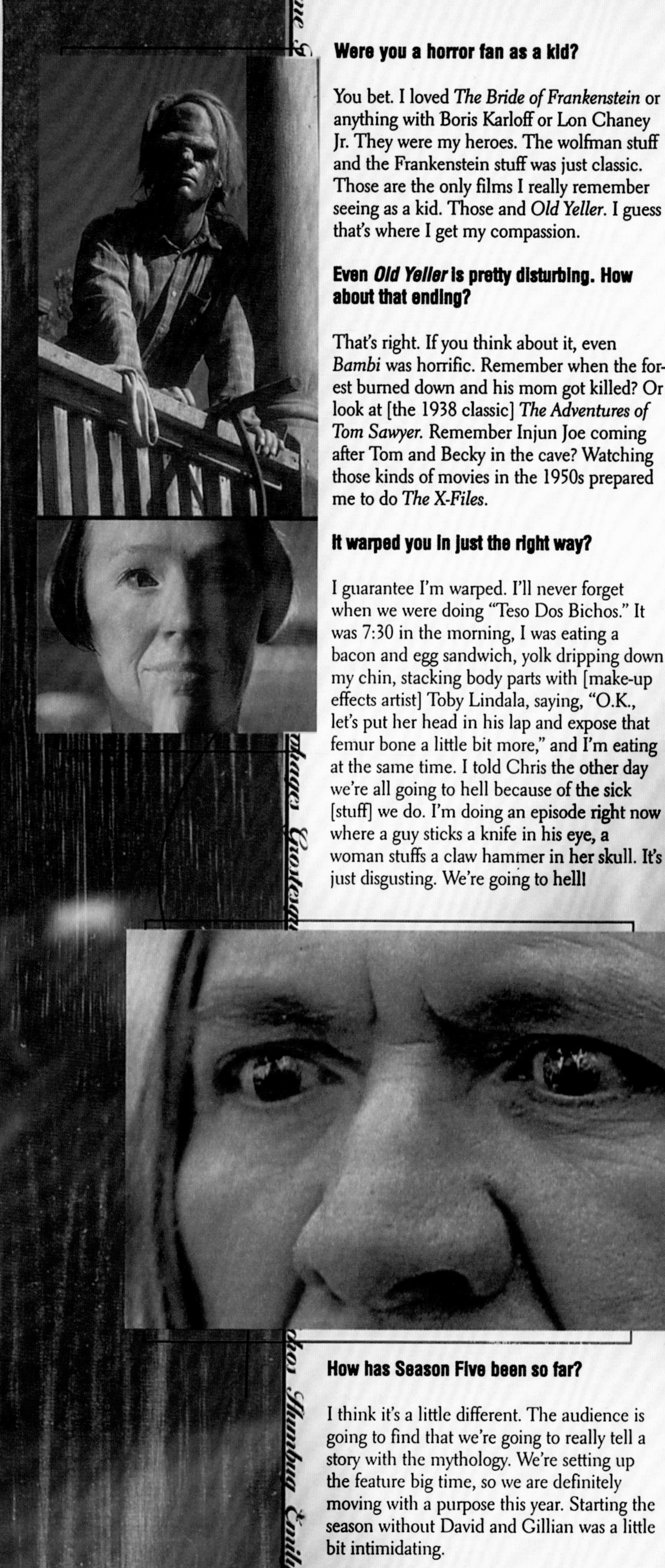

Were you a horror fan as a kid?

You bet. I loved *The Bride of Frankenstein* or anything with Boris Karloff or Lon Chaney Jr. They were my heroes. The wolfman stuff and the Frankenstein stuff was just classic. Those are the only films I really remember seeing as a kid. Those and *Old Yeller*. I guess that's where I get my compassion.

Even *Old Yeller* is pretty disturbing. How about that ending?

That's right. If you think about it, even *Bambi* was horrific. Remember when the forest burned down and his mom got killed? Or look at [the 1938 classic] *The Adventures of Tom Sawyer*. Remember Injun Joe coming after Tom and Becky in the cave? Watching those kinds of movies in the 1950s prepared me to do *The X-Files*.

It warped you in just the right way?

I guarantee I'm warped. I'll never forget when we were doing "Teso Dos Bichos." It was 7:30 in the morning, I was eating a bacon and egg sandwich, yolk dripping down my chin, stacking body parts with [make-up effects artist] Toby Lindala, saying, "O.K., let's put her head in his lap and expose that femur bone a little bit more," and I'm eating at the same time. I told Chris the other day we're all going to hell because of the sick [stuff] we do. I'm doing an episode right now where a guy sticks a knife in his eye, a woman stuffs a claw hammer in her skull. It's just disgusting. We're going to hell!

How has Season Five been so far?

I think it's a little different. The audience is going to find that we're going to really tell a story with the mythology. We're setting up the feature big time, so we are definitely moving with a purpose this year. Starting the season without David and Gillian was a little bit intimidating.

The first thing we [shot] was "Unusual Suspects." But it was a great show. Vince Gilligan put together a terrific script, and the Lone Gunmen—Tom Braidwood, Dean Haglund and Bruce Harwood—really came through. And the guest star, Signy Coleman, was perfectly cast. It really worked out. When it was funny, it was very funny, and when it was dramatic, it was very dramatic. That's what we were going for. We wanted to make the warehouse sequence really heavy, with low, wide angles and a lot of gunfire—dark and sketchy. But the rest of it we kept nice and light and funny. I thought that the blend worked really well.

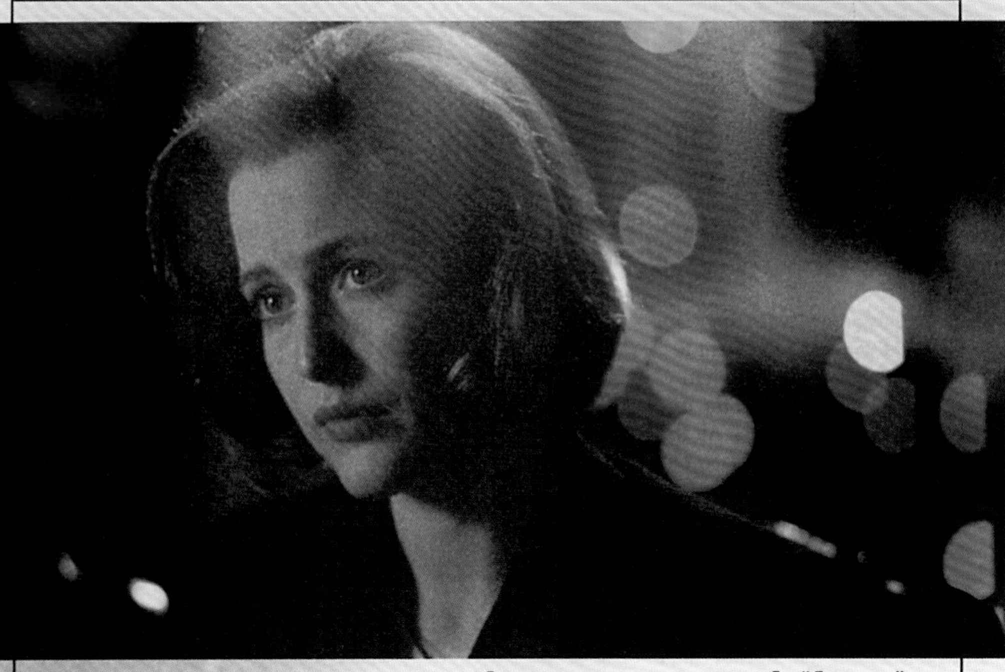

FACES OF FEAR: MANNERS DIRECTED [CLOCKWISE FROM ABOVE] "EMILY," "HUMBUG," "TESO DOS BICHOS," "DIE HAND DIE VERLETZT" AND "HOME"

Do you enjoy working on the more humourous episodes?

I enjoy all of them. I like the comedy because I feel I've got a knack for it. I really like "War of the Coprophages," "Unusual Suspects," "Humbug." But I also like the gory and the scary. I just like working on *The X-Files*. It's one of the few shows on television that I can truly say is a director's medium. It gives you an opportunity to do so many different things. You're doing high drama and comedy and some adventure and some real scary stuff. It's a real playground for a director.

"Humbug" was the first really funny episode. Weren't people nervous about making it?

I was scared to death. After "Die Hand Die Verletzt," they made me a producer. "Humbug" was my first episode as a producer, and it was my second [*X-Files*] episode ever. So the pressure was on. And here they hand me a comedy—not only a comedy, but one in which David Duchovny makes fun of himself. There we are with David posing on the steps of a trailer and somebody [pointing to him and saying], "Or I could look like an idiot, like him."

I thought the script was brilliant, but it was really blazing new territory. I knew I had to go in and make it really good and interesting, and I think that together we came up with a new *X-Files* [style]. You have the paranormal [episodes], you have the aliens [episodes] and now you have these little satires. [Writer] Darin Morgan opened up another door for us, and it's been a very successful door. Vince Gilligan has [kept that door open] with "Unusual Suspects," and I think Chris just did it with "The Post-Modern Prometheus." The Stephen King episode right now has a lot of that [flavour]. That's exciting for the fans, and also for me as a director and the writers and all of us involved with the show. We're doing a television series that's opening every door you can open, and the audience appreciates that.

Are there any new doors you're still hoping to open?

There's some special effects we could get into. But I shouldn't answer that. I would hate to see what the writers come up with that we haven't already explored, because I'll have to direct it and that could be a real pain in the [butt].

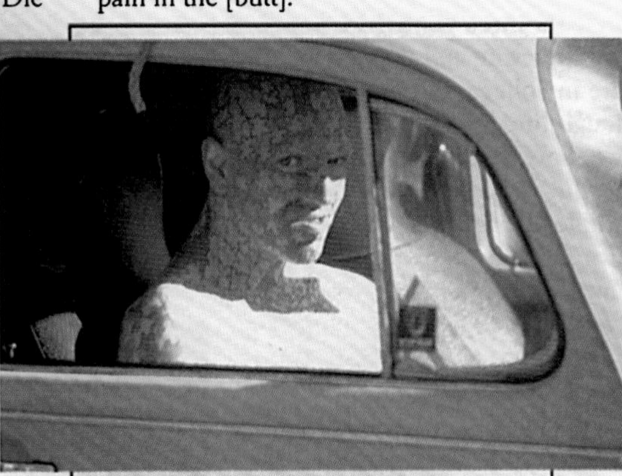

Is there a chance you would leave the show to do features?

I'm contracted for a sixth season. I'd like to do features eventually, but I don't want to jump into a film just for the sake of saying, "Oh, I did a feature." I've been offered three different features: two of them about gang violence, which I won't glorify, and a Vietnam story that was historically inaccurate, with guys cutting people off at the knees with machetes.

I only want to do a feature if it's right for me. I don't want to do a $50 million film. I'd like to do a $10 million film, something personal, something manageable for my first time out. And if I never do a feature, that's O.K. because I've done *The X-Files*. I know that after *The X-Files*, I won't be going back to do episodic television. I'll be very selective. So we'll see what happens. I'd like to do a film, but it's got to be on my terms.

How did you get your start in the television business?

I've been in the business all my life. I was a child actor in L.A.: I started acting when I was 3 years old. I was a day player on everything that you ever watched on television in the '50s and '60s: *Leave it to Beaver*, *Father Knows Best*, you name it. My mother took me on so many damn interviews. But I always wanted to be a director.

My dad tells a great story about that. When I was a kid, my dad produced [the classic kids' Western series] *Rin Tin Tin* and I used to go to the set every day and watch him work. There was a director on the show we called "Gramps" Beaudine. One day we were driving home from the set, and I said, "Dad, I want to do what Gramps does." And he said, "Why is that?" And I said, "Because he gets to tell the cowboys and Indians what to do." I was about 4 years old at the time. And here I am 43 years later fulfilling my life-long dream.

He's still at it. He just produced a *Waltons* Easter special. His name is Sam Manners. He was a real pioneer. He did shows like *Route 66*, *Naked City*, *Wild, Wild West*. If I wasn't working as an actor I was with pop on the set.

We travelled all over the United States with *Route 66*. It was the first time they ever took a television series on the road, and we travelled with my pop, went to school for three hours a day and then went to the set to hang out with the grips and electricians. It was fabulous. All the department heads would bring their children. I've got a brother and a sister. My brother's a production manager, Kelly Manners. He also works for 20th Century Fox. He just finished *The Visitor*. As a matter of fact, they wanted to put him on *The X-Files* next season if we move to L.A., and I told them, "No way!" I don't want him involved with this show. [Laughs.] And my sister's retired. She was a first assistant director. Her name's Tana Manners. She was the queen of movies of the week. She finally got smart and married a gaffer and they bought a ranch in Montana and now they raise horses.

She's the only smart one in the family. She got out of the business. Everyone else is addicted to it. I don't know anything else. This is it for me. And fortunately, I've been slogging through it long enough that I finally got onto a show like *The X-Files* where I can be proud of my work.

What kind of TV work did you do before *The X-Files*?

I've done around 240, 250 hours of television. *Simon and Simon*, *Matt Houston*, *Charlie's Angels*, *Hardcastle and McCormick*, *21 Jump Street*, *The Commish*. I cut my teeth directing second units for Aaron Spelling. He would send me out with a director of photography and we'd shoot car chases all over the world. We went to St. Thomas, Hawaii, all over the place. And then the first show I ever directed was a *Charlie's Angels*. Aaron told me, "As long as you keep two [breasts] at the bottom of the frame, it'll be alright."

I knew I could direct. I learned by watching directors who didn't know how to direct, who would waste time. I always marvelled at the directors who would go, "O.K., let's print that," and then go to the director of photography and say, "Now what do you think of something like this?" I'd think, "Jesus, this guy's only got 12 or 13 hours to shoot today. You'd think he'd come in a little more organized than that."

I take pride in coming in in the morning knowing exactly what I'm going to shoot. Exactly. I know what my last shot of the day's going to be. I go, "Cut it! Print it! We're over here!" *Bang*! I give the boys a setup and, *bang*, we light it. My last episode, "Emily," the crew did 25 setups in six-and-a-half hours after lunch. That's unheard of. Most crews don't do 25 setups in a whole day. Our crew is spectacular. They really are the best crew I've ever worked with in this industry. And that's saying something, because I've been around this business for 44 years.

You mentioned a possible move to L.A. Is that scary?

If it goes to L.A., I have no objections, because that's where I live. I've been up here for three years living in a hotel room with my wife and my dog. My daughters are in college, so I don't see them. It's a tough life. So I won't be broken-hearted if we move to L.A.

But we're going to have to train a whole different set of people. *The X-Files* is not a television series: It's an experience. This is not just going to work and doing 9 to 5 and picking up your paycheck on Thursday. This requires total dedication. Everybody involved in this television series gives it their heart and soul. To replace that in Los Angeles is going to be a tall order. I have never seen a group of people as committed to something in all of my life. It's like we work at NASA or something. We're putting up a space shuttle every week. It's amazing. ●

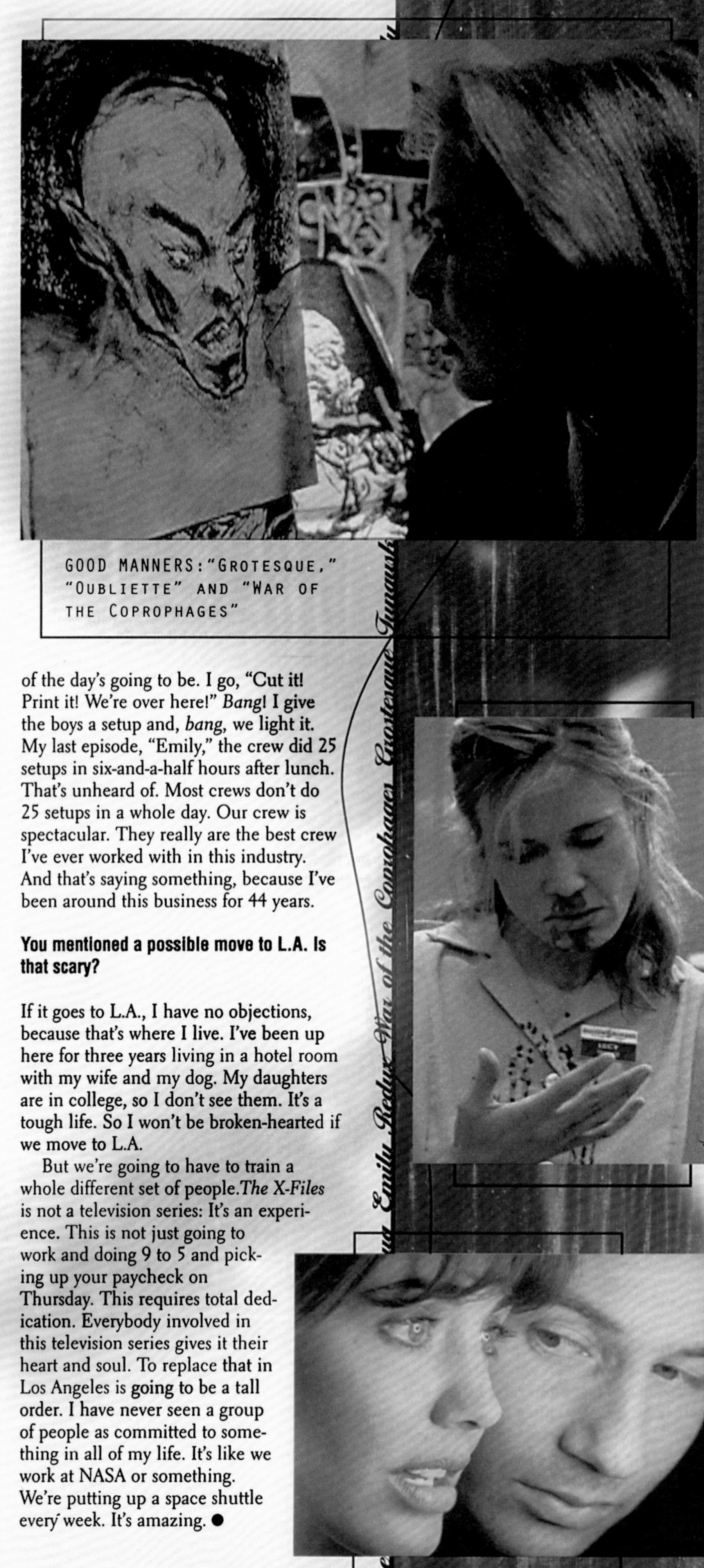

GOOD MANNERS: "Grotesque," "Oubliette" and "War of the Coprophages"

EPISODE GUIDE

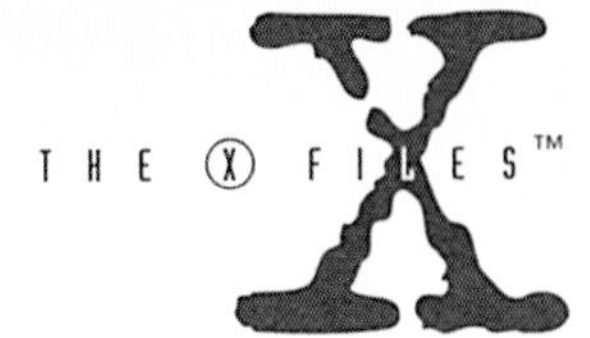

ipal Credits

oduced by	Ten-Thirteen Productions for 20th Century-Fox TV
eator and Executive Producer	Chris Carter
-Executive Producers	Howard Gordon, RW Goodwin
roducers	Joseph Patrick Finn, Kim Manners, Rob Bowman
o-Producer	Paul Rabwin
Music	Mark Snow

isode Credits

Written by	Howard Gordon
Directed by	Kim Manners
Special Agent Fox Mulder	David Duchovny
Special Agent Dr Dana Scully	Gillian Anderson
Assistant Director Walter S Skinner	Mitch Pileggi
Special Agent Bill Patterson	Kurtwood Smith
John Mostow	Levani Outchaneichvili
Aguirre	John Milton Brandon
Special Agent Nemhauser	Greg Thirloway
Special Agent Sheherlis	Susan Bain
Model	Zoran Vukelic
Glass Blower	James McDonnell
Young Agent	Kasper Michaels
Paramedic	Paul J Anderson

3.14: "GROTESQUE" Episode #3X14

Original US tx 2 February 96 Original UK tx 4 June 96

WASHINGTON, DC

A group of art students taking a life class are sketching a nude male model; however, one of them, John Mostow, draws a grotesque gargoyle, using his own blood as an equally grisly medium. After class, the model is attacked, murdered and mutilated as he leaves the faculty. Mostow is later arrested by an FBI team lead by Special Agent Bill Patterson, who finds a bloody razor blade at the scene. The case, it seems, is closed.

During questioning Mostow, a Soviet immigrant who came to the United States after a number of years in a sanatorium, confesses to the seven murder-mutilations of which he is suspected, but claims to have been possessed by a spirit which forced him to kill. Mulder, who had worked under Patterson as a rookie agent, but objected to his mentor's Nietzchian philosophy that in order to catch monsters, you must become one yourself, takes an interest in the case. Later, his interest becomes a great deal more focused when another murder occurs, bearing undisclosed – and unmistakable – hallmarks of Mostow's killings. Mostow, who has been busy etching more gargoyle images into the floor of his cell, seems unsurprised, stating that the spirit which possessed him has presumably found another host.

Mulder and Patterson clash over the case, with the latter sarcastically asking his former protegé if he suspects the involvement of "little green men"; Mulder refuses to rise to the bait, however, and later, during his own thorough search of Mostow's studio, discovers a secret caché of human corpses 'sculpted' into gargoyles. But as the murders continue, with the same pattern of facial mutilation common to Mostow's victims, Mulder begins to suspect that the murderer has passed the torch to a 'copycat killer' – one who has spent so long inside Mostow's head, he knows the killer intimately. Later, doubt is cast on Mulder himself when Scully discovers a blade at the scene of a crime. Examination of the blade reveals a set of Mulder's fingerprints.

F.Y.I.

Writer Howard Gordon, who, following his first season collaborations with Alex Gansa, has written "Sleepless", "Firewalker", "Fresh Bones" and "DPO" on his own, came of age with this extraordinary piece of television, one of the finest episodes of the third season. "I'm very proud of ['Grotesque']," he says, "because I think it illuminated a lot of Mulder, but also of this: that there really is a thin line between madness and sanity. We sort of walk around and act civilised, but there's this thin membrane between us and people who walk into McDonald's and start shooting things up."

Kurtwood Smith (*Robocop*) is brilliantly effective as Mulder's former mentor Bill Patterson, who graphically and grippingly demonstrates philosopher Friedrich Nietzche's axiom that "whoever fights monsters should see to it that in the process he does not become a monster." Patterson is loosely based on legendary FBI agent Robert K Ressler, who popularised the psychological profile.

Director of photography John S Bartley was the deserving winner of a 1996 Prime Time Emmy award for Outstanding Individual Achievement for Cinematography in a Series for this stunning episode. As Howard Gordon enthuses, "[*The X-Files*] has always been a very dark show, but on this one he dared to get really, *really* dark. His use of lighting was amazing. And to do this on an episodic schedule? I mean, it's one thing to see this in a feature film like *Se7en*, but to do it on *TV?*"

On its initial US broadcast, "Grotesque" rated the 29th highest show of the week, scoring a Nielsen rating of 11.6/18, equating approximately 11.1 million homes (18.2 million viewers).

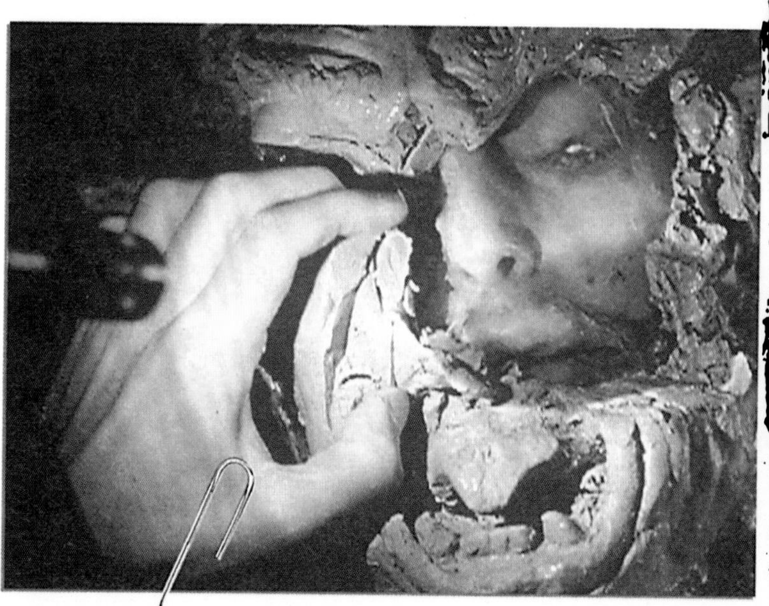

Noteworthy Dialogue Transcript

MULDER [to Patterson]: "Look at your hands. Now tell me what you're doing here..."

Meet FRANK BLACK

MULDER AND SCULLY ENCOUNTER ANOTHER PARANORMAL INVESTIGATOR FATHERED BY CHRIS CARTER IN THE LONG AWAITED **X-FILES/MILLENNIUM** CROSSOVER EPISODE by gina mcintyre

Ask any avid fan of *The X-Files* – one of the most essential elements to the series' successful formula is the singular chemistry between leads David Duchovny and Gillian Anderson. Together, their tireless characters have pursued all variety of monsters and travelled thousands of miles to track down the origins of a global conspiracy, forming a (potentially temporary) platonic bond thousands of times stronger than any pair of co-workers in television history. Now, all of that is about to change – at least for the time being.

After years of speculation, the long-awaited *X-Files/Millennium* crossover has finally made its way onto the burgeoning roster of Season Seven episodes, meaning that Mulder and Scully have a new partner – the enigmatic Frank Black. A conspiracy theorist after Mulder's own heart, Black, played for three seasons on Chris Carter's series *Millennium* by genre favorite Lance Henriksen, studied and infiltrated the mysterious Millennium group, an organisation whose warring factions fought to seize control of the imminent apocalypse. He is now an integral part of the FBI duo's final investigation of the 20th century.

Penned by the writing team of executive producer Frank Spotnitz and co-executive producer Vince Gilligan, the crossover episode, appropriately titled "Millennium," had been the subject of much debate by Carter and company for several years. Sensing that this might indeed be *The X-Files*' final year on the air and thus the last opportunity to meld the two series, Spotnitz and Gilligan decided the time was right for the trio to meet. And even though introducing Black into the conspiracy-heady *X-Files* world was not a new idea, it still managed to be a tricky endeavour.

"It's obviously something that had been proposed and thought about for three years while *Millennium* was on the air," Spotnitz explains. "We never did it because we felt that it would be done for the wrong reasons. Now that the show is off the air, when we can't help the ratings of *Millennium*, it just felt like a great thing to end Frank Black's run, to let him reach the year 2000. It was fun to put him together with Mulder and Scully. The idea was fun, but it proved to be a very, very hard story to figure out."

Spotnitz says the episode, a tale about a small group of retired FBI agents who share a terrible allegiance to one doomsday-eager sect of the Millennium Group, evolved very slowly and required much effort to successfully capture the unique spirits of both series. While the two shows shared a dark mood, there were subtle differences that needed to be preserved.

"We went through so many completely different versions of what the story was about," Spotnitz says. "The hard part was making it an X-file yet making it [seem like an episode of] *Millennium* and finding things for all three characters to do that made them all heroes. That was really the challenge, but I think we finally figured it out. We ended up finding a way to use the Millennium Group, to really touch on so many things that were essential to the show without confusing *X-Files* viewers who may not have been familiar with *Millennium*. That was really what we kept telling ourselves – pretend like you've never seen *Millennium*. Pretend like you've only seen *The X-Files* and make this make sense. Hopefully, we succeeded."

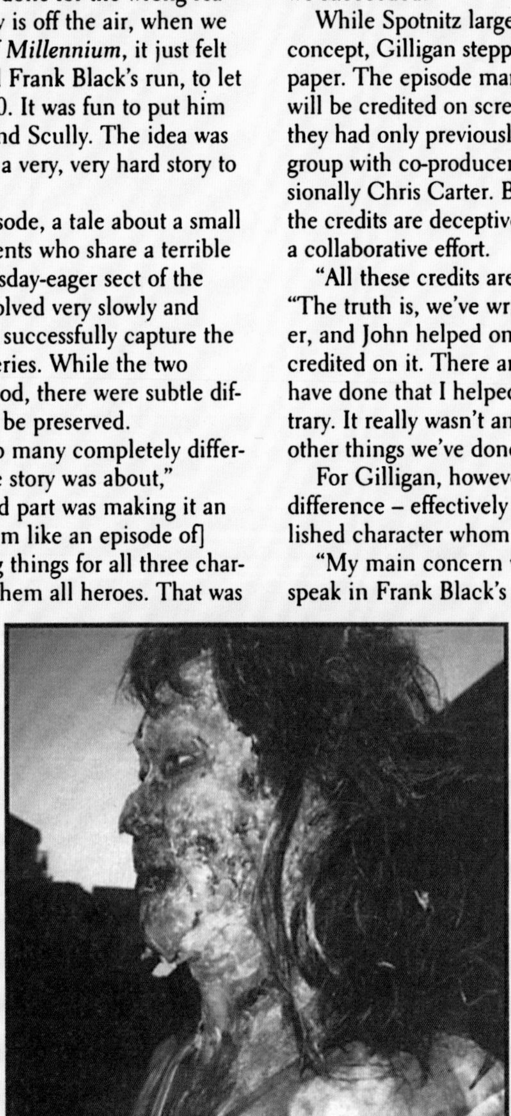

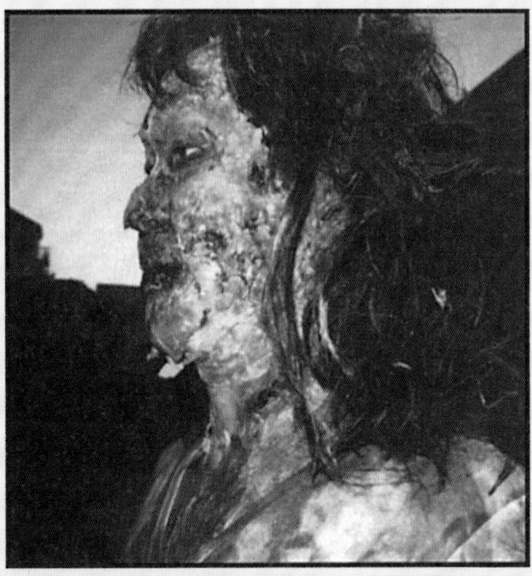

While Spotnitz largely developed the episode's concept, Gilligan stepped in to set the story on paper. The episode marks the first time the pair will be credited on screen together as partners; they had only previously teamed up as part of a group with co-producer John Shiban and occasionally Chris Carter. But Spotnitz cautions that the credits are deceptive – "Millennium" was still a collaborative effort.

"All these credits are insane," Spotnitz says. "The truth is, we've written many things together, and John helped on this even though he's not credited on it. There are things John and Vince have done that I helped on. It's just kind of arbitrary. It really wasn't any different than any of the other things we've done."

For Gilligan, however, there was one distinct difference – effectively recreating a well-established character whom he'd never written before.

"My main concern was to have Frank Black speak in Frank Black's voice," Gilligan says. "I wanted to make sure I was doing the character justice. I should say that I watched a bunch of old *Millennium* episodes, but the truth is, I didn't really. I just sort of started writing. At the end of the day, it really is an *X-Files* episode in which Frank Black is a guest character. As I said, I just wanted to stay true to the voice of Frank Black. I've always thought that Lance Henriksen is a great actor and I always loved the character of Frank Black."

Henriksen, for one,

"It was the weirdest thing for the first time on film seeing Mulder and Scully with Frank Black. They're all Chris' children in a way, all together in the same universe." -Frank Spotnitz

thinks Spotnitz and Gilligan realised their goals. The pensive actor admits he was surprised but pleased when he got the call to come to *The X-Files*' Los Angeles set to reprise his role as the beleaguered uber-profiler. In all honesty, he says, he never expected the crossover to take place.

"I think the only reason it did was because *Millennium* got cancelled," he says. "The cancellation was sudden, so Chris Carter felt he could wrap it up more completely [with a crossover]. And a lot of people wanted to see it."

Most notably, the upset viewers who were shocked to see *Millennium* disappear from television. Although the series never had the same kind of powerful mainstream appeal as *The X-Files*, the show claimed a smaller but equally devoted cult following.

"Apparently, Fox got 30,000 letters saying, 'What are you doing taking *Millennium* off the air?'" Henriksen says. "I think it was the scariest show on television. It wasn't as scary as the news at night. In the whole three years that we did it, nobody got killed or hurt – only on screen."

And in the crossover, people do get hurt... on-screen, of course. In fact, Mulder and Scully first come into contact with an institutionalised Black while investigating the suspicious circumstances surrounding the gruesome death of a former federal agent.

"We had what I think was an interesting way into the story, which was starting off Frank Black sort of in really bad shape," Gilligan says. "He starts off in a mental hospital. Granted, he's checked himself in, but he's not in the heroic pose we hoped he would be in when we last saw him in *Millennium*. In the series finale of *Millennium*, the last time we see Frank Black he's driving off into the sunset with his daughter. This [episode] starts up with him really down and out in a mental institution. We didn't want to put the character through hard times so much. We just wanted to start him off someplace

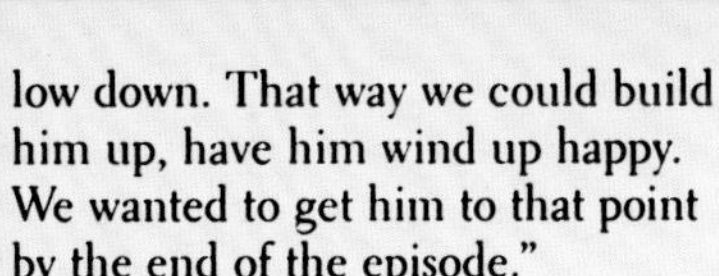

low down. That way we could build him up, have him wind up happy. We wanted to get him to that point by the end of the episode."

While a number of *X-Files* guest stars have gone on record expressing their amazement at the long hours required of the show's cast and crew, the 14-hour minimum days came as no surprise to Henriksen. A season veteran of the Carterian work day, the actor was well aware of the standard of perfection expected for every take. The actor says shooting *The X-Files* was just like another *Millennium* episode.

"It was identical," Henriksen says. "The only difference is *X-Files* is so successful that there's no [hesitation] to spend money, which is a nice thing to watch. They can polish it up like a good gem. And [director] Tom [Wright] and I did half of all the *Millennium* [episodes] ever done. He and I almost talk in shorthand, which often happens with actors and directors who work together a lot. Tom's very talented."

Wright could safely be considered the Kim Manners or Rob Bowman of *Millennium*, having helmed more instalments of the show than any other director. Spotnitz says he was hand-chosen because of his intimate knowledge of the Henriksen-led series.

NEW YEAR'S EVIL: [clockwise from above] executive producer Frank Spotnitz; Lance Henriksen as Frank Black; one of the episode's ghouls; the basement set created for "Millennium" [previous page] Mulder and Scully investigate strange goings-on in "Millennium"

MEN IN BLACK: [above] Frank Black and Agent Mulder in 'Millennium'; [below] a "Millennium" zombie

ferent generations of FBI agents, essentially. They're opposite sides of the same coin, I always felt. Maybe that's reading too much into it. I don't think Frank Black would be into all the UFOs and whatnot, but he'd probably have a more open mind about that stuff than Scully would."

"We thought that was appropriate because Tom directed so many episodes of *Millennium* that he really deserved to direct this," Spotnitz says. "Also, I thought it was great for Lance that it would be an *X-Files* crew and an *X-Files* episode but he'd be there with the director that he knew best."

Henriksen seemed to have no trouble blending in; he says he found *The X-Files'* cast and crew gracious and welcoming.

"It went really well," the actor reports. "David and Gillian and I had never worked together before, but when you put these three characters into the same room something unexpected happens. David was saying he would do another year if I was on the show. I thought he was so generous; he's a bright guy. Gillian and he have these characters down so well. They're doing a great job. It was a pleasant time."

Watching the actors interact was something of a surreal experience, Spotnitz says. "It was the weirdest thing for the first time on film seeing Mulder and Scully with Frank Black. They're all Chris' children in a way, all together in the same universe. [Mulder and Frank Black] actually have a lot in common. They're both profilers, but Frank has a stature that Mulder would be respectful of. He's not big on authority for authority's sake, but Frank has earned the right to be respected."

Gilligan says he remained cognisant of the pair's similarities when writing their dialogue. "I sort of picture it as the old guard and the young turk as it were," Gilligan says of the relationship between Black and Mulder. "[They're] two different generations of FBI agents, essentially. They're opposite sides of the same coin, I always felt."

In this case, he'd have to, for Mulder and Scully come to him with a case that appears to involve the dead returning to life in zombie-like form. And when such grave matters arise, it's up to make-up artist Cheri Montesanto-Medcalf to resurrect the unfortunate victims, who in this instance happened to be stuntmen hired by stunt coordinator Danny Weselis.

"What we wanted to do is make them spooky but not over the top," she says. "It was really important to us that they have really good decaying skin, yet we see photos of these FBI guys earlier, so there has to be something that you can kind of tell that they were these people. We were really into having movement so we used acetates and stuff so when they move their faces and their necks, it actually looks like rotten, decaying skin. It actually comes lose, it moves, it turns with them. It was really pretty cool, plus it picks up some light."

It took multiple make-up artists five hours to transform the stuntmen into the zombies; they were then required to remain buried beneath the elaborate make-up for an exhausting 17 hours.

"We stained their tongues with food colouring to make their mouths all gross," Montesanto-Medcalf says. "One man actually let me build something up [on his tongue] so when he opened his mouth, you saw hanging skin between the lips. That was really, really good."

Fortunately, Henriksen was spared such torturous treatment and was instead given the opportunity to focus on bringing his character to life during the day and returning to his Los Angeles home – and his brand new baby daughter – at night, something the actor says he missed when *Millennium* was filming in Vancouver. "When I did *The X-Files*, I thought what a nice thing it is to be in L.A. and do this, sleep in my own bed at night. It was really wonderful."

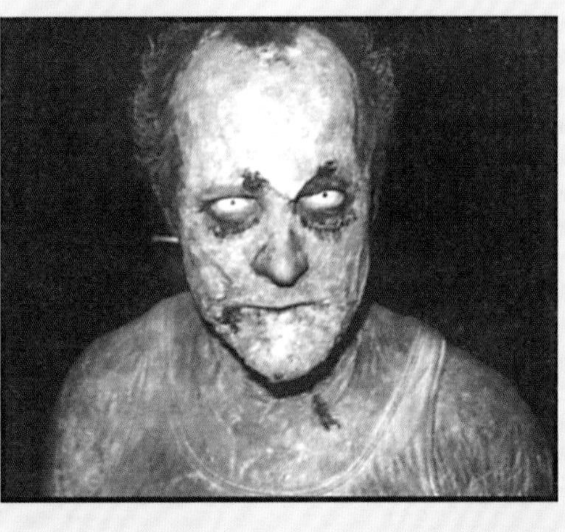

Although the episode sees Frank Black usher in the new, Armageddon-free millennium, Henriksen says he's not quite ready to see his alter ego disappear into the sunset.

"*Millennium* doesn't seem like it's gone away," he says. "What I'd love to do next with *Millennium* is if Chris did a film of it. It's a possibility. I don't know what that means. This business has more twists and turns with language than politics. But there is a quality thing about always leaving them wanting more." ●

EPISODE GUIDE

3.17: "PUSHER" Episode #3X17

Original US tx 23 February 96 Original UK tx 25 June 96

Principal Credits

Created by	Chris Carter
Produced by	Ten-Thirteen Productions for Twentieth Century Fox TV
Creator and Executive Producer	Chris Carter
Co-Executive Producers	Howard Gordon, RW Goodwin
Producers	Joseph Patrick Finn, Kim Manners, Rob Bowman
Co-Producer	Paul Rabwin
Music	Mark Snow

Episode Credits

Written by	Vince Gilligan
Directed by	Rob Bowman
Special Agent Fox Mulder	David Duchovny
Special Agent Dr Dana Scully	Gillian Anderson
Assistant Director Walter S Skinner	Mitch Pileggi
'Pusher'/Robert Patrick Modell	Robert Wisden
Agent Frank Burst	Vic Polizos
Agent Collins	Steve Bacic
Deputy Scott Kerber	D Neil Mark
[Agent] Holly	Julia Arkos
Judge	Don MacKay
Defense Attorney	Meredith Bain-Woodward
Prosecutor Brent	JD Sheppard
Lead SWAT Cop	Darren Lucas
SWAT Lieutenant	Roger R Cross
Nurse	Janyse Jaud
Lobby Guard	Ernie Foort
Bailiff	Henry Watson

LOUDOUN COUNTY, VIRGINIA

Robert Modell, a killer who called the FBI to confess to a series of murders in which he used the power of his will to force his victims to commit suicide, is apprehended in a supermarket – only to escape his captors on the way to jail by mentally willing the driver to crash into a truck.

At the scene, the word 'RONIN' fingerpainted on a police car alerts Mulder to a mercenary magazine, *American Ronin*, in which he finds an advertisement for someone who "solves problems". Staking out the payphone which corresponds to the listed contact number, Mulder receives a phone call from Modell, who calls himself 'Pusher', daring the agents to prove their worth by following his trail. Later, Modell wills one of the arresting agents to douse himself in petrol and set himself alight as a horrified Mulder and Scully look on, powerless to stop him.

Modell seems sure that his subsequent arrest is merely a temporary setback: a prophecy which is fulfilled when a judge, seemingly swayed by Modell's will, releases him. Although Scully suspects that Modell's confession of guilt was simply a ploy to gain attention, Mulder is clearly both appalled and fascinated, asking Modell, "How do you do it?". Soon, it becomes apparent that Modell is equally fascinated with Mulder, considering the agent to be "a worthy adversary" and selecting him as his next victim.

A desperate game of cat-and-mouse ensues, with Mulder and Scully finally tracing Modell to a hospital, where 'Pusher' draws the agents into an even deadlier game – Russian roulette...

F.Y.I.

"Pusher" was the first episode written by Vince Gilligan (see exclusive interview on page 14) after he had joined *The X-Files'* writing staff in October 1995 as a story editor; his earlier script, "Soft Light", had been written as a freelancer. Gilligan is now a co-producer with the show, and author of some of the fourth season's finest stories, including "Unruhe" and "Paper Hearts".

One of *The X-Files'* subtlest digital effects appears – albeit briefly – in this episode, giving former visual effects producer Mat Beck one of his frequent headaches. "Loudoun County is where Vince Gilligan is from," Beck explains, "and there's a scene that takes place at the Loudoun County courthouse [in which] the sign on the wall outside somehow got spelled L-O-U-D-O-N. So when Vince noticed it he said, 'I'm never gonna be able to go home again unless we do something!' Of course, it was a moving, tracking shot with people moving in front of it, and if you're *adding* something – an additional letter that has to fit in with a whole bunch of other letters which are really in the scene, so that you have a reference of how it's supposed to look – it's harder still! So when you look at it, one letter in there is artificial, and the others are real. It actually turned out pretty good."

On its initial US broadcast, "Pusher" scored a Nielsen rating of 10.8/18, equating approximately 10 million homes and 16.2 million viewers. Here in the UK, a record-breaking 10.8 million viewers tuned in for its BBC airing last summer, making it the first episode to break the 10 million mark *and* the highest rated episode of all time.

Noteworthy Dialogue Transcript

MULDER: "It was like you said: he was always such a little man. This was finally something that made him feel big."

EPISODE: 6x02

PATRICK CRUMP

"Drive"

The dictionary defines syncronicity as "coincidence of events that seem to be meaningfully related." In the case of actor Bryan Cranston, syncronicity means having the chance to play distraught fugitive Patrick Crump in the Season Six episode "Drive," all because he didn't shave.

"I wrote, directed and acted in an independent feature called *Last Chance*," Cranston says. "It just so happened I was playing kind of a redneck guy with a big, bushy mustache and longer hair. When I edited the movie, I decided I wasn't going to shave, I would just concentrate on the work. That's when my agent called and told me about *The X-Files* audition. They said the character was a bigoted, backwoods type of guy. I said, 'If I can act the part then I have the part, because I completely look it.'"

BRYAN CRANSTON

© 20TH CENTURY FOX TELEVISION

Chameleon-like transformations have become a staple of Cranston's busy career. A veteran character actor who starred in his first commercial at age eight, Cranston has since appeared in dozens of movies and television shows. Currently, he plays a clean-cut, albeit off-kilter, dad in the hit Fox comedy *Malcolm in the Middle*.

"I meet *X-Files* fanatics all the time who tell me they watch every episode," Cranston says. "I'll say, 'I did an *X-Files* once.' You can see them thinking and thinking about what episode it could've been. I'll finally tell them I was in the back seat of the car with David Duchovny in 'Drive.' They'll be amazed and say, 'That was you?'"

What might surprise X-Philes more than Cranston's new look is his complete lack of familiarity with the show. "I hadn't seen the series before," he says. "[Director] Rob [Bowman] and David were just slack-jawed when I said, 'So, what do you do?' [David said,] 'Um, I'm an FBI guy.' I didn't know the show at all. But I did run out and see *The X-Files* movie. I told Rob, 'Remember how much crap you gave me for not knowing your series? I can tell you honestly I was into your movie, and I didn't know the background of the characters.' That says a lot."—*Annabelle Villanueva*

ALSO KNOWN AS:

2000: "Hal" in *Malcolm in the Middle*
1998: "Buzz Aldrin" in *From the Earth to the Moon*
1997: "Witch Lawyer" in *Sabrina the Teenage Witch*
1995: "Dr. Tim Whatley" in *Seinfeld*
1983: "Doug Donovan" in *Loving*

1999: "Lance" in *Last Chance*
1998: "War Department Colonel" in *Saving Private Ryan*
1996: "Father Brophy" in *Street Corner Justice*
1996: "Virgil 'Gus' Grissom" in *That Thing You Do!*

EPISODE: 3x20

JOSE CHUNG

"Jose Chung's 'From Outer Space'"

PHOTO BY ALBERT ORTEGA

X-*Files* fans know Charles Nelson Reilly because of his hilarious performance in the Season Three classic "Jose Chung's 'From Outer Space.'" And game show afficionados fondly recall Reilly as a '70s-era fixture on such series as *Match Game* and *Hollywood Squares*. But the role Reilly is most proud of is the one the general public knows least—that of teacher.

"I've been an acting teacher since 1960. I taught Bette Midler, Lily Tomlin, Liza Minnelli, Gary Burghoff and Peter Boyle," says Reilly. "I've had wonderful pupils, and they're all working in TV and movies. So if I don't get a [part], it doesn't bother me. I'm a teacher first."

CHARLES NELSON REILLY

Though Reilly also sidelines as a director of plays (he was nominated for a Tony for his production of *The Gin Game*) and operas, he says Hollywood still pigeonholes him as a wacky game show regular. "I direct plays on Broadway, but they go, 'Yeah, but wasn't he on *Celebrity Bowling?*'" he says.

Fortunately, Chris Carter and former *X-Files* writer/producer Darin Morgan didn't let Reilly's game show past keep them from casting him as Jose Chung. Reilly would love for Chung to return—even though the eccentric author was seemingly murdered at the end of a *Millennium* episode, "Jose Chung's 'Doomsday Defense.'" "He could have faked his death. His books would sell better if he's dead," says Reilly, whose *Millennium* appearance won him an Emmy Award nomination for Outstanding Guest Actor in a Drama Series. "I think it would be so funny to see him watching his own funeral from a car, wearing sunglasses, saying, 'That's not a bad crowd, is it?'"—*Steve Hockensmith*

ALSO KNOWN AS:

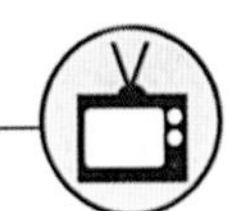

1995: "Mr. Hathaway" in *The Drew Carey Show*
1987: "Mr. Toad" in *The Wind in the Willows*
1975: "Uncle Croc" in *Uncle Croc's Block*
1971: "Hoodoo" in *Lidsville*
1968: "Claymore Gregg" in *The Ghost and Mrs. Muir*

1998: "Dinghy" in *The First of May*
1997: "Mr. Dumpty" in *Babes in Toyland*
1997: "Mr. Rudnick" in *Boys Will Be Boys*
1993: "King Llort" in *A Troll in Central Park*
1991: "Hunch" in *Rock-A-Doodle*
1989: "Killer" in *All Dogs Go to Heaven*
1987: "Vic Carson" in *Body Slam*
1984: "Don Don" in *Cannonball Run II*

IN "MILAGRO," A MYSTERIOUS LONER COMMITS CRIMES OF PASSION ON THE X-FILES' SET

BY GINA MCINTYRE

PHOTOS BY KHAREN HILL

TO LOVE AND DIE IN L.A

GILLIAN ANDERSON IS ABOUT TO HAVE HER HEART RIPPED OUT,

and no one on *The X-Files'* crew seems concerned. In fact, as three o'clock rolls around, hungry glances are exchanged and thoughts turn to what's for lunch. The work day, now six hours old, is only midway through its course; and the members of the series' dedicated behind-the-scenes team have summoned quite an appetite.

So far, they have spent Tuesday shooting scenes for the eighteenth episode of the year, a psychological thriller titled "Milagro," inside Mulder's apartment, which stands in the dark and deceptively chilly confines of Stage Six on the Twentieth Century Fox lot. When they return from the break, Dana Scully will face off with a killer who has the unfortunate habit of ripping the still-beating hearts from the chests of his victims. For now, Anderson lies on the ground, sobbing and clinging to co-star David Duchovny, until director Kim Manners yells, "Cut" for the final time, sending everyone in search of sustenance.

"Milagro," which is Spanish for "miracle," is aptly named. Although every episode of *The X-Files* is something of a miracle—just the fact that all of the necessary elements come together every week is nothing short of astonishing—the episode marks another stop in the journey of discovery that has become Season Six. A risky move to Los Angeles, more comedic episodes than any previous year and a somewhat different approach to Mulder and Scully's will they/won't they relationship has come to define the show's sixth year; "Milagro" continues the series' evolution.

Born from a collaboration between executive producer Frank Spotnitz and writer/producer John Shiban, the episode introduces fans to Mulder's next door neighbor, Phillip Padgett, who holds a strange power over the events about which he writes and harbors an unhealthy fixation with Scully that is not entirely unrequited. While Mulder stumbles onto a series of unexplained murders, Scully meets the amorous Padgett, who has left a medallion bearing the insignia of the sacred heart at the door to the basement office she shares with Mulder. As the investigation continues, Scully becomes drawn inside the writer's world, possibly embarking on a fatal attraction.

"It's actually a very personal story in a way because it's more about what we do than any other *X-Files* we've done," explains Spotnitz. "In a way, what the writer in 'Milagro' does is what we try to do on the show every week, which is create a character and make it seem real. It becomes an X-file when you create a character and the character actually

TWO OF HEARTS: Two scenes from "Milagro" [top and bottom]; a souvenir from the set [center]

is real. It's all stuff that we could totally relate to. He's got these cards that he uses to write his novel that are exactly like the cards we use to write *The X-Files*. There's a lot of things in there that echo with our personal experiences."

"We had talked for some time about doing a story about imagination and the power of imagination," Shiban adds. "Being writers and storytellers first, it's a really important part of our lives and of our jobs. We started talking about what if the worlds that we create in our heads actually became a reality. There's a good side to that and then there's the dark side to that, especially on our show and the kind of things that we come up with."

It's safe to say that Padgett is a good deal more eccentric than the show's writing staff. The character is solely devoted to his craft and forsakes the trappings of the physical plane. His apartment holds little furniture, and he owns few possessions, only what is necessary. He lives as a recluse, dwelling in the realm of his imagination.

"The other thing that we wanted to deal with in the story was sort of the acetic life of the artist and whether that's an admirable thing or something to be weary of, and how this man gets out of touch with reality because he lives in his imagination, which is something that happens to all of us I think," Shiban continues. "That's what we wanted to explore with Scully, too, the idea that she's on this quest with Mulder, this in some ways creative endeavor, and is she missing something. Is she missing love in her life because of that? What is the sacrifice that you give for your work? All those issues are kind of things that we talked about and then found this character to embody."

The character, played by actor John Hawkes, brings a unique energy to the episode. Usually, lead guest roles in *X-Files* episodes consist of cancer-consuming paramedics or 16th century Spanish conquistadors who have petrified into creepy tree-men. In "Milagro," however, the emphasis is on internal struggle, not external conflict. Yes, there is a killer on the loose, but some of the episode's creepiest moments involve the workings of the eerily omniscient Padgett's mind.

"I THINK ALL OF US HAVE FALLEN IN LOVE WITH THESE CHARACTERS THAT WE'VE SPENT SO MUCH TIME WITH AND THINKING ABOUT AND DREAMING AND IMAGINING AND WATCHING HUNDREDS UPON HUNDREDS OF HOURS OF FILM OF THESE ACTORS. IT WAS VERY EASY FOR US TO IMAGINE THIS GUY FALLING IN LOVE WITH SCULLY."

—FRANK SPOTNITZ

ONE FROM THE HEART: "Milagro" [top]; executive producer Frank Spotnitz [above]

"He's a little creepy, but if one were a good enough writer, one could do what Padgett does in this story, which is meet someone and because you observe them so perfectly, imagine what they're thinking in every situation, imagine what they would do given a certain provocation or idea," Spotnitz asserts.

"It's a little bit of what Sherlock Holmes does, I think. He observes somebody very carefully, observes their cane, observes their shoes, the coat, what's threadbare on the coat. That's what a really great writer does. I think Scully senses that about this guy. It's not that he's a stalker; it's that he has great insight into people. There's a terrible sadness about it, too, which I think is appealing. He draws such a perfect portrait of her and understands her so well that I think she feels a little unmasked by him and that's intriguing. It's frightening, but it's intriguing at the same time."

Padgett's affection for Scully, Spotnitz confesses, mirrors the feelings of *The X-Files* writing team. After five-and-a-half years of living with such strong characters, the team cherishes the FBI duo. If Mulder is the one with whom they identify, it's Scully they adore.

"When you're a writer on a show like this, you can't help but fall a little bit in love with the characters," he says. "I think all of us have fallen in love with these characters that we've spent so much time with and thinking about and dreaming and imagining and watching hundreds upon hundreds of hours of film of these actors. It was very easy for us to imagine this guy falling in love with Scully and the obsessiveness about Scully and Gillian Anderson. I think she was a little embarrassed, a little flattered but a little embarrassed when she read it. Honestly, it was kind of fun to be able to find a story to express that kind of obsessiveness you feel as a writer toward this character."

LOVE STORY: Actor John Hawkes as Phillip Padgett [top]; two scenes from "Milagro" [above]; director Kim Manners [right]

OBSESSED IS PERHAPS THE PERFECT way to describe not only Padgett, or even Mulder and Scully, but also life on the series. The level of dedication demanded from everyone on the show—the actors, the writers, the directors, the producers—is dizzying, particularly as the end of the year approaches. With only seven weeks remaining until *The X-Files* breaks for hiatus in April, four additional episodes must be written, polished, prepped, shot and edited. As such, time is a precious commodity. Because of the scheduling constraints, Spotnitz and Shiban carefully planned each thread of the narrative, then turned over scripting duties on "Milagro" to Chris Carter.

"We sat down and we carded the story beat by beat, all the characters and the ideas, and then Chris made it into this beautiful whole," Spotnitz says. "He found all the nuances and shadings and developed a lot of the ideas that were in the boards."

One of the key themes running through the episode is the dynamic nature of Mulder and Scully's relationship. During the course of the episode, Mulder must confront his feelings of jealousy toward Padgett, and Scully must examine her own emotions, specifically, whether or not she can allow another man into her life. "As always we're committed to their relationship remaining of a certain type, but we wanted to get to the whole issue of love, which comes to the forefront in 'Milagro,'" Shiban explains. "That's what the main character wants and that's what Scully sort of wants and maybe doesn't know it but realizes through this man that she might already have it. She might have the perfect love and that love doesn't have to be sexual and marriage and relationship. There are other kinds of love that are just as fulfilling. I think we've done a good job of tantalizing, yet keeping Mulder and Scully still themselves, keeping true to their characters."

A hermetic writer with a crush on Scully, increasing tension between the two leads and a host of mysterious, gruesome murders—it's a witches brew, but one that veteran director Manners is well-equipped to handle. On this fourth day of shooting the episode, Manners exhibits his standard demeanor; efficient, polished, professional, he guides the crew through a number of emotionally gripping scenes, sometimes talking at length with Duchovny or Anderson about the action.

"It's going to be a different *X-Files*," Manners says of "Milagro." "It explores some areas we haven't explored really. It's unlike 'Never Again' where we saw a wild side of Scully. This is a little different side. We see Scully here as a moth drawn to a flame. She's very curious about this man, as weird as he is. There's something about his honesty as a person that she's very curious about, even though she finds him slightly dangerous. She is attracted to him, not so much physically as to the man himself. If I can pull off how this man affects Scully, there's almost this curious danger about him, if I can pull that off without Scully looking foolish then we're going to have a great hour of television. That's what I hope to do."

AIDING MANNERS IN HIS QUEST to bring a gritty realism to such a powerful story are the other behind-the-scenes principals on the show. Production designer Corey Kaplan seems surprisingly collected for someone simultaneously working on five episodes. Perhaps the award she recently took home for outstanding production design on the spooky holiday outing "How the Ghosts Stole Christmas" is keeping her spirits bright under the stress, or it could be that creating Padgett's modest home was a slightly more straightforward assignment than most.

"The great thing about Padgett is he's a spartan," Kaplan says. "There's nothing in his room, so the decorator got to put five dollars on that budget. That's fun. Doing Mulder's lobby is fun and we got to do a bathroom, so we get to expand on his building."

The same standing set doubled as both Mulder's and the writer's apartments; the rooms were just dressed differently to accommodate what scene was filming at a given time, explains art director Lauren Polizzi, who works with Kaplan on the even-numbered episodes. "We've done more to [Mulder's] apartment," she says. "We're changing it over to another character's, the writer who lives next door to Mulder. We had to change it around. He gets a different

ART ATTACK: Production designer Corey Kaplan [top]; writer/producer John Shiban [bottom]

"MAYBE [SCULLY] DOESN'T KNOW IT BUT REALIZES THROUGH THIS MAN **THAT SHE MIGHT ALREADY HAVE THE PERFECT LOVE AND** THAT LOVE DOESN'T HAVE TO BE SEXUAL AND MARRIAGE AND RELATIONSHIP. THERE ARE **OTHER KINDS OF LOVE** THAT ARE JUST AS FULFILLING."

—JOHN SHIBAN

OWNER OF A LONELY HEART

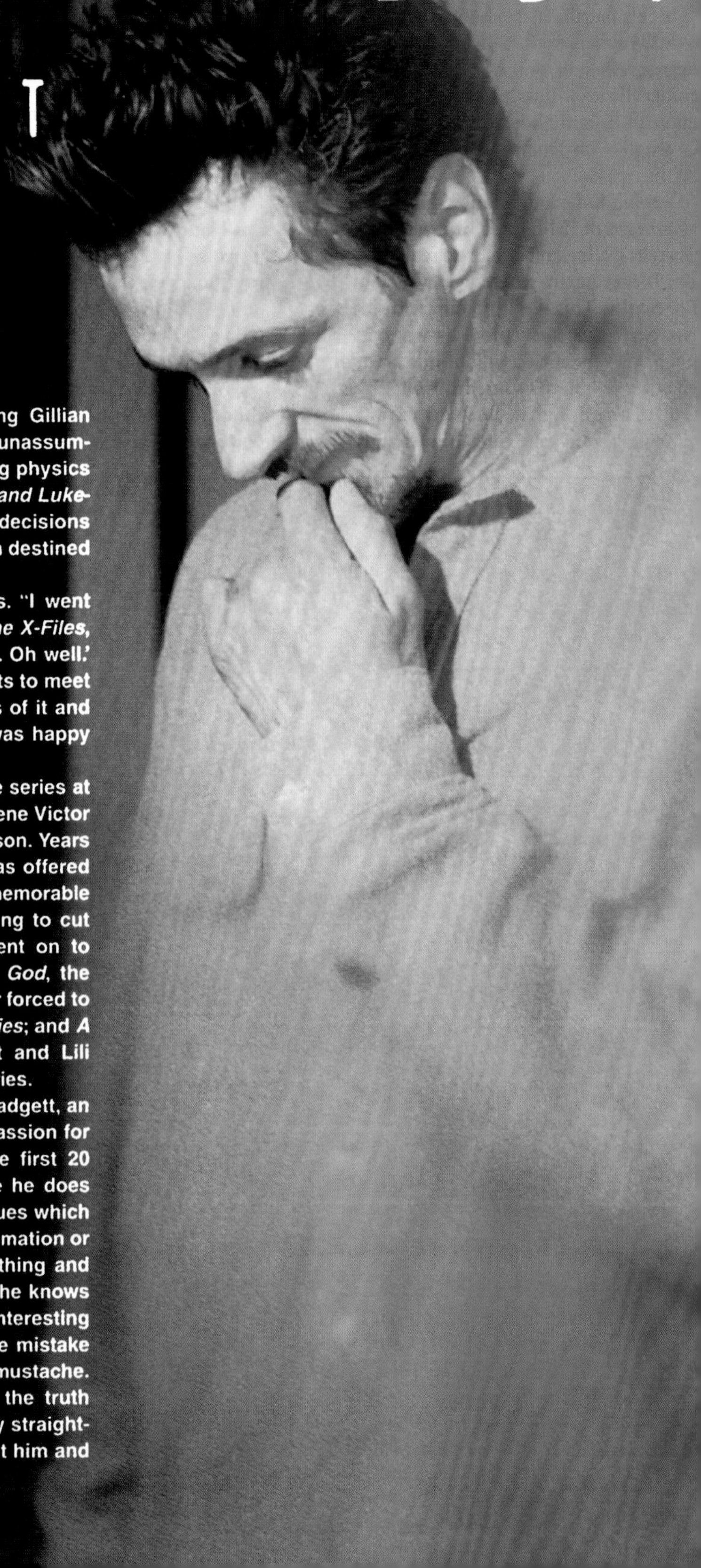

JOHN HAWKES HAD NO INTENTION of stalking Gillian Anderson's alter-ego Dana Scully; it just happened. The unassuming character actor first auditioned for the role of walking physics experiment/ex-con Pinker Rawles in "Trevor," the *Cool Hand Luke*-inspired stand-alone preceding "Milagro." As casting decisions would have it, though, he was instead chosen as the man destined to pine for Scully.

"I read [for Rawles] really well," Hawkes remembers. "I went home and my agents called and they said, 'Oh about *The X-Files*, they chose someone else.' I said, 'That's hard to believe. Oh well.' The next morning they said, 'Chris Carter called and wants to meet you for the next episode.' He'd written the first 25 pages of it and they [sent] that to me. I read it over the weekend and was happy because it was maybe even a better part."

It seemed inevitable that Hawkes would appear on the series at some point. He originally auditioned for the part of Eugene Victor Tooms, losing the role to his good friend Doug Hutchison. Years later, after a successful turn on *Millennium*, the actor was offered an audition for the lead in one of Season Four's most memorable outings, "Musings of a Cigarette-Smoking Man." Unwilling to cut his hair for the part, Hawkes declined. Instead, he went on to appear in three films with ties to *The X-Files*: *Playing God*, the action/drama starring David Duchovny as a former doctor forced to work with a mobster; the Vince Gilligan-penned *Home Fries*; and *A Slipping Down Life*, with co-stars Veronica Cartwright and Lili Taylor, both of whom enjoyed guest star turns on the series.

Now, Hawkes is bringing to the screen the lovelorn Padgett, an odd but appealing recluse who harbors a deep-seated passion for Scully. "It's exhaustive," Hawkes says of the role. "The first 20 pages, the character doesn't speak. Then the first time he does speak, he doesn't shut up. It's these long, long monologues which you never see in television unless a lawyer's doing a summation or something like that. It's wonderful because he says nothing and then when he does speak it's all about Scully and what he knows about her from lots and lots of time observing her. It's interesting because it's not a typical kind of stalker role. I think the mistake would be to play it menacingly or figuratively twist your mustache. I think it's very neutral and in fact the guy just tells the truth throughout the whole episode. This guy's just steadfastly straightforward and truthful. I think that's what Scully likes about him and why she is drawn into his world." —*G.M.*

bedroom and a bathroom, just making it different but similar enough that people know where they are."

The lighting, too, will differentiate between the characters' apartments, with shadows helping create a mood of isolation and detachment, explains director of photography Bill Roe. "It's very stark," says Roe, fresh from his own win for outstanding cinematography on the cross-country adventure "Drive." "It will be very, very lonesome looking. There's nothing in there. I think there's a bed, a table and a light. We'll get in there and we'll see what's there. We constantly think on our feet all the time."

As Padgett's minimalism extends to the items inside his apartment, property master Tom Day took an understated approach to the show, procuring only a typewriter, a manuscript and story outline cards for the set. Somewhat more challenging for Day was creating the actual medallion Padgett gives to Scully.

"Because it has to be something that is manufactured and since it is an art piece, it's awfully hard to get something that's going to work for everyone," Day says. "Since the sacred heart is an actual symbol you can find, that was going to be our first step, [to] see if we could find something. That didn't pan out because on most of the medallions, the actual sacred heart part of the medallion is too small for the camera to read it well. We've had to have someone sculpt a blown-up version of just the sacred heart. Right now, I'm on my third version. They needed it last week and we had to use a stand-in. We found a medallion of the right size and shape to shoot from the back side. We'll incorporate that so when we have the real item it'll match. No one will know the anxiety I felt."

No one except the other members of the crew, that is. For the scenes involving the heartless murder victims, costume designer Christine Peters almost had to reinvent the bra. "They thought the greatest way to do it would be to stick the—it's about the size of a man's fist, not a woman's fist—throbbing, dripping blood heart in her bra cup," Peters says, "so the guy could just reach in and pull it out of her bra cup. I said, 'So you're casting a really flat-chested person, right, because something else is usually in those bra cups, boys.' We were going to have to build a bra. It sounds like such a joke, but it would have been really expensive to do, and we would have had to do a lot of them. So we're not doing that."

Instead, special effects supervisor John Vulich and his team devised a special appliance to lie flat on the victims' chests; the appliance has a pocket that allows the actor playing the killer to reach inside and remove the heart. "Special effects will run a little tube underneath the appliance and they've got a pump that they can turn on when they need the blood to really bloom and it will magically just come blooming out," Peters says. "It's a lot of smoke and mirrors to get it to happen. There are so many factors. You're going to have a bloody, beating heart and everyone has to be in white or light colors so the blood will show when they rip their bodies open. So if you're going to put a throbbing, bloody heart in a white bra, it's not going to be white very long. We worked it out so now they've got the thing, and he'll reach in and it'll be all bloody and it will be fine."

MIRACLE WORKERS: (clockwise from above) property master Tom Day; art directors Sandy Getzler (left) and Lauren Polizzi (right); director of photography Bill Roe; costume designer Christine Peters

Anderson herself will square off with the heartstopping madman—as soon as the crew returns from lunch. In the meantime, a hush falls over the cavernous reaches of the dimly lit stage. No co-workers chat, no bells sound, no cameras roll. Mulder's apartment stands empty. After the rush of filming, the stillness is almost jarring, but it is only temporary. The voices that call to each other just beyond the stage doors will return only too soon to embark on their mission: bringing *The X-Files* to its devoted audience each week. Considering the size of the undertaking, they deserve a break. ●

ALIEN N

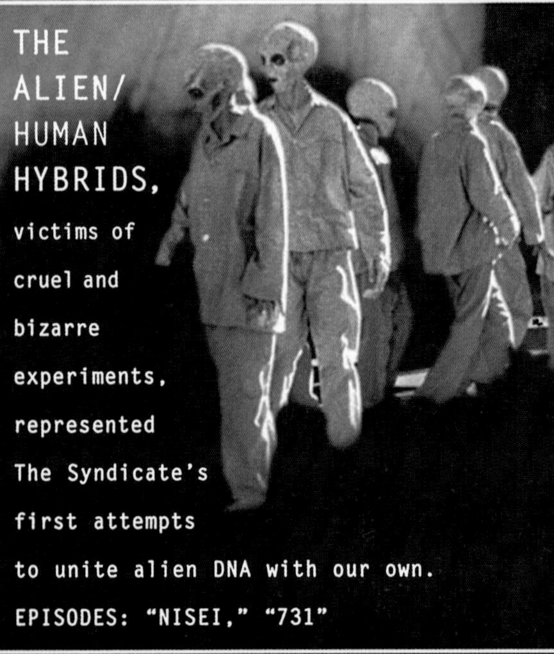

THE ALIEN/HUMAN HYBRIDS, victims of cruel and bizarre experiments, represented The Syndicate's first attempts to unite alien DNA with our own. EPISODES: "NISEI," "731"

THE ALIEN BOUNTY HUNTER dispatches green-blooded clones and alien rebels with a deadly stiletto. The seemingly unstoppable morphing menace is *The X-Files'* answer to the Terminator. EPISODES: "COLONY," "END GAME," "TALITHA CUMI," "HERRENVOLK," "PATIENT X," "THE RED AND THE BLACK"

LORD KINBOTE [left] was actually named for a character in Vladimir Nabokov's *Pale Fire*. The book deals with interpreting experiences in such a way as to confirm existing personal opinions. The ubiquitous GRAY ALIEN [right] derived its name from a more obvious source, its skin color. EPISODE: "JOSE CHUNG'S 'FROM OUTER SPACE'"

in THE X-FILES' galaxy, extraterrestrial biological entities are more than just LITTLEGREENMEN

ATION

BY Gina McIntyre

THE FACELESS ALIEN REBELS are out to prevent the imminent colonization of Earth; their extreme methods include torching UFO abductees. The mysterious beings cauterize their features to stave off infection from the deadly black oil. EPISODES: "PATIENT X," "THE RED AND THE BLACK," "TWO FATHERS"

THE BLACK OIL, one of the first species to inhabit the planet, infects humans on contact and controls them. The only reported defense against the substance is an experimental vaccine. EPISODES: "PIPER MARU," "APOCRYPHA," "TUNGUSKA," "TERMA," "PATIENT X," "THE RED AND THE BLACK"

THE DINO-ALIEN [right] gestates inside a human host until clawing its way through the torso, birthing itself. After a period of time, it sheds its reptile-like skin and assumes the form of the more docile gray alien [left]. EPISODE: "THE BEGINNING"

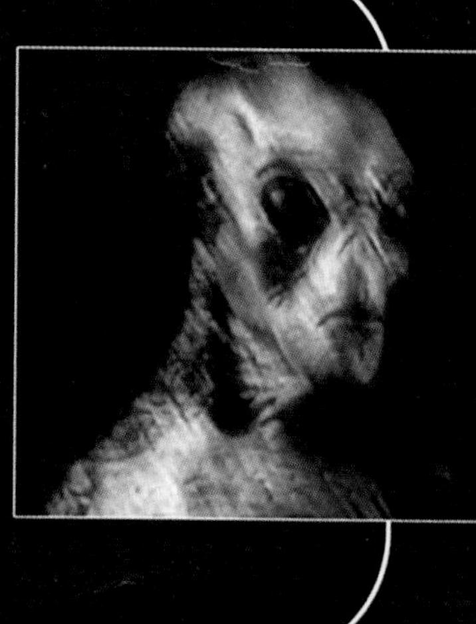

fan-Bleeping-tastic

Kate Anderson takes a look at an *X-Files* episode that spectacularly messes with your head – "Jose Chung's 'From Outer Space'"

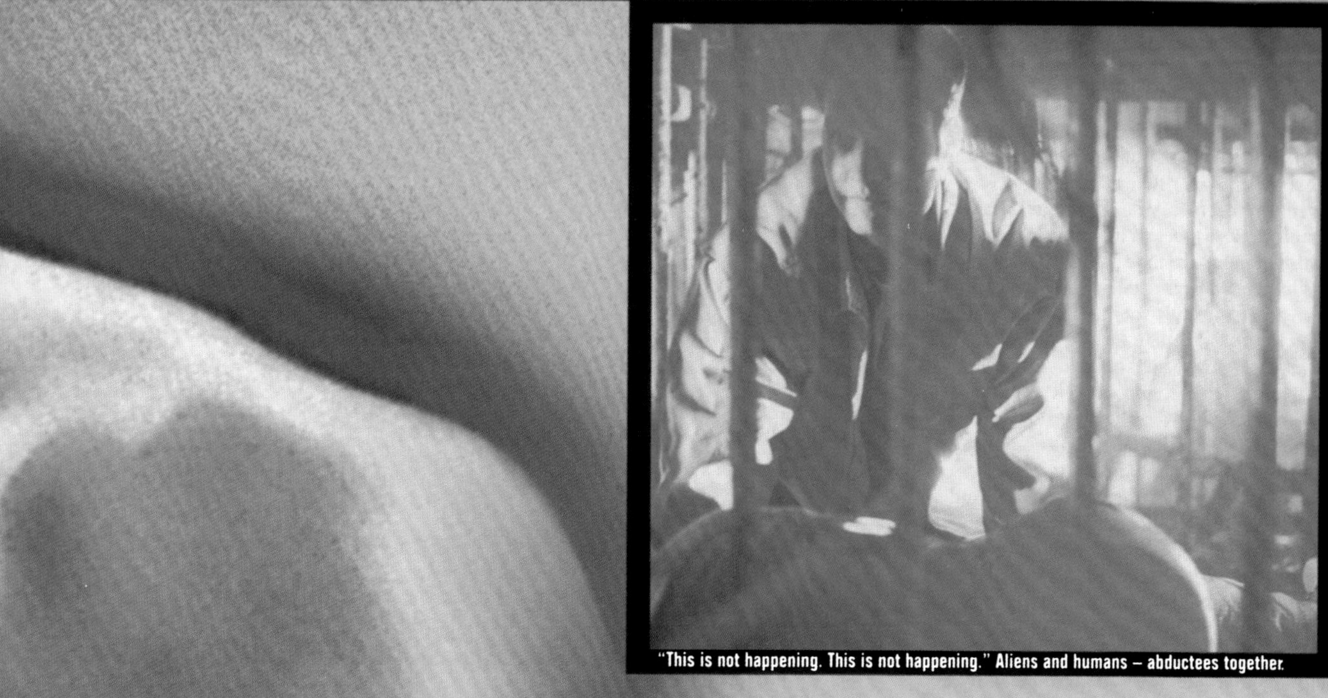

"This is not happening. This is not happening." Aliens and humans – abductees together.

Bizarre. Surreal. Extraordinary. "Jose Chung's 'From Outer Space'" is all this and much, much more. Clever, witty, effective, and very tongue in cheek, it brings together the best in sci-fi lore and UFO mythology clichés – military cover-ups, mysterious Men in Black and multiple interpretations.

Writer Darin Morgan – who began his *X-Files* career playing the Flukeman in season two's "The Host", and who also penned "Humbug", the Emmy Award-winning "Clyde Bruckman's Final Repose" and "War of the Coprophages" – delivers a deeply satisfying episode, the third season's jewel in the crown. No mean feat, especially for a season that brought us a heady concoction of episodes which enhanced the ongoing mythology arc and gave us some of the show's finest stand-alone moments.

From its bizarre teaser (involving two grey aliens with American accents and a *Power Rangers* lookalike villain called Lord Kinbote) to Chung's closing statement ("Although we may not be alone in the universe, in our own separate ways, on this planet, we are all... alone.") "Jose Chung" is ultra-funny, ultra-smart and razor sharp. It is a humorous and sometimes surreal treatment of the whole abduction phenomenon, with best-selling author Jose Chung interviewing Agent Scully and a motley crew of characters, all of whom have conflicting stories concerning the alleged abduction of two teenagers. But the plot soon thickens as evidence is uncovered of abduction, counter-abduction, conspiracy and counter-conspiracy.

Primarily a comic writer, Darin Morgan said that his unique style evolved in part because humour was essentially the only way he knew how to approach the show. He stresses that despite the comedic undercurrents of the episode, he nevertheless felt compelled to stay within the show's parameters.

"From the moment I joined the writing staff, I knew that I had only so many *X-Files* scripts in me. I had the pieces of this story for a really long time," he explained. "I had done research on hypnosis and had read a book about UFOs where the author felt that [they] aren't alien crafts but actually [piloted by] human beings who are able to manipulate time and space. It was really a show that was jam-packed with stuff, which you don't usually see on an hour of television. There was a lot going on.

"I was always very conscious of having it still be an X-file," he added. "I wasn't trying to do parody. You make some jokes at the show's expense, but I never wanted to parody it."

In little more than a year, Darin Morgan went from playing a giant flukeworm to being an acclaimed script writer. With a tremendous flair for black comedy, his take on *The X-Files* instantly struck a chord with fans, not to mention cast and crew. Fellow writers like executive

producer Howard Gordon expressed deep admiration for Morgan's ability to craft hours that could provide a lighter touch, without undermining the series' ongoing mission.

However, with season three the growth in the show's popularity spawned much closer scrutiny of each episode. Even the slightest inconsistency is picked up and often becomes a centre of debate among X-Philes. Not everyone was impressed or indeed appreciated Darin Morgan's efforts. No sooner had "Jose Chung" aired in the USA, than fans on the internet complained that Morgan was making fun of everything Mulder and Scully were doing.

Veteran *X-Files* director Rob Bowman was initially bewildered by Morgan's complicated story. In fact, he had to read the script "fourteen to fifteen times" before he really understood everything. "There's so many details in the script, I knew the audience wasn't going to understand it unless I told it in a way that they could see into the story – using repetitive staging and anything I could do to give them hooks along the way to remember how things tied together and allow them to be along for the ride.

"Darin Morgan has his own voice and maybe his scripts are not quintessential *X-Files*, [but] they are certainly entertaining," says Bowman.

"It was just a fun bit of orchestration and a show that really put a spin on the expectations of an *X-Files* viewer," he adds. "They turn the show on and see the episode and say, 'Boy, you can never predict what you are going to get on this show.'"

While often criticised for 'recycling' its guest stars, over four seasons *The X-Files* has featured many intriguing visitors. And none more so than Charles Nelson Reilly. An entertaining and engaging character, Reilly was extremely excited about getting to appear on *The X-Files* and is full of praise for everyone associated with the programme.

"I have been a fan of this extraordinary show since the beginning. It was a very good experience for me to be on the programme and it looks like the character could come back some time – the crew have threatened to quit if I don't come back!" (Reilly recently returned to the role in the second series of *Millennium* , in an episode called "Jose Chung's 'Doomsday Defense'" wri ten and directed by Darin Morgan.)

"I just thought it was so good, so clever – like a play within a play," continued Reilly. "Television has been going on for ages but when you see this programme, and you love like I do, I think what you see is entirely new has its own fabric which has never been seen before on television."

Reilly managed to captivate virtually every one on set with his antics, which included c ing "Nurse! Nurse!" every tin he needed to consult with the script supervisor. And at a tin in the production year when many were beginning to drag and feel their energy fading,

Above and left: **Scenes from the teas as 'aliens' menace humans and are th in turn menaced by the terrifying Lor Kinbote. *Below:* Scully and Jose Chun discuss the facts. *Right:* What the..?**

his enthusiasm gave them all a huge lift, as executive producer Bob Goodwin recalls.

"The most fun on that episode was the casting of Charles Nelson Reilly. I couldn't wait to watch the dailies [raw footage of that day's filming] because he is hysterical when he is doing the dialogue but even funnier when he goes off it. He forgets his lines. If you saw the dailies, you would die. I don't know how Gillian could continue to act because it was so funny," said Goodwin.

Not surprisingly, the actress herself cites "Jose Chung" as one of her personal favourite episodes from season three. She praises director Rob Bowman for how slickly the episode was produced and says that working with Charles Nelson Reilly was "delightful".

""Jose Chung" had such a smart script, sharp and tight. It was so well written and fabulous. It had some wonderful twists and turns in it," Anderson commented. "Charles was excellent in it. I thought that Rob Bowman, who directed that one, really did it justice. He pulled it together in a way that I don't think any of us expected when we first read the script. In reading it, it was great but confusing. Overall, it turned into what I found to be a really exciting, tight episode."

Over the top but nevertheless clever, Darin Morgan's unusual tale managed to re-invent the entire UFO mythology that *The X-Files* was built around from the beginning, using an ability to send itself up while staying within the series' established structure and boundaries.

"Darin wrote this episode knowing, I think, it would be his last ever and wanted to achieve perfection. And in fact, I think that's what he's done here." said series creator Chris Carter. "It put Mulder and Scully into funny roles. He got to explore their characters and make them seem fun and silly and the episode is a romp. I know Darin thinks of it as his tour de force of the four episodes he's written for the show," says Carter.

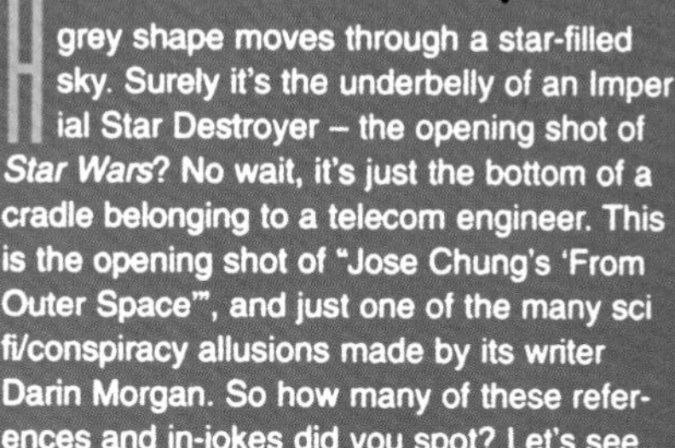

Clever, Clever

A grey shape moves through a star-filled sky. Surely it's the underbelly of an Imperial Star Destroyer – the opening shot of *Star Wars*? No wait, it's just the bottom of a cradle belonging to a telecom engineer. This is the opening shot of "Jose Chung's 'From Outer Space'", and just one of the many sci fi/conspiracy allusions made by its writer Darin Morgan. So how many of these references and in-jokes did you spot? Let's see...

The Writings of Jose Chung

- We learn that one of Jose's earlier works is called 'The Caligarian Candidate', a reference to the films *The Manchurian Candidate* and *The Cabinet of Dr Caligari* which both deal with hypnosis and perception, issues dealt with in this episode.
- And did you see the cover of 'From Outer Space'? Spookily similar to the cover of Whitley Streiber's alien abduction novel 'Communion'.

The Men In Black

- Just one of the many aspects of the UFO phenomenon. The first MIB we meet is played by Jesse 'The Body' Ventura (famous American wrestler). His partner is played by Alex Trebek, host of American game show *Jeopardy* – particularly significant since David Duchovny appeared on a celebrity edition. (He lost.)

The Men In Black 2

- Amateur conspiracy theorist Blaine Faulkner meets (what he thinks are) a different pair of Men In Black. "One of them was disguised as a woman, but wasn't pulling it off... her hair was red, but it was a little too red". No prizes for guessing it's Scully, and a reference to the fact that Gillian Anderson is actually blonde.
- And the second MIB: "the tall lanky one... his face was so blank and expressionless... he didn't even seem human. I think he was a mandroid". Here, Darin Morgan pokes fun at Duchovny's acting style and also refers to his appearance on (brother Glen Morgan's) *Space: Above and Beyond* as an artificial human being.
- Look out also for a subtle reference to Duchovny's appearance on *Twin Peaks* as the transvestite Dennis/Denise. His sweet potato pie munching in the Ovaltine Diner (an actual landmark) echos *Twin Peaks'* Agent Dale Cooper's similar mannerisms with cherry pie.
- Mulder and Scully make it into Chung's novel, albeit cunningly disguised as Diana Luscy and Reynard Muldrake ('reynard' means 'fox' in French).

Anything else?

- The episode takes place in Klass County, a reference to UFO writer Philip Klass.
- Lord Kinbote alludes to a character called David Kinbote in the Vladimir Nabakov novel *Pale Fire*. Like Chung (and the whole episode with its narratives within narratives), Kinbote is an untrustworthy narrator.
- The mashed potato sculpture created by Jaques Schaeffer refers to a similar creation in the classic UFO film *Close Encounters of the Third Kind*.
- The 'bleeping' Detective Manners is named after *X-Files* director Kim Manners, renowned on set for his foul language.
- Finally, look for the return of the Stupendous Yappi promoting his Roswell style video "Dead Alien: Truth or Humbug?", and the return of the actor who played the museum curator in "Humbug" as well as the tarot reader from "Clyde Bruckman's Final Repose". All have connections with Darin Morgan-penned episodes.

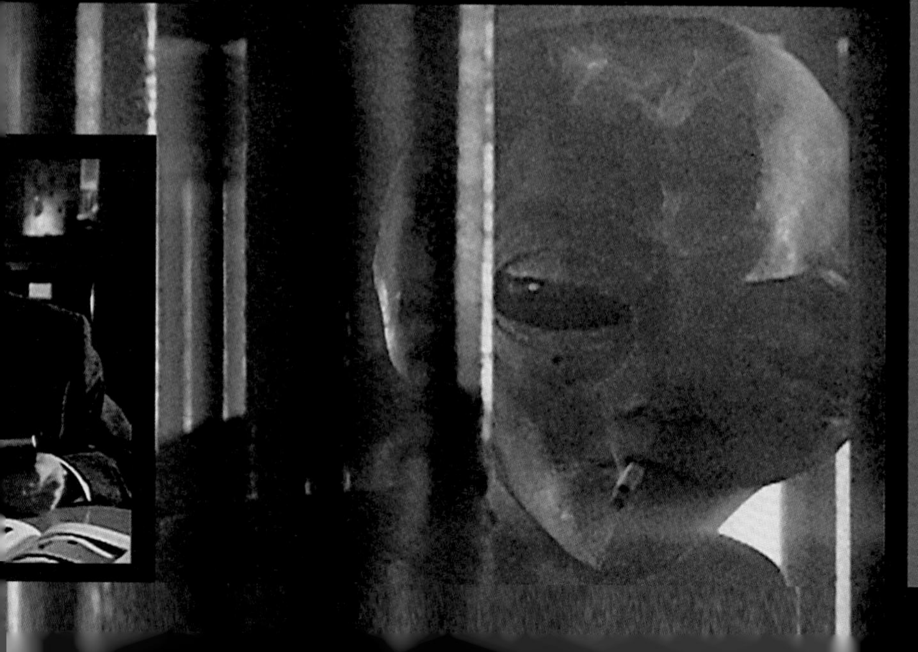

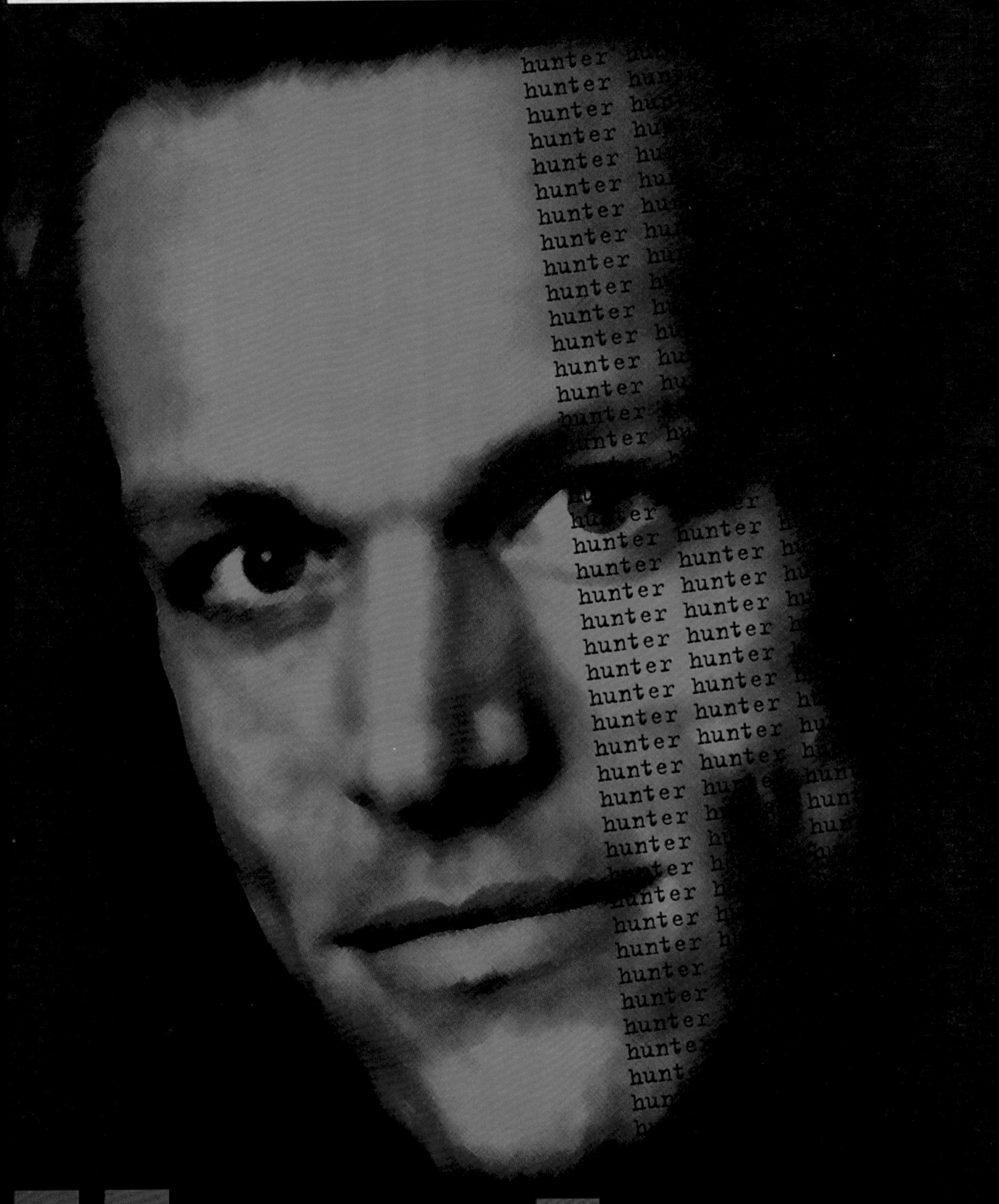

Hunter Thompson

Brian Thompson - *The X-Files'* hulking, terrifying alien bounty hunter - rolls *sushi*? Dave Hughes investigates...

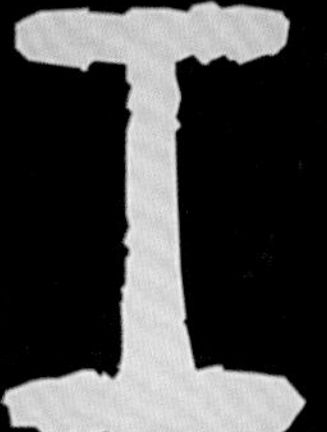

f *The X-Files* has taught us anything, it's that appearances can be deceptive. It is therefore just as well that I have been paying attention for the first hundred or so episodes of the show, for meeting actor Brian Thompson is a sharp reminder that things - and especially people - are not always as they seem, not only in the twilight world of *The X-Files*, but in life as well. Of course, one doesn't like to make snap judgements based on appearance alone, but who could honestly be prepared for the fact that a bodybuilder best known for his on-screen body counts would turn out to be a Shakespearean-trained thespian, a classical pianist and an expert in hand-rolling sushi?

Thompson's face - or, just as likely, his physique - should be familiar by now; the actor portrayed the imposing and anonymous alien bounty hunter in four *X-Files* episodes to date, beginning with the "Colony" and "End Game" two-parter (which finally made its way onto video in September after a disorientating 12 month postponement), and most recently in "Talitha Cumi" and "Herrenvolk". However, it's more than likely he was already recognizable by the time he landed his UFO in the Arctic and began systematically hunting down and killing a series of cloned abortion doctors. But where had you seen him before?

Was he the well-built barfly whose clothes Arnold Schwarzenegger borrowed in *The Terminator?* Could he have been the leader of the evil gang faced by Sylvester Stallone in *Cobra?* Did those Hurculean looks put the 'evil' in medieval in the fantasy epic *Dragonheart?* Or was that him under Klingon make-up in the classic *Star Trek* episode "A Matter of Honor," and again in *Star Trek: Generations?* The answer is it could be any or all of the above, although Thompson himself feels the video exposure of the Schwarzenegger and Stallone vehicles helps most people's memories. "The part from *Cobra* is memorable to most people," he says. "I can't stop still where there's a group of boys or men twenty-five or under, and not be recognized."

The day of our interview turns out to be a good time to talk about *The X-Files*, being the day after an 'admission' by the CIA that the US Defense Department was responsible for some fifty per cent of all UFO sightings during the 1950s and 1960s, thanks to their covert and covered-up testing of high-altitude spy planes conveniently painted in sun-catching silver. Coming as it did only a few weeks after the US military changed its story about the Roswell crash for the *n*th time – admitting (or rather, claiming) that there were bodies recovered from the scene, but that they were high altitude test dummies – the CIA's latest message did more to confuse than defuse the current UFO mania (or 'UFOria' as it has been coined), and Brian Thompson, for one, isn't buying it for a second.

> "*THE X-FILES* WAS ONE OF THE NICEST SURPRISES THAT HAS EVER HAPPENED TO MY CAREER."

"My personal feeling is that it's too little information too late," he says. "Why are they bothering to say they're responsible for fifty per cent of sightings? What does that mean? What does that mean? They were responsible for fifty percent of the sightings in the fifties. So? A lot of bugs hit a lot of windshields going through the highways of Nevada in the fifties, too. So I kind of line up those two statements as being about equal in how they're going to affect my life. I'm a little bit left wing when it comes to that kind of stuff – the CIA, covert operations, the NSA and all that.

"That's a whole topic for a bunch of other articles that would get you kicked off a lot of papers. I have a very good friend who is working on a top secret space program, [and] he freaks out about [it] when you ask him about it. [My wife and I] are this guy's best friends, and he won't tell us crap about it. He knows of some people who have worked in Area 51, [and] he will tell us the things that have happened to people who they've thought leaked information, and it's real cloak and dagger stuff – blackmailing people's families; ruining their careers; sending them down the gutter. So you understand where I'm coming from on this."

Mulder and the bounty hunter in "End Game"'s show down. (Ok, it's not Thomps but this is a shapeshifter, remember?

Like many of the show's fans, Thompson believes that the popularity of *The X-Files* has as much, if not more, to do with the public's mistrust of government as it does with the current popularity of all things extra-terrestrial – put another way, it's more para*noiac* than para*normal*. "*The X-Files* has succeeded because everybody believes that there's a huge amount of information out there which the government has decided we are not adult enough to assimilate for ourselves," he says.

> "*THE X-FILES* GOT THE GOLDEN GLOBE? I'M ON THE BEST SHOW ON TV? HOW THE HELL DID THAT HAPPEN?"

"Just simply to sum up what these people are involved with: the whole NSA, and the National Security Act and the formation of the CIA – all of that is about power. Power in its utmost, purest, darkest form. It's about secrecy, and about secret power, and when you start looking at the mindset that wants that kind of power, you start asking yourself why are they keeping things secret in Area 51? Well, it obviously has something to do with power and control, and if they do have a spacecraft that was capable of something, what is it and what do they want to use it for?" Whatever it is, you can bet it's not in the public

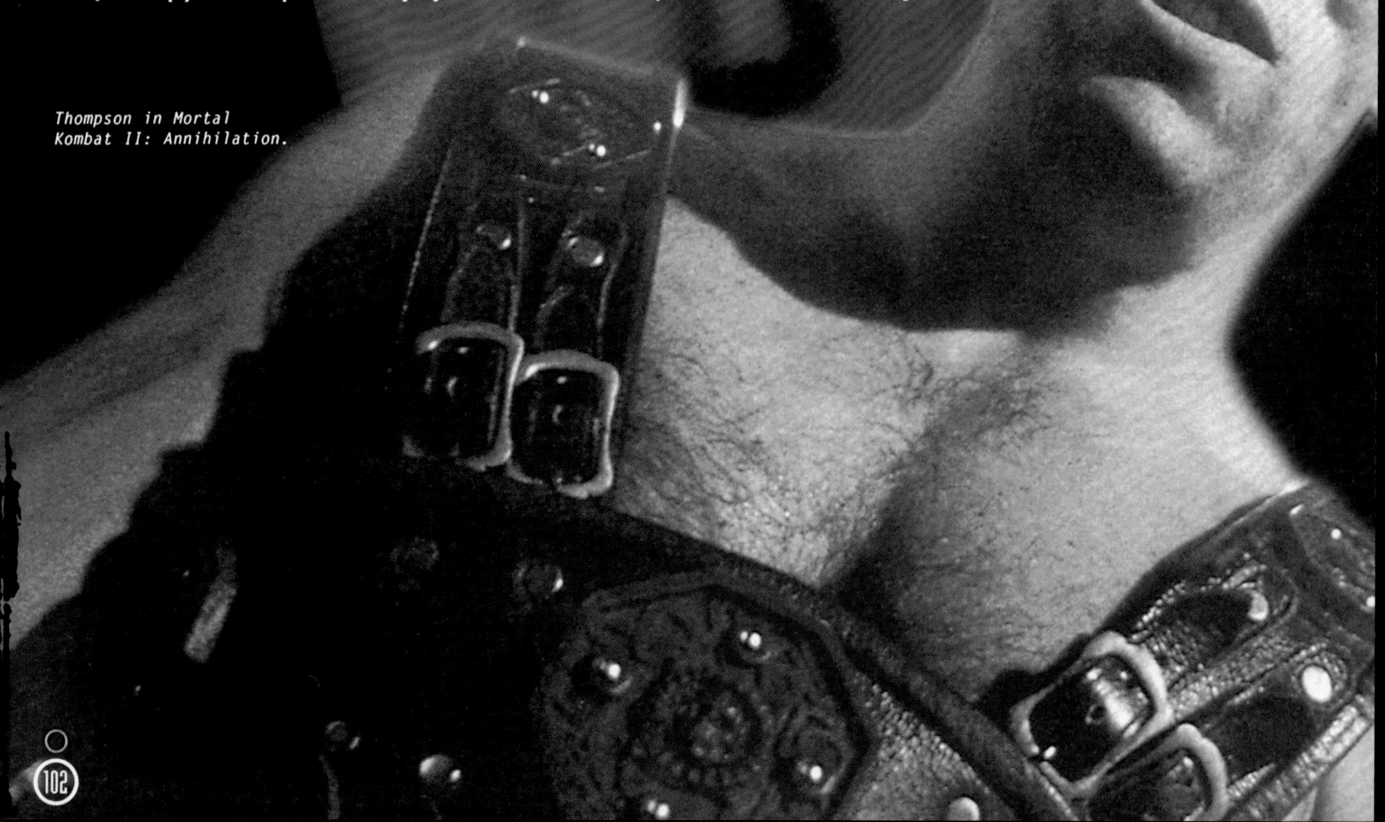

Thompson in Mortal Kombat II: Annihilation.

nterest. "Absolutely not. Absolutely not."

Since conspiracy theory is obviously one of his pet subjects, it is something of a surprise to learn hat Thompson had never watched an episode of *'he X-Files* before he was cast in "Colony". "*The X-Files* was one of the nicest surprises that has ever happened to my career, honestly," he says. "I had been out of the country for almost six months, and had just returned from making *Dragonheart* in Slovakia when all the buzz was happening over here in the first season. The first I knew about it was when my agent called and told me I had this science fiction show."

Thompson remembers attending a meeting with "Colony"'s co-writer Chris Carter and director Rob Bowman, who had previously directed him in *Star Trek: The Next Generation*. "Knowing Rob, and meeting with Chris Carter who I heard was a big surfer – and I'm a big wind surfer – it just seemed like they were all in the right frame of mind; it seemed like they were decent people to work with," he says. "So I went up there to Vancouver, BC, and I filmed for a week, came home, spent the weekend with my family, and on Sunday night I got back on a plane to go back to work the next day. And when I got to the ticket booth at the international terminal, the gal at the desk said, 'Hey, congratulations.' And I said, 'For what?' And she said, Your show – you just won the Golden Globe for Best Dramatic Series last night.' '*What?*' 'Yeah, *The X-Files*.' 'It got the *Golden Globe*? I'm on the *best show on TV*? How the Hell did *that* happen?'"

"TO HAVE DONE FOUR SHOWS AND HAD THE CHARACTER DISPLAYED SO PROMINENTLY IN THIS PRETTY TIGHT STORYLINE WAS PRETTY LUCKY."

No wonder Thompson found it gratifying when he discovered he would play a recurring role in the 'mythology' shows. "Herrenvolk", the next story conceived by the *X-Files* star, was the first in more than a year to call upon the services of the bounty hunter last seen holding Scully hostage in "End Game". "That was David's idea," says Thompson, to bring back the character in the third season. And that ended up being the season closer and then the season four opening. So, to have done four shows and had the character displayed so prominently in this pretty tight storyline was pretty lucky."

Not only that, but as killers go, the alien bounty hunter is more complex than most. "Not like those wacky guys in *Cobra*," he laughs. "My take on the bounty hunter is that he works for a benevolent political force out there in the cosmos who has a design for Earth, and they're trying to allow it] to develop as much on its own as possible with minor calculated interference. But any interference that isn't authorised by us is absolutely wrong." So the fact that the bounty hunter's work fits in with the Cigarette Smoking Man's agenda is merely serendipitous coincidence. Besides, as Thompson points out, his character does not kill indiscriminately; his only victims are the "unauthorised growth forms" created as part of covert government projects such as Purity Control.

"MY TAKE ON THE BOUNTY HUNTER IS THAT HE WORKS FOR A BENEVOLENT POLITICAL FORCE OUT THERE IN THE COSMOS."

"At the end of 'Herrenvolk'," he continues, "they have me save Mulder's mother to show that this man who has been running around killing people is capable of benevolent acts and performing miracles." Thompson also notes an important dialogue line in that episode, when the bounty hunter says to the Cirgarette Smoking Man, "I need to know the reasons why this should be". "That showed that he's not just a cybernaut, [but] a person who obviously has some authority of his own." And a conscience. "Absolutely. And if he has a conscience, we can infer that the people who have sent him and empowered him have a conscience as well."

It was not always thus. When the character first appeared in "Colony", Thompson had little to do, the bounty hunter seemed to be little more than a cold-blooded contract killer. "That's all I had to be in the first episode," he admits. "At that point I just made him as efficient a killing machine as possible. You always try to give someone human traits, you know – to show some struggle or some bit of warmth. Like when the guy's trucking down the hallway and they're doing close-ups of his face; it's not hate that's running through him – it's efficiency."

Indeed, there's a total absence of malice in the character: even when he effectively takes Scully hostage in "End Game", there is no malice intended on the bounty hunter's part; Scully is simply a means to an end. "When was with her in the car, I never felt that he intended any malice towards her," Thompson concurs. "I felt a gentleness towards her, which is easy to do – she is a very kind, loving woman with the most infectious giggle I've ever heard..."

Career-wise, Thompson says that, unlike many actors, he has no particular preference for television or film work; he is more interested in the strength of the material. "Initially, the philosophy was 'get a job'," he admits. "And then it moves towards 'get more money', and then it comes down to satisfying my heart again, *please*, because that's why I started acting. When you're in college," he adds, "you get to speak the best lines ever written, [because] you're doing the classics. And then you get to Hollywood and figure out twenty different ways to say, 'Don't f***in' move or I'm

Mulder arms himself with the only weapon that can stop the bounty hunter...

...But - oh no! - he's got one too.

gonna kill you.' Or maybe it's, 'Don't move, or I'm gonna f***in' kill... myself.'" He laughs. "I've done twenty-five movies now, and probably four times as many television shows."

So what does he look for in a role these days? "You look for a part that scares you a little bit; that you're not sure you can pull off; that you know has marvelous possibilities. Those are the good ones, [and] you don't get many of those auditions every year. And second to that, I try to just work on any that's worthwhile, like *The X-Files*. I'll hold a spear in a worthwhile project." Speaking of those, Thompson has a dream project of his own; *Crossings*, a script he is developing and will ultimately produce, about a champion wind surfer who crosses between countries separated both by geographical and political divides. Of his principal motivation for this, he explains, "I once asked Sylvester Stallone how it was I could get better parts, and he said, 'Start producing your own material.'"

In the meantime, Thompson will be seen as the main bad guy in *Mortal Kombat: Annihilation*, the sequel to the best and most successful movie based on a computer game. "I think that movie is going to be good," he says. "I do play the villain in the piece – he is the biggest, baddest warlord in the universe – but there's many sides to him. I believe it's the first time, as the villain in a movie, that I have a father, a mother, a daughter, and I have a normal relationship with all of them! I actually am sane with them." So, in other words, the main bad guy in a sequel based on a computer game had more depth and motivation than the lead villain in *Cobra*? "A hundred per cent," he laughs.

"I ONCE ASKED SYLVESTER STALLONE HOW IT WAS I COULD GET BETTER PARTS, AND HE SAID, 'START PRODUCING YOUR OWN MATERIAL.'"

"I went over to the director [George Cosmatos] and said, 'What are we doing? Why are we killing these people?' And he said, 'You have to ask Sly – he wrote it.' So I said, 'Okay, Sly, what are we doing?' And Sly says [adopts accent], 'Well, basically, you guys are doing what Hitler did when he was exterminating the Jews.' And I said, 'well, okay, I can see that, but you know, we're not showing that we're killing with any form of discrimination, Sly.' And he shrugged. So that was my character development conversation on *Cobra*."

With special thanks to Monica Rivas

You have been watching
BRIAN THOMPSON

who played the alien bounty hunter in...
"Colony"
"End Game"
"Talitha Cumi"
"Herrenvolk"

He also appeared in these feature films...
Mortal Kombat: Annihilation (1997), *Dragonheart* (1995), *Star Trek Generations* (1994), *Moon 44* (1990), *Alien Nation* (1988), *Three Amigos* (1986), *Lionheart* (1986), *Cobra* (1985), *The Terminator* (1984)

and these television shows...
The X-Files, Hercules: The Legendary Journeys, Star Trek: Deep Space Nine, Star Trek: The Next Generation, Conan the Librarian, The George Burns Comedy Show

Far left: Samantha and Mrs Mulder.

Left and top: Mulder approaches the Submarine and his first battle with the bounty hunter.

THE X FILES™

SEASON: 9

LUCY LAWLESS

GUEST GALLERY

EX-*XENA* STAR AND CURRENT *X-FILES* GUEST STAR LUCY LAWLESS, SHARES HER THOUGHTS ON HER *X*-PERIENCES, AND DISCUSSES HER OPINIONS ABOUT HER CHARACTER, SHANNON McMAHON, AND WORKING WITH GILLIAN ANDERSON AND ROBERT PATRICK.

LUCY LAWLESS

"MY TRUE-LIFE MOTIVATION for taking up the offer to appear on *The X-Files* was that about five years ago I went to the Emmy Awards ceremony with my *Xena* sidekick, Renee O'Connor [Gabrielle]," Lucy Lawless recalls. "We just went there to look at famous people! Renee bustled up to [series creator] Chris Carter at the end and said hello to him. I'd met him once at the NATPE (National Association of Television Program Executives) convention, years before that. [Chris] was tremendously nice to us and talked to us, even though we were really nobody. We were waiting outside to get our cars and when our limo pulled up they called our name. Chris came running across the road and opened the door for us. I was so charmed and grateful that somebody like that could be so gracious towards us, so when, almost five years later, he rang up and said, 'Hey, how would you like to guest on the season opener of *The X-Files*?' I said, 'I'd love to do that with you.' And that was that!"

The result, of course, was the two-parter that kicks off Season Nine of *The X-Files*, "Nothing Important Happened Today". Lawless is cast as Shannon McMahon, an old associate of Doggett's who suddenly and quite unexpectedly arrives on the scene. "She's causing a lot of trouble and Doggett has to clean up the mess," Lawless says carefully, determined, like most *X-Files* guest stars, to offer up tantalizing hints but not give too much away. "She was once in the military with Doggett and now she has information to impart that will affect how people see Scully's baby. Is McMahon a good witch or a bad witch? She's not manipulative. That's the beauty of it. If she's manipulating you, she's so damn good at it. She's very credible. She could be your best friend or your worst nightmare.

"Being a guest on *The X-Files* was a total pleasure. They were very welcoming. I must confess that I had a morbid curiosity. I just wanted to study Gillian Anderson. I wanted to see her up-close and see how nine years on a show might affect a human being. And she was lovely and so pleasant. She was very calm. She knows what she's doing. Women are very competitive animals and sometimes it's peculiar, going onto other women's shows. But there was none of that with her. She's obviously been there so long. She's very secure of her place in the world and it was a pleasure to work with her. I also had a lot of fun times with Robert because I play this character from his past and I spent half my time absolutely naked… or seemingly. He and I got on like a house on fire. He's a fun guy."

Lawless arrived on the *X-Files* set several months after completing her long stint on *Xena: Warrior Princess*. The show wrapped its sixth and final season last June in a two-part finale in which the show's protagonist was brutally beheaded! Right now, Lawless is back in Auckland, New Zealand, where she lives with her husband, former *Xena* and *Hercules: The Legendary Journeys* producer Robert Tapert, and her two children, the oldest of whom is a "mad" *X-Files* fan. She's reading scripts and looking forward to starring in a production of

REYES, SCULLY AND SHANNON MCMAHON IN "NOTHING IMPORTANT HAPPENED TODAY"

"[GILLIAN ANDERSON] WAS LOVELY AND SO PLEASANT. SHE WAS VERY CALM. SHE KNOWS WHAT SHE'S DOING."

the play *The Vagina Monologues* that will be staged in Auckland in February. "I went to a play-reading the other night and all of a sudden I remembered why I got into this business in the first place," says Lawless, who will also turn up as a punk-rock chick in the upcoming big-screen version of *Spider-Man*, which was directed by Sam Raimi (her husband's producing partner) and features an appearance by Bruce Campbell, who played Wayne Weinsider in the "Terms of Endearment" episode of *The X-Files* and was originally among those considered by Chris Carter and [executive producer] Frank Spotnitz for the role of John Doggett. "I was so excited because I'd forgotten what it was I loved about acting. My job on *Xena*, unfortunately, wasn't all about the acting. I was more like the morale leader, the camp leader on set, and the acting certainly came second. So I'm excited about doing this play and getting back to basics."

And what about getting back on *The X-Files*? Lawless would be "open" to reprising her role as Shannon McMahon, but…

"That's entirely up to Fox and to Chris," Lawless replies as the conversation comes to an end… for now. "If Chris feels that the character will serve his show, she might be back. I know how producers think. They just want to do what's best for their show and for the ratings. My being back remains to be seen."
– *Ian Spelling*

ADVANCED ALIEN AIRCRAFT TECHNOLOGY? WISE-CRACKING MEN IN BLACK? WHAT MYSTERIES LIE INSIDE THE TOP-SECRET MILITARY FACILITY KNOWN AS

AREA 51?

NEXT STOP: DRE

WARNING

MILITARY INSTALLATION

RESTRICTED AR

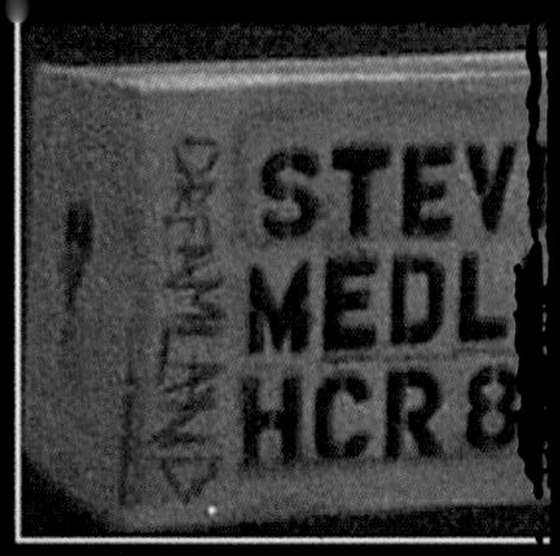

BY CHANDRA PALERMO

ILLUSTRATION BY SONJA SLONE SAUL

AMLAND

Even if the small trailer town of Rachel, Nev., were large enough to have a bureau of tourism, it couldn't hope to generate the kind of publicity the hamlet received thanks to a television news broadcast on local station KLAS in 1989—a segment that placed Rachel on the map and captured the imaginations of conspiracy theorists and alien aficionados across the globe.

Technical engineer Robert Lazar announced his now-famous claim that he had worked at mysterious air base Area 51—a top secret facility embedded in the U.S. military's Nellis Air Force Range in the Nevada desert—in sector S-4, reverse engineering one of nine captured alien spacecrafts. Lazar asserted that researchers could learn enough about extraterrestrial aviation technology to advance current aircraft beyond what was previously thought possible. Lazar's ease with engineering lingo and vivid description of the security and goings-on at Area 51 lent him credence, although a failed lie detector test and false claims about his education later cast aspersions on his integrity. The doubt about Lazar's character aside, the wheels of change were set in motion.

UFO devotees flocked in droves to see the spacecraft stored at Area 51, and Rachel, home to only 100 permanent residents, became a cult favorite tourist destination. A nearby stretch of road was renamed the Extraterrestrial Highway. A one-time roadhouse was converted into the Little A 'Le' Inn, featuring a sign reading "Earthlings Welcome." And a local rancher's mailbox now served as a gathering spot for those hoping to catch a glimpse of a UFO.

While the fringe populace embraced the facility, it took the release of the 1996 summer blockbuster *Independence Day* to introduce Area 51 to mainstream America. Even without a Will Smith action flick, the location of Area 51 (its restricted airspace is referred to as Dreamland on aviation frequencies) was bound to attract attention sooner or later. The facility, named for its designation on old test site maps, sits on the Groom Dry Lake bed in a desolate region just 100 miles north of Las Vegas, which, with its ostentatious lights and replicas of the New York and Paris skylines seems like an alien theme park based on Earth.

Fueling the imaginations of the conspiracy-minded is the fact that the government, for years, refused to confirm the existence of Area 51, which was quite bewildering—and slightly humorous—to visitors who had clearly seen the restricted area signs warning of the authorized use of deadly force, the camouflage-clad security guards who enforce border patrol and, of course, the base itself. Now that the facility has been officially recognized, information about the site remains sketchy. Spokesmen will say only that the Nevada outpost is used to test new aircraft technologies, further igniting the fervent imaginations of those who so badly want to believe.

"The Air Force is not in the UFO business. That's not what we do," Pentagon spokesman Capt. Joe Della Vedova says. "Our business is to supply air supremacy for America when we fight our wars. That's what the Air Force is about."

Curious about the conflicting reports, famed Area 51 expert Glenn Campbell headed to Rachel to investigate for himself. "I had read in the UFO magazines about people having sightings out there," says Campbell, a former Boston-based computer expert. "I took those articles in hand and went out to see if I could see the same things myself. I did see the same things myself, and I came to realize that these were routine military exercises. There were big glowing orbs that people reported as UFOs, and I came to see those as ground-launch flares, and as various other things that if you're not used to the night sky and you want to see UFOs, you'll see UFOs."

"[The Air Force's] version of the Top Gun school is [at Nellis]," Della Vedova explains. "Basically, they simulate the first 10 days of an air war because the first 10 days really decide who's gonna have control of the skies and space, which is absolutely essential in today's military environment."

The realistic wargames above Nellis provide quite a sight. "Almost every night you'll have these very active dogfights going on over Rachel and the surrounding area," Campbell says. "There are a number of flares that are released that could look like UFOs if that's what you're looking for. But that's just extreme aircraft maneuvers. Picture those images you saw of the Gulf War over Baghdad, all the tracers in the sky and a lot of activity in the sky, and that's what it would be like over Rachel and this area."

Campbell set up shop in a Rachel-based trailer, founding the Area 51 Research Center. Though a skeptic concerning the UFO lore, he still found his interest piqued by the secretive nature of the base and wrote and published a newsletter, *The Groom Lake Desert Rat*, and visitor's guide, *Area 51 Viewer's Guide*, which pointed out the best vantage points for getting a look at the installation. "I did my best to publicize the base, figuring that publicity might help crack some of those secrets," he explains.

In 1995, plagued by prying eyes, the government seized the land around the best of the viewing locations, known as Freedom Ridge. "It was a long, two-year process of seizing this public land that happened to overlook the base, where you could drive your four-wheel drive up to the top of a hill and actually look down on this base that didn't exist. And that was very embarrassing for the military," Campbell explains. "It made it more difficult to test whatever they want to test. So, they went through the process of seizing this land, but that process in itself drew enormous attention to the base. This is the first public acknowledgment they really had that there was anything out there, and that made it a mainstream story. If the government had not tried to seize this land, you wouldn't have ABC News out there. You wouldn't have CNN out there."

ALIEN NATION: [above and inset, top] scenes from *The X-Files*' trip to Area 51, Season Six's imaginative "Dreamland II"; [previous page, top right] artist interpretation of Rachel, Nev.'s most famous mailbox

And the news crews would come again. About the same time as the land issue raged, another legal war broke out centering on Area 51. Several former employees and one widow of an ex-worker filed a lawsuit against the Air Force, claiming illegal open-air burning of toxic and hazardous wastes at the base had caused many workers to develop various illnesses and horrible skin rashes. Testimony during the trial would require the description of the daily operations at Area 51—something the Air Force fought hard to prevent.

"The outcome of this is that the president himself, Bill Clinton, formally exempted the base from environmental reporting," Campbell explains. "Any sort of facility anywhere has to comply with environmental laws. The president himself has to exempt this base from those laws to avoid them having to file reports and provide information to the public.

"This lawsuit was taken on by a famous

attorney in Washington D.C., Jonathan Turley, and he saw it as a constitutional issue," he continues. "Can one part of the government claim government secrecy to hide its environmental abuses? And the outcome of the case was, yes, the government can do that. When the government invokes the secrecy privilege, it's absolute."

The new official statement admits a base is there, though its name is not Area 51 and details of its operations are still classified. "There are a variety of activities, some of which are classified, throughout what is often called the Air Force Nellis Range Complex," Della Vedova says. "The range is used for the testing of technologies and systems and training for operations critical to the effectiveness of the U.S. Military Forces and the security of the United States. There's an operation near Groom Dry Lake. Some specific activities and operations conducted on the Nellis range both past and present remain classified and cannot be discussed."

"Area 51 is shrouded with mystery and little facts, so people come up with crazy stories about what is going on there," offers Brandon Myers, creator of the Area 51: The Truth Web site (www.frontier,net/~gama/area51.htm). I mean, who doesn't like a good mystery and who hasn't ever thought that aliens have already been here? Some say that the government has spread the UFO information or misinformation to keep prying eyes focused on the skies and not on what is really going on there. And of course there are a few of the paranoid who think that interdimensional traveling devices are being tested, kind of like the transporters on *Star Trek* but with longer range."

Other more practical theories speculate that work is being done on a new stealth aircraft—The Aurora, said to fly in excess of Mach 5—which will replace supposed Area 51 graduates like the SR-71 and the F-117A. In this case, the government may have a very good case for keeping secrets—its proprietary interest in advanced military technology.

"You have this conflict in a free society,"

"The Air Force is not in the UFO business. That's not what we do."—PENTAGON SPOKESMAN CAPT. JOE DELLA VEDOVA

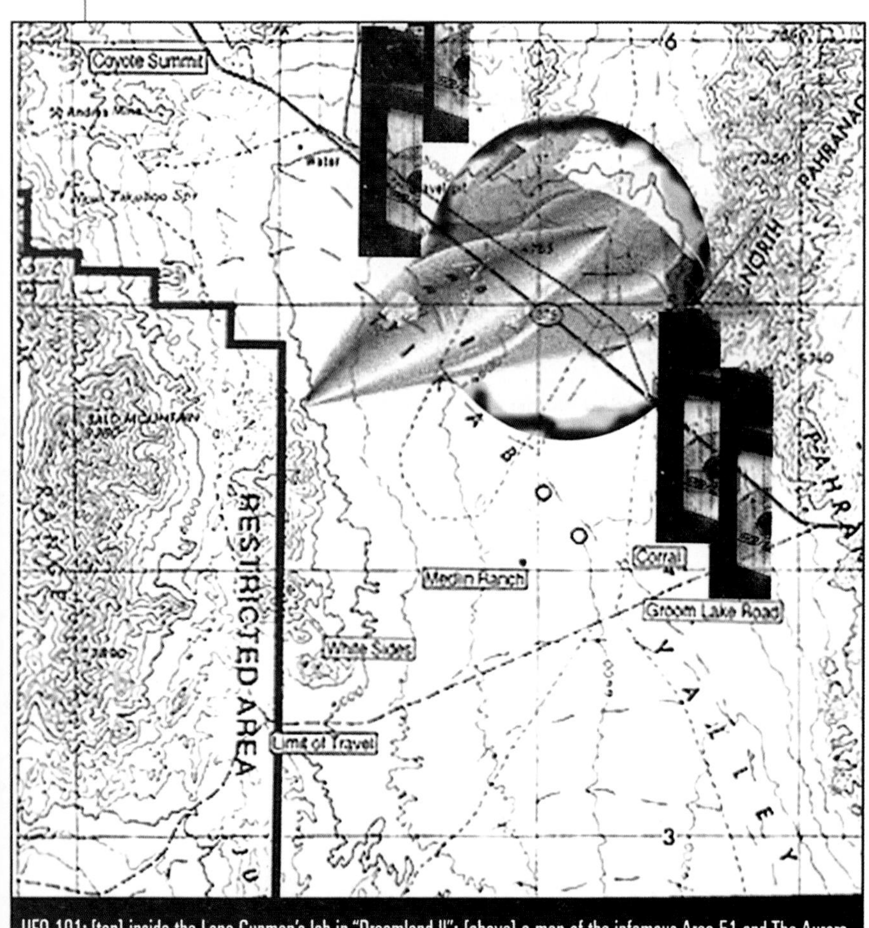

UFO 101: [top] inside the Lone Gunmen's lab in "Dreamland II"; [above] a map of the infamous Area 51 and The Aurora

Campbell says. "The military needs secrecy to fight wars. You can't be telling potential enemies what you're gonna do and what your weapons are. At the same time, a free society needs openness. There needs to be forces pushing in both directions. The military obviously always wants more secrecy, but there have to be people on the outside pushing for more openness."

Apart from the entertainment value inherent in stories of extraterrestrial contact or top secret military strategies, the phenomenon of Area 51 points to something perhaps more compelling: the unpredictable workings of the human mind. Campbell says he is amazed at the number of people who use Area 51 and the events at Rachel as evidence of greater forces at work in the universe and in their own lives.

"Area 51 is a blank slate that anybody can impress their own beliefs upon," Campbell notes. "If you believe that there are mysteries, that something is going on [outside] the realm of human experience, it must be going on out there because that can never be proven or disproved simply because it's unknown. It's one of the few terra incognitas out there. There's just so few mysteries left in the world that when one pokes up, people take notice. I'm interested in humanity, and this is cutting-edge humanity to me. People coming here and pressing their own beliefs on this base—that is fascinating." ●

He's the person without whom The X-Files would be nothing – Chris Carter. Ian Spelling caught up with the series' creator to discuss the past nine years of the show and his life – as well as what's in store for the future

THE UNCANNY X-MAN

It's a bittersweet time for Chris Carter. His television baby – The X-Files – is all grown up and moving out of the house. The kid's not quite gone yet; let's just say he's busily packing his bags – in other words, at the time of this conversation production and/or post-production was well underway on the last few episodes of The X-Files and on the two-hour series finale itself, "The Truth." During a short break, Carter sat down to talk with The X-Files Magazine and several other publications in an old screening room on the Twentieth Century Fox lot. Carter sounded by turns proud, realistic, sad, and enthusiastic about the situation. And well he should: he created the show, executive-produced all nine years of the program, wrote, co-wrote, or fine-tuned dozens of episodes, directed a good many hours, spearheaded the popular X-Files movie and even made cameo appearances in two episodes (namely "Anasazi" and "Hollywood A.D.").

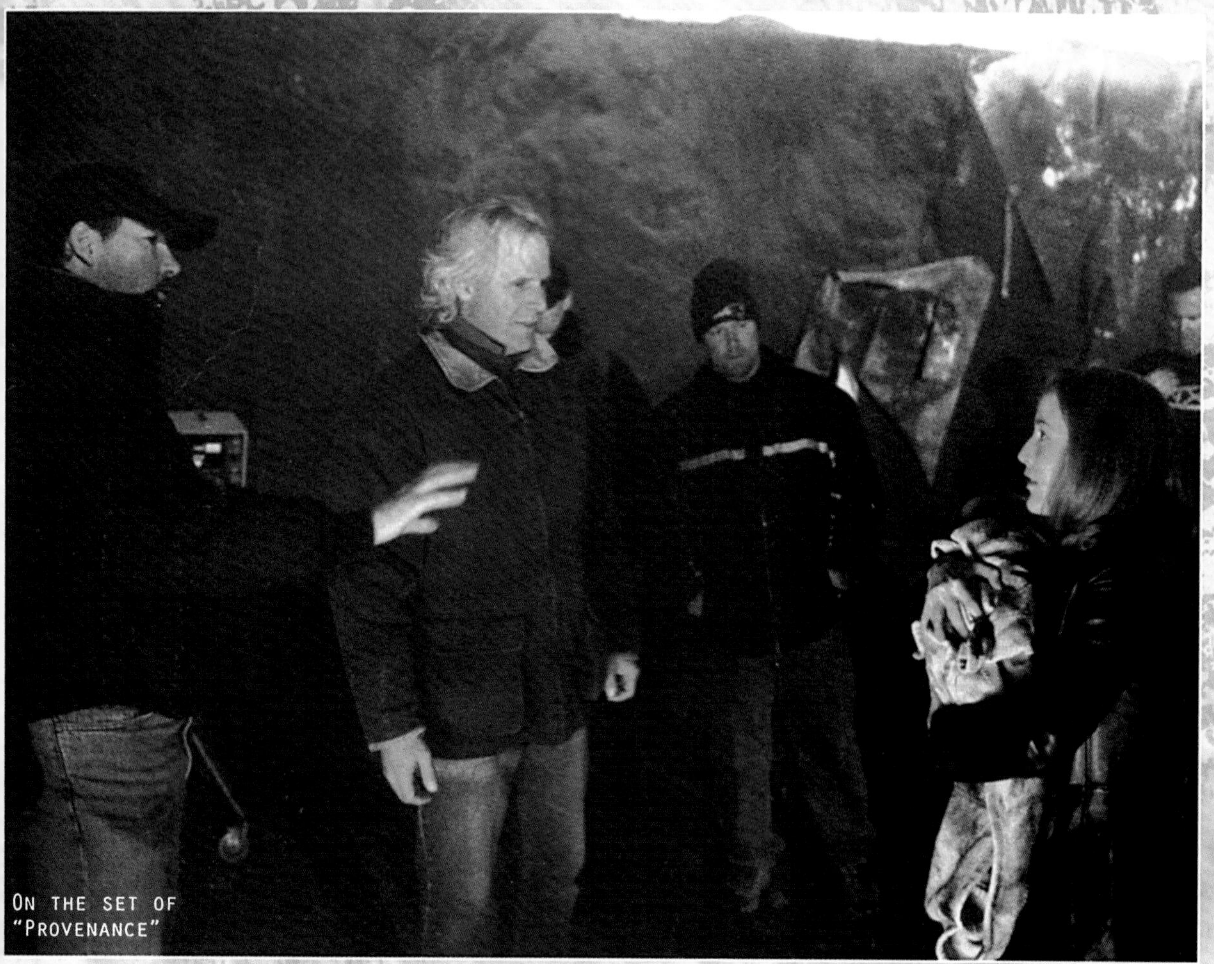

ON THE SET OF "PROVENANCE"

THE X-FILES MAGAZINE: How hard was it for you to make the decision to end The X-Files?

CARTER: Actually, it wasn't that hard to make the decision because we aired [Season Nine] against stiff competition. Our numbers were down from Season Eight. We'd always had the good fortune of being the winner for eight seasons, basically, and then this year the ratings were respectable, but we were sort of neck and neck with the competition. We'd been heavily counter-programmed. *Saving Private Ryan* was against us our first night. The next Sunday, the competition was Britney Spears on HBO. It was like we were taking flak, to use a war term. And so when the ratings had leveled off at about the sixth airing of the show, we came into Christmas vacation and I thought, "You know something, there are going to be articles written now about the show and what it used to be and they're going to take shots at Annabeth Gish and Robert Patrick, and they're going to take shots at the show." I thought that was pretty unfair because they were doing good work. I thought the ratings weren't justified. I thought the audience just didn't show up. It's not like they showed up and then decided they didn't like the show. They just didn't come for whatever reason. I don't know. It's a mysterious x-factor. So I just decided it was time to go and to go out strong and to look forward to the future, which is hopefully doing some X-Files movies. And I wanted to reward people for watching the show for nine years and to go out strong and give them something and have people say, "Wow, we didn't realize how good the show was, and now we're sorry to see it go."

You sound disappointed. Are you?

Well, hey, I created the show. For me it's been ten years now. It's been on the air for nine years or it'll be nearly nine years when we complete this year. It took me a year to get it off the ground. So I've been riding it 200 episodes worth. I haven't written every episode, of course, but it's something I've been doing for quite a long time

"I wanted to reward people for watching the show for nine years and to go out strong and give them something."

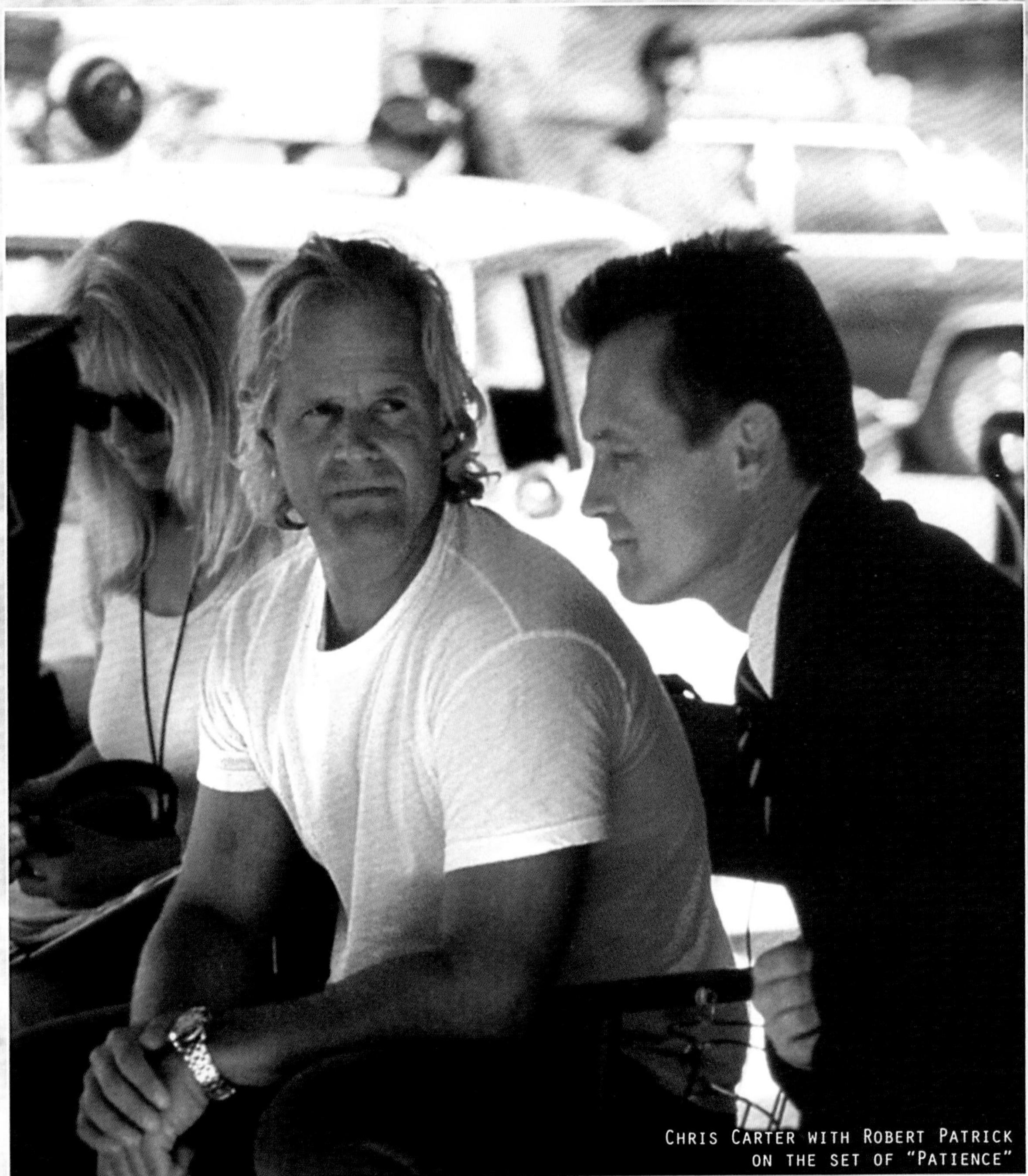

CHRIS CARTER WITH ROBERT PATRICK
ON THE SET OF "PATIENCE"

WITH ANNABETH GISH
ON THE SET OF "PROVENANCE"

and I just thought we were doing such good work this year that the disappointment is really the result of that good work.

How tough was it for you to pass along word of your decision?
It was very hard for me to do it. Actually, I had to kick myself because I started getting emotional. I'm very attached to the show, as you might imagine. I feel very fortunate to be working with the people that I work with. It's an amazing experience to work with a team, to feel a team spirit. That's one of the best parts of my job. So it was very difficult, and it was also very difficult to tell the actors.

Can you go back to the very beginning and then forward in terms of where the idea for The X-Files came from and how ideas come about at this point?
This idea was floating around in my head for a long time. There was nothing scary on TV in the early 1990s. When I was a kid there were good scary TV shows. I liked all these shows – *The Twilight Zone, The Night Stalker, The Outer Limits*. And so here I was, a television creator, and I was finally asked what I wanted to do. I said, "I want to do a good, scary show." And that's how *The X-Files* happened. And now, coming up with stories, they just come to you in the weirdest ways. One of the best experiences on the show for me has been having these other great writers that I work with come in and expand on what I originally did, and seeing what other people do with the show. I'm talking about people like Darin Morgan, Glen Morgan, and James Wong, and people like Vince Gilligan and Frank Spotnitz. They're the people who came in and expanded the idea of *The X-Files*.

X-FILES EPISODE CHECKLIST: CHRIS CARTER

SEASON ONE
"Pilot" (Writer)
"Deep Throat" (Writer)
"The Jersey Devil" (Writer)
"Space" (Writer)
"Fire" (Writer)
"Young At Heart" (Co-writer)
"Miracle Man" (Co-writer)
"Darkness Falls" (Writer)
"The Erlenmeyer Flask" (Writer)

SEASON TWO
"The Host" (Writer)
"Duane Barry" (Writer and Director)
"Red Museum" (Writer)
"Irresistible" (Writer)
"Colony" (Writer)
"F. Emasculata" (Co-writer)
"Anasazi" (Writer)

SEASON THREE
"The Blessing Way" (Writer)
"Paper Clip" (Writer)
"The List" (Writer and Director)
"Nisei" (Co-writer)
"Syzygy" (Writer)
"Piper Maru" (Co-writer)
"Apocrypha" (Co-writer)
"Talitha Cumi" (Writer)

SEASON FOUR
"Herrenvolk" (Writer)
"Tunguska" (Co-writer)
"Terma" (Co-writer)
"Memento Mori" (Co-writer)
"Unrequited" (Co-writer)
"Tempus Fugit" (Co-writer)
"Max" (Co-writer)
"Gethsemane" (Writer)

SEASON FIVE
"Redux" (Writer)
"Redux II" (Writer)
"Post-Modern Prometheus" (Writer and Director)
"Chinga" (Co-writer)
"Patient X" (Co-writer)
"The Red And The Black" (Co-writer and Director)
"The End" (Writer)

SEASON SIX
"The Beginning" (Writer)
"Triangle" (Writer and Director)
"How The Ghosts Stole Christmas" (Writer and Director)
"Two Fathers" (Co-writer)
"One Son" (Co-writer)
"Milagro" (Co-writer)
"Biogenesis" (Co-writer)

SEASON SEVEN
"The Sixth Extinction" (Writer)
"The Sixth Extinction II: Amor Fati" (Co-writer)
"Sein Und Zeit" (Co-writer)
"Closure" (Co-writer)
"First Person Shooter" (Director)
"Fight Club" (Writer)
"Requiem" (Writer)

SEASON EIGHT
"Within" (Writer)
"Without" (Writer)
"Patience" (Writer and Director)
"Per Manum" (Co-writer)
"This Is Not Happening" (Co-writer)
"DeadAlive" (Co-writer)
"Three Words" (Co-writer)
"Essence" (Writer)
"Existence" (Writer)

SEASON NINE
"Nothing Important Happened Today," Part 1 (Co-writer)
"Nothing Important Happened Today," Part 2 (Co-writer)
"Trust No 1" (Co-writer)
"Providence" (Co-writer and Director)
"Provenance" (Co-writer)
"Improbable" (Writer and Director)
"William" (Co-writer)
"The Truth" (Co-writer)

How do you go about wrapping up the show while simultaneously keeping enough of a hook to lure fans into the next film?
You know me well enough to know that I've always got a hook, and I do have a trick up my sleeve, but we really look to the movies as an opportunity to do stand-alone movies, not mythology movies. It's not like what we had to do with the first movie, which I thought was worthwhile, but it was really a movie where you couldn't have a beginning, middle and end – you could have a beginning and middle, but the end was going to come with the rest of the series, so it prevented us from really making it, I think, as big and blockbuster-ish as we might have. So I'm looking forward to just doing what we call stand-alone stories, but doing them as a movie franchise.

How quickly can we expect to see another X-Files movie?
I don't know. It depends on how long I take for vacation. I hope to write it over the summer of 2002 and I hope to prep it over the fall and spring and to shoot it in the late spring and summer of 2003. So I think you would end up seeing it in 2004.

Do you have the story in your head already?
I have rough ideas and I'm sort of deciding what to do. Frank Spotnitz and I will write it. It's one of those things where we will just sit down one day and throw out a lot of things and put in a lot of things. It's a process rather than just an idea that's in my head. It sort of takes shape.

Any chance that Annabeth Gish and Robert Patrick will be in the next feature?
We don't know. I'd work with Robert in a heartbeat and Annabeth, too. So we might find something. It just depends on the kind of story we're doing.

Were you at all surprised that David Duchovny agreed to return as Mulder for the finale?
I wasn't surprised because we've been in contact all year long and any differences that we had seem to have been something we've both gotten past. He and Gillian [Anderson] are both very anxious to do the movies. We've got to do them one at a time, so I'm only fantasizing about doing more than one. And so he realized that it was important to the future to participate in the present.

Take us through the process of David Duchovny both directing an episode in Season Nine and then reprising his role as Mulder. How did that all come together?
I approached him about the finale. I called him up and said, "Well, the show's over and I'm making the announcement." He said, "Congratulations, it was a good, long run." Then I think we spoke some time later about him being in the finale. We'd actually approached him before I had ever made the decision [to end the show] about possibly directing. That looked like it was going to go away because he was going to write and direct. When he ran out of time to write I said, "I'll write something for you," and I wrote the episode he directed.

In hindsight, was it a mistake to let Duchovny go?
I didn't let David go. David went. We could have tried to hang onto him, but he wanted to go. It wasn't a question of not trying. It was a life decision for him and you can't blame a person. When you do something for so long and you reach a point in your life, certainly around your 40s, you're going to want to try something else. You're never going to have another chance to be at that point in your life, so I don't hold it against him at all. And I still think we're doing great work. I think the reason that Fox brought the show back this year – and it was their decision to bring the show back – was because our ratings were still good and we were doing good work and David was only in roughly half the shows last year. It looked like the franchise was still very strong. That's the reason I came back. I didn't have to come back this year. The reason I came back was because I thought we had an opportunity to do good work and maybe even recast the show, as it were, in every sense of that word.

ON THE SET OF "TRIANGLE"

Some people think the spirit of the show changed when the production relocated from Vancouver to Los Angeles. What are your thoughts on that issue?
I disagree. We actually had more resources in Los Angeles, resources we didn't have in Vancouver. I thought we had more to work with, but you can look at it as pre-movie and post-movie. I look at it that way, but I think there was so much good work done after the movie on this show that it's hard for me to look at it that way. It changed, but I

THIS PIC AND LEFT: WITH BURT REYNOLDS AND ANNABETH GISH ON THE SET OF "IMPROBABLE"

don't think it actually meant that it changed for the worse. And every show has its season. You know, every show is built on a curve, unless you're *The Simpsons*, which seems to have a never-ending curve.

Why do you think The X-Files works so well all over the world?

Because people are scared of the same things. I think scared travels across borders very well and I want to knock some wood right now because I'm very fortunate to have created something that everyone seems to like. I get to write what I'm interested in and people like it, so that's one of those miracles.

Would you do another TV series?

If it were the right series and the right task with the right people. If I could surround myself with the right people. I've got lots of ideas.

Which episodes from the last season have you been most pleased with?

You know, I've been happy with the whole year. I'm trying to think of a specific episode that stands out for me and the one I'm thinking of right now is "Improbable", the Burt Reynolds one. It's very close to my heart because I wrote it and directed it and got to direct Burt. He's Burt, so I have to say that's a standout because it does what the best *X-Files* episodes do, which is to expand this sort of storytelling possibility, meaning I'm telling a story we've never told before. That's the beauty of the show. And if you're asking me why I seem disappointed [that the series is ending] it's because the show's format and storytelling structure was so incredibly elastic. It was a comedy. It was an intense drama. It was a melodrama. It was a horror show. It was a thriller. It could be so many different things and so that's what I'll miss.

It's got to be strange dealing with the finale. What's the experience been like for you?

It's interesting because we've gone so far from where we began and now, as I'm going back to where we began, it feels like just yesterday that we were there. This mythology that people always think is very convoluted and confusing, it actually all makes perfect sense. That, I think, will be very satisfying, that there's a beautiful structure to it all.

Did running your own show ever give you nightmares? Did you ever wake up in the middle of the night?

My trouble is going to sleep. I'm a very light sleeper. I don't sleep very much and so I tend to lie there and I work a lot even when I'm in bed.

So that's where your creativity comes from?

Yeah, that and the bathtub.

You've written countless episodes of The X-Files and directed a batch over the years as well. Do you have a preference, writing over directing or vice-versa?

Well, I'm a writer first and that's how I got into this business, but I have to say it's a lot more enjoyable to direct because the words are already on the page and you just have to figure out how to get those images you have in your head, the images the script gives you, and get them out on film. That's a trick, but looking at the blank page is probably one of the more daunting aspects of the business of what I do.

What's next for you?

There's a movie with Miramax/ Dimension that Frank Spotnitz and I have a deal to do. This one is about a guy who may be sort of a missing link. And then [I'm contracted to] Fox for approximately a year, and beyond that I was supposed to have written a novel a long time ago and I must get around to that. The novel is about one of two things. I have two ideas that I've had for a long time and it's really just which one I choose to do first. One is historical and the other is a little closer to home. So that's kind of the order of business.

Could you have done The X-Files for another 10 years?

Could I have done it for another 10 years? Yeah.

At this point, do you believe in aliens?

Me, no. But those aliens owe me a visit after all this time.●

Chasing the Unknown

REAL-LIFE GHOST HUNTERS TRACK APPARITIONS WITH A COMBINATION OF PLUCK, PATIENCE, TECHNOLOGY AND WHIMSY

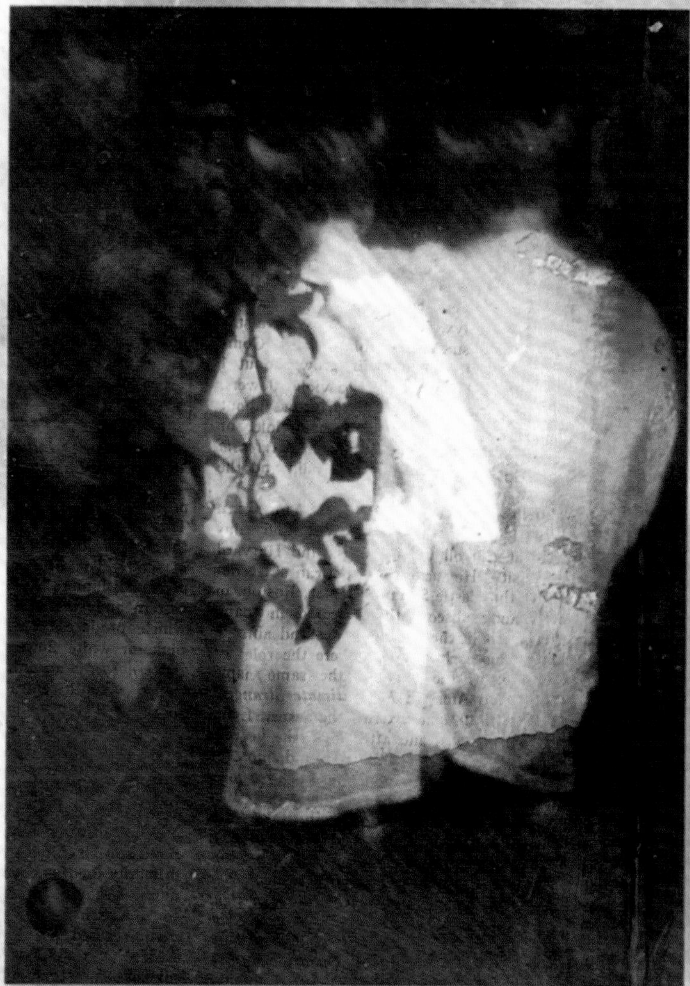

It was an unseasonably warm October day in the small seaport town of Astoria, Ore. Dave Oester and his wife, Sharon Gill, were shooting some footage with a local news crew at the town's Liberty Theater, an ornate opera house built in 1925. The crew, which was doing a special on the couple's line of work, were filming some interior shots as Oester and Gill told stories of their discoveries in the building.

They talked about "Lilly," the ghost of a woman whose throat was cut by her husband as she watched a play at the Liberty; she once dropped a pane of glass on a man in "her" seat—despite the lack of any windows or panes of glass anywhere in the building. Then there's "Paul," who threw a woman to her death off the theater's balcony, and who occasionally materializes to offer a menacing grin to horrified moviegoers. And there's the woman Paul murdered, "Mary," who sometimes locks women in the theater's bathroom stalls for hours.

BY KATHLEEN FLINN

because I didn't want to see a glowing face. All I could think was that my heart might

Ghost hunters Dave Oester and Sharon Gill

not be able to take it."

Oester bolted from the room, which surprised him. For him, feeling the bone-chilling breath of a ghost at his back is something of an occupational hazard. Ghost hunters by trade, he and his wife, Sharon Gill, have investigated thousands of cases of paranormal activity. They've written two books on the subject and head up the International Ghost Hunters Association from their modest home in St. Helens, Ore. And the Oesters aren't the only spook searchers out there: Believe it or not, following the trail of unquiet spirits is something of a growth industry these days. Newsletters, web sites and on-call ghost hunters are a standard part of the paranormal world that the Oesters and their colleagues call home.

The scare at the Liberty was a jolt, Oester admits, but the incident didn't diminished his love for his trade, which is booming these days. "We get about five people a week who request urgent help because someone is having a frightening experience and they can't deal with it because of their fear," he says. "Most of the time, the spirit just wants to be acknowledged. They're like kids—sometimes they do stuff to get your attention."

And they've been getting our attention for years. Documented cases of ghostly visits go back centuries (there's even a biblical reference to a ghost in the book of Job), and investigations into such happenings began in earnest about 300 years ago. England's famous Ghost Club was started in the late-1800s when spiritualism was all the rage, and since then, interest in the subject has only grown. When Oester and Gill established the International Ghost Hunters Association in September 1996, they signed up 700 members in 40 countries in less than three months, mostly through the Internet, and their youngest member is a 4-year-old boy from Kentucky.

Researchers say they are lured to the subject by the very fact that there are no firm answers, no solid evidence of visitors from beyond the grave. Ghosts, hauntings, poltergeists, spiritual apparitions, unexplained phenomenon seem to represent a perpetual mystery: Something's out there, they agree, but no one's sure exactly what.

"Ghost hunting stays fascinating for me because the phenomenon is so multifaceted," says Richard Senate, a longtime paranormal investigator based in Ventura, Calif. He claims to have personally seen 16 ghosts in more than 230 investigations. "The fact that there's so much to [paranormal investigations] is one of those things that doesn't come out on TV, including *The X-Files*. Ghost hauntings are really made up of a myriad of paranormal phenomenon. It's not just the dead coming back to do unfinished business, but a lot of interesting things that range from actual poltergeists to [lingering] images of historical events. Plus, I admit, there's a certain thrill to it."

The work isn't glamorous. Most investigators work the graveyard shift, sometimes in actual graveyards. In field investigations, they may wait for hours behind sensitive equipment only to capture nothing. Or, weeks of effort may turn up something small, like a recording of footsteps.

"I've sat in cemeteries for hours on end all night," says Troy Taylor, who heads the Ghost Research Society of Central Illinois. "It will be cold and wet, and there I am, taking time-interval photos."

On top of all that, it doesn't pay very well, either. Larry Montz, who runs a New Orleans business called "Hauntings Today," charges $100 per case. He claims to receive eight to 10 calls per week from potential clients, although the number of cases he investigates is significantly lower. Tucson, Ariz.-based investigator William Everist charges $125 per hour, with a two-hour minimum. "I've tried [full-time ghostbusting], but it's not a very lucrative profession," he says. "Usually what I end up doing is talking to people who call me, advise them

During the filming, Oester demonstrated his infrared camera, and once the shoot wrapped up, he decided to change the film. He wandered into one of the theater's dark cellar rooms, where a fourth, unidentified spirit is suspected of holing up. After Oester finished his task, he started toward the door. Suddenly, something hit him.

"I felt cold air engulf me. It was an icy feeling that spread against my back," he said later. "My hair stood up on end, literally. I didn't want to look behind me. For the first time in my life, I was truly afraid of the unknown. I knew standing there that I wasn't going to turn around

as to what might be happening and let them do their own personal inquiry."

Many investigators don't charge clients: Some academics look into possible paranormal activities in the name of science or as fodder for books; other investigators pursue ghosts in order to package "haunted tours," to which they sell tickets.

"I'd never charge for an investigation. I think it's tacky," says Taylor. "But most people are surprised because they do expect to pay." He agrees they probably get the notion from the movie *Ghostbusters*. "All I have to say about the movie is that I wish I had some of that cool equipment."

The Investigations

An investigation can last an hour, a night or, in one case Senate worked on, an entire year. The amount of scientific equipment can vary widely as well, but most investigators use the same group of tools. First and foremost is the electromagnetic field detector (EMF), the ghost hunter's primary spook-hunting device.

"In ghost hunting, when a ghost exists or materializes, it's usually as an energy anomaly, so it's detectable and can be measured," Oester says. Investigators measure the background electromagnetic "noise" of an area, then sweep through the area in order to find changes in specific spots.

A second vital tool is the digital readout thermometer, which is used to measure minute changes in temperature. "Cold spots" often indicate swirling vortexes of energy. To paranormal investigators, a sudden drop of temperature in a part of a room coupled with elevated EMF readings means they may have hit pay dirt. That's when they whip out ghost hunter tool number three: a camera. Any camera will do, although Oester likes Polaroid film (see sidebar) and many investigators swear by infrared film.

Beyond that, investigators often use a combination of infrared goggles and cameras, radiation sensors, microwave imaging systems, temperature sensors, movement detectors and high-frequency sound recorders. Oester looks for patterns to help track spirits. Hauntings seem to stick to lunar cycles, with the most activity occurring at full and new moons. Other researchers have suggested that most paranormal activity seems to occur at 3 a.m. and 3 p.m.—something that Oester says he's found to be true.

Typically, investigators set up a sort of "trap" with multiple indicators. During one famous stakeout, paranormal researchers tried to capture evidence of two shadowy, yet distinct ghosts that had been inadvertently caught on film by a hapless tourist. (Showing two delicate, translucent figures in the National Maritime Museum in Greenwich, England, it's one of the most famous ghost photos ever taken and a ubiquitous fixture in most books about ghosts.) Members of England's Ghost Club decided to do a full investigation, once Kodak assured them that its experts could detect no trace of tampering with the Greenwich photo.

In an all-night watch, they set up a network of devices to record atmospheric conditions and temperature, and additional tools included hypersensitive audio-recording equipment and various cam-

eras. The stair's railing was coated with petroleum jelly to check for fingerprints. Researchers then turned down all the lights and stayed quiet. Late in the evening, communication with the spirits was attempted through mediums, a Ouija board and automatic writing.

No ghosts showed themselves, but the researchers did record footsteps, weeping and something that sounded like muttering, along with the lonely, faint toll of a bell that was heard by all present.

But that was just one night of an investigation. Senate spent an entire year investigating hauntings at a hotel in Santa Paula, Calif. In addition to stakeouts, he and his colleagues held seances, wired rooms to record sound and interviewed 75 witnesses. They brought in a string of psychics, ranging from a housewife with a "special gift" to TV psychic Kenny Kingston. In the end, Senate and a team of researchers concluded that nine separate entities were present. They caught an otherworldly voice warning, "You will die" on one of their tapes, which was recorded in a room in which Senate was present. (At the time, he heard nothing.) Also, while staying in a room once occupied by Harry Houdini, Senate saw a figure appear at the foot of his bed.

"We also caught one image on infrared film of a man holding a deck of cards," Senate says. "It was consistent with the history of a cowboy who'd been gunned down in the hotel for cheating at cards."

For many researchers, the point of an investigation is to gain proof of an individual haunting, but some don't feel that they need concrete evidence that ghosts exist.

"Their methods—trying to record ghosts on tape or film—are pointless," says celebrated investigator Eddie Burks in his recent book, *Ghosthunter.* Burks believes that the only way to capture a ghost on film is if it is able to materialize through ectoplasm, which isn't very likely. As for noise, he believes that most "proof" usually consists of nothing more than recordings of slamming doors, floors creaking or windows banging.

"Those with psychic awareness know that this is an experimental thing. We don't need empirical evidence, we have to go along with what we experience," he adds.

Burks is possibly most famous for ghostbusting at Coutts, the Queen's Bank, in England in 1993. It seems that Thomas Howard, wrongly beheaded in 1572 after being accused of plotting to overthrow the monarchy, had taken a particular liking to the bank's main office. Howard's ghost reportedly showed up in the impressive main atrium routinely—without his head. The unquiet spirit also wreaked havoc with the bank's computers and dropped temperatures inside the bank low enough to make employees shiver. Not only that, he didn't even have an account at the bank. Clearly, he had to go.

Burks was called to communicate with the ghost and help direct it on its way. Unlike the Ghost Club members or other modern-day ghost hunters, he uses no electronic equipment. He says he communicated with the ghost intuitively and telepathically, urging it to let go of its hostility for its wrongful death.

"I was beheaded here on a summer's day not far from here," the ghost told Burks. After Burks' therapeutic visit, however, the ghost never showed up again.

GIVING UP THE GHOST

Burks' handling of the Coutts case does bring up a common theme: The best way to deal with a ghost is simply to figure out who it is, why it's hanging around, and then calm it down. Often, that's all people really want from a paranormal investigator—to stop the activity that's frightening them. But unlike the characters in *Ghostbusters*, real-life investigators don't have electronic equipment that will actually trap their prey. Many investigators don't think such grandiose gear is really necessary—and besides, do you really want to put your late grandma in a nuclear-powered spirit grid?

What needs to be remembered, say most ghost hunters, is that ghosts shouldn't be feared. Oester doesn't believe that religious ceremonies or exorcisms get rid of ghosts, for a very simple reason: Few ghosts are evil. "In life, you have good people and then you have rotten SOBs. If someone was a rotten SOB in life, then they will be [like that] in the afterlife as well," Oester says. But that usually means the spirit is just obnoxious, not evil. "Most of the time, it seems what the spirit wants most is to be acknowledged," Oester says. "That's why we suggest giving the ghost a name. Then, as far as they're concerned, you've acknowledged them and that's a sign of respect."

Some ghosts do go to a good deal of trouble to get people's attention. They hurl things, turn lights on and off, remove objects and replace them days later, and generally cause havoc in a household. But they aren't always the cause of such happenings, say researchers. Although the word "poltergeist" means "noisy ghost," it's believed that some aren't even really ghosts in the traditional sense, but perhaps some collective adaptation of negative energy in a household.

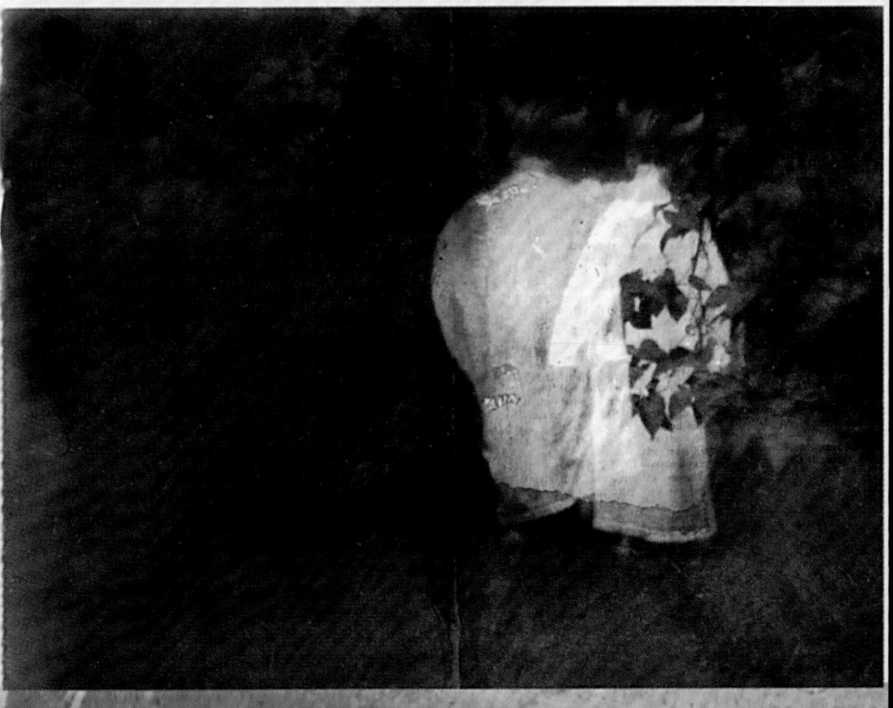

"It's almost like a psychokinetic hysteria that can be created by people," says William Everist, a researcher who teaches courses on paranormal topics in Tucson. "People are frightened by the unknown. So when things happen, they get more upset and possibly more activity occurs. It's a cycle. The occupants don't understand that they may be generating it themselves."

Everist was recently called upon to deal with a situation in a historic house where the silverware was moving around, various noises were heard at night, and the occupants began to be aware of an almost constant presence. "The family was really terrified. They were concerned when their youngest daughter was becoming more communicative with it." He checked out the location and explained to the house's occupants that family tension might be causing the problem; in a follow-up visit, he learned that the paranormal activity had greatly diminished.

More often, though, spirits don't want to leave and no one can make them. And maybe no one should try.

"Part of our responsibility as ghost hunters is to document events as they're occurring, but it's not our responsibility to make them leave, nor would we want to," Oester says. "When you order someone to leave, it's like sitting as a judge. What if someone is staying behind to watch over their family? To try to extricate them before their family is grown may ake [the ghost] angry. We have to respect the entities.

"As we open our minds and eliminate the fear that we have of the unknown, we may find that most places are what we might call 'haunted,'" he adds. "We may all have visitors— most people just don't notice."●

RADIOSHACK DAYS

Tools of the Ghost Hunting Trade

So you want to be a ghost hunter? Then what you'll need is some patience, a will to believe, a little discretionary income and a Radio Shack nearby.

"There is no need to travel to the ends of the Earth; [ghosts are] as close as the next room," says Donald M. Gibson Jr., a veteran paranormal researcher based in Providence, R.I. "And you don't need millions of dollars' worth of equipment or a full staff to study the world of ghosts and hauntings."

Still, having the right tools – expensive or not – makes all the difference for any job. That includes tracking down vaporous entities and other paranormal phenomena. Here are the basic tools of the trade, according to Sharon Gill and Dave Oester, who are the founders of the International Ghost Hunters Association.

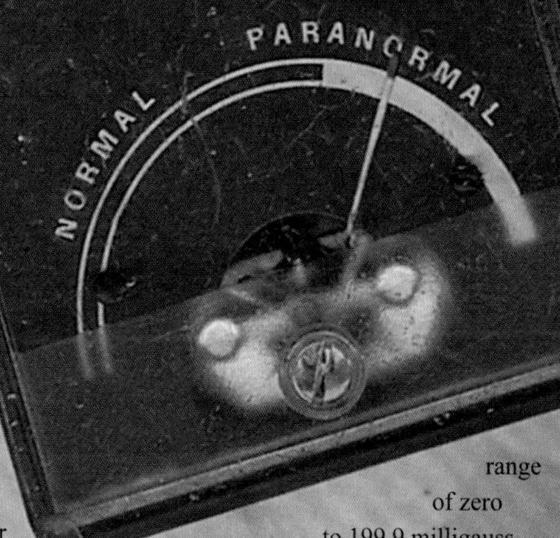

EMF Detector: Detects changes in electromagnetic fields. Such changes may indicate the presence of an entity. For researching their book, *Twilight Visitors*, Oester and Gill used a detector produced by A.W. Sperry Instruments, model EMF-200A. It comes with an EMF range of zero to 199.9 milligauss and a large LCD display. "You sweep the room to check for background 'noise' first, then look for anomalies, kind of like the tri-corders on *Star Trek*," Oester says.

Digital Readout Thermometer: Used to measure cold spots in a house, it's another indicator of possible entities, or "hauntings." You can find these items at Radio Shack.

Photography: You can use any kind of camera, since all types have been used to capture what are reportedly ghostly images. Many investigators prefer high-speed black-and-white infrared film; Dave Oester likes Polaroid film. He speculates that the embedded crystals that allow for the instant development may also polarize the light from an entity, making it visible. It is also impossible to double expose this kind of film. If you do use 35mm film, Oester suggests using a very fast speed like ASA 1600 or even the Kodak ASA 3200. – K.F.

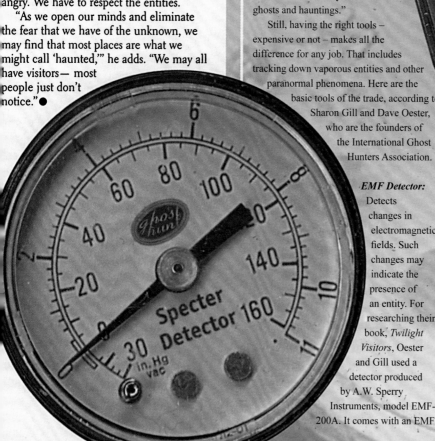

EPISODE GUIDE

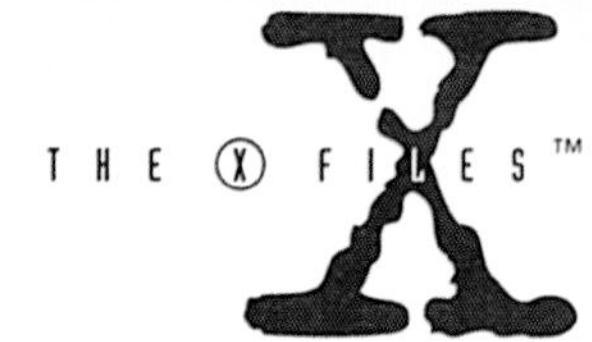

4.5: "THE FIELD WHERE I DIED" Episode #4X05

Original US tx 3 November 96 Original UK tx 16 February 97

APISON and CHATTANOOGA, TENNESSEE

After a tip-off about child abuse and stockpiled weapons, agents Mulder and Scully accompany other FBI and BATF (Bureau of Alcohol Tobacco and Firearms) officers on a Waco-style raid of the Temple of the Seven Stars, but find nothing but the cult's families. Mulder experiences a bizarre sense of *deja vu*, however, 'remembering' a secret hiding place in the temple grounds that he could not possibly have known about. Inside, they discover the cult's self-styled leader, Vernon Ephesian, and his six 'wives' about to poison themselves – but no guns.

The cult members are arrested and questioned in turn, and during the interrogation of one of Ephesian's wives, Melissa, her voice and manner changes to that of a New Yorker named Sidney – the name given by the caller who tipped off the FBI – who believes that Harry S Truman is still President. Scully believes her to be suffering from a multiple personality disorder, but Mulder has made a connection with the woman and is convinced that she is re-living a 'past life'. Mulder hides his theories from Skinner in order to pursue them, leading Scully to accuse him of being irresponsible. "You are responsible only to yourself," she says acidly.

The agents accompany Melissa back to the abandoned Temple, where further distinct personalities or past lives emerge, including a child named Lily and Sarah Kavanaugh, a nurse stationed in Tennessee during the American Civil War. Melissa/Kavanaugh describes the massacre of Confederate soldiers at the site on 26 November 1863. "I was here," she says, before turning to look directly at an awestruck agent Mulder, "as were you. This is the field where I watched you die..."

F.Y.I.

Glen Morgan and James Wong's second script since their return completes a loose trilogy which began with "Beyond the Sea" and "One Breath"; the difference in this story is that it is Mulder, not Scully, who is having a deeply personal experience with the supernatural. According to Morgan, the idea began with a comment made by Duchovny during one of the writers' regular field trips to Vancouver. "David said, 'I haven't had a show where I really kind of cut loose, you know? I'm doing a lot of exposition,'" Morgan explains. Thus, he and Wong decided to give Duchovny/Mulder something out of the ordinary to work with. "In most episodes Mulder knows before anybody what the paranormal thing is, he's two steps ahead of everybody. But this one, the case just drops in his lap, and he's the last to figure it out." Morgan and Wong also continued their plan to feature actors from their cancelled show *Space: Above and Beyond* in the four 'comeback' episodes, this time stretching Kristen Kloke as Melissa Ephesian.

Although "The Field Where I Died" scored one of the highest Nielsen ratings of the season – a 12.3/18 (approximately 11.8 million homes), the episode sharply divided audiences; while confirmed fans loved Duchovny's heartbreaking performance even as they complained about what they saw as continuity errors, *Entertainment Weekly* unkindly declared, "There's an evil conspiracy afoot, and it's the creative team responsible for this stultifyingly awful episode. The only thing Duchovny is channeling here is William Shatner." Morgan, for one, is unphazed by the negative critical reaction, naming it as his favourite episode. "I'm really happy," he says. "That show for personal reasons means everything to me, I was just so pleased with the way it came out."

Noteworthy Dialogue Transcript

SKINNER: "Ephesian had six women on the verge of suicide – you witnessed it. My concern is if the Temple members are released, any subsequent Federal investigation will ignite Ephesian's paranoia to such a degree that we won't have another Waco on our hands – we'll have Jonestown."

Principal Credits

Created by	Chris Carter
Produced by	Ten-Thirteen Productions for 20th Century-Fox TV
Executive Producers	Chris Carter, Howard Gordon, RW Goodwin
Producers	Joseph Patrick Finn, Kim Manners, Rob Bowman
Co-Producers	Vince Gilligan, Frank Spotnitz, Paul Rabwin
Consulting Producers	Ken Horton, James Wong & Glen Morgan
Music	Mark Snow

Episode Credits

Written by	Glen Morgan and James Wong
Directed by	Rob Bowman
Special Agent Fox Mulder	David Duchovny
Special Agent Dr Dana Scully	Gillian Anderson
Assistant Director Walter S Skinner	Mitch Pileggi
Melissa Rydell Ephesian/Sidney/Lily	Kristen Kloke
Vernon Ephesian	Michael Massee
FBI Agent Figgins	Anthony Harrison
Harbaugh	Doug Abrahams
Therapist	Donna White
BATF Agent	Michael Dobson

EPISODE: 5x12

SHERIFF HARTWELL

"Bad Blood"

In Season Five's "Bad Blood," X-Philes saw three sides to actor Luke Wilson. Mulder viewed Wilson's character, Sheriff Hartwell, as a buck-toothed hillbilly, while Scully considered him a good-looking charmer. By the end of the episode, Hartwell revealed himself to be a cunning, though ultimately merciful, vampire.

The versatility it took to pull off that tricky, multi-faceted role has paid off handsomely for the 28-year-old Wilson, who appeared in four movies last year: the buddy action/comedy *Blue Streak*, the romantic drama *Committed*, the wacky satire *Kill the Man* (which also features *X-Files* vet Michael McKean) and *My Dog Skip* with Kevin Bacon. That's a pretty astounding lineup for an actor who made his feature debut just three years ago in the indie film *Bottle Rocket* – which also featured his actor brothers Owen (*Armageddon*, *The Haunting*) and Andrew (*Never Been Kissed*). Wilson's performance in that film eventually led to a starring role in 1998's *Home Fries*, which was scripted by *X-Files* co-executive producer Vince Gilligan.

LUKE WILSON

© WARNER BROS.

"I got to know Vince a little during the filming of *Home Fries*, and after the movie was finished he called and said, 'Hey, would you ever want to do an episode of *The X-Files*? Because I've been trying to write a character for you,'" Wilson says. "I said, 'Yeah, I'd love to.' He called three weeks later and had this script, so I just went up to Vancouver to do it."

Wilson admits he was a little nervous about accepting the role, but the hospitality of the cast and crew set him at ease. Star David Duchovny even invited the actor to join in a between-takes game of hoops. "We shot baskets. I'm not good enough to go one on one with David," says Wilson, whose voice still has a hint of the Southern drawl he acquired growing up in Texas. "But we did play a few games of horse. I think that was pretty even, actually." —*Steve Hockensmith*

ALSO KNOWN AS:

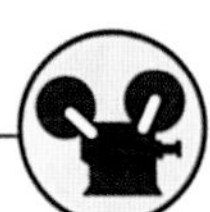

1998: "David" in *Bongwater*
1998: "Dorian" in *Home Fries* (above)
1998: "Dr. Peter Flynn" in *Rushmore*
1997: "Billy" in *Stab* (the film within a film in *Scream 2*)
1997: "Jesse Reilly" in *Best Men*
1997: "Henry" in *Telling Lies in America*
1996: "Anthony Adams" in *Bottle Rocket*

ILLUSTRATION BY ANASTASIA VASILAKIS

First Blood

by Gina McIntyre

Vampires were inspiring nightmares long before they gained TV and movie immortality

In 1931, a Hungarian stage actor named Bela Lugosi turned Count Dracula into a household name. Making his silver-screen debut in Tod Browning's masterful adaptation of Bram Stoker's classic novel, Lugosi's hypnotic portrayal of the undead aristocrat who beguiled his victims with his peculiar accent and mysterious demeanor captivated audiences. As well it should have. The actor radiated an alien intensity that came to define the contemporary vampire: A virtually indestructible fiend from beyond the grave, he is the ultimate seducer who lures his victims into a nocturnal existence, cursing them with an unquenchable thirst for human life.

Nearly 70 years later, Lugosi's Dracula remains the singular icon for a race of mythological creatures who have since saturated popular culture. No longer relegated to their traditional shadowy haunts, vampires have appeared in untold numbers of novels and short stories, as well as some 650 films and television programs. And with vampire novels (particularly those by Anne Rice) firmly entrenched on the bestseller list and more big-screen vamps in the wings, the demand for this most enigmatic of monsters shows no sign of waning.

GRAVE PERIL: "Bad Blood" [above and below]; **Dark Shadows** [above right]; bad Vlad [middle]; **Nosferatu** [bottom]

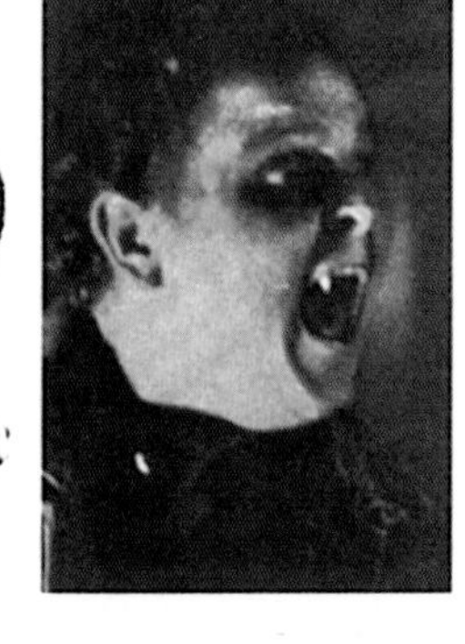

According to horror writer Poppy Z. Brite, our ongoing vampire mania stems from the nature of the beast. Vampires are appealing, Brite says, because they personify elements that people find fundamentally attractive – immortality, power and eroticism. "The vampire story always ends up coming back to blood and sex, which are two things that peopl are fascinated with, but it can be told in a million different ways with a million different spins on it," explains Brite, who has written her own vampire novel, *Lost Souls,* edited two anthologies of vampire stories and reviewed vampire novels for The *Village Voice*.

"The vampire does almost everything that is a taboo," she continues. "He is a cannibal of sorts. He has inherently unsafe sex. He represents anything of the dark side that you can imagine – night and violence and what I referred to in one of my introductions as dark dream side of ourselves – but he lives forever. He experiences all of our taboos but he's not actually subject to any of them."

Their refined ghoulishness may explain, at least in part, the resilience of vampires as predators throughout the centuries. The creature first surfaced in Babylonian mythology as a deity named Lilitu who was believed to suck the blood of infants, French scholar Jean Marigny explains in his book, *Vampires: Restless Creatures of the Night*. In ancient Greek myth, Zeus' lover Lamia transforms herself into a child-killing, blood-drinking monster after her own infant is murdered by the god's jealous wife. Those legends evolved to create a being called the succubus, a lustful female who preyed upon young men as they slept, seducing them in order to steal their virility and sometimes their lives. (For more on succubi, see *The X-Files* Season Thee episode "Avatar.")

But it was the introduction of Christian doctrine, however, that caused the vampire myth to boom. According to the religion, admittance to heaven was granted only to those who meet certain criteria – a final act of repentance, burial in consecrated ground, etc. It fell to the lot who didn't make the cut to wander the earth as soulless, undead monsters who murdered the living to survive.

Around the 12th century, Marigny says, sightings of the recently deceased, many of whom had been excommunicated, were reported in the British Isles. Eyewitnesses claimed that when the tombs of these newly dead were opened, their bodies were discovered wholly intact, their clothing spotted with blood. The somewhat logical conclusion that the "vampire" had been

Night Stalkers

When not rising from their graves at sunset or flapping about as bats, vampires are most often found drinking blood. But that unwholesome activity is not wholly confined to creatures of mythology and film. The red stuff is, in fact, the focal point of one particular group of fetishists, those who engage in what is called "bloodplay" or "bloodsports."

A faction of sadomasochism, bloodplay involves cutting or piercing oneself or a partner in order to draw blood for pleasure. (*The X-Files*' Season Two episode "3" mixed bloodplay enthusiasts with real-live—or real-dead—vampires.) The fetish doesn't necessarily include the consumption of blood, although a group of bloodsports participants known as "self-made vampires" do derive sexual pleasure from imbibing the liquid of life. The overriding caveat in all bloodplay, though, is "safe, sane and consensual," meaning that adults who choose to participate in bloodsports do so with great caution, given the dangers inherent in handling blood in today's world.

Then there are those who take recreational vampirism a bit too far, such as recent self-professed vampire Rodrick Justin Ferrell, who was convicted of murdering a friend's parents and burning the letter "V" into one of the bodies. The leader of a group of teens who engaged in bloodletting and group sex as part of what they considered "vampire" rituals, 17-year-old Ferrell insisted that he was a vampire even after he was convicted. He is sentenced to die in Florida's electric chair.—*G.M.*

buried alive and had wounded him- or herself trying to escape premature internment never occurred to medieval peasantry, and the unfortunate souls were declared cadaver sanguisugus (Latin for blood-sucking corpse) and promptly impaled. Nearly 200 years later, when the plague struck Eastern Europe, so did the undead. Large numbers of people who succumbed to the disease were promptly buried in an effort to contain the infection, but the haste virtually guaranteed that not everyone who was put into a grave belonged there. If these living dead were discovered, they were quickly branded vampires and dispatched accordingly, just as their predecessors had been thousands of miles away and hundreds of years earlier.

In spite of their increasing notoriety, vampires lacked any sort of individual identity or personality; like zombies, they aimlessly wandered the night in search of sustenance, shrinking in terror from the occasional cross, garlic clove or vial of holy water. That is, until 1431, when Vlad Tepes was born. Tepes (also known as Dracul, a name that translates to "devil" or "dragon") was a Romanian war hero with a nasty penchant for impaling his enemies on spikes. Tepes' cruelty remained unsurpassed until 1611, when Hungarian Countess Elizabeth Bathory was accused of kidnapping nearly 300 village girls in order to bathe in their blood to preserve her youthful appearance. Thank goodness for Oil of Olay.

Despite far-reaching reports of the atrocities committed by Tepes and Bathory, vampire fervour remained primarily confined to Eastern Europe, particularly among bands of local gypsies, for almost 200 years. Western Europeans turned their attention to the industrial revolution. The cultural shift toward progress and away from superstition forced the vampire to inhabit another realm: literature. It proved to be a realm in which they would flourish.

Samuel Taylor Coleridge's Romantic poem "Christabel" (1816) was among the first of this movement, followed three years later by John William Polidori's novel *The Vampyre* (1819), whose central character, the aristocratic Lord Ruthven, was commonly thought to be modelled after Lord Byron. "The fascination of the Byron vampire was that people could

Fangs for the Memories

Ever since Max Schreck's ghastly *Nosferatu* emerged from the expressionist shadows of 1920s German cinema, followed nine years later by Bela Lugosi in Tod Browning's classic *Dracula*, vampires have made themselves comfortable in the harsh lights of the silver and small screens. But not all of these creatures of the night have called Transylvania home.

Dark Shadows (1966-1971): Barnabas Collins (Jonathan Frid) set the tone for brooding vampires in the popular television series set in New England.

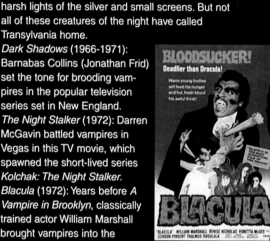

The Night Stalker (1972): Darren McGavin battled vampires in Vegas in this TV movie, which spawned the short-lived series *Kolchak: The Night Stalker.*

Blacula (1972): Years before *A Vampire in Brooklyn*, classically trained actor William Marshall brought vampires into the Blaxploitation subgenre. Pam Grier starred as a voodoo priestess in the 1973 sequel *Scream Blacula Scream.*

Martin (1977): Horror master George Romero's creepy black-and-white outing tells the story of a Pennsylvania boy with a thirst for blood.

Salem's Lot (1979): Vampires returned to New England in the legendary television mini-series (directed by Tobe Hooper) based on Stephen King's novel. —*G.M.*

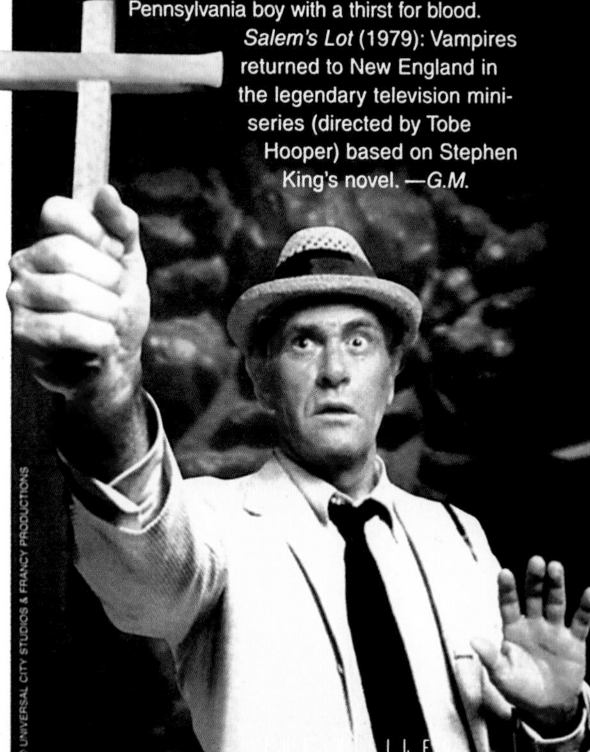

imagine that Lord Byron really was a vampire," explains Nina Auerbach, the John Welsh Centennial Professor of English at the University of Pennsylvania and author of *Our Vampires, Ourselves.* "I don't think those stories would have been popular at all if they hadn't been attached to Byron himself. The idea that the romantic poet, or at least the Byronic figure, was a real vampire transcending time really started [the public's fascination with vampires]."

According to Auerbach, the literary vampire was among the most free-spirited and sexually liberated creatures, real or mythological, to exist during Victorian England's notoriously strict moral doctrine, underscored in Sheridan La Fanu's 1871 short story "Carmilla." Carmilla is a bewitching, independent young woman who lives outside the authority of patriarchy (she is without a male guardian) and is therefore marked as alien and dangerous, Auerbach explains. In the story, the disturbingly unconventional Carmilla is revealed to be a vampire who befriends and seduces young women before putting the bite on them.

Vampires changed with the publication of Bram Stoker's *Dracula* in 1897: The Count is not concerned with befriending mortals. "When Dracula came along, we had really the first fascist vampire," Auerbach says. "He comes in from outside, and he mesmerizes people and moves them around and invades their minds. He's disgusting. He's very unphysical and unsensuous. He doesn't weep tears."

The book enjoyed immense popularity and was adapted for the stage in 1924. Lugosi took over the role in 1927 and, of course, starred in the silver-screen adaptation shortly thereafter. As often happens when novels are turned into films, some artistic license was taken with the character to make him more palatable to audiences: Lugosi's opera cloak and regal demeanor replaced the original character's beastliness.

"Through Bela Lugosi, [vampires] really entered the public consciousness. At this point, the vampire is totally a villain, but a loveable, sexy villain," explains J. Gordon Melton, author of *The Vampire Book* and *Videohound's Vampires on Video* and founder and president of the American chapter of the Transylvania Society of Dracula, an organization devoted to increasing tourism in Transylvania.

While Lugosi took his trademark role to the brink of parody with his appearance in *Abbott and Costello Meet Frankenstein* (1948), Christopher Lee returned the Count to his sophisticated roots in a slew of Hammer Horror films in the 1960s. Lee's Count, who was even more blatantly seductive, turned the character into something a little closer to a hero. "In the 1960s, in a number of different forms, not the least of which was *The Munsters* and *Vampirella*, the vampire became a good guy," Melton says. "In the 1970s, the vampire as good guy really came into full bloom."

Fred Saberhagan, the author of eight vampire novels, is partially responsible for the trend. After re-reading Stoker's novel, he became fascinated by the character's motivations, which are never directly addressed in the book. "It's part of the fascination of any villain, like a Richard III. There he goes doing what he wants, having a great time," Saberhagen explains. "It's the villain people usually identify with. You get to enjoy but you don't have to be staked or go to prison. For men, it's a feeling of, 'I can identify with this scoundrel and get away with all these things vicariously without really feeling guilty about it afterwards or being punished for it.'"

For women, the appeal is something slightly different, according to Auerbach. "The vampire would

BATMEN: Lugosi takes Costello under his wing [left]; Barnabas Collins [above]; Blacula fights the power [right]; '60s sucker Lee [below]

bring out these expansive sides of his female victims who weren't really victims but empowered creatures," she says. "They were opposed to paternalistic husbands and fathers, and they were very sexy. [The vampire] is a liberator. They represent power over authority at their best, power over time and power over death. They represent possibility, a dream of escaping."

It seems that the world community still dreams of escape. By the 1970s, vampires of all persuasions were wreaking havoc in cinema and literature. British film star

© AIP

Ingrid Pitt personified the lustful female vamp in *The Vampire Lovers*; a new, more sympathetic vampire emerged on television in *Dark Shadows*' Barnabas Collins; and disaffected bloodsuckers Louis and Lestat debuted in Anne Rice's *Interview with the Vampire.*

Rice's vampires have come to define the contemporary undead. They are beautiful creatures with artistic sensibilities; they have a profound hunger for knowledge, particularly about the history of their race within the world; and they are often plagued with an overwhelming sense of loss and alienation. And they have been embraced by millions of readers around the world.

The early '90s saw the first big-screen adaptation of Rice's work and the most recent version of Stoker's – both box office successes. And last year, the centennial anniversary of the publication of *Dracula* stimulated a new round of vampire fever – Bela Lugosi was even featured on a postage stamp. Not to mention that close to half of all the vampire novels ever written have appeared in the last decade. In fact, some 50 new vampire books are published each year in English alone.

"The vampire's going to remain popular. There are several different vampires out there, and the vampire good guy and the vampire villain still have a big audience," Melton says. "It's just too good of an archetype to die."

Interview with a Vampire

Ingrid Pitt set the standard for cinematic vampires of the femme fatale persuasion with her performance in 1970's *The Vampire Lovers*, Hammer Studios' adaptation of Sheridan Le Fanu's classic tale "Carmilla." The story of a vamp who preys on the young women she befriends, the film transfigured women in horror from victims to predators; Pitt's fang-baring (and breast-baring), not to mention the movie's homoerotic subtext, gave British censors something to chew on and American audiences a thrilling new villainess to fear.

But Pitt (née Natasha Petrovana) never realized the monster she was creating. In fact, the naivete she brought to the role —she had no real knowledge of vampire lore— was, she says, what gave the film the unique feel it needed to become a classic. "When I first started making *The Vampire Lovers*, I went to a priest [who] said that vampirism was invented by the church to keep the peasants under control and that it had nothing to do with sex. Vampires were not interested in eroticism; all they wanted was blood. With this thought in mind, I made a film which was quite innocent, I thought, although everybody else thought it was very lesbian. I don't think it was, and this, I think, saved the film," she says.

Pitt continued her love affair with vampirism in the horror anthology *The House That Dripped Blood* (1971) and countless other genre films, often co-starring with Christopher Lee and Peter Cushing. Now, the self-professed Queen of Horror is reliving her nocturnal exploits though her new book, *The Ingrid Pitt Bedside Companion for Vampire Lovers*. "It's a gentle jaunt through the myth of vampires through the ages," Pitt explains. "It's got a little bit about vampire cinema, not just judging films but saying what various films had to add to the myth of the vampire."

Pitt is now preparing to again expand the canon of vampire films with her own project, *Dracula Who*. Penned by the actress herself, the movie will explore the Count's adventures in vegetarianism. "It's going to be quite fantastic if it works out,' Pitt effuses. "I think there will be *Dracula Who 2* and *Dracula Who 3*. It's very, very funny."—*G.M.*

© HAMMER FILMS

virtual
persona

lity

by erik j. martin

Today, the computer is man's best friend—could it become his worst enemy?

"I THINK, THEREFORE I AM." That's easy for a human to say. But just try getting a computer to say it, understand it and really mean it.

In a sense, that's exactly what scientists and researchers across the globe have been trying to do for decades: Create machines and computers that can think for themselves, learn independently and achieve "consciousness." It might be common in science fiction—where talkative robot sidekicks and evil computer programs (like the ones which seek to destroy their human masters in *The X-Files* episodes "Kill Switch" and "Ghost in the Machine") have become a staple. But in the real world, machines with "artificial intelligence" (or "AI") are a lot harder to find.

John McCarthy, professor of computer Science at Stanford University and a pioneer in the artificial intelligence field since the 1950s, defines AI as "the science and engineering of making intelligent machines, especially intelligent computer programs." But hasn't that goal been achieved already? The standard home PC can take verbal commands (with the proper voice-recognition software) and beat the average human at chess. Isn't that "intelligent?"

Not really, according to most AI researchers. They believe that for a machine to truly be considered smart, it must be able to learn on its own while seamlessly mirroring human intelligence. In fact, the benchmark for gauging AI—the Turing test, created by English mathematician Alan Turing—has a pretty simple bottom line: If a machine can successfully pretend to be human to a knowledgeable observer, then it should be considered intelligent.

illustration by
michael morgenstern

Dr. Thomas Whalen says that's as good a measure of intelligence as researchers can devise at the moment because it "puts an emphasis on what the computer does, not on how it does it." According to Whalen, scientists don't even really understand how people think, making it pretty tough for them to figure out how anything else should.

"We don't know how the human brain works, so how would we know if a computer program works the same way?" says Whalen, a trained experimental psychologist and "natural language interface scientist" at the Communications Research Centre in Ottawa. "Your brain is probably more powerful than all the computers in the United States combined. With more than 10 billion neuron cells making 10 trillion connections, that's an awful lot of processing power. The question is, should we be trying to make our AI programs like the human brain?"

Dr. Paul Cohen believes he can answer Whalen's question with an unqualified "You bet." A professor in the department of computer science at the University of Massachusetts in Amherst, Mass., Cohen has been working in AI for 15 years. According to him, "The real quest is to learn more about how human beings think."

Part of Cohen's research involves two very interesting test subjects—Red and Blue, two Pioneer One-model robots made by Real World Interfaces. Each resembles a two-foot-long tugboat with a mechanized gripper arm. Cohen bought the robots to help him find an answer to a fundamental AI question: How does a hunk of hardware develop a mind?

"I look at how infants get minds by researching cognitive childhood behaviors. I try to develop similar theories that can be implemented into the [robot's] computer," he explains. "My goal is to get my robots to think like humans and to learn language. I've already got [them] learning very primitive activities and small words, like 'push.'"

The evolution of AI "is never going to go as fast as people would like because it's simply too hard," Cohen insists. "Things like speech and vision, which are easy for humans, are phenomenally difficult for computers to process." Nevertheless, his robots have "evolved" to the point where they can recognize objects in their environment by color, he says.

That sounds like a great step forward for researchers like Cohen. But, if science fiction has taught us anything, it's that the smarter a machine becomes, the more selfish and, ultimately, evil it grows, as well.

PHOTO BY JOHN BRENNER

"The question is, should we be trying to make our artificial intelligence programs like the human brain?" —Dr. Thomas Whalen, natural language interface scientist at the Communications Research Centre, Ottawa

Megalomaniacal computers have run amuck in movies like *2001: A Space Odyssey*, *Colossus: The Forbin Project* and the *Terminator* films and on television on *Star Trek*, *Doctor Who* and, of course, *The X-Files*. Yet AI experts like Whalen aren't too worried about having their computers turn homicidal in the near future.

"I wouldn't expect the possibility of artificially intelligent computers turning on humans for centuries," Whalen says. "Why is there the assumption that humans and robots would compete for the same resources? One must also consider the issue of whether being smarter is more adaptive in Darwinian terms. There are organisms like insects which are increasing in numbers as fast or faster than humankind. Insects can coexist with people, can't they? Computer brains are simply not powerful enough to turn on human beings."

They certainly are, however, in Tom Maddox's universe. Maddox, co-writer of *The X-Files*' "Kill Switch" episode, is also author of the science-fiction novel *Halo*, in which a computer system named Adelph acquires consciousness via interaction with humans. Only, unlike the malicious AI that runs rampant on the Internet in "Kill Switch," Adelph remains benevolent.

"With 'Kill Switch,' computer intelligence becomes an emergent phenomenon that evolves out of a sufficiently complex network—namely, the Internet," says Maddox. "Humans also derive their intelligence from a network that is their nervous system, connected at the front by the brain."

Though Maddox acknowledges that the malevolent-computer theme has grown a bit tired over the years, he thinks it is still a powerful means of expressing one of science fiction's central themes.

"One of the main things science fiction does is express our anxieties about change," he says. "Anything genuinely different is viewed as negative. And most people have superstitious feelings about computers, which are treated as magic machines on television and in movies. Some sci-fi writers aren't interested in writing about AI because they look at it as too magical. When the artificial intelligence is allowed to turn into a god, it becomes uninteresting. In reality, I personally don't see computers possessing artificial intelligence turning on humans because they're not competing with us for resources. It doesn't need to steal your land or your girlfriend."

Cohen is equally skeptical about any

human/microchip showdowns in the near future. "It will be a long time before computers deliberately go out of their way to harm people," he says. "Just imagine a toddler running the world—he might crash trains and wreak havoc just for the fun of it, but he wouldn't necessarily understand

COMPUTATIONAL HAZARD: Artificial intelligences wreak havoc in "Kill Switch" (above) and "Ghost in the Machine" (right)

that he was hurting people. There's no moral or common sense there, which is also true of the systems we're currently building. But imagine a machine with an adult's intellect running the world—it could do it responsibly, I would hope."

Whalen sees another reason not to fear the future. He admits that computer intelligence is increasing exponentially, but points out that—despite *Baywatch* and *The Jerry Springer Show*—humans are getting smarter, too. "Our human IQ has been going up thanks to things like increased specialization in the sciences, new research and proper nutrition," Whalen says. "Hopefully, we'll continue to get smarter faster than computers."

And therein lies Whalen's greatest fear—that artificial intelligence won't evolve and progress fast enough. "In our lifetime, we probably won't be able to point to a program and be able to say, 'Yes, it's intelligent.' Even if it were to progress, how do we know it won't be an alien intelligence? Will we be able to recognize it?"

Of course, there's one scenario that would make artificial intelligence hard not to recognise: A computer that flat-out tells you it's intelligent. Researchers are laying the groundwork for that now by improving the crude voice-recognition programs currently available. Unfortunately, these programs only work well when users talk slowly and succinctly, and the computer isn't expected to talk back at all. Yet human-computer conversations aren't too far off, according to Whalen.

"We're not very far away from having a computer which can converse naturally," says Whalen, who predicts that software vendors will have such products out on the shelves within a few years. "There are several different possibilities: You could have a system where you type the questions and get reasonable answers, or a system where you can ask fairly big and incomplete questions and get answers that will satisfy exactly what you're looking for. But there will remain a big gap between having something answer most questions and having something appear intelligent. The former is fairly easy. The latter is very difficult."

So difficult, in fact, that researchers like Cohen worry that artificial intelligence might not ever be possible, and that much of the R & D sunk into the field will have been in vain.

"It's possible that we'll find out that we just won't be able to understand how the mind works," Cohen says. "I honestly don't know if a computer can realise consciousness. When I look at what my robot experiences and I see its 40 sensors bouncing up and down, I know there are some physical correlates to its experience. But it still doesn't have the sensations that you and I experience. I ask myself constantly, 'What would it take for this robot to have that same sense of experience?' It's a fundamentally philosophical question, but then again, most of the good AI questions are." ●

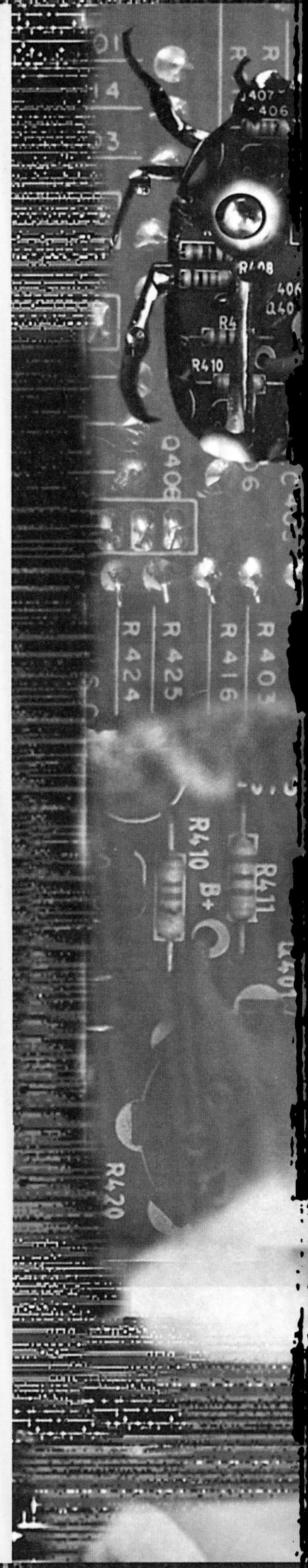

Fig.14
WASHINGTON
CAPE HATTERAS
ATLANTIC
OCEAN
Jacksonville
BAHAMAS
Tropic
La Habana
JAMAICA
Prince

Is the ***BERMUDA TRIANGLE*** *the doorway to another world – or just an epicentre for stormy weather?*

THE TWILIGHT ZONE

By Chandra Palermo

the year was 1945

The year was 1945. On a clear, sunny day, five pilots flew a routine mission in well-fuelled Navy Avenger bombers. Inexplicably, their compasses malfunctioned and they became lost at sea. The team, known as Flight 19, radioed for help, but just after the leader explained that things were beginning to look strange, the transmission was interrupted. With little warning, the planes disappeared, as did one of the aircraft in the search party sent to find them. No wreckage or survivors were ever discovered.

Flight 19 was historic for another reason: it almost single-handedly launched the legends about the area of ocean where the pilots vanished, the Bermuda Triangle.

Draw lines on a map from Florida to Puerto Rico, Puerto Rico to Bermuda and Bermuda back to Florida and you'll pinpoint one of the planet's most infamous hotspots for the disappearances of boats, planes and people, an area with such menacing monikers as the Devil's Triangle, Hoodoo Sea, Limbo of the Lost, Magic Rhombus, Port of Missing Ships, even the Triangle of Death.

During the last 100 years or so, more than 50 ships and 20 aircraft have vanished in the Triangle, according to information on the Naval Historical Center's website. The loss of as many as 1,000 lives has been attributed to the strange goings-on in the area. Paranormal devotees have cited everything from mischievous aliens to the sunken city of Atlantis as explanations for the disappearances. Even Columbus recorded seeing a "ball of light" in the area. But skeptics scoff at such silliness, saying that human error combined with tempestuous weather patterns are to blame. There is little proof to substantiate either claim.

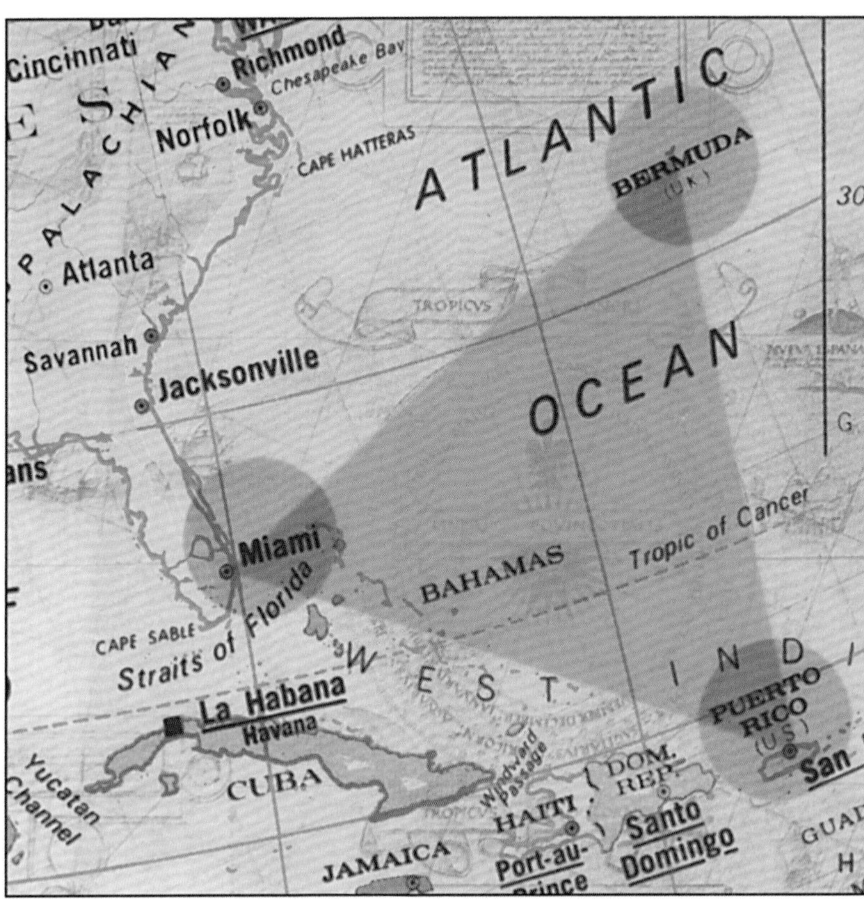

The first suggestions that something mysterious was happening in the Triangle came in 1950 in a short Associated Press dispatch written by E.V.W. Jones who, after stumbling across an abnormally high number of other disappearances in the area, hinted that Flight 19 suffered a curious fate. George X. Sand's 1952 article in *Fate* magazine, "Sea Mysteries at Our Back Door," reiterated his thoughts. But the name Bermuda Triangle wasn't coined until 1964 in an article written by Vincent Gaddis for *Argosy* magazine.

The major catalyst for debate came in 1974 when author Charles Berlitz plunged the theory of a paranormal malevolent force wreaking havoc in the Triangle into the mainstream by devoting an entire book to the subject. His book, *Bermuda Triangle*, quickly became a best-seller, garnering thousands of dedicated followers for its argument. But a sceptical tome, *The Bermuda Triangle Mystery – Solved by Larry Kusche,* soon followed, attempting to dispel what Kusche felt was the pure myth presented in theories like Berlitz's

"When I wrote my book, I started out thinking this thing was a mystery, but I collected all these articles and started putting all this information together, and I just noticed it was pretty slipshod," Kusche says, "So I started doing some intensive research on each of the incidents that at the time were mentioned. And every time I would do some research and find some legitimate information, I would find that there was a logical solution to these so-called mysteries. I found in virtually every case that the weather was involved."

The water surface tornados called waterspouts and sudden, harsh thunderstorms indigenous to the Triangle, Kusche says, can account for a majority of the disappearances, including that of Flight 19. And the facts Kusche found surrounding that particular mission paint a less than puzzling picture. Since the flight was a training mission, only instructor Lt. Charles Taylor had much experience, and he was reported to be suffering the effects of a hangover. The surface looked strange not only because Taylor was new to flying in the area and it was raining, but also because he thought he was flying directly over the Florida Keys when he and his men were actually heading farther out to sea. As for the search party plane that vanished, witnesses reported an explosion in the area where the plane was headed, and an oil slick was found near this spot. Planes of that type were known for faulty gas tanks.

As watertight as the explanation might seem, conspiracy-minded folks claim that too many of the answers are taken from naval records, which could easily be manipulated to hide the truth. "I always look at a 'cover-up' or a 'conspiracy' as the last resort of a sensationalist who really has no facts to back his so-called mystery," Kusche responds.

With no wreckage and no survivors to offer explanation, what really happened to Flight 19 is ripe for speculation. There are numerous other incidents occurring within the Bermuda Triangle with less conclusive explanations: As early as 1872, the Mary Celeste, a 103-foot ship, was found abandoned and floating with one lifeboat missing. In 1948, a commercial flight from San Juan to Miami vanished without a trace. No mystery is enticing enough for Kursche, who insists that there is a rational account for all the Triangle's strange activity. "According to the coast Guard and Lloyd's of London, this area is really no different than any other area," he says. "Lloyd's insures a lot of ships, and they don't charge any higher rates for anything going through there. People always talk about this tiny little area of the ocean, and in reality, a large number of the incidents they talk about as being mysterious happened nowhere near that area. The fact that they have to bring in the incidents that didn't even happen in that area shows they've got a weak argument."

The Navy and the Coast Guard are, not surprisingly, on Kusche's side. According to the Bermuda Triangle Fact Sheet prepared by the U.S. Coast Guard and the Naval Historical Center, the most practical theories "seem to be environmental and those citing human error." The sheet identifies the gulf stream, compass variance, sudden storms and a great number of inexperienced travellers as possible explanations for the disappearances and overtly dismisses any paranormal leanings: "The Coast Guard is not impressed with supernatural explanations of disasters at sea. It has been their experience that the combined forces of nature and unpredictability of mankind outdo even the most far-fetched science fiction many times each year."

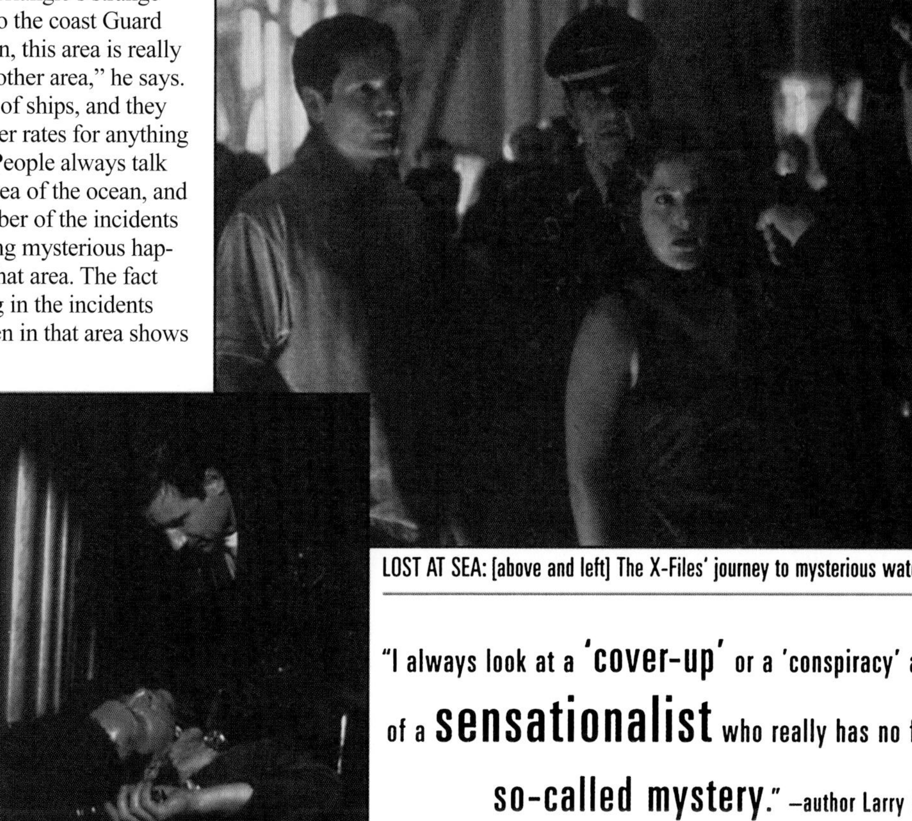

LOST AT SEA: [above and left] The X-Files' journey to mysterious waters, "Triangle"

"I always look at a 'cover-up' or a 'conspiracy' as the last resort of a sensationalist who really has no facts to back his so-called mystery." –author Larry Kusche

James Knickelbein, who maintains the Bermuda Triangle Home Page, wants to know why, if the Coast Guard so emphatically denies the existence of unexplained events in the Triangle, has it issued a fact sheet? "My theory is it's probably because of natural forces that humans don't understand right now," Knickelbein says. "There are scientists who have pretty much conceded that there are a lot of things about nature that they have no idea about, no understanding of whatsoever, and that area has a great amount of mystery behind that sort of thing."

No matter what really is the truth behind the Triangle, the area still generates an enormous amount of interest, Knickelbein says. "I've had 5,000 people [visit the Bermuda Triangle Home Page] since summer last year," he says. "I've had people from 74 countries visit. What amazes me is I get a lot of people from

Singapore, China and Australia. I only have 37 per cent that I can prove is from North America."

Many of those visitors don't doubt that something strange is afoot beneath the seas, and a large faction of these believers are UFO enthusiasts. Many suggest aliens actually come from oceanic depths and pre-existed man. Dr. David Jungelaus, author of *The City Beneath The Bermuda Triangle*, says he interacted with the aliens who live below the Triangle's ocean surface. "I went down into the Bermuda Triangle where there was a bubble city and was taken all around Neptune's Kingdom, which is what it was called," says Jungelaus, who has a PH. D in religious philosophy and now specializes in parapsychology.

"The reason the city was built was to preserve the knowledge of Atlantis," he continues. "In a way you can say it is a library in a sense because all their knowledge and all their technology and things are completely recorded and known. The people down there don't have contact with people on our planet. Very few come up to our planet because the vibrations are so much different. They are waiting for us to move into a more spiritual realm."

Jungelaus says the alien residents of Neptune's Kingdom often abduct Triangle travellers to examine, which accounts for many of the disappearances. He also espouses the gas hydrate theory, which is popular among some fringe scientists. The theory states that some areas of the water are less dense than others, causing boats to sink quickly.

The theory of the sunken city of Atlantis finding its final resting place beneath the Bermuda Triangle and affecting passing ships is championed, in some form or another, by many. In an article for the New Age-oriented site Spiritweb, Geoffrey Keyte explains the form most of the Atlantis theories resemble. "When Atlantis was destroyed, it sank to the very bottom of the ocean," Keyte writes. "While the ruined temples now play host to multitudinous underwater creatures, the great Atlantean fire-crystals that once provided so much of the tremendous power and energy that was found in Atlantis long ago still exist. And they are still emitting strong energy beams into the universe… From time to time, the force field emitted by these damaged Atlantean fire-crystals becomes very powerful, and any plane or ship coming within the influence of this force field disintegrates and is transformed into pure energy."

"I went down into the **Bermuda Triangle** where there was a **bubble city** and was taken all around **Neptune's Kingdom**." –Dr. David Jungclaus

What remains indisputable about the Bermuda Triangle is that it is, at the very least, a great source of entertaining tales. Skeptic Kusche says even he enjoys a good Triangle story, but he believes everyone should also want to know the truth about the area. "I get a little concerned that there are so many people who believe all this business just on the basis of a few things they've heard," Kusche explains. "I've had several people say, 'Oh, I was really disappointed when I read your book because I wanted it to be a mystery.'"

The real truth is we may never know what is behind the mystery surrounding the Triangle. Ships and planes have disappeared, but little evidence has been found to explain their fate. No diving expedition has combed the ocean floor searching for shipwreck debris or the ruins of Atlantis, as depths in the area abruptly drop to thousands of feet past the continental shelf a few miles out from the shore. In fact, the deepest point in the Atlantic Ocean, the approximately 30,100-feet deep Puerto Rico Trench, lies within the Bermuda Triangle. And no shipwrecked sailor has washed ashore to tell of surviving a terrible storm. Thus, the enigmatic Bermuda Triangle remains a mystery.

OTO COURTESY OF DAVID J

THE X FILES™

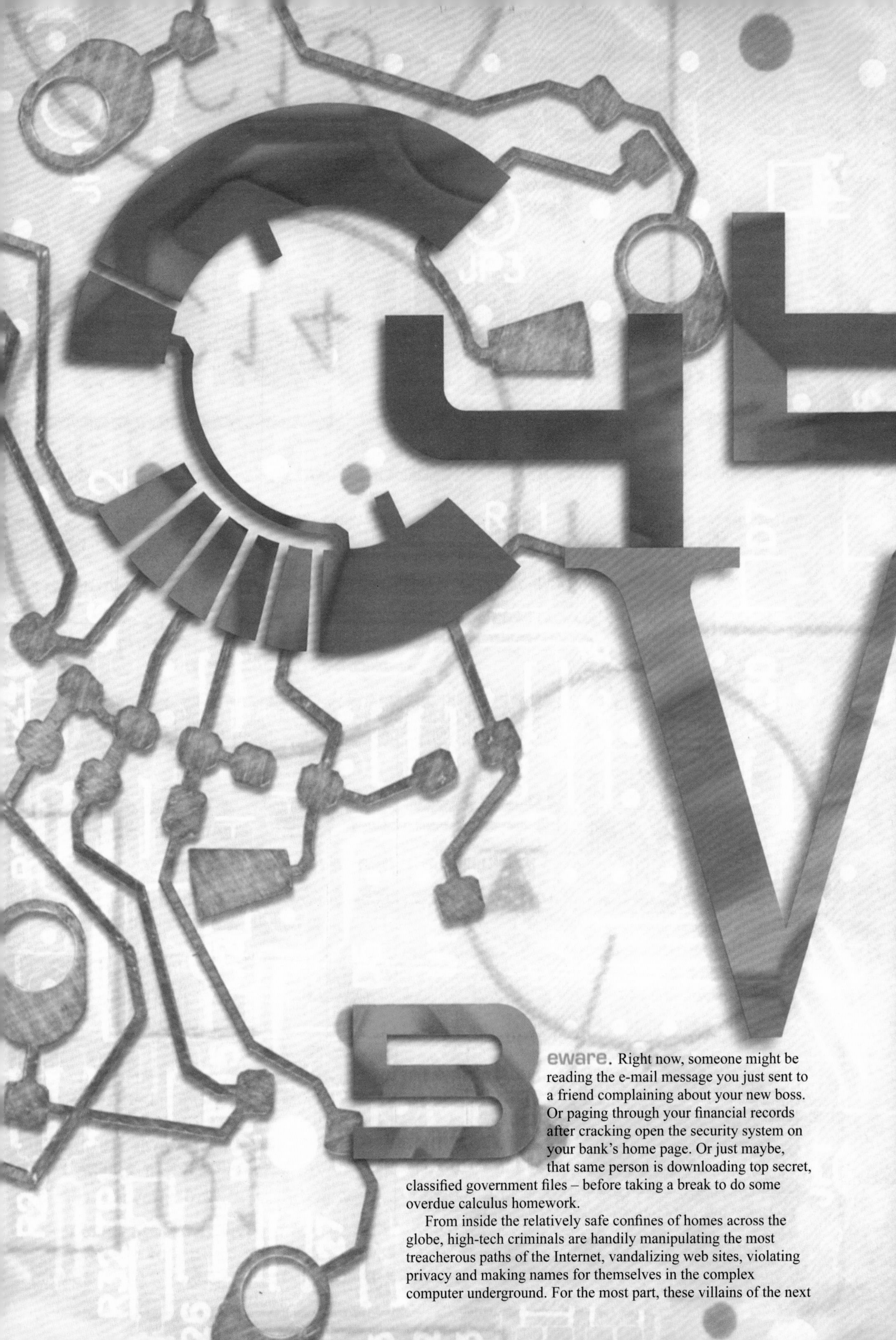

Beware. Right now, someone might be reading the e-mail message you just sent to a friend complaining about your new boss. Or paging through your financial records after cracking open the security system on your bank's home page. Or just maybe, that same person is downloading top secret, classified government files – before taking a break to do some overdue calculus homework.

From inside the relatively safe confines of homes across the globe, high-tech criminals are handily manipulating the most treacherous paths of the Internet, vandalizing web sites, violating privacy and making names for themselves in the complex computer underground. For the most part, these villains of the next

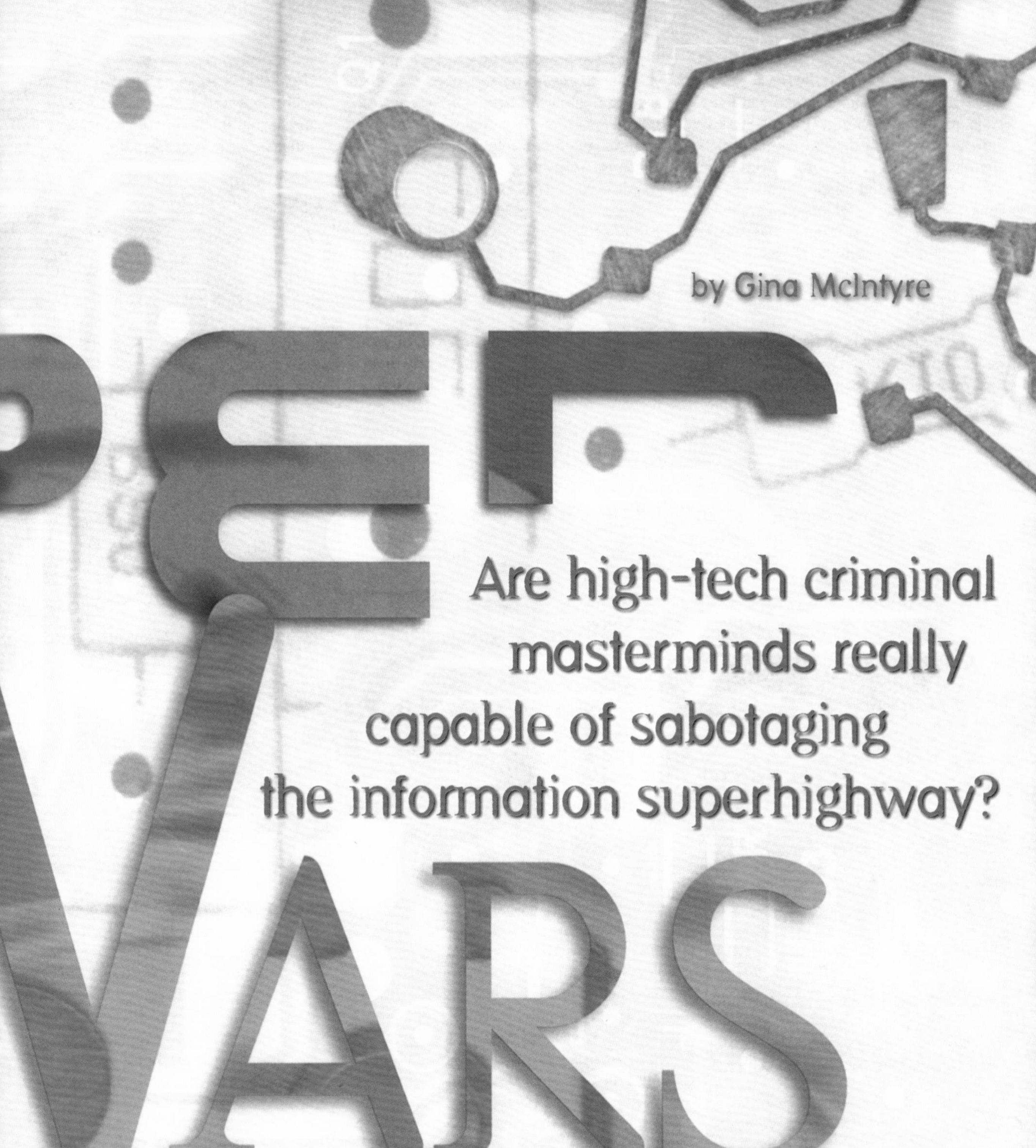

by Gina McIntyre
Are high-tech criminal masterminds really capable of sabotaging the information superhighway?
VARS

millennium are not career criminals; they are innocuous high school students who, by night, don the mantle of electronic mischief makers ready to sabotage our increasingly computer-dependent culture. They are computer hackers.

While many computer experts maintain that the majority of hackers pose no kind of real threat to private industry or the public at large, they have nevertheless caused a significant stir. Early this year, President Clinton announced a $1.46 billion plan to help the U.S. guard against computer attacks by developing improved methods of detecting hackers and recruiting more computer experts into the government's ranks. Some of the country's largest financial institutions are adopting vigilante stances against hackers – deface a web site and risk a visit from a baseball bat-wielding thug from First Financial U.S.A. And so-called super-hacker Kevin Mitnick, who was arrested four years ago and charged with accessing corporate software without permission and copying proprietary software, sits in a California jail, awaiting a trial that is expected to set a new precedent in the punishment of computer crime.

Although there are numerous cases of hackers causing system glitches, the notion of malicious outlaws looking to rob unsuspecting citizens and overthrow governments is exaggerated, explains Bruce Sterling, author of such cyber-friendly books as *Islands in the Net* and *The Hacker Crackdown: Law and Disorder on the Electronic Frontier*. Sterling says most hackers are brainy teens curious about technology, not vicious criminals.

"The typical hacker profile is a young white male,

suburban, [who has a] high SAT [score and is] mathematically gifted. His parents are undergoing some kind of marital strain and they buy him a computer to keep him occupied while they are carrying out their divorce. This is the absolute psychological breeding ground for electronic mischief," Sterling says. "[Hackers are] people who are going to break in and deface your web site and leave taunting messages or get rude on your system. It's basically a voyeur crime. It's like panty raiding – 'Boy I got in there and look, I've got some panties!" These are a different group from people who are career criminals and happen to have discovered computers and cell phones."

Computer underground expert Gordon Meyer has been following hacker culture since the early '80s and takes a similar line. "While some of what hackers do is, technically, illegal, it is not committed as a criminal act from which they reap profit," Meyer says. "It's a fine technicality I suppose, but it's important to keep context

and intent in mind. I believe the current 'hysteria' over computer criminals is the natural result of politicians, reporters and courts who don't understand technology, I don't believe they are dangerous at all. Unprotected computer systems, bad company policy and poor security [are] the real dangers, in my opinion. The courts, law enforcement and certainly the media have exploited hackers for their personal gain without having an even basic understanding of the culture or technology involved… Private citizens don't need to worry about hackers."

What drives hackers to break into systems is the same force that persuades other teens to venture into different sorts of trouble – the thrill of exploring the unknown. They hack their way into private systems looking for nothing more than bragging rights; often hackers will leave their codenames or private messages to prove that they made it into a supposedly protected area. In some cases, hackers might leave behind viruses or steal information, but the motive is always to demonstrate their electronic prowess, their power over technology.

A would-be hacker known as Dissident posted an essay titled "The Ethics of Hacking" on the Anti.Online web site offering a first-hand account of the allure of hacking: "A true hacker doesn't get into the system to kill everything or to sell what he gets to someone else. True hackers want to learn, or want to satisfy their curiosity, that's why they get into the system – to search around inside of a place they've never been, to explore all the little nooks and crannies of a world so unlike the boring cesspool we live in…"

Their pursuit of knowledge isn't always without serious consequences in the outside world, however. In 1997, a Massachusetts teen hacked his way into a Bell Atlantic computer system, causing a crash that disabled phone service to a nearby town and interrupted communication at the Worchester, Mass., airport for six hours; he became the first juvenile charged in federal court with computer hacking. One year later, an 18-year-old master hacker known as "The Analyzer" was arrested after he allegedly helped two California teens break into hundreds of US military and university computer sites. In January, the former leader of a hackers group call Virii, 21-year-old Sean Trifero, was sentenced to prison when he was convicted of tapping into five academic and commercial computing systems without permission, causing some $67,500 worth of damage, prosecutors claim. Members of Virii have been linked to break-ins at NASA and the Pentagon, among other agencies.

Jim Thomas, criminology professor at Dekalb, Ill.-based Northern Illinois University, maintains the Computer Underground Digest, an online newsletter/journal related to computer culture. Given the grave nature of such highly publicized cases – and the public's lack of real understanding about contemporary technology – Thomas says its only natural that hackers are considered armed with secret knowledge and dangerous. He, too, insists that the reality of the menace is often very different from the way in which it is perceived.

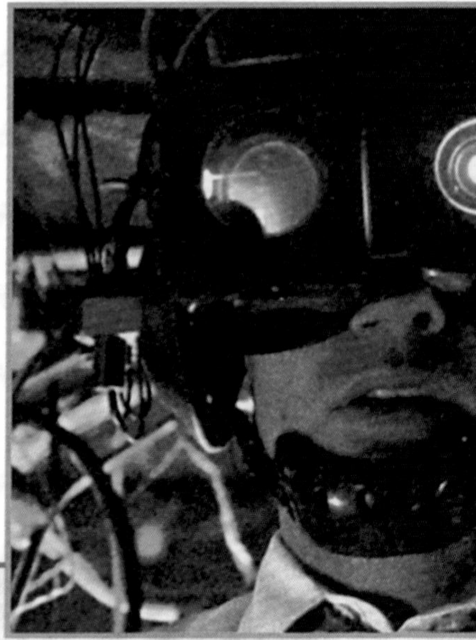

"A true hacker doesn't get into the system to kill everything or to sell what he gets to someone else. True hackers want to learn, or want to satisfy their curiosity, that's why they get into the system…"

—would-be hacker Dissident

"You have people out there with names like Legion of Doom and Marauding Killer," Thomas explains. "I think there's this whole kind of [image that] law enforcement might see legitimately as a real threat. If somebody's out there talking about bringing the state to its knees, well, they should raise an eyebrow. On the other hand, when you see that it's a 16-year-old kid who does this mostly just by posturing, well, maybe we're overreacting."

One of the most famous cases of the government overreacting involves a former Chicago prosecutor William Cook, who founded the now defunct Computer Fraud and Abuse Task Force. In 1990, Cook dispatched Secret Service agents to a Texas publishing house, Steve Jackson Games, to retrieve a confidential document he believed was stolen by hackers. The company was nearly forced out of business when its computers were seized, even though it had nothing to do with the disappearance of the missing document. A lawsuit was filed and the task force was disbanded. The event was the subject of Sterling's book *The Hacker Crackdown*.

"[Cook] was collecting data on this huge conspiracy, which he imagined to be soothing on the scale of Whitewater," Sterling explains. "He was tracking a criminal conspiracy of people who were mostly teenagers operating under pseudonyms, and doing things like phone fraud and credit card fraud. In particular, he was pursuing one document which he thought had something to do with the police 911 emergency system. He thought he was going to find this document inside those computers, and this would prove that [the company] was a nest of criminal conspirators. In point of fact, they had nothing much to do with anything. One of their employees was a running buddy with some hackers."

Still, a number of laws exist to curb the potential threat hackers pose. The Electronic Communications Act of 1986, an amended version of the "anti-wiretapping" act passed in response to Watergate, prohibited unauthorized eavesdropping and outlawed access to messages transmitted via computer, among other things. Ten years later, Congress passed the Database Investment and Intellectual Property Antipiracy Act to prevent tampering with databases. Also, the FBI and the Department of Justice created special details designed to curb computer crime.

While the number of technically-savvy criminals might be on the rise, Thomas says the time for alarm about teen hackers is past. "Certainly what we're calling the hacker heyday [has peaked]," he explains. "The learning curve now is so high that it's very hard to be a 16-year-old kid and start cold. Nowadays to be a good hacker you have to know a minimum of two computer languages. You have to have a sense of modems. Operating systems are more sophisticated. Security and the complexity of the software makes it more difficult to just pop in cold."

Sterling advises that concern about hackers be directed elsewhere. "If you spend all your time worrying about teenage guys, you really need to register and vote," he says. "Who's more dangerous – Bill Gates, young hacker boy, or Bill Gates, richest man on Earth? He's the same human being, it's just that he has billions of dollars and appears in front of the Senate. He still fights for his geek agenda, but he's a super-powerful mogul. A super-powerful mogul is someone you ought to pay more attention to than a young computer delinquent." ●

hollywood hackers

The undeniable mystique of breaking into top secret computer systems goes a long way toward explaining the appeal of hacking to technologically inclined teens. But roaming through unexplored matrixes makes for great cinematic entertainment, too.

Even before hacking was a full-fledged phenomenon, Hollywood presented audiences with the almost-too-believable scenario about a curious high school student breaking into a military central computer to begin World War III. The film was 1983's *War Games*, starring a baby-faced Matthew Broderick and Ally Sheedy, as the two teens who must find a way to end their game of Global Thermonucelear War before their electronic opponent can launch deadly missiles that will destroy the world.

On the heels of the film's success, a short-lived series called *Whiz Kids* showcased the adventures of a group of teen hackers who doubled as private eyes. The show lasted only one season, but computer hacking surfaced in movies ranging from *Real Genius* and *Weird Science* to *The Armchair Hacker*, which featured a villainous hacker who broke into homes as well as computers.

By the '90s, hackers were a staple in almost every science fiction or action movie — *Jurassic Park*, *GoldenEye* and *Mission: Impossible* all made reference to the phenomenon. 1995 saw two offerings devoted exclusively to the subject: *Hackers*, in which a group of young computer enthusiasts are framed by a career criminal, and *The Net* featuring Sandra Bullock as a computer afficianado who loses her identity when she becomes the target of a conspiracy. Three years later, cable network USA spawned a syndicated series of the same name from the premise.

HACK & CRACK: [Clockwise from top] WarGames, The Net, Hackers

More offerings are in the wings, including *Takedown*, starring Skeet Ulrich and Mitch Pileggi. Based on the story of computer hacker Kevin Mitnick, the film should arrive in cinemas soon. *G.M.*

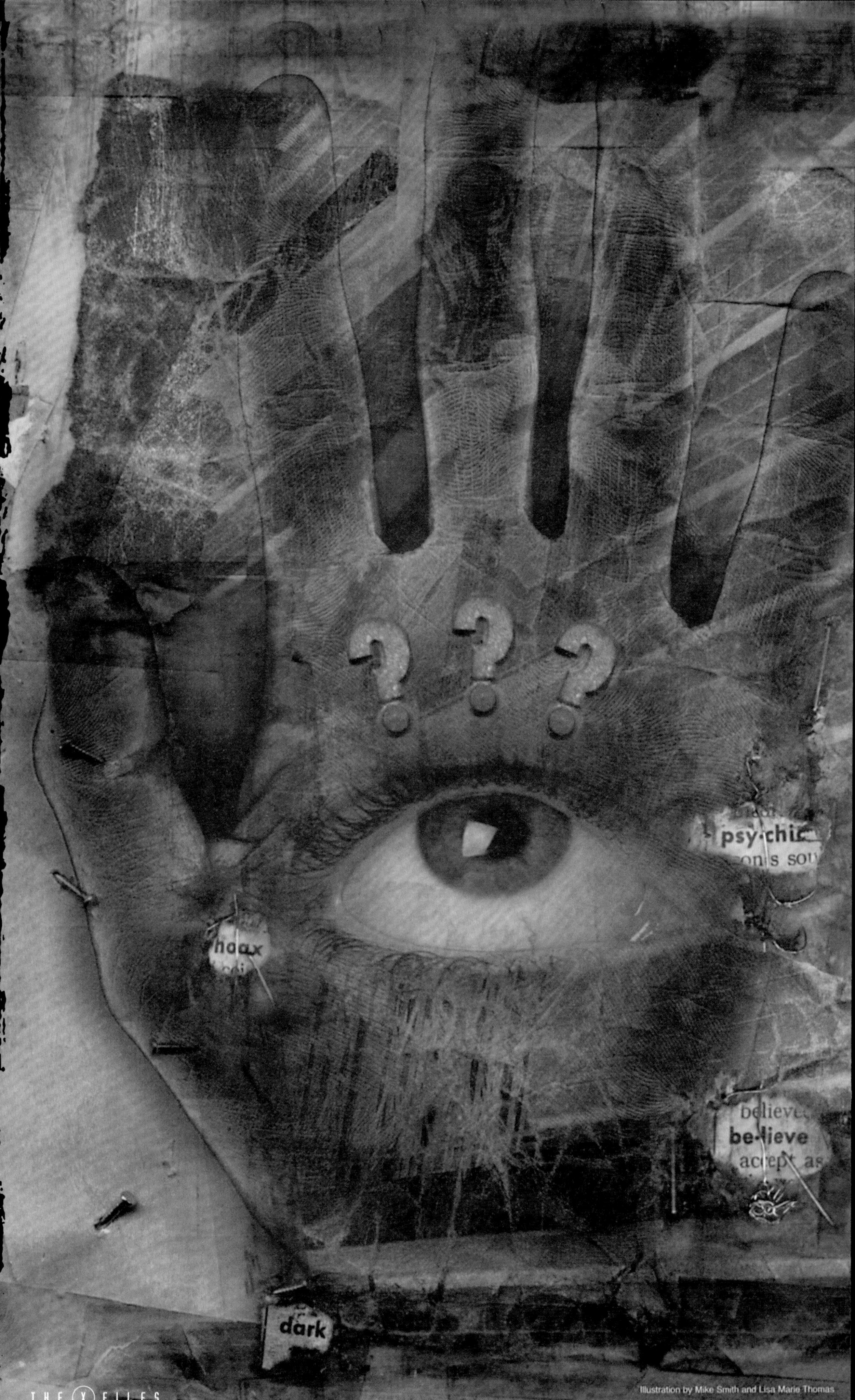

Illustration by Mike Smith and Lisa Marie Thomas

In an exclusive excerpt from The X-Files Book of the Unexplained Volume Two, Jane Goldman investigates law enforcement's psychic connection

False Prophets?

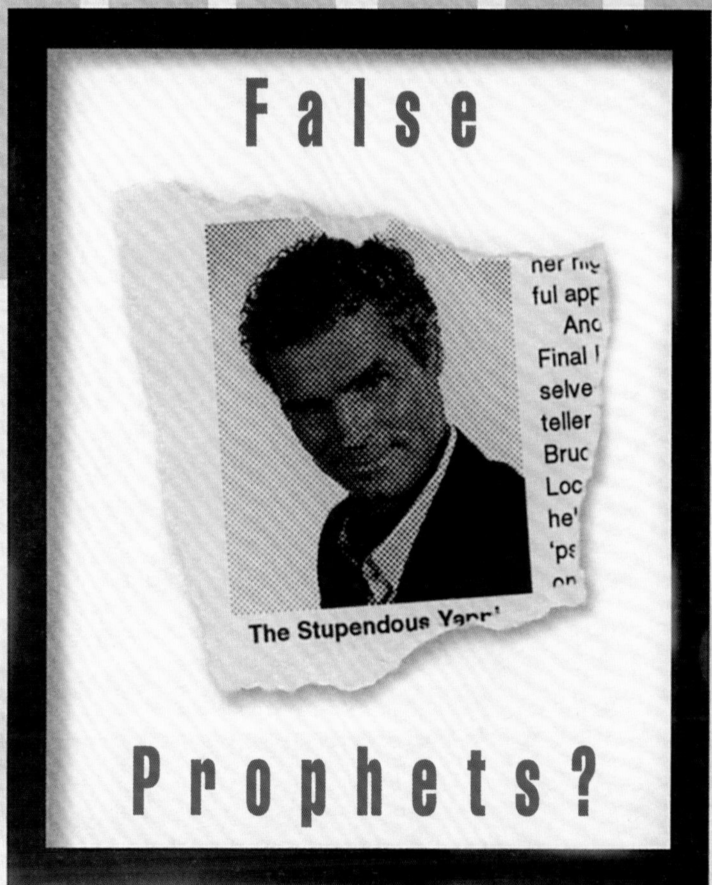

Information garnered by anomalous means has helped Mulder and Scully in their investigations several times. In Season One's outstanding "Beyond the Sea," a death row inmate's channeling abilities help lead the agents to a homicidal kidnapper. Two seasons later, in "Oubliette," a former kidnap victim finds herself inexplicably reliving the traumas of her abductor's latest victim. With Mulder's sympathy and trust, her nightmarish visions result in the successful apprehension of the perpetrator.

And in the exceptional "Clyde Bruckman's Final Repose," Mulder and Scully find themselves hunting a killer who is targeting fortune tellers with the help of reluctant psychic Clyde Bruckman, a depressive insurance salesman. Local law enforcement, meanwhile, enlists the help of the Stupendous Yappi, a flamboyant "psychic detective." The episode was the second written by Darin Morgan, following "Humbug."

"'Humbug' was a terrible experience for me," says Morgan. "I was very happy with the script, but then everyone freaked out like it was going to destroy the show. The network was terrified, saying it was a comedy and *The X-Files* is not a comedy, and the director was petrified. I didn't think I would ever come back to the show, but I survived, and it was very popular with the fans and then it was: 'We want you back.'"

"I looked at 'Humbug' again, then I watched 'Beyond the Sea,' which my brother [ex-staffer Glen Morgan] wrote, and which is still my favorite episode. And I thought if we could do an episode of that quality every week, this would be one of the greatest shows of all time. So I planned something much more serious. I said: 'I'm going to show everyone. I'm not going to have any jokes, it's going to be very serious, very depressing. I want this episode to be the most depressing thing ever.'

"In our research library we have this book with actual crime scene photos from homicide investigations. It used to be on my desk, and people would come in and they'd surf through it, and I'd warn them not to. I'd say, 'This is going to bother you for days,' and they'd ignore me, and then they'd come back afterwards and say, 'Man, I couldn't sleep, this was really disturbing.' And so I figured that if a psychic could know the future, theoretically he would be able to see everybody's eventual future, which is their deaths. You wouldn't be able to live with that. You'd go insane and you'd kill yourself."

For all his plans to write a sombre tale, Morgan was (to the delight of his fans) unable to suppress his unique humour. "Fortunately, the gruesomeness of the idea was sort of lost along the way," he admits. "But I think it was clear enough that the character had seen so many deaths that he was depressed all of his life."

The idea of psychic ability as a curse also influenced Morgan's creation of the killer. "I gave him some psychic ability but not enough to really figure anything out. In the script I called that character the Puppet because I just wanted the idea that his guy felt like a puppet. He could see his future and he wasn't in control of it."

It's a haunting notion, and one to which Morgan gave much thought. "I don't personally feel that things are predetermined, and yet, if I were to find out that they were, I wouldn't be shocked. I think it basically comes down to the feeling of: Who am I to say?"

As a writer, Morgan managed skillfully to stalk the middle ground by contrasting Bruckman, with his genuine gift/curse, with the Stupendous Yappi, a shameless charlatan. A voracious researcher, Morgan read dozens of books on psychics, [concentrating on] "psychic detectives"—people who claim to put their extra sense to good use by helping the police solve crimes.

His main source was a book called *Psychic Sleuths*, for which 11 researchers spent a year investigating well-known psychics. Reading it left Morgan's opinion on the subject profoundly changed. "You think maybe it's possible, or you don't really think about it. You go: 'They borrowed a psychic and he found a body...wow, that's weird.' Then if you start to look closer, look at specific examples, you go: 'Oh, it's so obvious that it's not.'

"They are wrong so much of the time, and they say things that are very general. I did so much research on that angle, and all it came down to was those few lines of Mulder's [dismissing psychic advice]. Charlatans don't irritate me, but I believe it's wrong. There's a difference between what Barnum did, which was a sense of: 'I'm fooling you and you've got to try to guess how,' as opposed to the psychic detectives who go, 'I can help you find your missing boy' when people are emotionally dis-

Peter
while

traught. Getting people's hopes up can be very harmful, I should think."

Many psychic sleuths are inveterate self-promoters. After all, it isn't just the media that hypes them. How many police agencies are eager to spread the word that a psychic with a mystic vision was able to crack a case they couldn't solve? And only successful psychic input gets reported. For every miraculous, spot-on psychic deduction, there are perhaps thousands of useless paranormally generated clues—placing the correct ones well into the realm of random chance.

Nonetheless, there have been cases through the years in which a psychic has provided such detailed and accurate information that even the most determined skeptic would have to reconsider. Arthur Lyons and Marcello Truzzi claim to have begun researching their book on psychic detectives, *The Blue Sense*, with a healthy dose of cynicism. Truzzi was even a member of a prominent skeptics' association. Yet both authors ended up championing some of the people detailed therein.

So let's meet some of the men and women of the Paranormal Patrol.

GERARD CROISET

The reputation of Gerard Croiset, whose specialty was locating missing persons—dead and alive—rests on his good fortune in attracting a supporter with impeccable academic credentials: Professor William Tenhaeff, a lecturer in parapsychology at Urecht University. Croiset submitted himself to Tenhaeff in 1956 for long-term study, and when he died in 1980 it was with the sobriquet "world's most tested psychic."

For this reason, it is hard to contest Croiset's record. In several instances, he was able either to find a missing person or predict when and where the person—or the body—would be discovered (he himself claimed an 80 percent success rate in accidental disappearances).

Croiset began his career, and made his fortune, as a psychic healer. He also claimed precognition as one of his gifts, and would perform a stunt devised by Tenhaeff in which he would "project into the future," predicting details about an apparently random person who would be sitting in a specific chair a week or so hence.

Psychic Gerard Croiset made his fortune as a psychic healer.

Commendations: Besides being one of the few psychics to submit to "scientific" testing, Croiset would accept no money for his body-locating services (although his fame in this field certainly boosted his considerable income from psychic healing). His "hit ratio" of located persons appears to exceed chance.

Complaints: Collusion? Professor Tenhaeff had as much to gain from supporting Croiset as Croiset had from Tenhaeff's endorsement. And the "chair test," with its flamboyant showmanship and many opportunities for cheating, seems more like a magic trick than a demonstration of genuine clairvoyance.

PETER HURKOS

Hurkos, a Dutchman like Croiset, craved and cultivated fame, along with an eccentric mystique. He tried to insinuate himself into many notorious cases, including that of the Boston Strangler (for which he fingered the wrong man, yet still claimed credit for helping with the investigation) and the Tate-LaBianca murders, for which he came nowhere close to describing the Manson Family and even misidentified the victims. He was also under the delusion that he had solved the murder of a priest in Amsterdam and had received a letter of commendation from the Pope—neither of which ever happened. Nonetheless, his claims were rarely disputed, and, self-propelled, he rode to fame on the airwaves of Europe and the U.S.A.

Hurkos, born Pieter van der Hurk in 1911, supposedly gained his powers after a fall from a ladder while painting Nazi barracks in the Hague during World War II. Although he claimed many powers, his speciality was psychometry: divining details through touching appropriate objects. Regardless of his dubious gifts, Hurkos knew instinctively that the media would gladly

...edly gained his powers after a fall from a ladder ...barracks in the Hague during World War II

report a clever hoax as true in order to feed the public appetite for such stories, and he clearly had a masterful grasp of publicity.
Commendations: He clearly had what the Yiddish call "chutzpah", or what the Spanish call "los cojones grandes."
Complaints: He was undoubtedly a fake.

NOREEN RENIER

Noreen Renier stakes her fame on two "forecasts" she issued in 1981. According to her P.R. machine, she successfully predicted both John Hinckley's shooting of Ronald Reagan and the assassination of Egyptian president Anwar Sadat. On the heels of those triumphs, the FBI's former head of profiling, Robert Ressler, invited her to speak about psychic detection at the FBI academy at Quantico. In her profession, it doesn't get any better than that.

So why quibble and point out that she had earlier predicted that Jimmy Carter would be re-elected in 1980 and then assassinated on the White House lawn, and that his vice president, Walter Mondale, would commit suicide? Or that in fact she had indicated that Reagan, not Sadat, would be killed by machine-gun fire in the autumn of 1981. ('See, I knew it would be a president," she reportedly said.)

Renier claims that she relives crimes psychometrically, suffering as the victim suffered, by holding objects associated with the deed. Ressler confirms that she has worked on cases for the FBI. "I invited her to the Academy. I work with her off and on. I had her at the Academy as a lecturer to my classes, [and] I used her in a couple of cases, and the Bureau went bonkers—they said, 'You're using psychics and that's voodoo and witchcraft.'"

The assassination attempt on President Reagan was foreseen by Noreen Renier

Ressler describes the first time he watched Renier's technique. "I met Noreen back in the '70s at a conference on parapsychology down in southern Virginia," he says. "She came up and did her little routine. People put these metal objects in envelopes and sent them down front and put an identifying initial on it, then she'd pick it up and say, "Oh, let's see, this guy is a big tall guy, and he's young, robust, well built." That described most of the cops in the room. "And he likes speed and excitement." I thought, most cops do. Now she says he had an operation, he has a scar on the back of his left leg, he's single. Then she says he's got black hair, no, he's got white hair, no, he's got black hair, no, white hair—I don't understand this.

"Pretty soon a guy steps up. He's a young guy, tall, muscular, big chest and shoulders. He says, 'I have a motorcycle, I have a Corvette, I like speed and I drive like a maniac even though I'm a cop.' He fits the general pattern.

"He had a baseball cap on. He had jet black hair. She says, 'Well, I said you had black hair. I guess I was right.' He takes his hat off: He's got a white lock right up the center of his hair."
Commendations: Has impressed many people in the media and law enforcement. Speaking at Quantico and working with the FBI was a considerable coup.
Complaints: Has exaggerated or misrepresented cases she has predicted or solved. Makes numerous appearances on vacuous daytime TV shows.

NELLA JONES

Probably no case ever thrust psychic detection into the spotlight as intensely as that of the Yorkshire Ripper. July of 1979 saw a tabloid frenzy of psychic predictions and sketches. Frustrated police brought in a stream of psychics and followed up on countless dead-end clues. Weighting in with her own vision of the killer—by far the closest that anyone came to describing Peter Sutcliffe, who was arrested in 1981—was Nella Jones.

Nella told a tabloid journalist that the Ripper was a transvestite who also donned priestly vestments now and then. This was incorrect. But she said that his name was Peter, and that he lived in a large house, number six on the street, on an elevated site in Bradford, Yorkshire. She said he was truck driver, and that the cab of this truck was emblazoned with the company's name, which began with the letter C. She also said he would kill again on November 17, 1979. All of this was true.

Until recently, she was called upon regularly by Scotland Yard. And although it is difficult to confirm whether her information has ever conclusively solved a crime, she has made a large number of accurate declarations. She says she has worked on 150 cases and [claims that] "I've never been wrong yet, love, not yet."

"It started in 1970 or 1971," recalls Nella, "with the big Vermeer [painting] robbery from Kenwood House [a museum in London]. I was watching the television news, and they were talking about this painting [and] I thought: They won't find it, because they are looking in the wrong place. I sat down and drew a map, and put a cross there and a cross there, and I rang up. I tried to explain that I was clairvoyant. Ten minutes later, the phone went again: 'Mrs. Jones, can you come up and help us?' So I took them to Kenwood House."

There, at the crosses on Nella's map, the police found the frame and the alarm system from the painting. "I was taken to Superintendent Arthur Pike. His first words—I shall never forget them as long as I live—were, 'Well done, Nella. When did you put them there?' I said, 'Typical copper—I go out of me way to help you, and this is all you can say.'"

Nella went on to describe a cemetery where she said the painting was hidden. The police thought it sounded like nearby Highgate, but the ensuing search proved fruitless. "They still thought I'd done it. Arthur Pike said afterwards that he was on the point of arresting me twice. Where did they find the picture? In the cemetery—the next one down from Highgate. I would have liked some of the reward money I was entitled to. They had a reward up for the painting. I didn't get a penny."

(In fact, the painting had been stolen by the IRA, who threatened to burn it on St. Patrick's Day. The cemetery they had hidden it in was in the City of London—more than ten miles from Highgate—and it was found by a policeman from another force.)

Nella once submitted to a test conducted by James Randi in which she examined several items, one of which had been used in a gruesome crime. "Nella failed miserably," says Randi. "She gave totally wrong histories and then made all kinds of excuses: 'Well, if you want to test it, this isn't the correct way.' The correct way is to make her look good."

"They'll never get it to work under scientific conditions," says Nella. "It's got to be absolutely free, absolutely natural. The minute you start putting labels on it, it doesn't happen."

Randi is unimpressed. "She gave all kinds of horrendous histories for objects that had been taken directly off the assembly line with plastic gloves and had never been touched by anybody who even had an evil thought. And when she came upon the fireman's ax that had actually been used not only to murder two people in bed, but also to chop their bodies into little pieces, she said this was used to force entry into a room. I think you'd call that missing the

...ently, Nella Jones was called upon ...y by Scotland Yard.

point somewhat. It was totally miserable failure. But the audience was on her side. There are so many people who believe her, and media people dote on her because she's a good story. Nella Jones fails? Well, that's a non-story."

Commendations: Good calls on numerous cases. Great call on the Ripper case, but it did not contribute to his capture. Scotland Yard once sent Nella an official letter of commendation.

Complaints: Failed Randi's test. Openly bitter about the lack of financial reward in psychic detection.

One problem seems to be that everyone debates whether or not psychic detectives really are psychic—forgetting the more important question of whether they really are detectives. And the answer, for now, seems to be negative. The researchers of *Psychic Sleuths* were unable to find a single case that could not have been solved without the "assistance" provided by a psychic.

Yet Robert Ressler remarks that after observing the FBI Behavioral Science Unit at work, Noreen Renier informed him that the most talented criminal profilers were those who had some psychic ability.

"I don't disagree, you know," Ressler offers. "I don't particularly agree. I'm open-minded." ●

SEARCHING FOR THE TRUTH

While Jane Goldman's beliefs were put to the test during her research for both volumes of *The X-Files Book of the Unexplained*, the author feels she has managed to find a happy medium between science and faith.

"I think I'm much more of a middle-ground sort of person," Goldman says from her home in London. "What I like about the series is, as it has progressed, Mulder and Scully both reflect that it's really hard to be firmly in one corner."

Goldman, a prolific writer of books and magazine articles, says she was captivated by *The X-Files* at the beginning of the first season and knew early on that she wanted to write a book that would delve into the historical inspirations for each episode. Since then, she has researched *X-Files*-ish phenomenon like reincarnation, feral humans, voodoo and various physical anomalies.

"When I interviewed the writers [from the series], one of the things I really wanted to know was what provided the inspiration for each episode," Goldman says. Based on the writers' input, Goldman delved into months of in-depth research: "I had to [do that] because there are so many different subjects and things touched on as minor points in the show, as well as in the topics covered in the main storyline."

The research, which consisted of interviewing countless scientists, paranormal experts and investigators, was exciting particularly because Goldman says it made her re-evaluate her own beliefs.

"I think I've been through so many different changes of mind while I was doing it," she explains. "It depends so much on who you speak to—there are so many interesting people, and some of them have such strong arguments. When I got off the phone with one of the biggest skeptics in Europe, I was feeling very [cynical]. But then you do come across some strange things that we don't yet understand. I sort of wound up somewhere in the middle, even though I veered violently from side to side for a bit."

The second *Book of the Unexplained* covers the series through Season Three and was released late last year. Goldman, who cites "Beyond the Sea" and "Clyde Bruckman's Final Repose" as her favorite episodes, is not sure whether she will write another *Book of the Unexplained*, but she does say that she is impressed by show's fourth season.

"I think the show is as strong as ever," Goldman says. "It's tempting [to write a third volume]. I'm really enjoying Season Four, and I'm finding it hard to watch without thinking, 'Hmmmm, another volume would be really interesting.' I never say never."

—Kristin Kloberdanz

THE X-FILES BOOK OF THE UNEXPLAINED Vol 2 is published by Simon & Schuster at £17.99. To order a copy (p & p free within the mainland UK) please call 01624 675 137.

THE X FILES

10 Best teasers

By Kate Anderson

The object of a pre-credits sequence is to a reel a viewer in hook, line and sinker. Teasers are designed to **keep you glued** to your television for the next 55 minutes. Not surprisingly, after nine seasons, The X-Files has an abundance of memorable teasers. Some are **shocking**, some are surprising, and some are **downright scary.** But they all have one thing in common - they keep you watching. They say first impressions last, well this is our countdown of the ten best...

10 "Bad Blood" (season five)

WHAT HAPPENS: A man (whom we soon discover to be Mulder) chases a teenage boy through a wood. The teenager cries out for help but suddenly stumbles and falls to the ground. After a brief struggle, Mulder plunges a wooden stake into the boy's chest. When a slightly out-of-breath Agent Scully arrives on the scene, Mulder draws her attention to the boy's vampire fangs. But they turn out to be plastic! "Oh shi...!"
WHY IT WORKS: Largely because it's so funny. It's a classic chase scene with a surprising twist; the false fangs are a hoot.

"The post-Modern prometheus" (season five) 9

WHAT HAPPENS: Shaineh Berkowitz sits alone watching *The Jerry Springer Show*. She fails to notice a canvas sheet being draped over her window. In her kitchen someone is burning something on her stove. Pretty soon, smoke fills the house. Suddenly, the door to Shaineh's room slowly opens to reveal a horribly disfigured face. Outside, the house is completely covered by a large striped tent.
WHY IT WORKS: Because it's so quirky – even by *X-Files* standards. Filmed in black and white and accompanied by a Cher soundtrack, *The X-Files* continues to break new grounds in television. In short, it's visually stunning and a lot of fun.

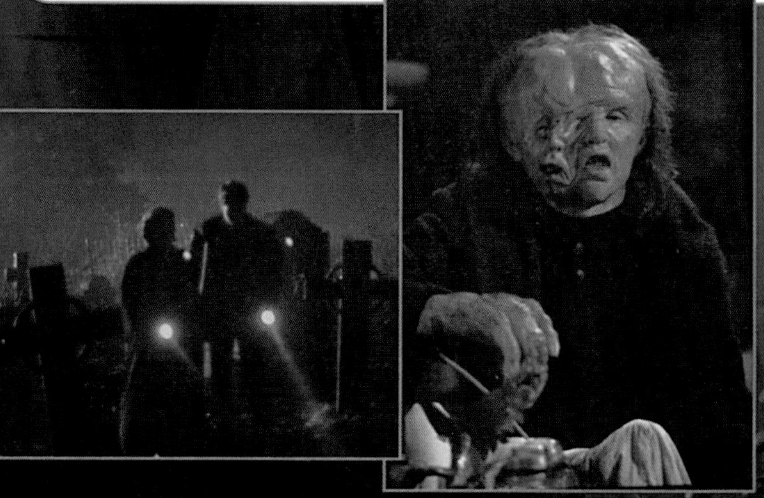

"Jose Chung's 'From Outer Space'" (Season Three) 8

WHAT HAPPENS: A couple of teenagers on their first date are out driving. Suddenly their car stalls and a bright light shines down from above – it's a spaceship! The teenagers pass out and then two grey aliens try to drag their bodies towards their ship. But then another spaceship arrives and a huge ugly growling alien interrupts them.

WHY IT WORKS: A fantastically bizarre teaser from an episode that from beginning to end intentionally makes fun of everything *The X-Files* is about. A show that doesn't take itself seriously is definitely at the top of its game. And this pre-title sequence is a mouth-watering taster of what's to come.

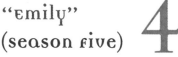

"Our Town" (Season Two) 7

WHAT HAPPENS: A car comes to a halt on a lonely highway. A young woman exits the car and runs off into the woods. The other passenger, a man, follows her. But the girl disappears. Lost and alone, he loses his footing and falls to the ground. When he stands up he's confronted by a wood full of strange lights, and a man in a scary tribal mask holding an axe. The man screams as the axe blade comes down...

WHY IT WORKS: Because it's so scary! Anyone who has watched *The Blair Witch Project* knows that no one in their right mind goes into a wood at night, particularly on their own! This is one of those shouting-at-the-TV-moments we all love!

"The Calusari" (Season Two) 6

WHAT HAPPENS: At a park, an unseen presence unhooks a toddler from his childproof halter. The child follows a floating helium balloon, which appears to be pulled along by the same unseen presence. The boy is led onto the park's railway track, just as a miniature train closes in on him.

WHY IT WORKS: It's a deeply disturbing teaser sequence. There's no blood or gore and something as innocent as a balloon is used to entice the little boy. What you see is what you get, and this is a classic example of suggestive horror being more effective than any gory revelation.

"The End" (Season Five) 5

WHAT HAPPENS: A packed audience watches as a young boy and a Russian grand master play chess. On a catwalk above a balcony, a man opens a suitcase and pulls out a sniper's rifle. Just as the boy moves to make his checkmate, the shooter fires… and a bullet rips into the Russian, killing him instantly – and accidentally.

WHY IT WORKS: Wow! Where did that come from? One minute we're watching a game of chess, the next witnessing a murder. The boy being the target was something of an unexpected move. We have to stay tuned to find out why.

"Emily" (Season Five) 4

WHAT HAPPENS: We see a desert sandstorm and through the blinding gusts walks a barefoot Dana Scully wearing a flowing black dress. We can hear her thoughts as she falls to her knees and reaches for something in the sand: a gold cross. She picks it up and stares at it. Slowly the color drains from her face and hair, as she turns into sand, dissolving into the storm.

WHY IT WORKS: A profound and hauntingly beautiful moment, this dream sequence succeeds on every level to make you feel the weight of Scully's loss.

"colony" (season two) 3

WHAT HAPPENS: We hear Mulder talking about his sister's abduction. Then a bright light in the sky gradually gets closer – it's a helicopter. Then we see Mulder on a stretcher; clearly barely alive, he is rushed into a military hospital's emergency room suffering from extreme hypothermia. They put Mulder into a frostbite tank. Then Scully bursts in. She tells the E.R. doctor that Mulder will die if they don't get him out of the tank – the cold is the only thing keeping him alive!
WHY IT WORKS: A refreshing way to keep the show inventive by telling the story in flashback. The adrenaline-filled teaser is reminiscent of an episode of *ER* and it packs a powerful punch.

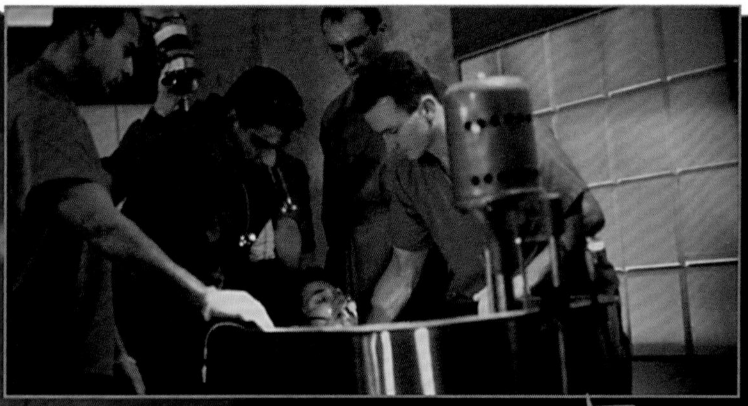

"memento mori" (season four) 2

WHAT HAPPENS: We hear Scully's voice and at the end of a long tunnel, we can see a small rectangle of light. As we get closer towards the light, we find Scully dressed in a hospital gown. She is studying a MRI film of a skull. A small dark mass is clearly visible on the film.
WHY IT WORKS: An ambitious trailer attached to an equally ambitious episode. Although not the first time *The X-Files* has used a dialogue-heavy teaser sequence, it's never been quite so exquisitely written as it is here.

"ice" (season one) I

WHAT HAPPENS: A snowstorm ravages a remote installation base. Inside, everywhere is a mess and there's a dead body lying on the floor. Another man appears; he's wounded and clutches a gun. He sits down in front of a video camera. He barely has time to record his message when another man jumps him from behind. Their violent confrontation ends with both men pointing guns at each other – then at their own heads. Outside, we hear two shots ring out.
WHY IT WORKS: This opening sequence is so claustrophobic it's undoubtedly one of the show's most tense and dramatic moments ever. Nine seasons down the line, it remains just as unforgettable as it did first time around.

...And let's not forget these 10 just bubbling under...

"Squeeze" – George Usher has his liver ripped out.

"Beyond the Sea" – Scully's dad dies and Dana has a vision.

"Talitha Cumi" – a man goes a little nuts in a fast food restaurant.

"Little Green Men" – cool Mulder voiceover.

"Nisei" – Japanese doctors gunned down during an alien autopsy – or maybe not.

"Terms of Endearment" – women being impregnated by an evil demon – but with a twist.

"DeadAlive" – Mulder's funeral... sob.

"Roadrunners" – probably the most violent teaser – *ever*.

"Pilot" – how it all began.

"Patient X" – faceless aliens and people set on fire.

EPISODE: 7x14

ORELL PEATTIE

"Theef"

A COUPLE OF years back, the uncertainty of whether or not Season Seven would happen may have been sheer torture for X-philes, but it turned out to be beneficial for actor Billy Drago. He might not have played Appalachian voodoo man Orell Peattie in Season Seven's "Theef" otherwise.

"Once it became clear at the end of [Season Six] that they were unsure how much longer they'd be running, they said, 'We've got a wish list of people we always wanted to do an episode with but never had the opportunity. Just in case the show's finishing, let's try getting these people on,'" Drago explains.

Drago's relationship with co-executive producer and director Kim Manners placed him on said wish list seasons ago. Manners directed Drago in the series *The Adventures of Brisco County Jr.*, and since its cancellation had been looking to find Drago a guest spot on *The X-Files*. The show's shooting schedule, however, never seemed to mesh with Drago's chaotic film work.

"I do a lot of films overseas and a couple times they called and said, 'We think we got one,'" Drago says. "And I'd say, 'Darn, I'm leaving for Russia a week from Monday, so I don't think that's going to work.' This time everything worked out perfectly, which I was very happy about."

Unbeknownst to Manners or anyone else, Drago was well versed in the folk magic and medicine Peattie practices in "Theef." "I have some cousins and aunts from one particular branch of my family that live in the Ozarks and down in the Appalachian Hills," he says. "As a child, my parents and I would go visit them and voodoo is fairly prevalent in the area. It's so insulated and rural that there aren't many modern medical facilities there. If you get sick, you're treated with folk medicine. The home remedies and all that come from the people who settled there, so a lot of that tradition remains."

The chant Drago used in "Theef" is actually used by modern voodoo practitioners for cursing and healing. It was so authentic, he blames it for causing him back pain throughout the shoot. "We're doing that scene with the landlady who has the back problems, and during one of the set-ups, I started to sit down and my back went out," he says. "For the rest of the show, I was going to the acupuncturist at night. That's what we get for using real dolls that they bought at a magical shop and a real chant by an actor who grew up in that area."—*Josh Schollmeyer*

BILLY DRAGO

ALSO KNOWN AS:

1999-'00: "Barbas" in *Charmed*
1997: "Gallindo" in *Assault on Devil's Island*
1993: "John Bly" in *The Adventures of Brisco County Jr.*
1986: "Rat" in *North and South II*

1999: "The Dog Catcher" in *Soccer Dog: The Movie*
1997: "Mannix" in *Convict 762*
1997: "Keith" in *A Doll in the Dark*
1993: "Danny Bench" in *Cyborg 2: Glass Shadows*

A KIND OF

BY JOSH SCHOLLMEYER

Though the mere mention of hexcraft conjures images of goofer dust and spell books, modern-day practitioners focus on cures, not curses. We inestigate the truth behind season seven's "Theef".

F

AGIC

When Silver RavenWolf cuts herself, she never reaches for a bandage – not when she can stop the flow of blood on her own.

"It's very easy," RavenWolf says. "It's a chant, and you just say it over and over and over again while you concentrate. The trick is you have to be able to visualise that there is no blood flowing. That's all there is to it. You just close your eyes and do it. It does work, and the more you do it, the better you get. That's the other thing – it takes practice. But then again, none of this is really magic the way people understand Hollywood magic, even though it's called that. This is really the incredible power of the mind, and how someone perceives the world around them and what they believe in, which takes you back inside your own head."

RavenWolf is a hexcraft practitioner, and staunching blood flow is just one of many uses of the folk magick. Although urban legend would have the general populace believe it to be some form of malevolent sorcery, hexcraft, or pow-wow as it is locally known in Central Pennsylvania, has less insidious origins and applications.

Isolated from the rest of the colonies, the German immigrants who settled Pennsylvania in the late 17th century practiced hexcraft to treat ailments, induce a plentiful harvest, promote animal husbandry and, yes, cast hexes. Every family used it, and each of their nightstands contained a copy of John George Hohman's *The Long Lost Friend*, a book of hexcraft remedies such as, "To cure whooping cough, thrust the afflicted three times through a blackberry bush."

Today's hexcraft, though still certainly outside the bounds of conventional science, is not as embedded in superstition. The form RavenWolf and her contemporaries practice is more "modernised." Since writing the book *Hexcraft: Dutch Country Pow-Wow Magick* five years ago, RavenWolf has used a combination of hypnotherapy and pow-wow chants to treat sicknesses ranging from the common cold to cancer. "What we've discovered is for standard things like colds, flus, minor infections and teeth extractions, the healing process is actually faster by using the pow-wowing," RavenWolf says. "However, you could also pray, and, if you're focused, it could work faster, too. A lot of this has to do with the psychology of the human mind. It's not woo-woo."

HEX APPEAL: [right] Silver RavenWolf; [below and opposite page] scenes from Season Seven's "Theef"

Especially with cancer patients, RavenWolf requires certain criteria be met before she is willing to attempt treatment. First, the client must be open-minded and a fighter. Secondly, in addition to the hypnotherapy and pow-wow, the client must be undergoing treatment from a licensed physiciar "Most of those today who practice [pow-wow] d believe you go see a physician and then you go to the pow-wow," RavenWolf says. "You do both You just don't pick one and hope for the best. You do everything you possibly can."

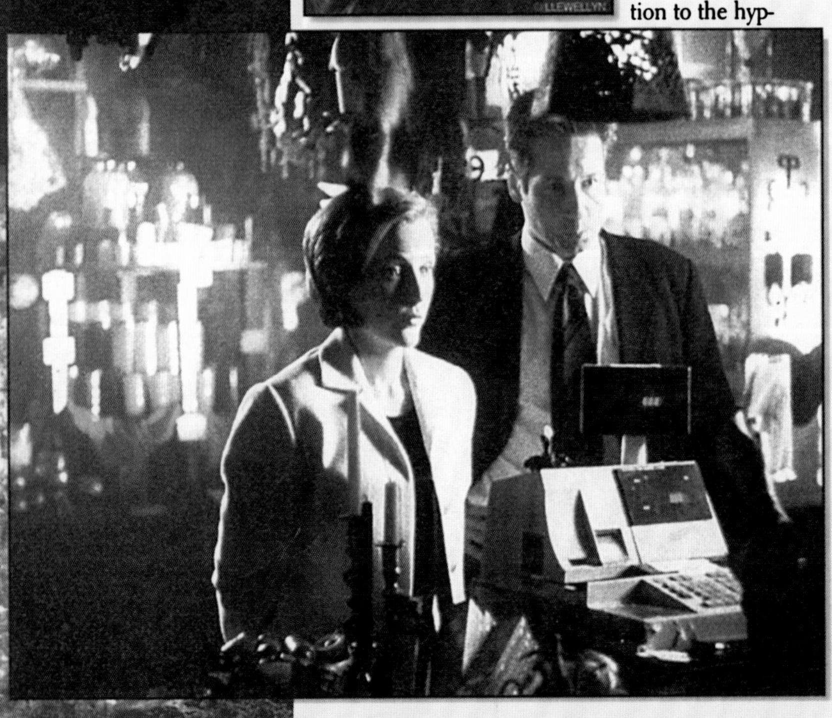

RavenWolf begins her therapy by speaking softly about a safe place in an attempt to lull clients into the semi-conscious alpha state. Once there, she instructs them to visualise something to represent their tumours – often, this is a large dragon. She then asks them to continually shrink the dragon until it disappea The pow-wow consists of a healing chant repea ed three times while the client is in the alpha state. When brought back to true consciousne people are surprised at the session's normality. "It's funny because the first time you bring the out, they go, 'That's it?'" And I'm like, 'Yeah, that's it,'" RavenWolf says. "'But I heard you th whole time.' 'Yeah you did.' They sit there and kind of smile. It's like, 'That was pretty cool. I like that.'"

Each pow-wow session lasts about an hour, and there are three sessions per week for six weeks. In addition to the sessions, RavenWolf gives clients a frequently used key word such "flower" that triggers thoughts of healing ever time it's heard. She also videotapes the sessio so people can relive the pow-wow when they' at home. She claims incredible results from her treatment.

"[One female client] went back to the docto and they had to do another MRI or whatever it was before she went into surgery so they'd know where to cut, when to cut and all that stuff," RavenWolf says. "So [her doctor] comes back i the office and wants to know, 'What the hell ar you doing?' And she says, 'Why? What do you mean?' And he says, 'If I hadn't done both of these [MRIs] then I would have believed there was an error. But I know I did these, and I know they're yours. I want to know what the hell you're doing.' And she said, 'Why?' And he said 'Because you know that [tumour the size of a] softball? It's the size of a pea. We're cancelling the surgery. What are you doing?' She told hir and he laughed in her face."

For generations, no one but the Pennsylva Fancy Dutch – a nickname for German s tlers in the area – knew anything about hex Even into the Roaring '20s, as the rest of the world became more industrialised and embraced modern medicine, the Fancy Dutch preferred hexcraft.

Then John Blymire came along.

Blymire was a Fancy Dutchman whose gran father and father were noted faith healers. But when the sick and wounded of York County, P visited Blymire, he couldn't even cure their sni fles. The situation completely baffled him. In the Fancy Dutch culture, magical powers were passed from generation to generation differently in each family – in some it was mother to son, in others it was father to daughter – but in the Blymire Family they obviously transferred from father to son. And they never skipped a generation. The only explanation for Blymire's magical ineptitude was a hex.

"This was a true gift within his family," says David Laubach, an English professor at Kutztown University who teaches a course in hexology. "There would be no reason he would lose his gift unless someone wanted to take it away from him."

Blymire became obsessed with the hex. He paid numerous magical doctors to cast it away and locate its source, but they all failed – despite always claiming to be close to revealing the origin's identity. Finally, he sought an audience with a powerful witch outside of Harrisburg who uttered the name, "Rehmeyer." Blymire had worked for a man named Nelson Rehmeyer as a boy and became convinced this was the Rehmeyer who robbed him of his ability to heal. He immediately attempted to reverse the hex by obtaining Rehmeyer's copy of *The Long Lost Friend*. When Rehmeyer resisted, Blymire and two cohorts killed him – effectively, at least in Blymire's mind, restoring his power to heal.

The national media pounced on the story. "What was shocking to everybody was that it was 1929, and here was a corner of the country where somebody would actually kill somebody because they thought they'd been hexed," Laubach says.

The York Chamber of Commerce and the judge presiding over the trial did their best to cover up any hexcraft connection to Rehmeyer's death – maintaining Blymire and his accomplices killed Rehmeyer for money. But they fooled no one. Hexcraft was too prevalent in the Fancy Dutch community. According to local folklore, even Rehmeyer was a powerful hexenmeister who had a buried fortune from all the hexes he cast.

"[Hexenmeisters] were people who walked the line," RavenWolf says. "They did [faith healing and cursing]. And if they did something for you, you owed them. A lot of the other pow-wowers worked on barter, and, 'Oh honey, if you don't have anything, you'll get back to me.' Hexenmeisters were better accountants, like, 'Excuse me, you asked me to curse this pig, it died. Fine. Pay up, or your pig is next.'"

The negative publicity from the trial effectively ended hexcraft's practice in every Fancy Dutch household – forcing its older, lifelong practitioners underground. "What happened was the [American Medical Association] came in and made the practice of folk healing in this area illegal," says Dave Fooks, the General Manager of the Kutztown Pennsylvania German Festival. "They claimed it was practicing medicine without a licence, and it was pretty well shut down. And those people who practiced it more or less had to disappear."

When researching her book, RavenWolf found the majority of the people who grew up using hexcraft now reside in Pennsylvania nursing homes. Since the '60s, there has been a resurgent interest in the hexcraft culture and Blymire's trial – it has inspired a book, an opera and a movie starring Donald Sutherland (*Apprentice to Murder*) – but it remains largely a novelty item for tourists. The last of its admitted practitioners, like RavenWolf, use solely its folk remedies.

In the most rural areas of Central Pennsylvania, though, no one is willing to say the complete practice of hexcraft – hexes and all – has been halted. "*The Long Lost Friend* is still sold in old country stores – always under the counter," Laubach says. "When we did this play concerning it at the folk festival two years ago, we got copies of *The Long Lost Friend* from the York Historical Society, and we sold out the first day we had them. We had a guy come here from [Penn State University-Harrisburg], and he said there are no more power doctors in Pennsylvania. But I think on the road he drove from Harrisburg up to Kutztown, if he made the right turns at the right places, he would find people still practicing hexcraft." ●

"A LOT OF THIS HAS TO DO WITH THE PSYCHOLOGY OF THE HUMAN MIND. IT'S NOT WOO-WOO." – Hexcraft practitioner Silver RavenWolf

Illustration by Rich Borge

INVASION OF THE BODY SNATCHERS

Are aliens kidnapping us in our sleep...or is it our imaginations that have run amok?

By Katherine Flinn

Classic Alien Abduction Scenario

"I was in my bed sleeping when I awoke to hear a beeping sound. I saw flashes of blue light outside the window. I suddenly became aware of four aliens standing in my bedroom. They seemed to have come through the walls or otherwise materialized. I tried to move or scream, but I couldn't. I was paralyzed. Suddenly, I was being moved from my bed and sort of 'floated' until we reached their craft. There, I was tied down to the table by a transparent material stretched over my body. They performed a number of tests, including an excruciating gynecological exam in which they extracted an egg from my ovaries. The aliens were gray, with big heads and black eyes and seemed to communicate with me telepathically. At the time, I was about 7 and they implanted some sort of device under the skin of my arm. Now, when they come back for me, it hurts. I know they are coming. But I can't stop them."

Five Million Believers

Missing time, unexplained scars, and strikingly similar stories of exams by sinister entities. Big-headed aliens who do naughty things to us may be the new bogeymen, replacing that monster we long suspected lurked in the closet. There may be a lot of speculation about Bigfoot and the Loch Ness Monster, but no one is claiming that Nessie or Sasquatch abducted them to perform painful experiments on their private bits, either.

More than 23 million Americans claim to have seen a UFO, while some 2 percent of the population (about 5 million) reported experiences consistent with alien abductions, according to a 1992 Roper poll. Did you get that? *Five million*. Since 1957, researchers have documented reports from nearly two dozen countries of close encounters of the fourth kind (i.e., involving actual contact). Unlike UFO sightings, of which all but about five percent are ultimately explained, the majority of abduction cases are not. People pass lie detector tests and come up with scars and scoop marks or burns as "proof." They have a profound belief that this experience truly happened. And for now, all we have is their word.

So the question is pretty simple. Are people really being abducted, or are their stories the result of some collective psychological maladjustment, a sociological phenomenon or even a widespread hoax?

"We have an enormous amount of information on abduction cases, but we really don't know very much," says author Don Berliner, a member of the executive committee for the non-profit Fund for UFO Research. "We know that something's going on. But we don't know what it is. [Abductions] are a very complicated aspect of the UFO mystery. You can speculate all you want, but it's pointless."

Beyond Belief

Abductions have proved divisive even within the UFO research community. The believers battle a "lunatic fringe" label slapped on them by a skeptical scientific community. Believers point to similarity in stories, especially from children and reports from outside the U.S.

Among the true believers is Budd Hopkins. In his 20 years of researching abductions, he's studied more than 600 cases and documented his findings in a best-selling book, *Intruders*. Hopkins says there are too many coincidences to just dismiss the whole phenomenon as something that happens in people's heads.

"In case after case, the details are completely parallel, even to the point of some out-of-the-way details," Hopkins says. He points to indications of strong psychological damage suffered by abductees, including post-traumatic stress disorder. The range of people reporting these accounts also is telling, Hopkins says, from housewives to lawyers, and even eight psychologists.

Another believer is John Mack, a professor of psychiatry at Harvard University, whose recent book *Abduction: Human Encounters with Aliens*, details the experiences of 13 abductees. Mack claims to once have been a major skeptic, but after considering more than 70 such abductions cases, he's a convert.

However, scientists have questioned Mack and other abduction investigators' methodology. Researcher Donna Bassett posed as a patient, crashed his study and later reported publicly that although Mack was well intentioned, his procedures were flawed. Bassett asserts that by relying heavily on hypnotherapy, such investigations cannot be considered scientifically sound. Hypnosis doesn't necessarily invite people to tell the truth, but rather to dredge up memories in their subconscious that may *seem* real, such as dreams, delusions or fantasies. In such research, there's always the danger that interviewers will "lead" patients, even subconsciously, and therefore skew results.

Meanwhile, skeptics note that while there are many similarities in reports, there are also noteworthy discrepancies. Some abductees report aliens as gray, others as blue. Some say they have no faces at all. Some get "tours" of the ships, and those accounts can vary dramatically. Even the descriptions of aliens have shown cultural and generation-based differences. Until recently, aliens encountered in the U.K. were typically described as blond and Nordic, while in the U.S. they've changed from little green men to the standard gray variety.

Many psychologists believe that the aliens materialize from "sleep paralysis" or collective mental neurosis by fantasy-prone individuals. (More on both of these later.) Still others speculate that these "aliens" may even be a coping mechanism, acting as a stand-in for truly traumatizing experiences, such as child molestation or rape. Even laymen have been quoted as believing that some abductee stories might just be a means for a quick buck or public attention.

Others see it just as a strong indicator of just how ingrained aliens are as a pop culture phenomenon. The scary, creepy narratives of alien experiences make for good consumption, as demonstrated by widely popular movies such as *Close Encounters of the Third Kind*, best sellers such as *Communion* and successful TV shows such as the abduction-heavy *X-Files*.

"It's not as if each abductee has been hermetically sealed from the outside world and has no input about what others are saying," the late Carl Sagan noted in an interview with the TV program *Nova*. "It's all cross contaminated and it has been for decades. I think that's the clearest evidence for it not being good evidence—that so many people tell the same story."

ALIEN NOTION: E.T.s appeared in "Redux" [above] and "Duane Barry" [below]

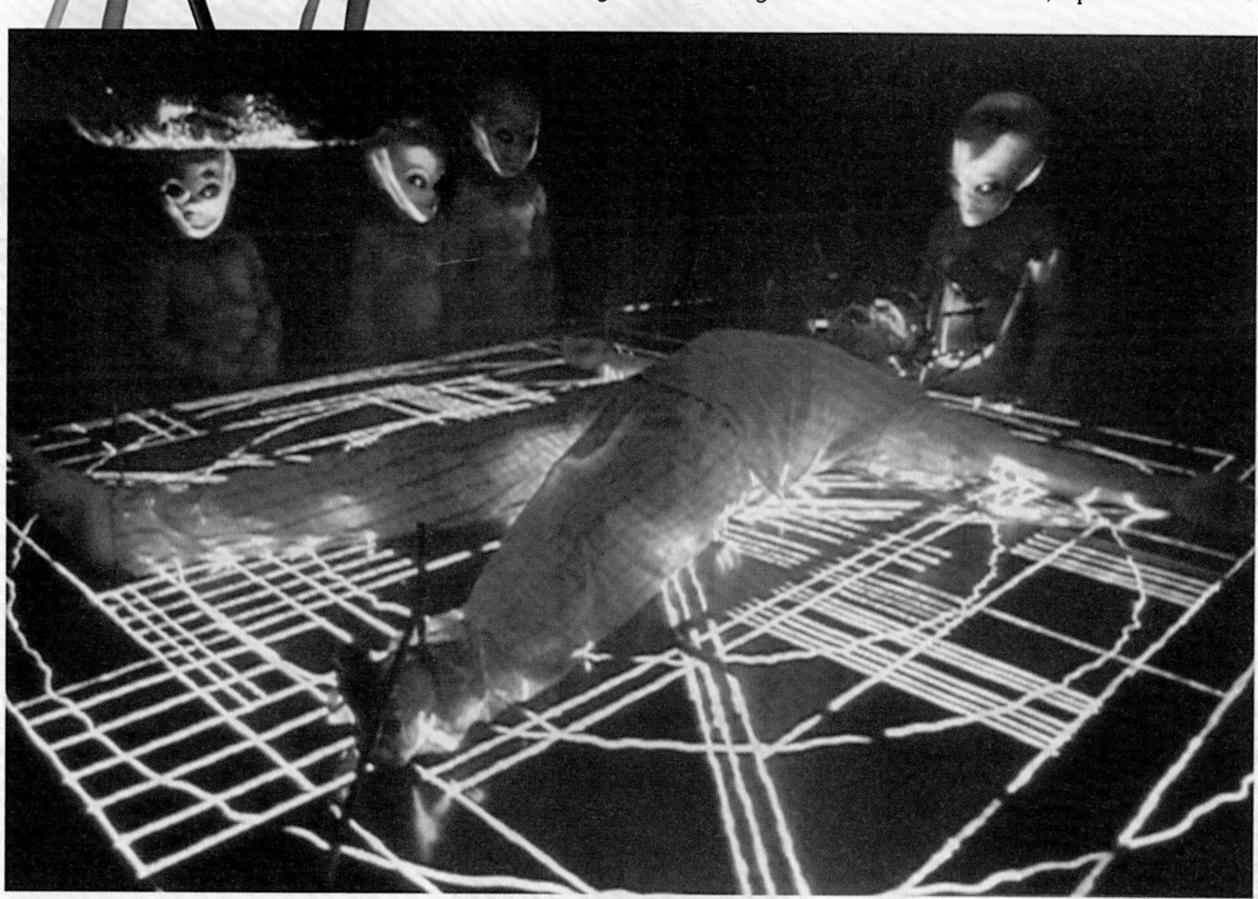

In the Beginning

Many acknowledge that the Bible's account of Ezekiel's vision of a "wheel within a wheel coming as a whirlwind" may be the first documented UFO sighting. But few recall that the old man also reported that four strange beings took him aboard the mysterious craft and landed on a distant mountaintop. As a young girl in 1425, Joan of Arc is said to have seen a brilliant light with strange creatures inside, which she perceived as a religious experience, according to a U.K. ufologist. Jacques Vallee, an astrophysicist and folklorist, has recounted numerous tales in literature of objects in the sky and occasional run-ins with strange inhabitants.

A young South American farmer reported the first modern abduction in 1957. Antonio Villas-Boas claimed that he watched a saucer land in a field, and then aliens took him aboard, stripped him and left the room. A semi-humanoid female entered. Villas-Boas had sex with her and, once done, she pointed to her stomach, then the sky.

But what first took hold took hold of the American collective imagination was a fateful night's drive by a couple in the foothills of the White Mountains in New Hampshire. In 1961, Betty and Barney Hill spied a large, luminous object from the window of their car. They stopped, Barney got out and took a look, getting close enough to see aliens inside. They drove home. Later, the couple realized they had "lost" more than an hour of time. Betty began to have nightmares about aliens. Under hypnosis with Dr. Benjamin Simon, the pair independently recounted a detailed account of their trip aboard the ship, including painful medical experiments. Betty also remembered being shown a star map noting where the aliens hailed from in the star system Zeta Reticulli.

It's worth noting that Simon later said that he felt the account was a "shared" fantasy that resulted from Betty Hill telling her husband her dreams of aliens.

Since that time, reports of other encounters trickled in. In one highly publicized case in 1975, six loggers traveling home from working in the mountains of northeastern Arizona saw a large, red object hovering above the trees. They stopped to get a closer look and one man, Travis Walton, jumped out of the truck. He was knocked back by a bolt of light. His companions fled in fear. When a massive manhunt failed to turn him up, authorities began to suspect Walton's co-workers of murder. Five days later he showed up, dehydrated and traumatized, with a tale of silent alien creatures and harrowing medical exams that was later used as a basis for the book (and later movie) *Fire in the Sky*.

But it wasn't until the late '80s that the floodgates of abduction reports broke wide open. Publication of books such as Whitley Strieber's *Communion* and Hopkins' *Intruders* drew a flurry of media attention. Both books outlined the emergence of a classic abduction tale, one that evolved from the Hills' account into a more specific and sinister paradigm. This one includes suspicions that the aliens are stealing human eggs and sperm for some ongoing genetic experiment to create hybrid creatures. They also revealed accounts of repeated abductions from childhood.

While earlier, well-known cases involved individuals picked up in remote locations or from their cars, *Communion* and *Intruders* both focused on right-from-their-own-beds abductions. In that, many people seemed to find a kindred experience.

"After those books came out, I was taking a phone call a week from people who said that they had been abducted who hadn't talked to anyone else," Berliner said of the calls he fielded at the Fund for UFO Research. "There would be a pause, and then the person would invariably say, 'You're not going to believe this.' Many, many of them attributed their decision to come forward to one of those books. I think they felt like, 'Well, this happens to people. I'm not alone."

With this sudden flood of reports, skeptics had to work overtime. They've come up with a few basic explanations for why all these people might be telling abduction stories. Here are the two most prevalent.

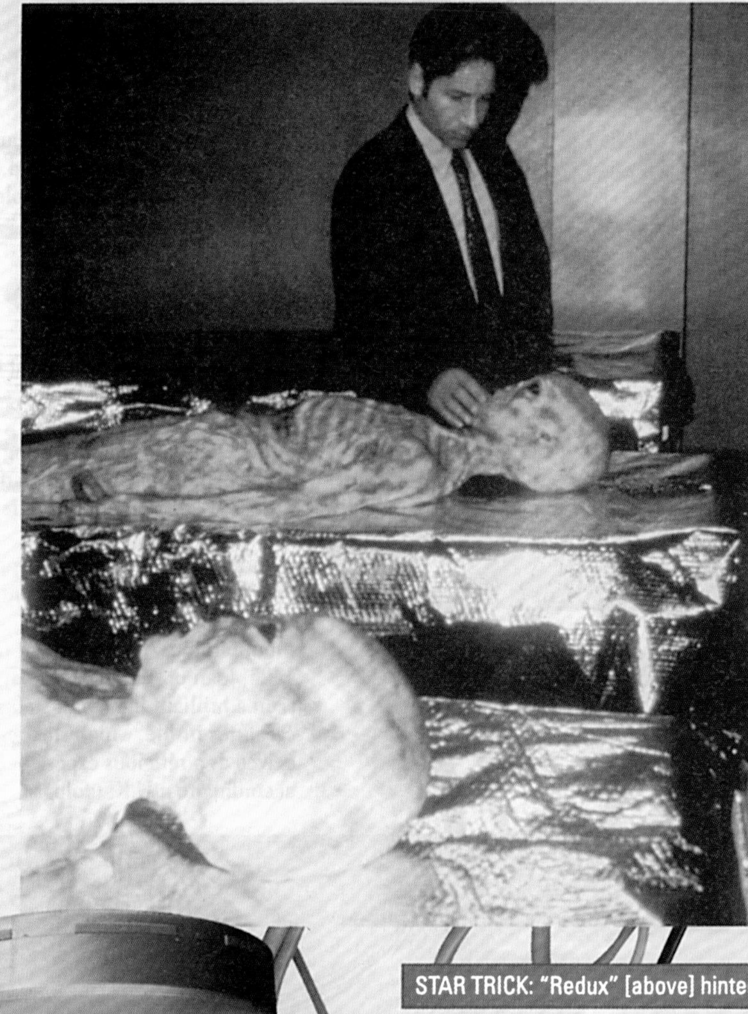

STAR TRICK: "Redux" [above] hinted at a hoax

Skeptic Explanation #1

They know when you're sleeping

Many psychologists and investigators blame sleep paralysis and the phenomenon of 'waking dreams' for the majority of abducted-out-of-bed stories. In one study of 95 abduction cases, a researcher found that 79 took place in the abductee's residence, usually the bedroom. Ten subjects reported being taken from their cars, six from a cabin or campsite.

"I was reading Whitley Strieber's book and right in the middle of it is this extremely accurate description of sleep paralysis," says Dr. Robert Baker, professor emeritus of psychology at the University of Kentucky and a noted researcher of the paranormal.

Sleep paralysis is the psychophysical mechanism that keeps us from acting out our dreams. We all experience it, but it usually only becomes noticeable in that twilight between sleep and waking, when some people report a sense of falling or floating. It can also be experienced as the inability to move—a feeling of being "paralyzed." If you've ever "jerked" involuntarily as you're falling asleep, you've experienced sleep paralysis setting in for the night. At the same time, senses can be heightened. Combine this with an intense "waking dream," and you've got an experience that can seem profoundly real. It's estimated that five percent of all people have these kinds of "night terrors" at one time or another.

Put into the context of history, the link between the "night terrors" of the past and the "abductions" of today seems clear, Baker says. Tales of attacks while sleeping go back to the Middle Ages, when a "succubus" or female demon, would sexually assault men while they slept. Male versions would attack women. ("This was often reported in clusters at nunneries, which was then used to explain why some of the nuns turned up pregnant," Baker says.) A variation on this theme was the "old hag" incidents, when

sleepers reported being attacked by an old witch, who would sometimes perform spells on them. Ghost researchers encounter similar stories from people who say they see ghosts sitting on the edge of their bed, talking with them or attacking them while they lie paralyzed, Baker says.

But believers such as Hopkins are quick to point out that this theory doesn't explain away other abductions. "What happens to this theory when there are six people in the car and they're all wide awake? What happens when there's an abduction in broad daylight?" Hopkins asks.

This also doesn't explain cases such as the one described in his most recent book, *Witnessed*. In it, he relays the accounts of eight eyewitnesses who watched a women float from her bedroom accompanied by small beings—12 stories off the ground. Skeptics would say she suffered from sleep paralysis, Hopkins says, but then how do they account for all these witnesses?

Skeptic Explanation #2

It's all in your head

Some researchers say that the alien abduction phenomenon is not unlike near-death experience reports—including the element of remarkably similar stories—and there's some similarity in the types of people who report them.

Baker and other researchers note that many people who file reports of extraordinary experiences such as near-death, alien abductions and even religious visions show signs of what psychologists call "fantasy proneness." Those who have this abnormal personality type have specific tendencies, including having imaginary friends as children, belief in their own psychic powers and physiological effects, such as getting a rash when they erroneously think they've come into contact with something that would give them one.

These individuals are also easily hypnotized, and some researchers believe they are possibly more likely to fall prey to even subconscious "leading" by well-meaning hypnotherapists. In *The Omega Project*, researcher Kenneth Ring notes a "consistent tendency" for abductees and near-death experiencers to admit childhood abuse and trauma.

This conclusion is echoed by another researcher, Jim Lorenzen. He has noted, "One thing we have learned when we have gone into the background of persons who claim to have been abducted by UFOs is that for the most part they have had a history of being battered children or to have had sad histories in other ways."

That becomes especially important when you consider that some psychologists believe that fantasy proneness might be a protective device crafted during a troubled childhood.

"There's probably not one thing as a fundamental cause of this," says Shaun Vecera, a cognitive psychologist with the University of Utah. "We delude ourselves all the time. Sometimes this is a good coping mechanism.

"But some people are better at deluding themselves than the rest of us," Vecera continues. "Couple that with a belief in extraterrestrials and you've got an ideal candidate for someone who will not only look for these cues of having been abducted, but once they have a couple of cues they will start to piece things together. 'Gee, not only do I have some missing time, but I have this funny scar.'"

But Hopkins has a response to this argument: He says that less than half of all reports he's studied are based on memories culled through hypnotherapy. He also says that a "troubled childhood" could result from an abduction at an early age. He adds that some abductees recall both an abduction and sexual molestation as children, so the abduction scenario isn't a "stand-in" for the other event.

While many abductees may be candidates for fantasy-proneness, Hopkins believes that a significant number are not. "Some of these people are the most rational you'll ever meet," Hopkins says.

No Smoking Laser Gun

No one's ever proved that UFOs are really alien craft. Sure, there are photos and videos, but they've yet to be authenticated beyond a shadow of a doubt. Some researchers point to the disturbed ground near landing spots. Radar has tracked mysterious blips for nearly 50 years. Multiple eyewitness accounts dot the books.

One researcher, Derrel W. Sims, is known as the "Alien Hunter," for his proactive search for evidence. Sims believes that some initial findings may eventually prove that abductions are not just in people's minds. Among them: about one-third of abductees he's examined have developed rare allergies to drugs such as Novocaine, compared to the normal one percent of the population, and about five percent of abductees have had some "fluorescent" type markings on their skin following reported contact with aliens, Sims says.

Still, skeptics consider none of this definitive proof. They point to hoaxes, such as the video footage of a supposed alien autopsy released two years ago or the two blokes who admitted to being behind the U.K.'s enigmatic crop circles.

Yet Sims and other believers say they're dedicated to finding real, irrefutable proof that aliens are visiting Earth. "I don't need 5,000 cases that are true. I just need one," he says.

So what happens if the skeptics are wrong and someone finds the proverbial smoking gun of alien abductions, some souvenir that's so irrefutable it can't be questioned?

"I think there would be a lot of red faces amongst the scientific community," Hopkins says. "But we really don't know. It would depend on what we could find out. If all a president could say was, 'Gee, these aliens are real, we can't do anything but they are abducting our men, women and children on a regular basis. They seem to be conducting an ongoing, long-term study on genetics, but we don't know why. Thank you and good-night, America.' How do you expect people react to that?"

Hopkins thinks he knows what the response would be—sheer panic. "At that point," he says, "I'd rather be in the liquor business than the bond market." ●

THE X FILES

10 BEST CLIFF-HANGERS

BY KATE ANDERSON

To be continued... three little words. But not just any three little words; they encompass a range of emotions and feelings: anticipation; excitement; and awe. Which is one thing our pick of the 10 best *X-Files* cliff-hangers all have in common...

10

"Requiem"
(Season Seven)

WHAT HAPPENS: Skinner visits Scully in hospital and breaks the awful news to her about Mulder's disappearance. Scully takes his hand and tells him that she already knows. They both become emotional and Scully tells Skinner that she will find Mulder – she has to. Although she can't begin to explain it, she's pregnant!

WHY IT WORKS: The mother of all cliff-hangers – excuse the pun! – and one of the most talked about. Set tongues wagging as to whom the father was – not to mention how the supposedly barren Scully could conceive in the first place!

9

"The Blessing Way"
(Season Three)

WHAT HAPPENS: Mulder's apparently dead and Scully could be next. With Mulder out of the equation, Scully doesn't know who she can trust – even Skinner. At Mulder's house, she pulls her gun on her boss – who draws his at the same time – and they face one another in a stand-off.

WHY IT WORKS: A terrific double bluff making us think that Skinner has been sent to kill Scully. Bursting with tension, we're left on tenterhooks – the next episode can't come soon enough.

"Christmas Carol" (Season Five)

WHAT HAPPENS: It's Christmas morning and Scully's staying with her family. An F.B.I courier delivers the results of a D.N.A. test on a little girl Scully believes to be her sister Melissa's child. But the test reveals that Melissa isn't the child's mother – Dana is!

WHY IT WORKS: The look on Scully's face says it all! It's a great moment and in typical *X-Files* fashion, it answers a question only to pose half a dozen more!

"Colony" (Season Two)

WHAT HAPPENS: A shape-shifting bounty hunter has been killing doctors at abortion clinics across the country. The alien can change his appearance and become anyone he chooses. Mulder turns up at Scully's motel room, just as she takes a phone call – from Mulder!
WHY IT WORKS: A classic example of a cliff-hanger; it's riveting, exciting and chock-full of suspense.

"Patient X" (Season Five)

WHAT HAPPENS: Scully and other abductees are 'called' to Ruskin Damn where Scully's surprised to see Cassandra Spender in the group. Then all of a sudden, a bright light appears in the night time sky, just as faceless men appear and start to set people on fire. One of the faceless aliens advances toward Scully…

WHY IT WORKS: A visually stunning climax. Again they play the Scully-in-peril card but in this instance to great effect.

AND LET'S NOT FORGET THESE 10 JUST BUBBLING UNDER...

"REDUX I" – THE CURE FOR SCULLY'S CANCER IS… DE-IONIZED WATER?!

"TALITHA CUMI" – MULDER AND SCULLY FACE OFF AGAINST THE ALIEN BOUNTY HUNTER WHO HAS COME TO KILL JEREMIAH SMITH.

"TUNGUSKA" – MULDER BECOMES A TEST SUBJECT FOR THE BLACK CANCER A.K.A. THE BLACK OIL.

"PIPER MARU" – KRYCEK VISITS THE MEN'S ROOM AND COMES OUT 'A NEW MAN'.

"PILOT" – UNFORGETTABLE IMAGE OF THE CSM IN THE HUGE PENTAGON STOREROOM.

"BIOGENESIS" – SCULLY STANDS ON A SHORELINE STARING IN AWE AT AN ALIEN SPACECRAFT BURIED IN THE SAND.

"THE END" – SCULLY HOLDS MULDER AS HE SURVEYS HIS FIRE-DAMAGED OFFICE.

"DREAMLAND, PART ONE" – THE REAL MULDER TRIES TO CONVINCE SCULLY THAT THE MAN SHE BELIEVES IS HER PARTNER ISN'T – OKAY, HANDS UP IF YOU'RE CONFUSED!

"ESSENCE" – ALIENS IN THE F.B.I.. AGENT CRANE HAS AN ALIEN VERTEBRA ON HIS BACK!

"TWO FATHERS" – CASSANDRA SPENDER BEGS AGENT MULDER TO SHOOT HER!

"Anasazi" (Season Two)

WHAT HAPPENS: In New Mexico, Mulder discovers a pile of what look like alien bodies in a train boxcar. The Cigarette-Smoking Man arrives on the scene and orders his troops to set the boxcar on fire – with Mulder inside!
WHY IT WORKS: "Oh my God, Scully. What have they done?" Mulder's starting to put the pieces of the puzzle together and so are we. On that note, we're left on tenterhooks and waiting for the next season to begin is going to be tortuous.

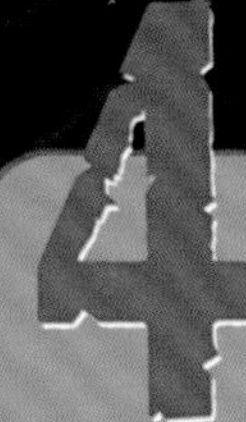

"The Erlenmeyer Flask" (Season One)

WHAT HAPPENS: Deep Throat dies in front of Scully, warning her to 'Trust no one'. And an emotional Mulder phones Scully to inform her that they are to be separated and the X-files division shut down.
WHY IT WORKS: Talk about pulling no punches! The death of an important character like Deep Throat so early into the series is a huge shock. The final moments, although not a traditional cliff-hanger, have a terrific impact nonetheless.

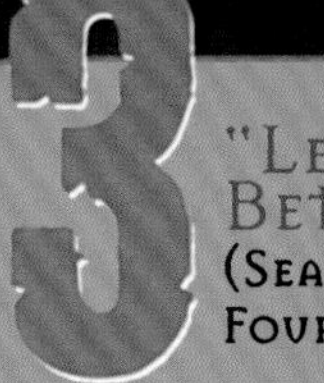

"Leonard Betts" (Season Four)

WHAT HAPPENS: Cancer-eating fiend Leonard Betts attacks Scully in the back of an ambulance. Their confrontation is brutal, with Betts telling Scully that she has something he needs. He's too strong for Scully; she manages to use a pair of defibrillation pads to kill him. But she is left to ponder her condition. Later, Scully wakes up in bed with a bloody nose.
WHY IT WORKS: Betts' attack on Scully is horrifying enough but the realization that Scully has cancer is way more shocking. The sight of blood pouring innocently from Scully's nose leaves you feeling completely numb.

"Gethsemane" (Season Four)

WHAT HAPPENS: We see Mulder's tear-stained face and then the scene switches to Scully facing an F.B.I. committee. She's very emotional as she explains that she was called to her partner's apartment in order to identify a body. Her voice trembles as she informs them that Mulder is dead! Apparently, he died of a self-inflicted gunshot wound to his head.
WHY IT WORKS: One of the best ever *X-Files* cliff-hangers, as we're led to believe that Mulder has killed himself. Of course, it's just a bluff but nevertheless the wait for the next season is agonizing. And that's how any successful cliff-hanger should be.

1 "Duane Barry" (Season Two)

WHAT HAPPENS: At a supermarket, Agent Scully accidentally scans a piece of metal she took from Duane Barry. The machine goes berserk and later Scully calls Mulder about it, leaving a message on his answering machine. Suddenly, Barry appears outside her window. We hear lots of crashing and a desperate Scully yelling for help.
WHY IT WORKS: The first ever two-part story ends on a high with a superb cliff-hanger. Both gripping and intense, this is edge-of-your-seat stuff. Never were the words 'To be continued' loathed so much!

EPISODE GUIDE

Principal Credits

Produced by: Ten-Thirteen Productions for 20th Century-Fox TV
Creator and Executive Producer: Chris Carter
Co-Executive Producers: Howard Gordon, R W Goodwin
Producers: Joseph Patrick Finn, Kim Manners, Rob Bowman
Co-Producer: Paul Rabwin
Music: Mark Snow

Episode Credits

Written by: Chris Carter
Directed by: Rob Bowman

Special Agent Fox Mulder: David Duchovny
Special Agent Dr Dana Scully: Gillian Anderson
Detective Angela White: Dana Wheeler-Nicholson

Margi Kleinjan: Wendy Benson
Terri Roberts: Lisa Robin Kelly
Bob Spitz: Garry Davey
Madame Zirinka: Denalda Williams
Brenda Jaycee Summerfield: Gabrielle Miller
Jay 'Boom' DeBoom: Ryan Reynolds
Dr Richard W Godfrey: Tim Dixon
Minister: Ryk Brown
Young Man: Jeremy Radick
Scott Simmons: Russell Porter

3.13: "SYZYGY" Episode #3X13

Original US tx 26 January 96 Original UK tx 28 May 96

COMITY, CAROL COUNTY

In Comity, 'The Perfect Harmony City', a candle-lit service is held by a group of high school students – among them a jock named Jay 'Boom' DeBoom and two pretty blondes, Margi and Terri – in honour of a friend, apparently murdered by a group referred to as "the cult". Having learned that this sinister group intends to make a blonde virgin its next victim, Terri and Margi entice Jay with an unusual come-on line: "Maybe if we weren't virgins, we wouldn't be so scared." The next morning, the young man is found hanging from a cliff, while the two girls (unseen by the police) play 'He loves me, he loves me – not!' on the rocks above.

An unusually argumentative Mulder and Scully arrive on the scene during a service for Jay, the third victim in a series of mysterious deaths supposedly linked to the local satanic cult. Scully, aware that the FBI has debunked virtually all so-called cases of satanic worship linked to serious crimes, is sceptical, and is none too impressed by the investigative methods employed by local detective Angela White. When DeBoom's casket spontaneously combusts at the service, however, Mulder feels that the locals may have a point. The agents interrogate Terri and Margi, whose literally identical stories of demonic possession and black-robed cultists sacrificing human babies make both suspicious of their motives.

Later, Scully finds a burn mark on DeBoom's body which Mulder and Detective White both believe resembles "a hornéd beast," prompting Mulder to use the innuendo "I was hoping you could help me solve the mystery of the horny beast" to talk his way into the attractive detective's apartment; together, they visit local numerologist and astrologer Madame Zirinka, who tells the bemused pair that a rare alignment of Mercury Mars and Uranus is imminent – an event she believes may be responsible for the town having "lost its marbles". But is this portentous 'syzygy' responsible for the student body's growing number of bodies – not to mention the "naked movie-star games" that the high school principal believes are being played by local devil worshippers – or are Terri and Margi hiding more than their motives?

F.Y.I.

An odd one this; unjustly villified by X-philes on its initial broadcast, "Syzygy" is actually very well conceived, written and executed – a *Heathers* with a neat satanic spin. Carter, seemingly inspired by the totally fresh approach taken by "Humbug" writer Darin Morgan, has a great deal of fun with his characters, demonstrating a keen ear for dialogue, most notably the inane Generation X-isms spouted by Jay 'Boom' DeBoom and the girls ("Hate him – wouldn't wanna date him," *et al*), and Scully's sudden liking for the *Clueless* catchphrase, "whatever."

Mulder makes explicit reference to the seven year McMartin trial, in which workers at a private day care centre were accused – and ultimately acquitted – of an almost laughable catalogue of satanic crimes involving pre-school children. Those interested to know more should check out *Indictment: The McMartin Trial*, HBO's Emmy award-winning dramatisation of the trial starring James Woods, currently available to rent or buy on video.

"Syzygy" scored a Nielsen rating of 10.8/17 on its initial US broadcast, equating 10.36 million homes – not bad for a much maligned episode.

Noteworthy Dialogue Transcript

DET. WHITE [upon hearing that the satanic cult's next victim is supposed to be a blonde virgin]: "Excuse me."
SCULLY: "Where's she going?"
MULDER: "You don't suppose she's a virgin, do you?"
SCULLY: "I doubt she's even a blonde."

Unexplained Plot Discrepancies

The deteriorating Mulder/Scully relationship displayed in this episode, and Scully's petty reaction to the attractive Detective White, irritated many X-philes, who seemingly failed to realise that the agents were under the same astronomical influence as the rest of Comity. "That's one of the risks you run," a bemused Carter shrugs, "that people become so hopeful and familiar and comfortable with something that when you turn it on its head, they don't understand it." It is odd, however, that everyone refers to Comity as a town except the city limits sign, which calls it a city.

THE X FILES Personality Test

Who's your favorite X-Files character – and what does it say about your personality?

Fox Mulder

You've always been a bit different – someone who marches to the beat of their own drum, rather than falling in with the crowd. On the surface you appear confident but in reality you're quite shy.

You've always been a bit of a loner and you don't make friends easily. Trust is a big issue with you too and only a few close friends are worthy of it. You have a droll sense of humor, not to mention a sharp, intelligent and open mind.

As a self-confessed workaholic, you don't seem to have much time for a social life. You're not great with relationships either, and you rarely show any emotion. Sometimes you look as though you're carrying the weight of the world on your shoulders.

A firm believer in, well, just about anything, you can sometimes be too gullible for your own good.

John Doggett

You're very much a 'by the book' kind of person. Some would even say you're a conformist. And you don't like to draw attention to yourself. You're happy to stay in the background and get the job done. You're pretty thorough and on the surface you can appear somewhat hard-nosed. But you do have a gentle side, it's just that you usually keep it very well hidden!

You're a very down-to-Earth person; with you, what you see is what you get. You're not a great believer when it comes to conspiracy theories and the paranormal. In fact, the only way you'll believe something is if you can see it, smell it and touch it. Otherwise, it just doesn't exist.

Monica Reyes

You might not look it, but underneath your conventional exterior lies a bit of a wild child. You're quite a spiritual person and you have an interest in mysticism. Although you don't like to call yourself either a believer or a skeptic, you do have an open mind. You're willing to believe in extreme possibilities and you don't have to see something with your own eyes to believe it.

You are a genuinely compassionate, caring and sensitive person. And you are responsive to other peoples' feelings and moods. It's no surprise that you have a great faith, a belief in your own instincts.

Dana Scully

At heart you're a skeptic – although your skepticism has eroded a bit over the last few years. Still, nine times out of ten, you believe that everything has a logical explanation and that science can provide all the answers. You're very conscientious and have a stubborn streak – when you make your mind up about something it stays that way!

You're extremely reliable, determined and very career minded. A consequence of all your hard work seems to be your loss of a social life; you're all work and no play!

Let's face it, it's been so long since you let your hair down and enjoyed yourself, you've probably forgotten how to have a good time!

Walter Skinner

You're the strong, silent type; you see silence as strength and showing your emotions as a sign of weakness. You can be way too serious for your own good and sometimes not as patient as you would like. You don't like to let people see the real you and as a consequence, you often appear cold, sometimes even hostile. But at heart you're loyal, honest and reliable and when push comes to shove you can always be counted upon.

In a crisis you keep a cool head and you have great leadership qualities. And you're always willing to stand your own ground, to stand up for yourself – and for your friends.

The Cigarette-Smoking Man

You like to make your presence felt and you'll willingly risk everything to get what you want. Power is your aphrodisiac. And the more power you have, the more you crave. You are quite mysterious; no one knows who the real you is – maybe not even you.

It's a good thing that you're used to getting your own way because you do have a dangerous, somewhat sinister side. You want people to respect and admire you. But more often than not, you mistake their respect for fear. In short, you're unpleasant, loathsome and altogether a rather nasty piece of work.

Yes, people may well remember you. But more for the wrong reasons than the right ones.

Alex Krycek

Charm may well be your middle name but you also have a ruthless dark side, which you keep well hidden. You can be extremely selfish and always seem to have your own agenda; you look after number one.

Words to describe you range from devious and underhand to untrustworthy and spineless. You don't care who gets hurt just so long as you get what you want.

To you, no one is expendable – and woe betide anyone who gets in your way! I mean, do you even *know* what a guilty conscience is? Where were you when they were handing them out – the back of the queue? Guilt is certainly an alien concept to you.

THE X FILES™

OTHER GREAT TV TIE-IN COMPANIONS FROM TITAN

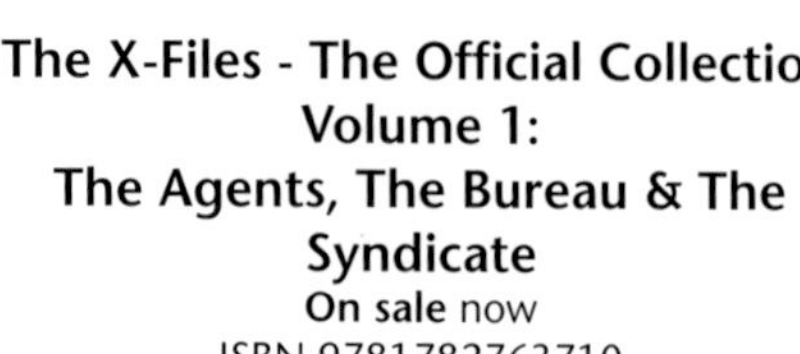

The X-Files - The Official Collection Volume 1: The Agents, The Bureau & The Syndicate
On sale now
ISBN 9781782763710

Buffy - The Slayer Collection Volume 2: Monsters & Villains
On sale March 2016
ISBN 9781782763642

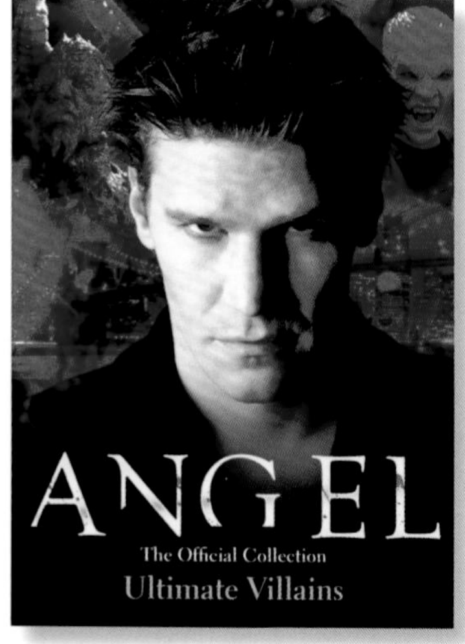

Angel - The Official Collection Volume 2: Ultimate Villains
On sale May 2016
ISBN 9781782763680

COMING SOON...

The X-Files - The Official Collection Volume 3: Conspiracy Theory - The Truth, Secrets & Lies
On sale June 2016
ISBN 9781782763734

For more information visit www.titan-comics.com

TITANCOMICS

Welco
Bizarre

FRE GEEKS! AND AMAZING PEOPLE!

The planet's most incredible individuals tell us what makes them tick

Contributors The photographers who made the whole thing possible

Neville Elder
Now living in New York, Neville shoots the weird and wonderful for *Bizarre* all over the USA.
Nevilleelder.com

JOE PLIMMER
Joe is a people snapper and believes everyone has a story to tell, and a great photo in them.
Joeplimmer.co.uk

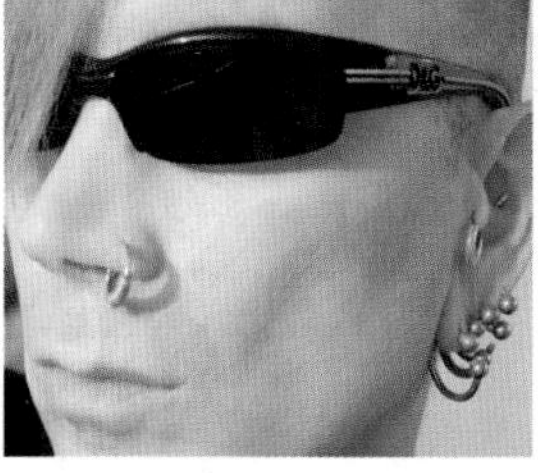

ASHLEY
Since 1989, Ashley has been one of the UK's most respected photographers of alt.culture.
Savageskin.co.uk

Sam Scott Hunter
Sam is a portrait and music photographer from London, and shot Selene Luna for this book.
Samscotthunter.co.uk

Mark Berry
Mark hails from Bristol, but now lives in LA snapping weird photo features for *Bizarre*.
Hot-cherry.co.uk

Biff Yeager
Biff shoots incredible portraits, and is well-known in the USA as an events photographer.
Yeagerfotografix.com

James Stafford
As well as snapping Amanda Lapore, James has shot many vixens for *Bizarre* covers.
Jamesandjames.net

Bizarre Big Book Of FREAKS! GEEKS! AND AMAZING PEOPLE!

CONTENTS

112

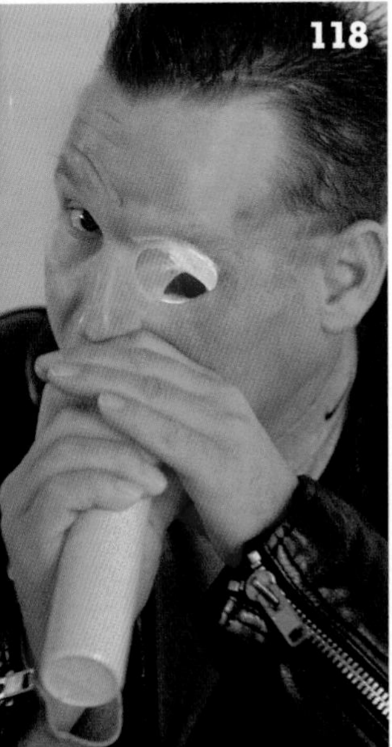
118

154

88

BIZARRE
BIZARREMAG.COM

30 CLEVELAND STREET, LONDON W1T 4JD
TEL (020) 7907 6000 EMAIL BIZARRE@DENNIS.CO.UK

EDITORIAL
Editor David McComb
Production Editor Eleanor Goodman
Deputy Editor Kate Hodges
Senior Writer Denise Stanborough
Staff Writer Alix Fox

ART
Art Director Mike Mansfield
Art Director At Large Dave Kelsall
Picture Editor Tom Broadbent
Picture Researcher Emily McBean

COVER PHOTOS
Mark Berry, John Little, Joe Plimmer, Sam Scott Hunter, James Stafford

CONTRIBUTORS
Words Mark Berry, Paul Cheung, Alix Fox, Marc Hartzman, Kate Hodges, Victoria Hogg, John Little, Maki, David McComb, Ben Myers, Jack Ruby Murray, Chris Nieratko, Denise Stanborough, Jeffery R Werner
Photos Ashley, Barcroft Media, Mark Berry, Neville Elder, Joe Plimmer, Sam Scott Hunter, James Stafford, Biff Yeager
Special thanks Victoria Hogg (extra words), Darren Brooke, Dave Kinnard, Katie Brooke (repro superstars)

SUITS
Digital Production Manager Nicky Baker

MANAGEMENT
Bookazine Manager Dharmesh Mistry
Production Director Robin Ryan
Managing Director Of Advertising Julian Lloyd-Evans
Newstrade Director Martin Belson
Chief Operating Officer Brett Reynolds
Group Finance Director Ian Leggett
Chief Executive James Tye
Chairman Felix Dennis

MAGBOOK
The Magbook brand is a trademark of Dennis Publishing Ltd, 30 Cleveland Street, London W1T 4JD. Company registered in England.

Bizarre Big Book Of Freaks! Geeks! And Amazing People! ISBN 1-906372-74-8

LICENSING
To license this product, please contact Winnie Liesenfeld on +44 (0) 20 7907 6134 or email Winnie_liesenfeld@dennis.co.uk

LIABILITY
While every care was taken during the production of this Magbook, the publishers cannot be held responsible for the accuracy of the information or any consequence arising from it. Dennis Publishing takes no responsibility for the companies advertising in this Magbook.

Printed at Butler, Tanner & Dennis

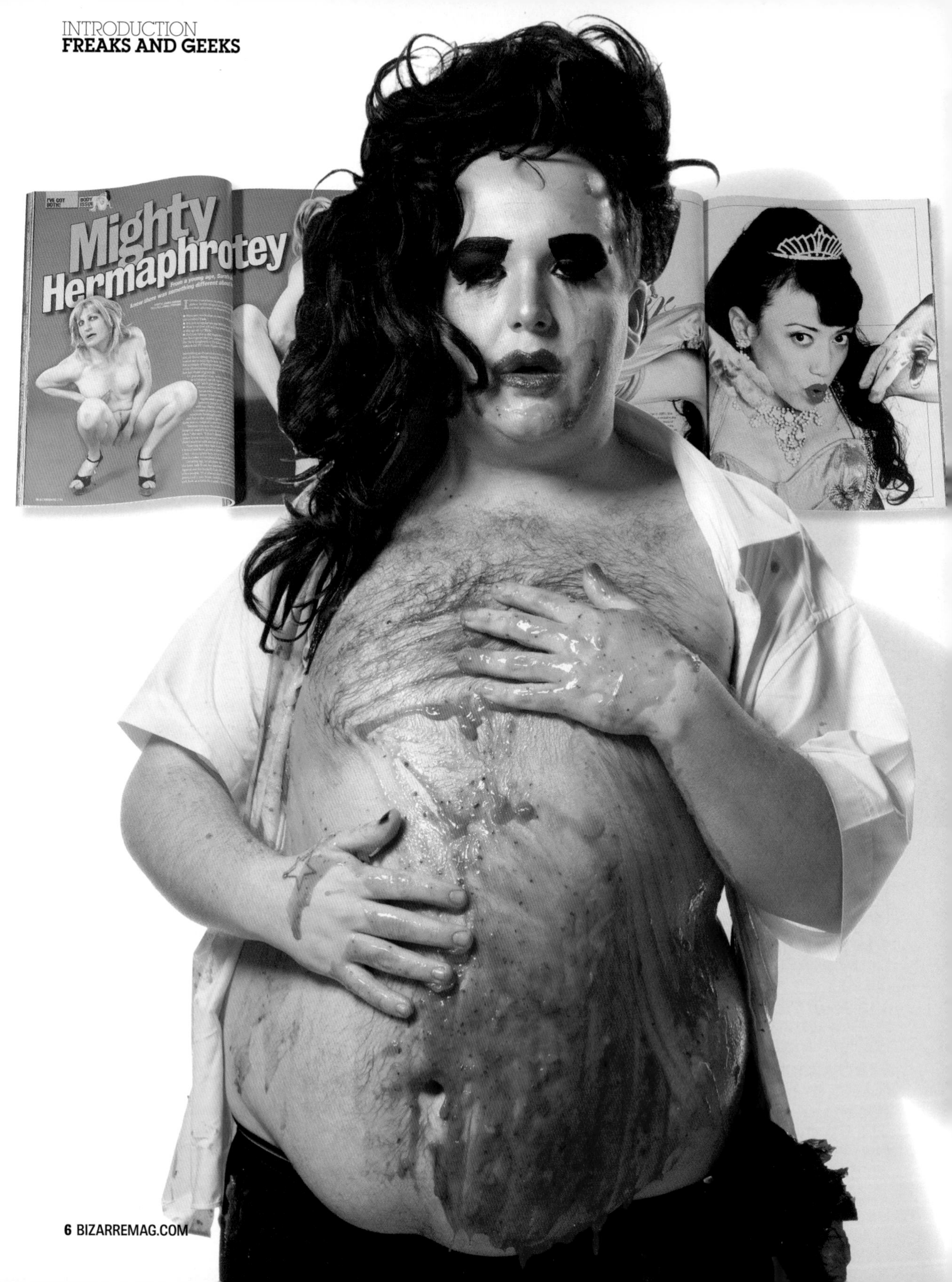
I'VE GOT BOTH!
BODY ISSUE
Mighty Hermaphrotey

SUPER FREAK!

No.2

SYBAN V

She's neither a fetish nor burlesque performer – although she combines elements of both. She's simply Syban V and she's "absolutely fantabulous, darling"

In the beginning

PAMELA PEAKS

TWIN PEAKS

Meet the adult actress who's cooking up a feast of depravity in the kitchen. Live

SUPER FREAKS!

Bizarre has been interviewing amazing people since 1997. This Magbook is a collection of our favourites...

When quizzed about what makes working on *Bizarre* the best job in publishing, most people expect us to ramble on about the wild parties we've been to and the depraved sights we've witnessed in the name of journalism. Others think pouring over photos of naked girls day-in, day-out is what makes our job a (wet) dream come true... that, and popping along to covershoots and seeing our models sashaying around in their scanties, of course. In reality, what makes working on the world's #1 alternative magazine so much fun is the incredible people we get to meet.

From Mexican midget wrestlers who never remove their masks to guys with metal Mohawks embedded in their heads – via alt.artists, rogue taxidermists, pervy performers, body modifiers, freak show acts, madcap musicians and a hundred other indefinable outsiders – working on *Bizarre* gives our writers direct access to the world's →

CHI CHI LARUE

TRANNY MAGNET

She's Big, Brash, Bawdy and Ballsy – best get out the way of the runaway locomotive that is Chi Chi LaRue

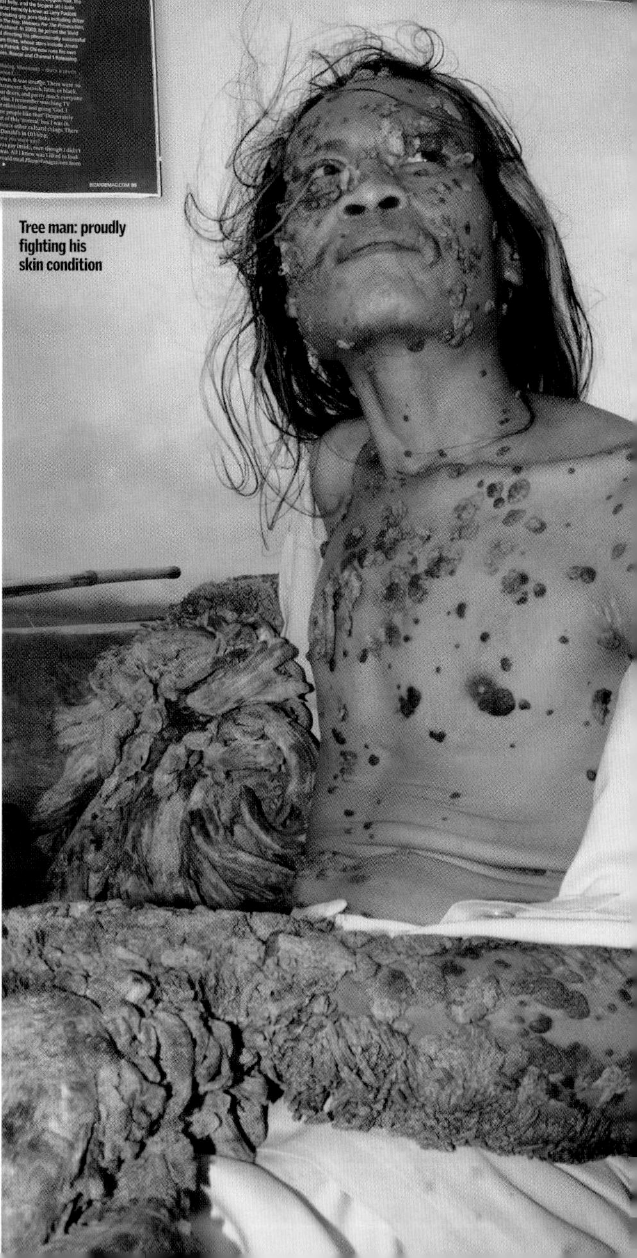

Tree man: proudly fighting his skin condition

"We get access to the world's most fascinating people, who refuse to compromise"

most fascinating people; individuals who refuse to compromise, who are content to buck the norm, and are happiest when ploughing their own furrow in life or dancing to their own tune.

This inaugural *Bizarre Big Book Of Freaks! Geeks! And Amazing People* Magbook collects some of our favourite interviews from the past decade of *Bizarre*, with loads of unseen photography and new quotes that are guaranteed to make your hair stand on end. **GASP!** As you read about the man who can drink beer through his empty eye socket. **SWOON!** As you meet the gorgeous twins whose stage show toys with the taboo of incest. **HOWL!** As the freakiest performers on the British cabaret scene reveal the amazing stories behind their ascent to notoriety. And **CRY!** as the heart-breaking tales of Tree Man and Teen Wolf show how even the unluckiest of folk can rise above the cruel tricks played on them by Mother Nature, and defy humdrum societal rules that declare all people should look and act the same.

Bizarre is dedicated to celebrating difference, and in every page we dare our readers to stand out in an increasingly grey and homogenous world. And without the incredible people featured in this book, planet Earth would be a much, much duller place.

DARK STARS

The British alt.performance scene is hotter than hell right now, so we cornered four of its greatest talents for the *Bizarre* treatment…

THE VIVID ANGEL

From her flaming red hair to her dazzling smile, The Vivid Angel is Europe's premier showgirl

WORDS **DAVID MCCOMB**
PHOTOS **JOE PLIMMER**

Whether she's leaping barefoot into a pile of broken glass, hammering nails up her nostrils or driving skewers through her flesh, you can't take your eyes off The Vivid Angel. A devilish tsunami of freak show thrills, slinky burlesque and showgirl pizzazz – all delivered with a cheeky smile and self-deprecating sense of humour that make her shows utterly charming – Vivid is Europe's premier fetish performer and has set venues alight, from the hardcore clubs of Amsterdam to the main stage at the inaugural Bizarre Ball. But who is this delicious bundle of weirdness? We thought it was about time for a proper introduction...

True believer

Elizabeth Jansen – better known to her friends as Lisett – was born in 1969 in the Dutch city of Leeuwarden, birthplace of exotic dancer Mata Hari, who was executed by the French government for being a German spy during World War I. But while Vivid's performances are the work of the devil, it was young Elizabeth's Christian upbringing that set her on the road to hell.

"I was raised in a religious background and went to church every Sunday," Vivid smiles broadly, flashing a row of pearly whites that always twinkle from the stage. "What stuck with me most, though, was →

Vivid gets her teeth into her art

a Sunday school lesson when I was seven, where the teacher asked, 'Who's the most important person in your life?' Most kids said, 'Jesus!' or 'My family!' but I was the only one who said, 'Me!' The teacher agreed, and said we had to be good to ourselves or else we'd get nothing out of life. That idea's always lived with me – be respectful of others, but always look after yourself."

Buoyed with the confidence to follow her heart – and supported by her mother, who'd also harboured dreams of stardom in her youth – Vivid soon began performing in her local church and entering dance competitions. But while the church had been the foundation for her burgeoning art, a traumatic, pre-teen experience destroyed Vivid's faith and changed the course of her life forever.

"I was abused by strangers before I'd reached my teens," she says. "It had nothing to do with my family, and I've met lots of people who've gone through worse ordeals. But the abuse scarred me deeply, and my anger came out in rebellious behaviour when I got into punk and new wave music. But while my experience was horrifying, it meant I had two strong sides to my life – I had the nice, angelic side, but I'd also come face-to-face with darkness. And that's the reason I chose the name The Vivid Angel – the dark and light sides are both vital parts of me."

"I fell in love with the fetish world but never touched anyone's genitals!"

Technicolour dreams

When she was 15, Vivid had her first taste of fame on Dutch TV. "My dance school became the studio dancers on Holland's equivalent of *Top Of The Pops*," she says. "Suddenly, I was on primetime television every week! A few years later I won a dance competition, and the prize was a modelling course. Sadly, I failed on the catwalk because I swung my arms too much – I had too much energy!"

After leaving home in 1990, Vivid worked as a go-go dancer around Holland during the days of acid house raves, dancing her "arse off in front of 5,000 people" a night. But while her performances to date had been mostly mainstream, a visit to the Demask store in Amsterdam steered Vivid into fetish heaven.

"I went shopping with a friend who wanted a rubber dress for himself," she says. "I was amazed – I'd never seen clothes like that. I tried on this tight, knee-length latex dress with cut-out sections and a collar, and it made me feel classy and beautiful. It turned out that the owner was a fetish designer, and later he asked me what I wanted to be in my life. 'I want to be a star,' was my reply, and he told me about these fetish events he managed called Europerve, and how fashion shows could help me achieve my dreams."

Soon, Vivid was the face of Demask. "Fetish parties were a new world for me," she continues. "I remember being →

scared at first – there were people walking around in rubber masks with breathing tanks on their back; hardcore S&M guys, not the fashionable fetish crowd. I remember leaving the club in shock – it was like Sodom and Gomorrah right before my eyes!"

Undeterred, Vivid stuck with the fetish scene and found a new home in Amsterdam's smaller, less hardcore clubs. "I felt better when I realised that women were the ones in charge at these places," she says. "You'd get these half-naked men coming up to you and asking, 'Can I touch you?', and you could say whatever you liked. It was empowering as I could be sexy without people touching me or taking advantage. So I fell in love with the fetish world – I played with a lot of people and got inside their heads and aroused them, but never touched their genitals. And with my history of sexual abuse I found it amazing that I felt comfortable sharing something so deep and emotional."

However, things were quickly changing in the fetish scene and becoming overtly sexual – an evolution that wasn't to Vivid's tastes. "When I started out, fetish play wasn't driven by sex," she says. "It was more like a serenade, and was extremely theatrical with whips, movement and so on. However, parties started getting harder on the gay leather scene and, before long, people in every club wanted to suck and fuck. I was more into mind games, so I didn't like the way things were. Luckily, it was around this time that I was able to move into performance art."

Meat your maker

In 1996, Vivid was offered a 15-minute slot at Europerve and told she could do whatever she wanted. But no one could've predicated what happened next. "I was quite morbid in those days," Vivid recalls. "I had this idea that I wanted to crawl out of a cadaver and be a spirit. I linked up with another performer, Crazy White Sean, and we made this fake human body, put it on a table, then filled it with raw meat and blood. Sean would come on stage and start cutting the body open, and suddenly I'd fly out of its guts and send blood and meat everywhere. I still have a love for raw meat to this day!"

A video of this gruesome show soon did the rounds of the Euro fetish scene, and the two – who'd since then become lovers – started working full-time as Lisett and Sean. "We were both into being gross and over-the-top, and became renowned in fetish clubs," Vivid says. "For a time fetish events were a huge deal in Holland and TV crews went to every party, so Sean and I were interviewed on mainstream telly all the time. We were ambassadors for the scene, and even had our own 40-minute TV show."

At a crossroads

But while Vivid was becoming more renowned in mainland Europe, her uncompromising attitude to fetish performance brought her to the attention of party animals Torture Garden. "I was doing a show called 'Sex Change' at the time," she says. "I went on stage and cut off some fake boobs and a fanny, then sewed on a penis and ended up in a bowler hat doing a little dance. Torture Garden loved it, and asked me to work on the door and as a club hostess. They flew me over to London once a month, but each time they tried to persuade me to stay."

In 1999, Vivid relocated to London with nothing more than a suitcase, make-up bag and £800 cash; and although she initially found it hard to get to grips with the sprawling metropolis and its cold inhabitants, she stuck with it and developed friendships with performers who've since emerged as *Bizarre* favourites.

"I'd fly out of a fake human body and send blood and meat everywhere"

"I got to know people such as Lucifire, Miss Behave and Empress Stah," Vivid says. "I was an illusionist and known for my horror effects, but my friends were into the real stuff and taught me how to eat fire, and stub a cigar out on my tongue."

Before long, Vivid had moved beyond special effects and began pushing her body further and further. "I was doing all kinds of crazy stuff," she says. "But then I started doing real things on stage, like cutting my arms and chest with a straight razor. I was really into method acting, so before a show I'd work myself up from mid-afternoon, becoming quieter and weirder and rocking myself back and forth in a tin bath. My best friends cried and thought I'd gone too far, but I didn't agree. I didn't even feel the pain – I was in another place. When I looked at my scars the day after a show, I felt free. I realised my body would recover each time, and that's when I became proper hardcore. But that also meant I had to take a break from performing, as most →

She's definitely
a fiery one!

Fluttering her eyelashes... in her own unique way

established clubs wanted to pigeonhole me as the 'illusionist girl'. I didn't like that. I'd spilt my blood on stage, there was no going back, and for a time I had to stay goodbye to performing."

Faith, hope and clarity

With performance in her blood, of course, nothing could keep Vivid off the stage, and for a time she pursued a music career with her current boyfriend JROK. Their band, Swetbox, were often compared to System Of A Down, and played extensively around the UK in 2003 before securing a showcase in Los Angeles' legendary Whiskey A Go-Go. This gig brought Swetbox to the attention of several high-profile producers and record labels, but relocating to LA wasn't right for them at the time, so their dreams of global domination began to peter out.

"As Swetbox came to an end, I started getting back into doing my own performances," Vivid says. "And it was so much fun. I'd turn up with my own shit, be in control, then get paid and enjoy all the applause! It felt like a fresh start for me, and for the past two half years I've been performing regularly."

"It's great now as I'm getting more commercial and corporate work, rather than focusing exclusively on the fetish scene," she continues. "It's funny to look out and see all these posh men and ladies in nice suits and dresses, while I'm whirling around like a dervish with weighted chains hooked to my eyelids!"

But while the British alt.performance scene is reaching saturation point, and there's no shortage of dancers and freaks willing to go to extremes, Vivid's years of experience means she knows how to connect with her audience, no matter if they're fat-cat bankers or drunken metalheads at the Download festival. "If you don't connect with the audience, you're not an entertainer," Vivid says. "A performance is all about the audience, not about you, and if you don't connect with the crowd you're just another sexy girl wiggling her arse. I don't ever want to be that girl!"

But as she turns 40, has Vivid considered hanging up her props and costumes forever? "No way," she scoffs, her infectious laughter ricocheting around the walls. "I'm lucky, because my arse is in the same place it was 10 years ago. I often share dressing rooms with younger girls, but I never feel any pressure. I don't want to be young – I'm happy where I am. When certain performers walk on stage you know they're going to be around for a while because they look relaxed and have a natural sparkle – people such as Missy Malone and Vicky Butterfly. And that's the way I am – there's no ego, and I don't need to walk around going 'look at me!'. I'd like to be like Bruce Forsyth or Barbara Windsor – I love them! They've been around forever, and are still funny and charismatic. They're an inspiration to me. One day, I'd like to be like that." B

SPREADING HER WINGS

How The Vivid Angel made it from Amsterdam clubs to the Bizarre Ball

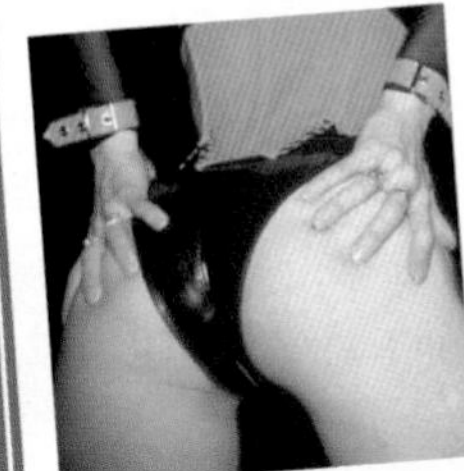

GO GO
"Ha-ha! I used to dance so hard and fast at the go-go clubs in Holland that they only ever seemed to get my ass in the shot!"

DEMASK CATALOGUE
"I love this photo from one of Demask's old fetish catalogues. Around the world, people told me they loved this shot."

CUTTING SHOW
"When this photo was taken I'd just finished cutting myself and the blood was really starting to run. My expression scared my friends and fans!"

BIZARRE BALL
"This is one of my characters, Betsy Vaudeville, who went down well at the Bizarre Ball. The act involves stomping on glass!"

SCOTTEE

This performance artist is revolting – against his mum, body fascism, and bad lip-synching…

WORDS **ALIX FOX**
PHOTOS **JOE PLIMMER**

"The bits that look like chocolate sprinkles are supposed to be spiky little pubes, as though she's had a Brazilian wax but then let it grow out until it's scratchy and beardy," says Scottee. "I'm a faggot though; I've been dating a male illustrator for five years, and haven't seen real-life lady parts since I was 16, so it might not be an accurate depiction."

Scottee's chatting about a woollen vagina he's sewing, the latest product of an embroidery hobby he took up because he "likes the idea of keeping a threatened female craft alive, plus it keeps my hands busy while my ass is parked in front of *EastEnders*."

As a so-hot-right-now experimental performance artist, DJ, host of what he calls "art-fash club bash" events, and omnipresent London gay scenester, the 24-year-old is at the centre of one of the capital's most creative social circles – but one that can also be hideously self-indulgent, catty and pretentious. You might expect Scottee to be a hyped-up, cocky nitwit. Instead, he's a witty knitter, who's likeable and surprisingly down to earth.

Pop Art

When trying to describe Scottee, you may be tempted to compare him to the late Leigh Bowery – the performance artist, designer, 1980s alt.club legend and inspiration behind Boy George's musical *Taboo*. After all, there are strong echoes of Leigh's 'Birth Show' – where he pretended to give birth to his friend and future wife Nicola Bateman – in Scottee's 'Diet Coke', where he plays a downtrodden middle-aged woman who pops out a Coca-Cola child. But Scottee has his own stories and ideas, and protests that "any fat guy who likes to wear make-up and a vaguely spherical outft is bound to get compared to Leigh – it's a compliment, but also a lazy comparison".

"I always formulate my acts by picking a vivid memory or an image that's had a strong impact upon me, then extrapolating it by →

asking 'Now, what would happen if...?'," Scottee explains. "During the 1990s, there was a TV advert where these women in an office would take a 'Diet Coke break' to perv at a builder taking his top off outside. I found it homoerotic – the guy was gorge! I wondered what would happen if the dumpiest lass in the company managed to somehow hump this hunk, then got pregnant with his Diet Coke baby."

From carbonated children to bursting bolognese boobs, Scottee's 'Lady In Red' act sees him becoming a busty secretary. Tired of colleagues talking only to her chest and valuing her solely for her body, she decides to use scissors to chop off her breasts – made from plastic pouches filled with tomato pasta sauce.

"This character's based on someone I only got a fleeting glimpse of, but who I've never been able to forget," Scottee says. "It was a lady slumped against the entrance of a bar bawling her eyes out while her work Christmas party continued inside, with red wine all down her white shirt, pockets full of stationary, and a ratty bit of tinsel round her neck. When you see a woman blubbing in the street, it sort of feels like art – it's so raw and real, and such a contrast to everyone else around who's keeping their shit rigidly together and their regulation 'public face' in place. Weeping women are fabulous. This sounds quite dark, but I always thought my mum was at her most beautiful when she was crying – mascara and kohl smeared down her face, sobbing along to Lisa Stansfield songs."

"I always thought my mum was at her most beautiful when she was crying"

Keeping mum

Scottee's mum cried a lot. She might still cry a lot now, but Scottee doesn't have a clue; he hasn't spoken to her for three years. "Gay men are supposed to have a special affinity with their mothers, but I had to cut ties with mine to preserve my own mental health," he begins. "I grew up on an estate in north London, home to the Camden Boyz gang, who left a man brain damaged during a fight with concrete slabs, baseball bats and knives in 2005. It's the kind of area where violence is so commonplace that no-one comments on it.

"My parents fought tooth and nail. At age 12 I discovered the man I lived with wasn't my real dad, and spent years asking about my biological father – but my parents refused to tell me more than 'he's Greek'. I was frustrated that they withheld information I felt I had a right to know; I was permanently shaky and fractious, worrying about their behaviour. I began to meddle with substances, alcohol and bingeing to cope with how stressed they made me. I couldn't do it any more. To keep my sanity, I consciously stopped having a relationship with my folks, and my life changed. An enormous deadweight was lifted."

Before making this decision, still trapped at home, the teenage Scottee used to find relief by escaping on the number 24 bus to a youth theatre group. He soon landed small roles in *The Bill*, and also worked as a stunt double in a Harry Potter film aged 16: "It was more boring than it sounds, unfortunately; most of the time I was just standing in as the back of a Hogwarts student's head."

These dull days put Scottee off movies, so the young thesp moved onto fringe theatre instead – but that was also a disappointment, "full of 'conceptual' buffoons pretending to push themselves over while philosophising about apples" – so he joined a community arts group called Spare Tyre Theatre Company. →

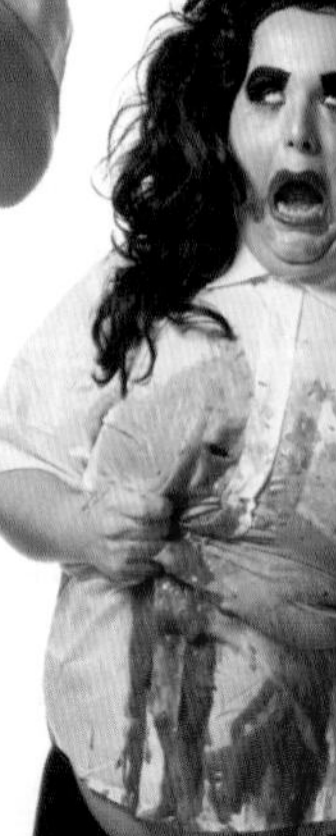

"Noooo! My favourite shoes!"

"Just keep on pushing!"
"Now I make a living rolling around in my own vulgarity, vanity and vomit!"
Diet Coke

"I collaborated with a group of elderly people to produce a musical all about their lives in the 1930s and 40s, called 'Same Meat Different Gravy,'" Scottee enthuses. "Off the back of that, the government hired us to put together anti-ageism training packages for carers who deal with older people. I discovered how much I loved performing pieces that had a political slant to them, pushed boundaries, or offered a social commentary, and this philosophy continues in the work I do today. However, when Spare Tyre put a project together to tackle homophobia in educational establishments, but only garnered interest from a pathetic two schools, I became disillusioned again. I quit mainstream acting companies altogether and hit the gay and fashion-forward club scene hard. I worked – and networked – like a motherfucker, got a name for myself as part of several influential party-organising crews – including Kashpoint, Popstarz, Foreign, Yr Mum Ya Dad, and more – then began to introduce myself as a solo performance artist against a background of avant garde nightlife. Now I make a living rolling around in my own vulgarity, vanity and vomit!"

Regurgi-tate modern

Scottee's work is rife with references to sick – and weight. He sees his size as a tool he can use to his advantage, and frequently strips off on stage. "After a decade of diets and doldrums I had a revelation when I was 18, and realised that other people are more afraid and shocked by seeing my body than I am," he says. "The fact that I'm now comfortable with something that still makes them feel awkward gives me power and authority over them. But my acts aren't only about being fat. I use my gut as a prop, yes, but I go much further than that. Getting my stomach out is only one small part of a creative, varied show; it's not the sole big reveal. Not like a damned tassel twirl..."

Scottee faces up to 'fatherhood'

Not his cup of tease...

Aha. Burlesque. A subject Scottee holds more venom for than a pit full of pissed-off pythons. While he's got plenty of time for inventive performers such as Syban V and thinks Immodesty Blaize is "one of the most charismatic women I've ever met, who lives and breathes her art 24/7, and makes a striptease look like ballet", he slates most burlesque as "backwards, misogynistic, and incredibly boring."

Is there anything else that gets Scottee's goat? "I also can't stand lip-synching tranny performers getting lyrics wrong," he says. "For Christ's sake, they don't have to write the words – just remember them! To make my point, I made a video called LipSync Swim, where I did synchronised swimming in a bath full of water while wearing a peg on my nose singing The Supremes' 'You Can't Hurry Love'. And I didn't get a single line wrong." Ⓑ

GREAT SCOTT

Snapshots of Scottee's story so far

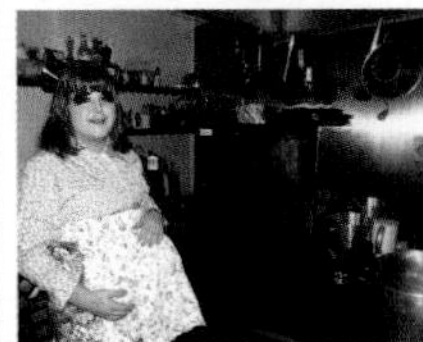

TORTURE GARDEN

"In my 'dressing room' before performing at London Torture Garden, ready to deliver 'Diet Coke'. They treat me so well."

DIGITARIA

"Thinking out of the box just before the opening of Digitaria, a gallery and art boutique I'm curating in Soho. I hold knitting clubs there."

JODIE HARSH

"On my estate, rocking a 'Harsh Is My Homegirl' T-shirt. Drag queen Jodie Harsh and I often collaborate and get along well."

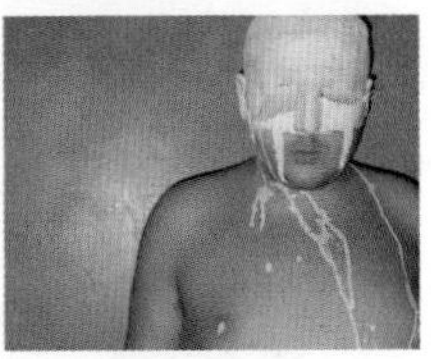

STAR DJ

The first ever 'look' I created to DJ for a Ministry Of Sound night called Nude. It wasn't the easiest cosmetic arrangement to work in."

From Cambridge drama luvvie to cabaret king, meet the delectable...

DESMOND O'CONNOR

WORDS **BEN MYERS**
PHOTOS **JOE PLIMMER**

From childhood punk to Cambridge drama luvvie to potty-mouthed Latin teacher, Desmond O'Connor is the new cabaret king of UK burlesque. If you've frequented club nights in London, New York or Amsterdam in recent years – or checked out some of the small stages at music festivals – there's a good chance you've come across Des O'Connor, who describes himself as a "rare male in a girl's world".

As MC and ringmaster of many a cabaret night, he's the man who holds it all together; as a politely spoken, ukulele-wielding, corpse paint-wearing songwriter he's responsible for one of the darkest and most hilarious songs currently gracing the world's stages. He's in demand, is utterly *Bizarre*, and we love him. Naturally we had to find out who the hell he is, where he's come from, and what it is about necrophilia that he finds so jolly entertaining...

Best foot forward

Imagine someone with the same cut-glass grasp of the English language and tempered demeanour as comedians Jimmy Carr and David Mitchell – with the delivery of Nöel Coward or performance poets such as Ivor Cutler or John Hegley – but with the subject matter of an extreme metal band, and you begin to approach →

"I'm a demon! Fear me!"

what Des O'Connor is about. Born in Northampton, Des (not to be confused with him off the telly, of course) first moved to Leicestershire, then, at the age of 12, to Romford in Essex – "which was quite a fucking shock, actually". Escape at that point came through performance.

"My earliest memories are of performing," Des explains. "I was basically a show-off. I gave my first performance at four years old, which I imagine was a bit gruesome for all concerned. I got into musical theatre shortly after that."

The young Des also found solace in punk and new wave music, especially the escapism offered by dandy-ish pop star Adam Ant. "I've always been quite bipolar in my tastes," he remembers. "The first single I bought was Adam & The Ants' 'Stand And Deliver', when I was about eight years old. I was a member of his fan club and used to get sent lots of deeply unsuitable material through the post. Being a punk got me in trouble at school, yet at the same I was also playing classical piano from the age of six and discovering Stephen Sondheim – and Andrew Lloyd Webber, before I realised how rubbish he was! So music and lyrics have been passions of mine, right from the beginning."

Des's first attempts at songwriting came while staging musicals as a child, but it wasn't until he won a place at the University Of Cambridge, where he joined famous student entertainment troupe the Footlights, that he found his theatrical footing. He happened to arrive during a particularly creative →

> "I sing thinly-veiled songs about my own neuroses, concerns and worries"

Des has a relaxing night in

"Magicus, magica, magicum"

era that has since spawned many of today's comedy successes, including Ali G, Borat and Brüno creator Sacha Baron Cohen, *Peep Show*'s David Mitchell and Robert Webb, Matthew Holness of cult TV show *Garth Marenghi's Darkplace*, and Richard Ayoade of *The IT Crowd* and *The Mighty Boosh*. In fact, after Desmond "had a year off university for good behaviour", David Mitchell asked him to be musical director of the famed theatrical group.

"You're never sure whether your Footlights generation is going to be a high achieving one," remembers Des. "It turns out mine was. In fact, I think Sacha did his first live sketches on the same night I did mine – I'm still playing catch-up with him. Footlights was full of very confident comics, and adept writers and performers, so it was daunting, but I worked hard to keep up and be a part of it."

It was only after Cambridge that he began to carve his own niche in cabaret. "I always think, 'Perhaps this is going to be my year and they'll all end up unemployed,'" he laughs.

The devil's in the detail

Latin to laughing

Des is certainly a star in waiting, and he's a genuine one-off: an ultra-polite and classically educated individual who you're almost shocked to hear swearing. In fact, he sounds like an old Latin schoolmaster. Wait a minute – he is a Latin schoolmaster!

"Yes, I currently teach at a well-known central London school," Des sheepishly reveals. "And that's why you won't find a lot of clips of my more risqué songs on the internet – because I could get in quite a bit of trouble. But I'm just in the process of finishing my final teaching stint. After this last summer term, I shall be doing cabaret and burlesque full-time."

> "People see my ukulele and hear my accent but end up shocked by the content"

While his performance is polished, heartfelt and utterly endearing, the artist we see today only began performing his current act three years ago as compere to London band The Shortwave Set, who were hosting a night called The Pawn Shop in Soho.

"At that point I had no sense of visual style whatsoever," he explains. "The burlesque and cabaret scene was enjoying a resurgence and – this is a desperately shallow thing to say – I realised that I'd never get my picture in magazines while dressed like a tramp. So I remembered my love of Adam Ant and dressing up, and I decided to make more of an effort with my clothes and make-up."

Was this sudden fondness for painting his face perhaps a way of adopting a mask as a barrier between the gregarious host we see onstage and the sensitive soul offstage? "Yes, completely," explains Des. "In fact, my new show is all to do with masks and identity. I'm known for singing rude and silly songs, but the majority of my work is serious, or certainly from the heart. I sing thinly-veiled songs about my own neuroses, concerns and worries. But as soon as I began to dress all that up in extreme make-up and present a flamboyant character on stage it allowed me to be honest about myself. I think it was (*Bizarre*'s own) Alix Fox who first said to me, 'Your songs aren't really comedy songs. They're really sad and serious'. And I took that as a compliment – the fact that I'm using subversive means to address issues that you wouldn't normally discuss in a comedy club."

Fucking your mum

So what exactly are these issues and neuroses that Des sings about? Well, anything, it seems. Incest, animals and a crowd-pleasing song →

The ukulele had been stringing him along

about necrophilia that contains lines such as: '*Love is great, romance is fab / When you're humping and pumping on a coroner's slab*'.

"I tackle anything that you shouldn't really be able to sing about in a cheeky and frivolous manner," he laughs. "For a long time I thought that necrophilia was the most extreme subject to sing about, but then I branched out. For a Mother's Day gig in Amsterdam I wrote a beautiful, touching song entitled, 'If You Were My Mum I'd Fuck You'. In fact, it was such a triumph I performed it at the Bizarre Ball in 2008."

Such subjects may be hard to digest, but Des's ability to sugar such bitter lyrical pills sets him apart from many of today's shockmeisters. And Latin's loss is the entertainment world's gain: Des's current schedule stretches around the world and well into 2010. It's all down to a combination of dogged determination – and good timing.

"Burlesque was a god-send to me," he says. "Before its revival I didn't feel there was the right outlet for what I was doing. Had it not been for burlesque I doubt I would've broken out of being an MC on the music scene. I'm very impulsive, so when I saw an advert for a new burlesque night at the Bethnal Green Working Men's Club I decided there and then that I wanted to be a part of it all. By that Friday, I was performing there and was spotted by Dusty Limits, who's a big name in cabaret, and who got me many more shows and has been a huge help to me. There aren't many men in burlesque – it's great to be a limited commodity – and hopefully I'm quite central to this new alternative cabaret scene."

Devilish charm

He's clearly a man in love with all aspects of the murky hinterlands of the new wave of vaudevillian performance, but he's also quick to point out that he leads a far from glamourous existence – most nights are spent "getting changed in dingy cupboards alongside mops and buckets".

Des's most recent show was called And The Devil May Drag You Under, a variety performance that he describes as "in your face, crazy, crude and a very fucked-up cabaret show", and which included circus performances, musical interludes, striptease and Des playing The Devil. It had the overall feel of the best illicit speakeasy you'd hope to find yourself in, with Des's customary dark humour defining the tone of the evening.

"I realised I'd never get my picture in the magazines while dressed like a tramp"

"People see me with my ukulele and hear the charming Englishman accent so have certain expectations, but end up being quite shocked by the content," he says. "It's all about working an audience – it's about taking people out of their comfort zone, but still putting them at ease."

As Des prepares to give up teaching, his thoughts turn towards his newest show, 'Desmorphia', which is set to shock even more. "I'm taking it to far darker places," he says. "I have a new song about an anorexic couple who fall in love and feed off their passion for each other, but nothing else. It's sweet, funny and very bleak. I also have a song about an impotent panda, which, as usual, contains many thinly-veiled references to myself.

"What else? Oh yes, I have a song about a haemo-phobic vampire. It's a song based upon duality that lies in all my songs. It's one to herald the end of my teaching life and welcome in the next stage of my career."

Going on past performances, it looks like this Dark Star is going to be a huge success. Ⓑ

Des and his invisible orchestra

CABA-HOORAY!

A cabaret comedy career

BETHNAL GREEN

"My cabaret career began when I was dragged from my quiet classroom life by indie art-rockers The Shortwave Set. Their weekly Soho gathering, The Pawn Shop, reignited my interest in writing and I went to perform at Bethnal Green Working Men's Club."

BESTIVAL

"I was quickly taken under the sequined wing of the burlesque community. Shortly after this photo was taken I started hosting Burlesque FreakOut in Amsterdam and The Tassel Club in Dublin. A year later I returned to Bestival as a presenter for MTV."

EDINBURGH

"At the Edinburgh Fringe I discovered the need to dress up, mess up and associate with important, lovely people. Amanda Palmer was incredibly supportive and booked me to play at her Best Of The Fringe soiree, then invited me to perform with The Dresden Dolls in New York."

AND THE DEVIL MAY DRAG YOU UNDER

"The support of *Bizarre*, Ministry Of Burlesque, Blond Ambition and Fletch Productions resulted in the success of my cabaret cavalcade And The Devil May Drag You Under. It became an award-winning show on The Brighton Fringe."

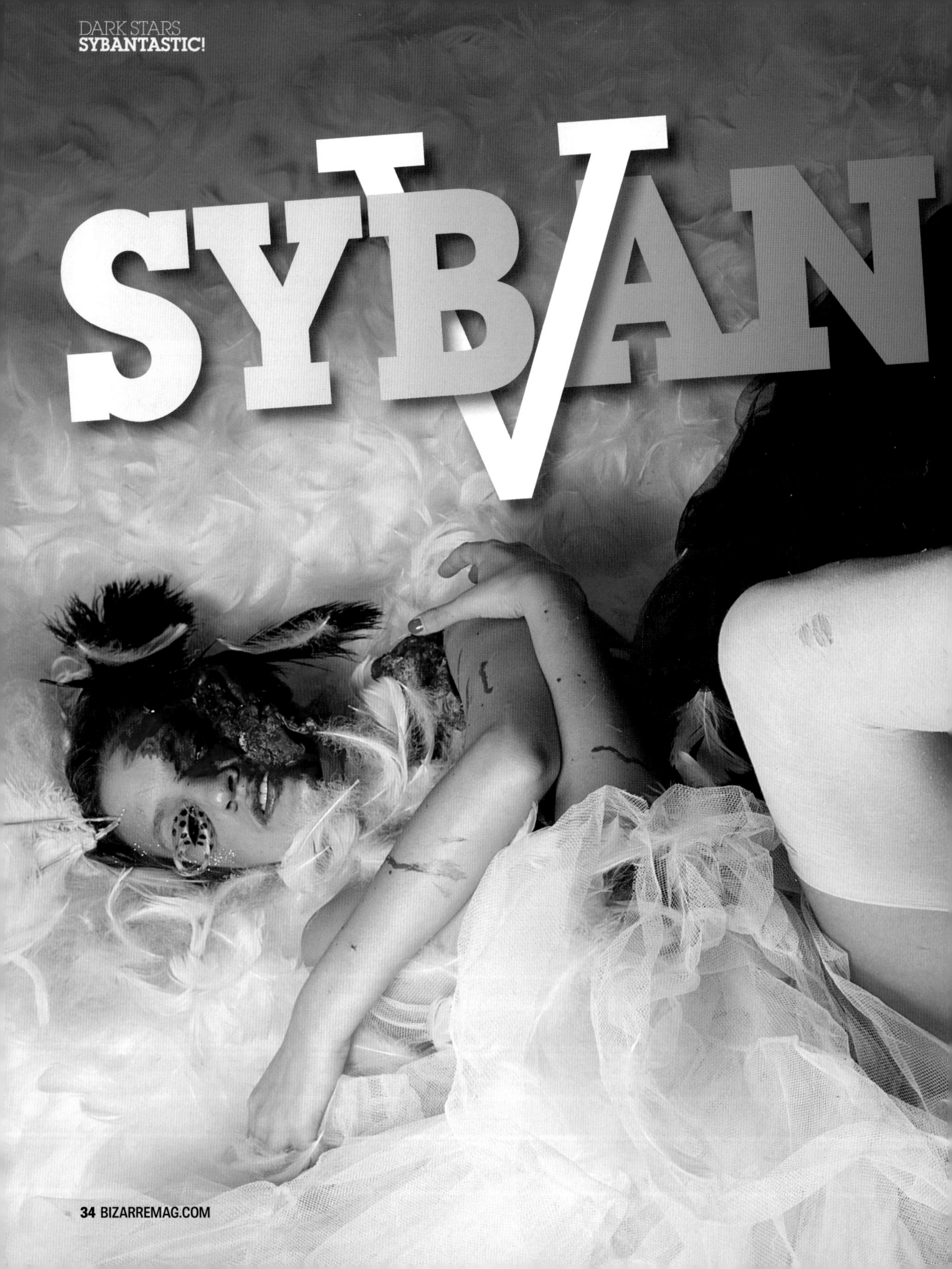

SYBVAN

Like a riddle wrapped in an enigma, this girl's a whole new kind of crazy

WORDS **BEN MYERS**
PHOTOS **JOE PLIMMER**

From working underage in London's fetish clubs to performing blood-splattered, one-woman versions of *Swan Lake*, Syban V's colourful life has been dedicated to dancing, travelling and performing, but mainly, in her own words, the endless pursuit of "shits and giggles". "None of this is a career for me," she explains. "It would never work. I don't have a website and I don't have a business card. It's strange – people and opportunities just seem to present themselves to me. I think perhaps it's because I'm the same person offstage as I am on it, so what you see is what you get. I suppose you could say I was a born performer."

And what do you get? A colourful ball of energy that's crammed more into her 21 years than most manage in a lifetime. Here's Syban's strange and wonderful story...

World of trouble

Born Syban Velardi-Laufer to Italian and Venezuelan parents and raised Jewish, Syban's life was never going to be conventional. Her formative years were spent in Italy, Israel and London, where she went to school in Chelsea's ultra-posh Sloane Square – when she wasn't spending three or four months travelling the world.

"I think travel is one of the best things you can do," she enthuses. "My mind was opened up to different cultures and languages, and I spent all my time around grown-ups. I was very privileged. To get so much visual stimulation at such a young age is a great inspiration. Also, my mother is a designer, so I was always exposed to creativity from a young age – I experienced theatre, ballet and dancing on a worldwide scale."

Taking up dance from the age of three, Syban was the young girl who liked dressing up, but never stopped. An epiphany of sorts came at the age of 12.

"I was a quiet child until that point," she remembers. "Though I liked dressing up and was a Barbie obsessive, I distinctly remember one night when I couldn't sleep that I had this realisation. I said to myself that I was never going to be quiet again, never going to be →

boring or mousey or conventional. Since that moment my life has been full of colour and craziness."

This 'craziness' began her teens, when Syban would turn up at school with pink hair and fairy wings. "When I was 16 I did a bondage show as an art project," she says. "I covered the art studio in plastic bags and tied up my friend, who was dressed as Catwoman. At that moment the headmistress walked in with a group of parents on an open day... but even then it was, like 'Oh, and this – *this* – is Syban...'. I existed entirely in my own bubble."

Little Miss Naughty

While still at school, Syban found herself spending more and more time in the spiritual home of British alt.culture: Camden Town. Despite being underage she got a job in a shop that was also a fetish club, and began working as a 'walkabout'. It wasn't long before she caught the eye of other key players on the scene.

"One night a performer didn't turn up for a medical performance," she remembers. "The people running the show said, 'Syban, you're crazy, do you want to do it?' and because I've always been insanely reckless I stepped in and did it without much thought. The next thing I knew they were sticking needles in me from my collar bone to hip. It didn't hurt at all, and it was at that point that I realised I have an obscenely high pain tolerance."

Medical performances lead to an interest in rope bondage, which lead to a job at Torture Garden – all while Syban was still 16. "People saw me dressed up around town," she grins. "They'd ask me what I did, and I'd say 'Er... I'm Syban and I'm fantabulous' and they'd say 'Cool, do you want to come and do a show?'"

If this sounds like dangerous waters for a impressionable teen, then rest assured – Syban claims she's always had a wise head on her shoulders. "I'm aware that bad things can happen out there, but I've been self-aware and lucky," she explains. "I've always known that drug use can alter the chemicals in the brain, so I'm anti-drugs, to the point where my friends tell me off for being too judgmental. I suspect I produce an unnaturally high level of serotonin as it is, and I've been told I'm batshit-crazy enough already. Plus, if everyone else is doing something I'm inclined not to do it, just to be different. I can actually hallucinate without drugs anyway, so instead I draw inspiration from the ultra-vivid dreams that I have every night. From these dreams come my characters, my clothes, my poems – everything."

Clowning around

Clothes and characters form the basis for all of Syban's performances today. She learnt how to make costumes during an 18-month internship at a couture fashion house, and has performed as a zombie, a pregnant clown, and her own twisted version of *Swan Lake*. Whether she's performing in country estates, churches, or overseas, she always provokes a response.

> "I decided I was never going to be boring, mousey or conventional"

"A pretty typical reaction is, 'What the fuck?'" she laughs mischievously. "I did this zombie show in Athens, where I cut parts of my body off. I cut my breasts off and then ate them, and then I cut my head open and ate my brain. I remember looking up and seeing someone masturbating at one side of the room and someone vomiting at the other."

Another performance is Pregnant Clown Lady, which came to Syban after she cut her foot open in Egypt and developed a fever. "The story of the Pregnant Clown Lady came to me in this weird state," she explains. "She's this huge, fucked-up character who drinks and smokes and has broken her body to such an extent that she can't give birth naturally. So she cuts herself open and pulls her baby out – it's dead and full of pink rose petals. I don't just put on a show – I tell a story." →

Syban found pregnancy hard to stomach

We bet Tchaikovsky never did this

The nutty professor

When asked how to categorise her show, Syban is – for the only time – temporarily lost for words. "It's not burlesque," she ponders. "And though I do fire stuff, piercing and stapling, I wouldn't categorise myself as any of those. I just find it amazing that as human beings we can continually recreate ourselves through new characters. What's most interesting is people's reaction to me. Older people might see me on the street and assume I'm deviant or a trouble-maker, but I'm really not like that at all."

"I draw inspiration from the ultra-vivid dreams I have every night"

Syban's certainly a one-off, though, referring to herself in the third person – "Syban is very happy today" – or littering the conversation with 'Sybantilisms', made-up words to describe fictional creatures or feelings in the fantasy universe that she immerses herself in: 'Sybantelope', 'Sybanticore', 'Sybantastistic' and so forth. She picked up the stage name Syban V while working for wrestling cabaret act and *Bizarre* favourites Lucha Britannia. And though she speaks to *Bizarre* today through the fog of jetlag having just spent five weeks sleeping on beaches in Venezuela, London is where she calls home, and where she's currently studying fashion at university by day and performing by night. And when she's not performing she's being "a crazy little scientist", working on new clothes and wigs.

"I love London because there are creative things you can do here that you can't do anywhere else in the world – but it can be toxic and crazy-ass too," she asserts. "It can send you mad. There are two halves to my life: one's all about these intense levels of theatrical creativity, making my own clothes and performing in them, and the other is escaping to the jungle or the beach... or anywhere. I just disappear in order to replenish myself."

Tonight she'll go home and stay up half the night making a cage that's also a skirt – or possibly vice versa. Either way, it'll be done in her own inimitable style. "There's no persona here," she concludes. "For some reason, people just seem to pay me to be myself. Maybe that's where the Salvador Dali influence comes in – art wasn't a job for him, it was who he was. It was his existence and his art was part of that. I see my life the same way: I am a fabricator and a performer at all times. I don't own a pair of jeans and I'm pretty much anti-Primark, anti-Topshop. I believe that life is full of personal choice and it's up to you to live as wonderful life as possible."

"SYBAN IS VERY HAPPY TODAY!"

The story so far, from little princess to hillbilly clown

PRINCESS CHEEKS!
"When you push things through your cheeks they make this lovely little 'pop' sound! Once I attached a big rubber mouth to my face."

ZOMBIE PRINCESS
"I went to The Amsterdam Clinic about two years ago, and it was the first time I'd performed abroad by myself."

THE TREE
"I'm fascinated by turning myself into something else. I'm never bothered about looking 'sexy' – I just love being surreal and making clothes."

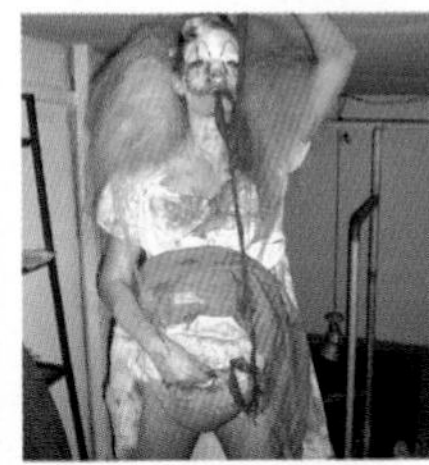

PREGNANT
"This was taken backstage in Athens after my hillbilly Pregnant Clown Lady show. She's fast becoming one of my favorite characters."

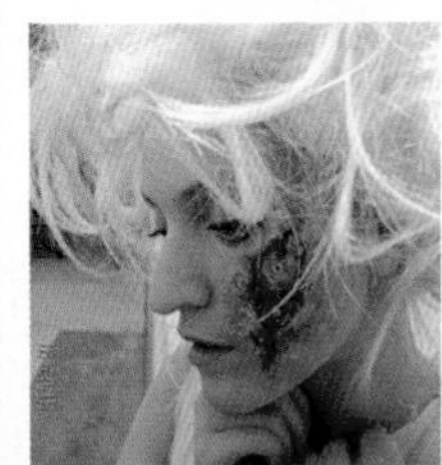

SYBANTIROBOT
"Although most of my friends think I'm a little crazy, what they don't realise is that I'm secretly a Sybantirobot. Can't you tell?"

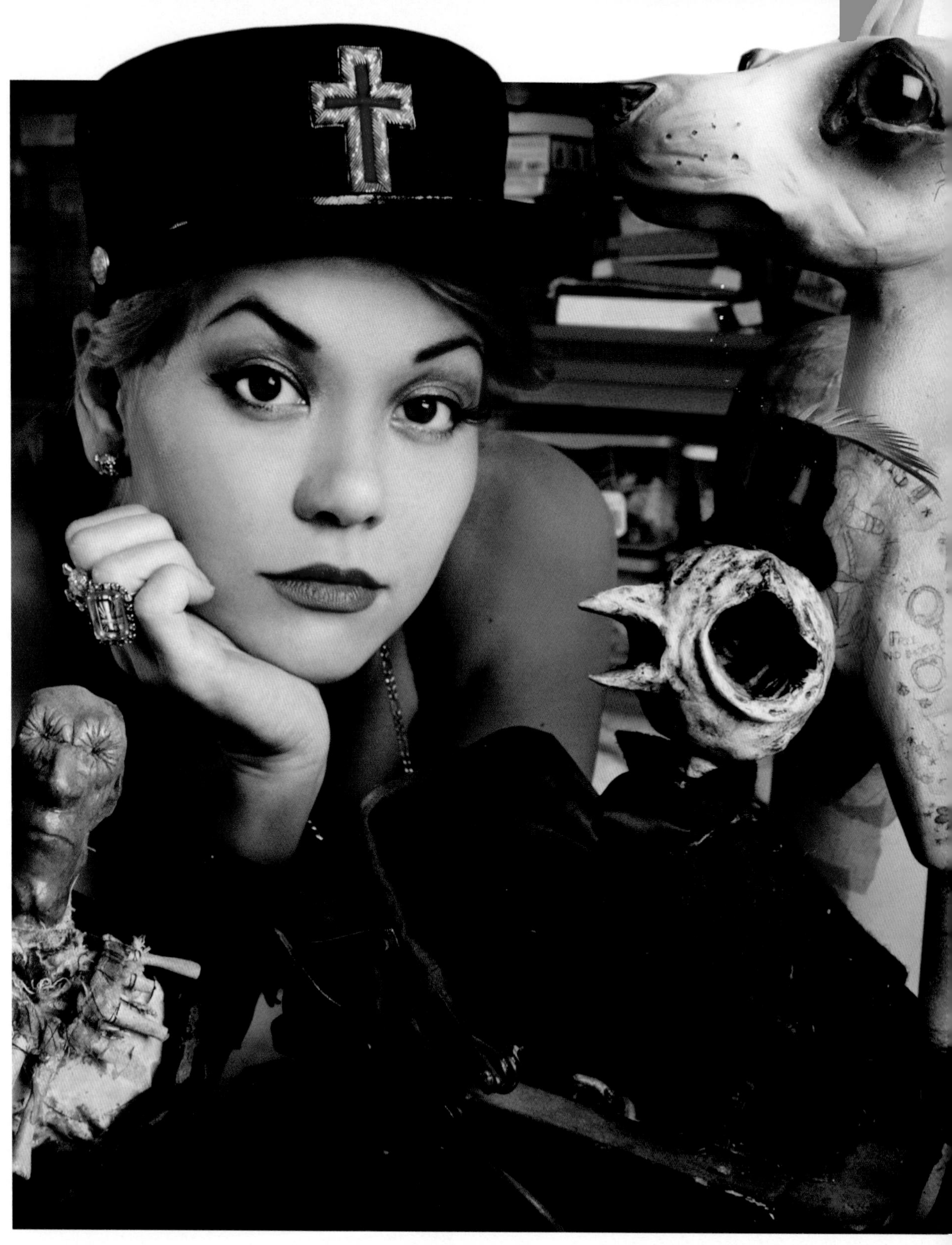

ALT. ARTISTS

Today, the mainstream is trying to gatecrash the alternative art scene – but *Bizarre* met its kookiest creators first…

42

66

50

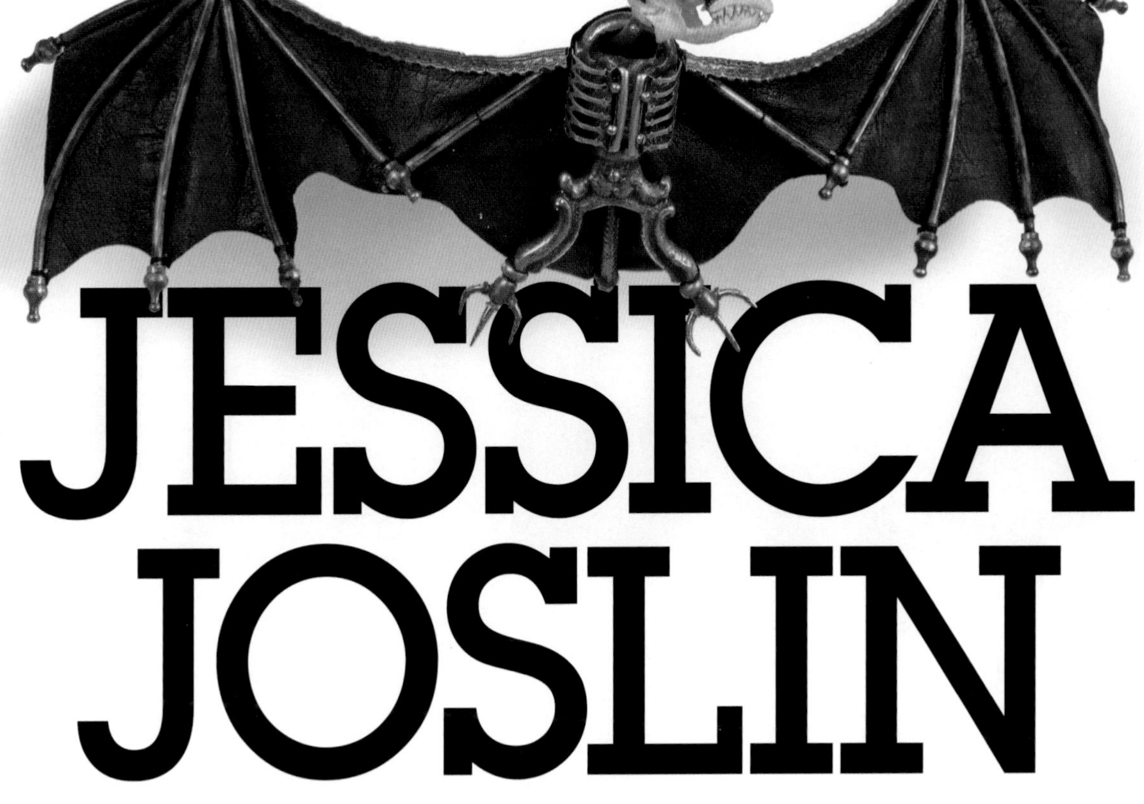

JESSICA JOSLIN

The alternative artist who turns animal corpses into sculptures of wonder

WORDS **JACK RUBY MURRAY**
PHOTOS **NEVILLE ELDER**

Jessica Joslin is an elegant woman with piercing grey-green eyes and pale skin, set off with a blood-red shock of hair piled high on her head. Dressed in black, the 37-year-old mixed media artist welcomes *Bizarre* into her home in Chicago to share the secrets of the 'Victorian clockwork' aesthetic that drives her eerie and magical artwork.

Jessica creates 'creatures' from the bones of animals and discarded scrap metal. The macabre figures evoke feelings most of us left behind a long time ago, when we put down childish things and took up the reins of adulthood. A monkey wearing a fez and riding a tricycle, and a deer decorated with a Cleopatra-style headdress watch *Bizarre* with dead black eyes as Jessica tells us how she assembled her menagerie.

"I don't go looking for roadkill any more," she says in a low, husky voice. "I buy the bones from osteological suppliers – and I know a lot of bone dealers. If you find a bone and you don't know where it came from, you can get into trouble for using it. Finding a skull on the street doesn't mean you can keep it."

Jessica shows *Bizarre* cabinets and drawers stuffed with the skulls and bones of birds and small mammals, all as bright and white as children's teeth. When she →

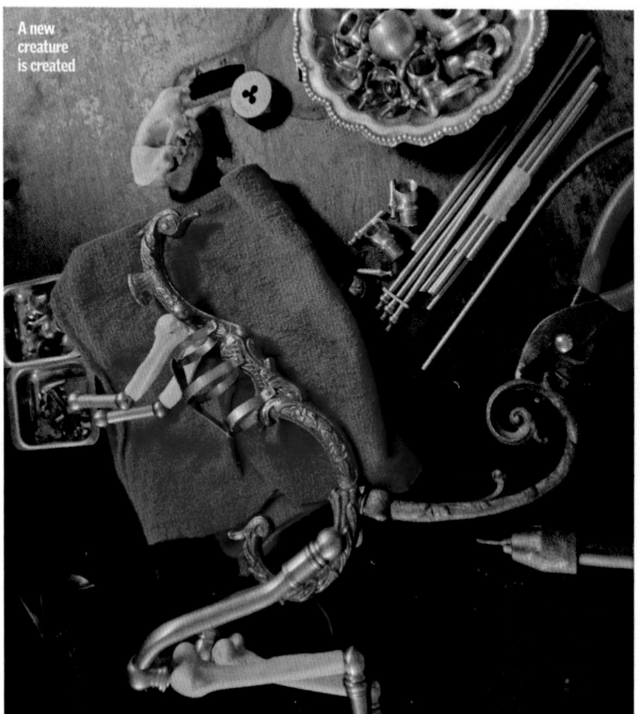
A new creature is created

"Any one peculiar item with a nice patina can be the starting point of a new pet," she explains. "I look for items that have an nice tone to them. I spent many years building architectural models where I needed an incredible level of precision. And I apply that to my art."

These creations aren't just glued together. Jessica takes the raw materials and fuses the pieces mechanically – drilling new threads to assemble the skeletons, as they may be made from different gauges of pipes, or linking solid lumps of brass with no identifiable origin. And the bones have their own peculiar characteristics to consider.

"The process needs to be over-engineered to compensate for the extreme differences in bones between species," she says. "For example, the outside casing of bird bones are extremely thin. The skeleton is composed of delicate lattice work that keeps it light for flight, whereas a cow bone is like rock – there's very little hollow area in it. It's dense because it supports all this flesh."

The animals' eyebrows and hair come from trimmings taken from objects such as embroidered gloves, or the fringes on vestment trims. These quirky touches give her work a sense of fun that defies the creepiness, and many of her beasts appear to be alive or animated. One of her favourite reference points is the Victorian circus – many of her animals balance on balls or ride bikes.

"I don't think of what I'm doing as dark, necessarily," she says. "Death is inherent in the work because of the bones, of course. But I see the work as part of the love for the living creature – and if they're going to have a life after death, I want it to be fun." →

"I'd find dead bodies in the woods and wrap them in chicken wire"

lived in the countryside, she'd go on roadkill scavenging trips and find the carcasses of birds and animals – but then had to work out how to clean her treasures.

"I'd find dead bodies in the woods and wrap them in chicken wire to protect them from being carried away by wild animals," she says. "I'd come back a couple of months later to find the elements had cleaned the bones."

Brass monkeys

The main structures of Jessica's sculptures are made from brass. Stuff found in junk shops and flea markets – light fittings, chandelier parts, decorative sconces, radiators and gas lamps – are also fair game. She's used to fitting strange things together as she also works as a commercial model maker, building prototypes of toys.

Jessica loves him skele-tons

Neville's proud of his plumed hat

'Til death do us part

Whimsical but perverse, these animals seem to have emerged from a forgotten era. Jessica admits influences such as the madcap taxidermy of British artist Walter Potter and the anatomically perfect etchings of John James Audubon, as well as the nightmarish paintings of Hieronymus Bosch. As a child her father would take her to the Harvard Museum Of Natural History in Boston, where she was intrigued by the ability to get close to the stuffed birds and animals and really study them. These Victorian collections came with the era's grandiose presentations: wooden cabinets with brass plaques are another obvious link to Jessica's work.

Though fascinated by the Victorian obsession of collecting anatomical specimens, it wasn't until she was studying photography at college that Jessica took her first steps towards the sculptures she makes today. She got hold of her first raw materials by collecting the bodies of birds who'd crashed into a huge mirrored wall at the base of the Art Institute Of Chicago, and fallen into the pond below. "It was a graveyard with all these incredibly brilliantly coloured little jewels," Jessica says. "It made me so sad to see guys fishing the dead birds out with nets and dumping them in the garbage. So I started taking them home and preserving them."

The bones are sorted by type

"I started taking dead birds home and freezing them"

It was around this time that Jessica met her husband, Jared. He saw her watching the birds circulating in the flow of the fountain, they started chatting, and discovered they both had a freezer full of dead birds! As Jessica says, "I gave him my phone number and offered to give him taxidermy lessons – and that was that!"

Jared, a wonderful artist whose style is rooted in the 1930s, has always been a great supporter of Jessica's work. "My earlier pieces had quite rigid poses," she says. "He was one of the first people to say, 'You need to figure out a way to make them more lively.' So I got them to bend, twist and pose."

No bones about it

Jessica's been showing and selling her work in Chicago since she left college, but finds local taste a little conservative. →

Her art sells thorough the Lisa Sette Gallery in Scottsdale, Arizona. She finds her exhibition openings are a good way to judge how her work is received, and smiles, "People are either horrified or delighted. There isn't a whole lot in between!"

As her work gets larger (her biggest piece, Francesca the ostrich, stands at eye level) she hopes to reduce the weight of her pieces by using wood instead of metal where she can. She also has an eye to creating the plinths and cabinets that enhance her Victoriana aesthetic, and trained by building sets for the Johnny Depp remake of crime drama *Public Enemies*.

> "I see the work as part of the love for living creatures"

Jessica sees beauty in the dead, but happily, she doesn't covet bones of the living. "I think of the animals I use as muses," she explains. "I never think, 'I wish I could get that bone out of that guy' but more like, 'come here and sit for me'. I'll pose and study my friends' pets for ideas." She thinks working with human bones would be cheesy – the art would be overwhelmed by the controversy of using such grisly materials – but says her own bones could be an exception. "I'd like my own remains to become part of a metal structure. I'd leave instructions on how to assemble it with my bones after my death."

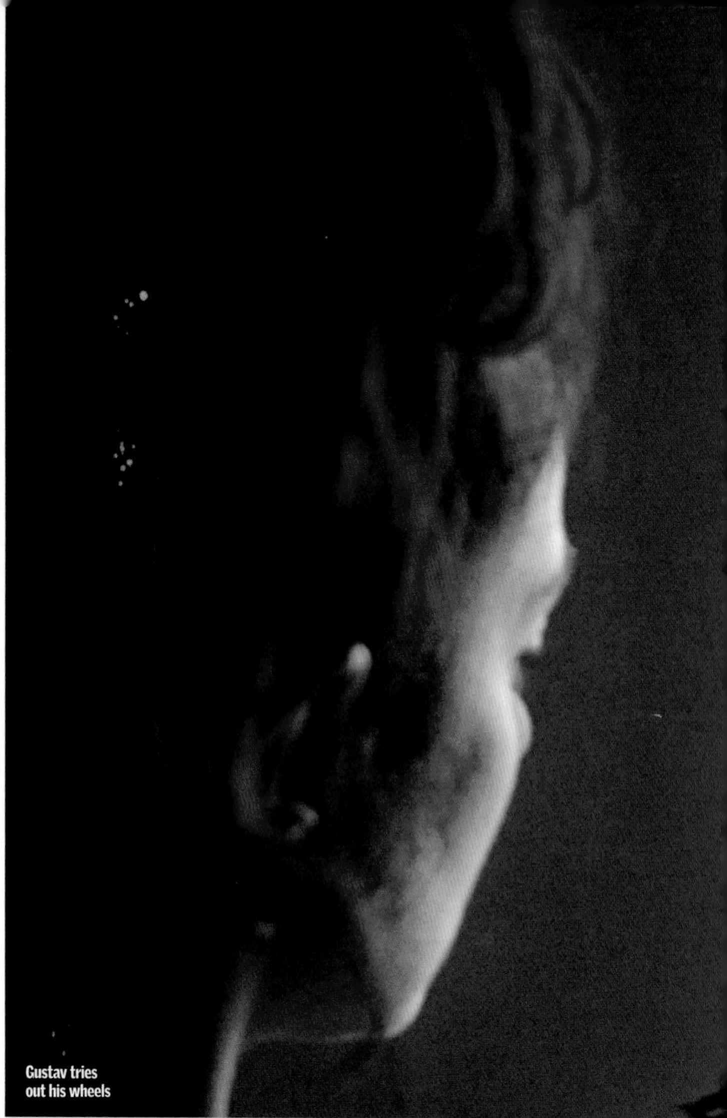

Gustav tries out his wheels

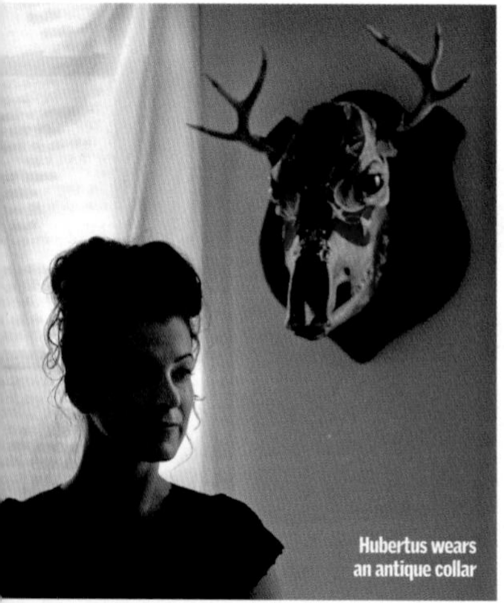

Hubertus wears an antique collar

Jessica's collection of oddities

SKELETONS IN THE CLOSET

The secret creatures with a second chance at life

HELMUT
DEER WITH WHEELED FOOT

"I found a deer skeleton by the road, and gave him a wheel as a tribute to one of Helmut Newton's photoshoots."

OTTO
MONKEY ON BALL

"My husband loved Otto so much that I made him one to keep for our 10-year anniversary."

LAUTREC
BAT

"Bats are small and fragile. For the delicate wing structure I used some tiny brass curtain rods made for a doll's house."

HAPPY
DACHSHUND

"I met a couple who said they had the skeleton of their pet dog – about a year later they sent me the bones."

GUSTAV
MONKEY ON TRICYCLE

"Each claw is cut from curtain rings and all of the ears and eyelids are made from antique opera gloves."

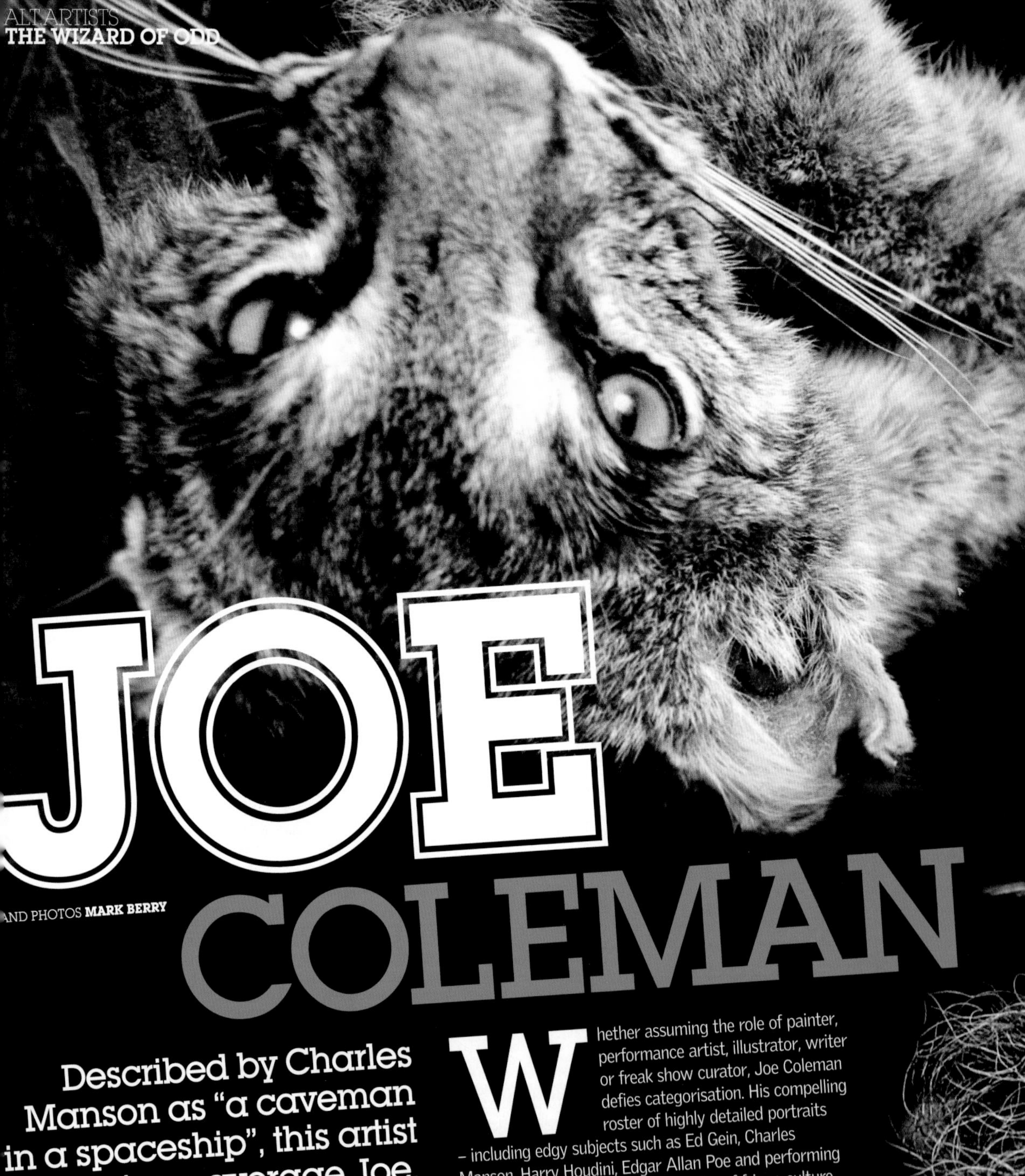

JOE COLEMAN

AND PHOTOS **MARK BERRY**

Described by Charles Manson as "a caveman in a spaceship", this artist is no average Joe. Welcome to his blackened mind

Whether assuming the role of painter, performance artist, illustrator, writer or freak show curator, Joe Coleman defies categorisation. His compelling roster of highly detailed portraits – including edgy subjects such as Ed Gein, Charles Manson, Harry Houdini, Edgar Allan Poe and performing freak Johnny Eck – explore the depths of fringe-culture icons. In the past he's even expressed himself by attaching exploding firecrackers to his body and biting the heads off rats in front of an unsuspecting audience. →

His beard deserved its own museum

'Ecce Homo'

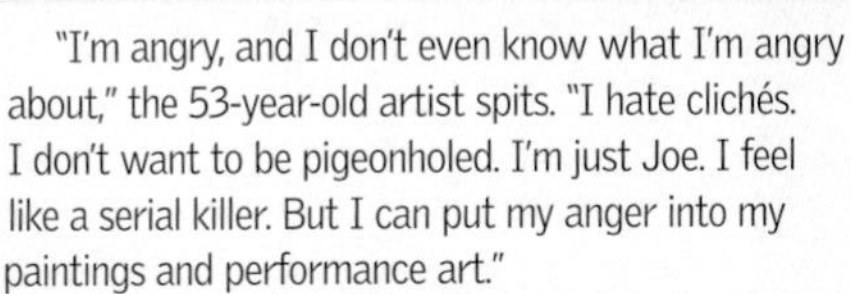

"I'm angry, and I don't even know what I'm angry about," the 53-year-old artist spits. "I hate clichés. I don't want to be pigeonholed. I'm just Joe. I feel like a serial killer. But I can put my anger into my paintings and performance art."

Magical mystery tour

Joe surrounds himself with vintage sideshow posters, serial killer paraphernalia, waxworks of murderers and religious icons. Dozens of glass eyes stare back from every corner of his studio in New York City, and framed curiosities cover the Victorian wallpaper. The front of his fridge displays photographs of famous personalities, including Johnny Depp and Iggy Pop, who've visited his home and bought his paintings. Even Joe's bathroom is macabre, filled with fish taxidermies and a tap that's dripped for so long it's left a muddy stain on the porcelain.

This 'Odditorium', as Coleman calls it, is one of the most comprehensive collections of weird relics. The collection is so huge that most of it languishes in a storage warehouse. Last year, at a retrospective exhibition in Germany, the Odditorium occupied four massive floors.

> "These items are my children, like my paintings"

"I feel a responsibility to my collection," Joe explains, stroking a stuffed cat. "I don't think I'd be a good father to a live child, but these items are my children, as are my paintings. They need a place where they're respected and have a chance to tell their story.

"I have no fucking choice but to house the Odditorium myself. I put relics in this room to try to own or possess my fears, to calm my mind and all the disturbances in my body. These objects have →

power. It's called 'magical thinking', and sometimes it's viewed with disdain. Psychiatrists say it's pathological to invest power in objects. A lot of items are here, not because I wanted them to be here, but because they have a will of their own.

"I also have a piece of Jesus, a fragment of bone. But the thing is, Jesus rose from the dead, so it's probably some sin that dropped off him when he came back to life."

Tainted love

Although Joe leads a reclusive life, he has a partner – photographer and dominatrix Whitney Ward. She offers him hope in what he sees as a terrifying world. It's so terrifying that he blocks out all the windows in his New York apartment and lives in darkness.

"The best thing in the prison cell that is my human carcass is Whitney," he says, sipping liquor from a mug emblazoned with a poster of Tod Browning's 1932 film *Freaks*. "I'm happy to see her come through the door. If I go to a hotel room – if I'm doing a tour or something and they put me in a room with white walls – that's fucking scary. But Whitney is sweet.

Left: 'The Elephant Man'

Below left: 'Albert Fish'

"We were once in a hotel and she saw how disturbed I was by the clean surroundings, so she put her hair extension on the bedpost. It looked like a shrunken head and that calmed me down.

"Sometimes, I don't see human beings for months. I'm in this cave and I don't even get any sunlight. It could be summer, it could be winter, it could be night or day. I spend eight hours a day living in a tiny little world about this big," he says, closing his index finger and thumb to a size smaller than a matchbox.

"I'm just Joe. But I feel like a serial killer"

"I know I'm sentenced to a prison called life, for the crime of being born," he continues. "But years ago I used to go out. I did performance art, strapping explosives to my body and going into strangers' homes and blowing myself up. There's an element of escape in that because I'm afraid of being in my body.

"My work from the beginning was about fear. Now everything's exploding inside me. It's funny because now there are these Middle Eastern terrorists using human bombs, and they're all copying me. Everybody's trying to be like Joe." →

Fancy a rom-com?
Maybe not...

Work of heart

Joe's painting technique consists of using a single-haired brush and looking through a pair of jeweller's lenses strapped to his head. His paintings take around six months to complete, and his last one sold for $250,000 (£126,000).

He's currently producing his most ambitious project to date – a self-portrait the size of a door. "It'll take four or five years to complete, but I have a backer for the first time and he doesn't care," Joe says. "It's like a diary. I only put down what I experience today, whatever the fuck is happening in my life at the time.

"It includes things in the Odditorium, serial killers, childhood experiences, or movies I'm obsessed with. But the main figure is me. It's a collection of thoughts, feelings, fears, desires and regrets – anything that might happen on a day."

Joe's efforts to defy categorisation make him antagonistic and confounding. Possessing a desert-dry wit, he also has excitable childlike moments when he beams a broken-toothed grin, and somehow oozes his own peculiar charm.

"A journalist once said I was pathological," he says. "I've always been uncomfortable with 'art'. When I hear that word I want to grab a gun and shoot someone. So I said, 'Yes, I'm a pathologist. That, I'm totally comfortable with.'"

"Sometimes, I don't see human beings for months"

Joe's cloning experiment didn't work

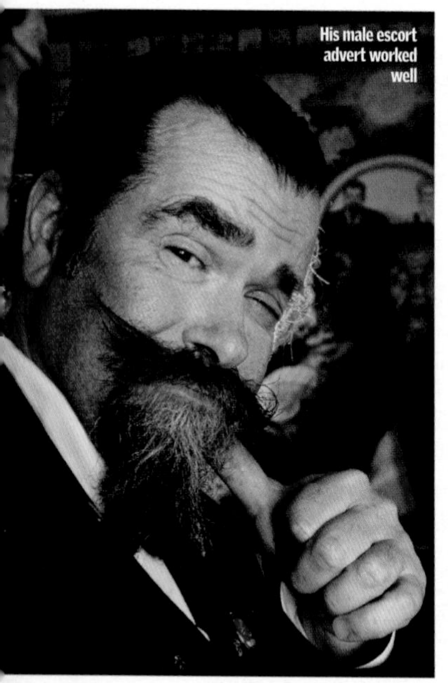

His male escort advert worked well

'Vietnamese Prostitutes'

1

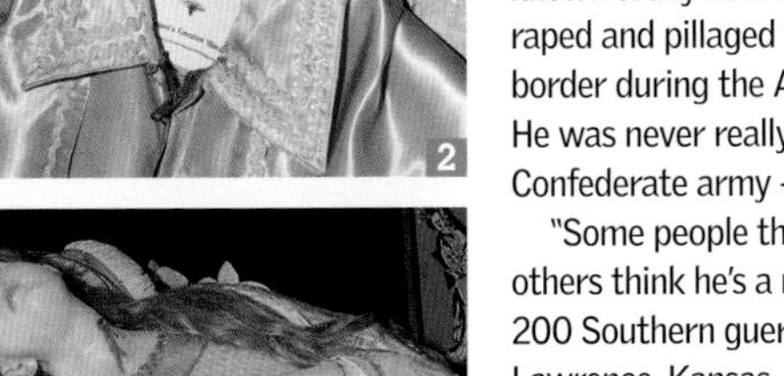

2

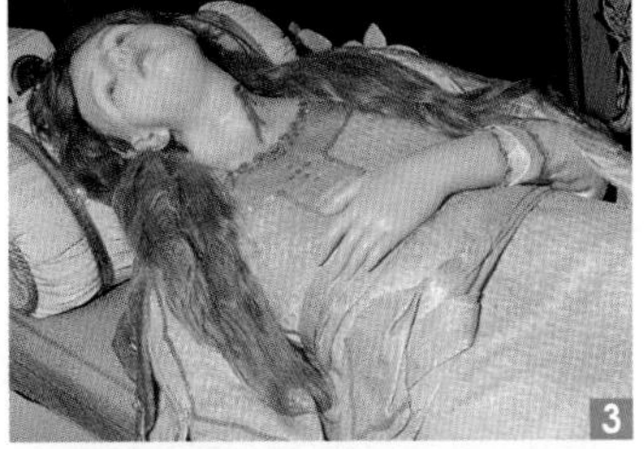

3

4

5

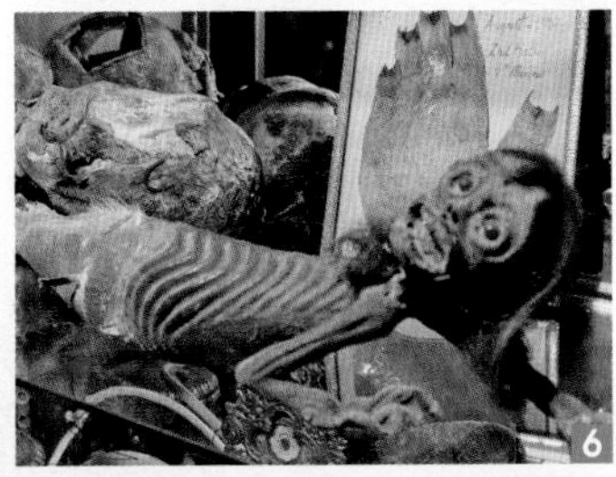

6

COLEMAN'S ODDITIES

A selection of curios from the Odditorium...

1 WILLIAM CLARKE QUANTRILL'S HAIR

"This is a lock of a hair from William Clarke Quantrill, from about 1864. He's known today as a Confederate raider who raped and pillaged the Kansas-Missouri border during the American Civil War. He was never really sanctioned by the Confederate army – he was a guerrilla.

"Some people think he's a hero and others think he's a monster. He rode with 200 Southern guerrillas and burned Lawrence, Kansas, to the ground. He was a schoolteacher there before he devised the attack, which makes it even more intriguing – he wanted to take revenge. This guy was a twisted motherfucker."

2 JOHNNY ECK'S PERFORMING COSTUME

"I'm proud to say this came from Forrest Ackerman's collection (the recently deceased Forrest coined the term 'sci-fi'). He was one of my heroes when I was a kid. Forry came to me and said, 'I don't know who's going to like this, Joe.' I said, 'Forry, I'll pay whatever you want.'

"Johnny Eck was such an amazing person, but his tragedy adds so much to the story (he was an American freak show performer who was born missing the lower half of his torso)."

3 ST AGNES WAXWORK

"This is one of my favourite objects – it's a waxwork, but underneath are human bones. It has real human teeth and supposedly it's the remains of St Agnes, the patron saint of chastity, who was executed at the age of 12.

"Catholics are obsessed by body parts and the idea of the reliquary (a sacred container used to store body parts). But, like, I'm Irish – we have the slide on it. So if you get the Celtic version of Catholicism, it's like 'Oh yeah, I get the reliquary. Body parts, yeah!'"

4 ALBERT FISH LETTER

"Albert Fish was a 1930s serial killer and cannibal, who was eventually convicted and put in the electric chair. I was looking to get a photocopy of his famous letter to the mother of Grace Budd, who he murdered and ate. When the secretary copied the letter, she handed me the actual papers and filed away the photocopy. I looked around and thought, 'OK', and that's how I knew Fish wanted it in my possession.

"It's like the letter has a life of its own, as I think all these objects do. In that filing cabinet, the letter couldn't speak. Now, for everyone that comes to the Odditorium, it's a story that can be told."

5 WILLIAM MARWOOD'S BUSINESS CARD

"This is my favourite autograph in my collection. It's the calling card of William Marwood, the English executioner, from 1879. The day he signed this was the day he hanged Charlie Peace, the notorious burglar and murderer. It helps you realise that the fascination and the desire to own a relic of horror – as well as something more spiritual – has always existed.

"William was the first hangman to devise the method of weighing the condemned person, measuring the drop and creating a knot that would cause instant death. He was actually humane."

6 FIJI MERMAID

"This is my Fiji (or Feejee) mermaid. Originally exhibited by grand huckster PT Barnum, Fiji mermaids weren't really half woman, half fish – as advertised to appalled audiences around the US – but were actually made from half a monkey, stuck on half a fish. Originally a form of religious icon made by fishermen in Japan and the East Indies, no 19th century freak show was complete without a mummified mythical beast in a dusty cabinet."

LIZ McGRATH

She's a beautiful freak with a rebellious streak: meet the first lady of lowbrow art

WORDS AND PHOTOS **MARK BERRY**

Eggshells pierced with pins, skull bunnies wearing purple ribbons in their hair, and paintings of eye-patched chicks screaming hungrily, "It's human tonight, bitches!" It's a truly black Easter Sunday at the home of Elizabeth McGrath and husband Morgan Slade, in a smog-laden neighbourhood of downtown Los Angeles.

Affectionately dubbed Bloodbath McGrath by her pals, Liz's creations are dream-like wonders and strange personalities from a freakish carnival sideshow. Like dark, Disneyesque sculptures, they're a patchwork mix of taxidermy, resin, paper, wood and textiles, with back stories of horror and humour. Some pieces are intricate dioramas, a few resemble warped interpretations of colonial-style animal heads, others are cute illustrations and distempered posters. Not surprisingly, Liz's singular vision has attracted attention from art collectors and critics across the globe, with shows in New York, Berlin, Tokyo and her hometown of LA.

Liz's current project – this finely-furnished series of Easter baskets stuffed with bloody goodies – is only the latest chapter in her career, but it's indicative of her ironic humour and cutesy-styled comic book horror, fused with a religious bent. →

Jesus freaks

"It's my Mom's birthday today, but I saw her yesterday because I knew that, if I went today (Easter Sunday), my parents would try and make me go to church," explains the youthful 36 year old, whose work has been partly shaped by a strict Catholic upbringing. Liz's father considered joining the priesthood as a young man, while her mother spent time in an English convent. When she hit 13, Liz's parents sent their rebellious daughter to a Fundamentalist Baptist correctional institution.

"I'd just done acid for the first time and my parents were like, 'Hey we're going to the zoo for your 13th birthday!'," Liz recalls. "I decided to go and keep them happy. At the time, my parents had this Isuzu van and I had a tri-hawk and Dr Martens with nails driven through them.

"So, we were on the road and I was sleeping because I was hungover. I woke up and saw we were going along this dirt track in the middle of nowhere. My folks told me we were lost. I was like, 'If we don't go the zoo, maybe we can go horseback riding?' But up ahead was what looked like a fortress. My parents got out of the van and I looked over and saw all these heavy metal chicks wearing culottes and pulling weeds. There was Christian music blaring, and I put two and two together. I started screaming and kicking, totally shredding all the vinyl in the van with my spiked shoes. A preacher guy came over and said, 'You're going to be staying here for a year.' I was like, 'Ugh! So this is victory for girls?'"

However vile and oppressive, the institution was where Liz began to hone her artistic craft by drawing for her fellow inmates and creating designs for greetings cards – mainly teddy bears and crosses. But when she left, things didn't get any easier.

"My parents had been instructed to burn everything I owned, including my photos and record collection," she says. "I had no →

"My parents had been instructed to burn everything I owned"

Right: 'Urban Deer' with tatts from hubby Morgan

Left: Liz paints a hedgehog in a top hat. Probably

Liz's pet chihuahua lives on

The cast audition for *Toy Story 3*

cool clothes, just a closet full of culottes. Of course, the first thing I wanted to do was to go and see my friends. I showed up all fat with zits and a bad haircut. I was like, 'Hey guys' and they were all, 'Who are you? What bands do you like? Do you even know who the cool bands are now?' But I didn't know anything because I'd been locked up for a year and a half! And they just totally shunned me. So I said, 'You know what? Fuck you guys!'"

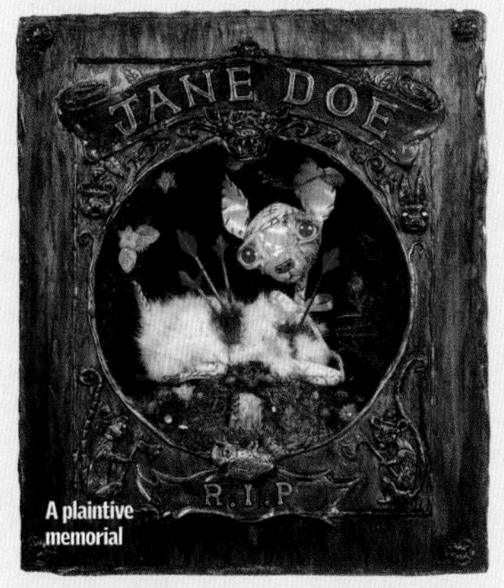

A plaintive memorial

Anarchy in LA

Before long, Liz had enrolled in art classes at Pasadena City College, and returned to music as a singer in cult experimental punk band Tongue.

"The whole premise for Tongue was just to get drunk and wasted," says Liz, who still enjoys a beer but has been a health junkie for years. "We started as an all-Asian punk band, but most of us were Mexican and just looked Asian. We were playing in east LA to an all-ages Latino crowd, and I always brace myself doing all-ages shows because kids are mean. But then all their gangster uncles started turning up. The pit was going crazy and these guys were just socking people in the face. A bloody fight started breaking out in the middle of the gig, with bottles being thrown into faces. Then someone pulled out a gun and started firing into the air and threatening to shoot people. It was then I thought, 'I'm not doing this any more. It's pretty fucking lame.'"

City of lost children

Not long after leaving Tongue, Liz was hired as a stop-motion animator, making pop videos with Fred Stuhr (director for metal outfit Tool) and learning the craft of sculpting miniatures. At this time, her evolution as an artist was also influenced by living in downtown LA, a hive of scum and villainy. →

"I'll see the guy with the giant foot, or the one with no arms and legs"

'Winter Wonder Where'

"I've seen maybe three or four dead bodies," she says. "Just hanging out on the corner I'll see the guy with the giant foot, or the one with no arms and legs who'll move about on a gurney he operates with weird tubes. There used to be this lady called Lisa. She once told me men attacked her who were into colostomy rape. This toothless, homeless woman was like, 'Yeah, they just want to get in this hole right here. They pay extra money for this.' Lisa got really sick and, when I saw her again, she said, 'The hole got infected. You just can't use it for that.' It was just wrong. I thought I was living inside a Joe Coleman painting. Seriously."

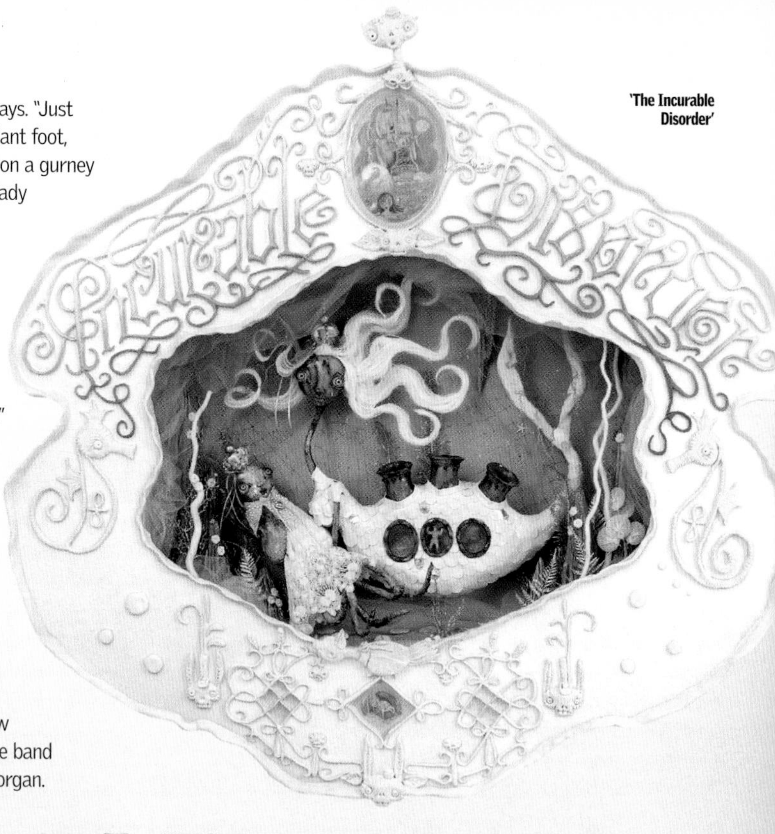
'The Incurable Disorder'

The high end of lowbrow

Liz, whose dead pet Chihuahua sits taxidermied on her dresser table, builds her living dead things while listening to audio books. And now that she's been "lumped in with the lowbrow art scene", her career has really begun to take off. She's currently working with kinky designer Jared Gold on a series of dark fashion accessories, including marionettes with embroidered faces, a selection of which were revealed at a celebrity-filled runway show that featured a performance from Miss Derringer, the band Liz fronts and whose music is penned by husband Morgan.

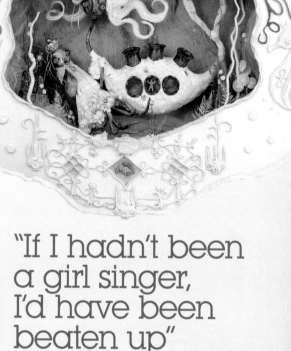

A strange little monkey

Man inside submarine (see above)

Singing in Miss Derringer

"If I hadn't been a girl singer, I'd have been beaten up"

Far mellower than Tongue, the darkness is still there in abundance, pouring from every country-tinged, heart-bleeding doo-wop number. Johnny Cash's influence is heavy, as is Blondie, whose drummer, Clem Burke, guests on the album. They toured with Bad Religion and played at the House Of Blues in California.

"The curtains opened and I saw all the skinhead dudes at the front," she says. "We started playing, doing choreographed dance moves, and there was just silence after the first song. By the second, there was just boos and calls of 'show us your tits'. At first I was like, 'Ugh!', but then kept thinking it was like a John Waters movie. Our guitarist Bill Woodcock said, 'You guys wanna hear a really fast song?' and the crowd went, 'Yeah!' Then we played our slowest number!"

"It was kind of an awesome experience. If it wasn't for the fact I was a girl singer, I'd have been beaten up. We got death threats for a while. But after getting booed by 1,500 people at that show, I know I can do anything now!" Ⓑ

'Deer House': a comment on nature vs mankind

THE GOLDEN AGE OF GROTESQUE

Liz McGrath's most peculiar pieces

DEER HOUSE

"This was part of a show called *The Incurable Disorder*, which was about how man's environment is always encroaching on nature and vice versa. In downtown LA you'll see these people that live under the freeways with tree roots growing into the mattresses they sleep on."

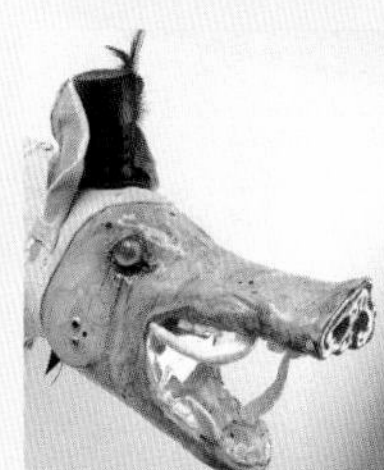

IN THE YEAR OF THE PIG FISH

"It was the Year Of The Pig when I made this. It's a giant pig with its mouth carved out. I put a tiny general store inside with kids skating around it. It was meant to be happy and cheery, but on the other side a girl is trapped under the ice."

SAVOY

"This piece was a kind of deer thing. I was listening to some book about Norse mythology – I won't tell you the name because it was a cheesy romance novel! But it was interesting, because in the story were these deer that were half-fish."

MILK BLOOD

"I was listening to an audio book of *The Man With The Golden Arm*, so you can see a lot of heroin references in the piece. I spent a lot of time in that tiny room by myself. All I had was a mirror and, unavoidably, after a while you start modelling things on yourself."

UNDER THE OWL LIGHT

"This is a piece from my show *Altarwise By Owl-Light*, which is a poem by Dylan Thomas that's a really dark, abstract telling of the story of Christ. Miss Derringer were on tour in Italy and I saw a window display of furniture covered in black resin. I really wanted that effect."

COOP

Artist, car enthusiast and Satanic priest... Come and hang with Mr Coop

WORDS **MAKI**
PHOTOS **MARK BERRY**

Voluptuous girls fucking futuristic sex robots, cigar-chomping devils with diabolical grins, monsters driving slick hot rods as they puff on skinny cigarettes; the work of Chris 'Coop' Cooper is instantly recognisable. His bold, comic book style, retina-sizzling colours and images seeped in 1950s Americana have made him one of the hottest talents to burst out of the lowbrow art scene, a deviant genre he shares with *Bizarre* favourites such as Jessica Joslin and Joe Coleman.

Coop's fiendish images first found notoriety in Kustom Kulture, a modern subculture borne from the car and motorbike customising enthusiasts of 1950s America. Since then, his gig posters and album covers have inspired countless alternative artists and musicians across the globe, and any tattoo shop worth its salt has a full set of Coop flashes in its collection, →

You don't see *her* at racing circuits...

"Oklahoma isn't really a place to be a weirdo"

including his famous red devil smoking a cigar (an image which was originally commissioned by lighter manufacturer Zippo).

Walking into his Los Angeles studio, Coop's workplace is everything you'd expect it to be: pictures of gloriously huge women adorn the walls, and a gleaming hotrod is parked in the front drive. His workshop also houses a stunning "army" of 7,000 obscure vintage toys – the result of years of incessant hoarding and a trip to Japan, the only missing pieces from this enviable collection being the toys Coop moans were "prohibitively expensive".

Coop lives in Silverlake, California, only coming into his studio to work on pieces that can take between four days and six weeks to complete. Like many artists, when he stops working he just wants to go home and "hide under the bed", or hunker down and watch Turner Classic Movies all day with his wife.

But even though Coop avoids the bullshit of the mainstream art world, get him on the topic of cars and he won't stop talking. "LA

is the fertile crescent of hotrodding," he says, his eyes twinkling. "It's still big here, really alive. The neat thing is that the history of the hotrodding scene is still relatively recent, so all the first- and second-generation guys are still here, still walking around and driving the incredible cars they built. One of the things that appeals to me as an artist is that the whole essence of hotrodding is taking a mass-produced item, pulling it apart, then rebuilding it to make it better. You're making it into an individual statement – and that's art."

Coop designs a new poster (see left)

Getting engines revved up!

Keeping it old school

Coop's art grew from his humble beginnings in Oklahoma – the heart of middle America – where, as a kid, he was "really into comics and *Mad* magazine". By 1984 he was knocking out posters for local bands, taking inspiration from artists such as Robert Williams, the 'father of lowbrow art' and pioneer of underground comics. Then, in 1988, Coop moved to California and his whole life changed. "As soon as I relocated to California, I immediately felt at home," he says. "Oklahoma isn't really a place to be a weirdo. By contrast, Los Angeles is the American capital of weirdness."

Once settled in LA, Coop began his professional career with a few small jobs for independent record labels and local gigs (including a few flyers for fellow Okie weirdos The Flaming Lips), before hooking up with the renowned Sympathy For The Record Industry record label. Working with established graphic artist Frank Kozik, Coop started to build his fanbase designing record sleeves and gig posters, and in the next few years he nailed the bold, confident and deliciously sexy style that has made him famous across the globe.

But even though Coop's career has brought him fame and fortune, is he bothered that he missed out on art school and the doors it can open? "Nah," he laughs. "When I started out, I didn't have any interest in going down that route. I didn't think I'd get what I wanted out of it. In retrospect, I'm happy I didn't.

"The idea of going to art school is to develop technical skills and learn how to do all these things I wanted to do. But art schools don't provide that any more. Instead, they provide four years of playtime for rich kids – and I wasn't a rich kid, so I didn't have that luxury. As far as educating myself in art history goes, I just went out and did it under my own steam. And I learned all about the skills I wanted to master by just by doing them."

From zero to hero

Surprisingly, while Coop's devil girls and oversized lovelies are often engaged in eye-watering wantonness, what has caused the most fuss with America's moral guardians is the fact his girls are curvaceous, defiant and confident, shirking the 'size zero' culture most obvious in the Sunshine State he calls home.

"These days I'm meeting a lot of people who look like the women I draw, especially now I've started doing photography – I'm finding more of these girls are just showing up at my studio! It's almost like I'm conjuring them. But I love women – I'm fascinated by them, I'm obsessed with them, and my work revolves around them." →

THE LOWDOWN ON COOP

Other lowbrow art heroes on Coop's appeal

DAVID PERRY
WEST COAST HOTROD AND PIN-UP SNAPPER

"I first heard the name 'Coop' at the Kustom Kulture show in Laguna Beach, California. Years later, I met the man himself through our mutual friend Frank Kozik (legendary concert poster designer). One afternoon, while toiling away in the darkroom, there was a knock on the studio door, and there stood Coop. I showed him the tattoo I'd gotten of one of his pieces – a beatnik eyeball driving Ed 'Big Daddy' Roth's Beatnik Bandit while drinking coffee with his beatnik girl. The beatnik eyeball has four arms, one working the stick of the Bandit, one holding a wrench (a paintbrush in the original), one a coffee cup, and one a camera (originally a copy of Ginsberg's *Howl*). They're peeling out in a burnout cloud of tyre smoke.

"One of my favourite images is in the fourth *Gearhead* magazine, where Coop portrays a slacker dragstrip beatnik-type dude, waiting for the bus. While encapsulated in a thought bubble he dreams of drivin' around in a hot muscle car while giving the finger, with his Bettie Page dream girlfriend." *Davidperrystudio.com*

JOE CAPOBIANCO
THE WORLD'S MOST POPULAR 'FEMALE FANTASY ART' TATTOOIST

"Wow, what can I say about Coop's artwork besides that it's been a huge inspiration over the years, since the first time I laid eyes on it, until this very day. The man has a way of capturing all of the most alluring aspects of the female form. Unique, and just drop-dead gorgeous." *Joecapobianco.com*

Coop forces us into submission

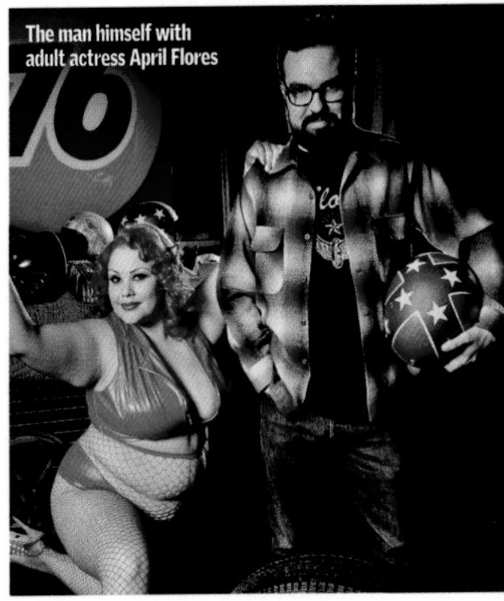
The man himself with adult actress April Flores

"I taught myself – art school provides playtime for rich kids"

Another of Coop's obsessions is the devil and the world of Satanism. And, not surprisingly for a man who made a career from doodling El Diablo, Coop is a member of the Church Of Satan and enjoyed a close relationship with the organisation's late founder, Anton LaVey – who even made Coop and his wife priests.

"Anton told me, 'What you're doing with your work and your life is Satanic,' and that's why he made me a priest," Coop says. "I thought that was a terrific honour. But I don't have to run around in a cape and scare people or anything."

Devil's in the detail

Although Coop is best known in Europe for his stunning gig posters for Foo Fighters, Rocket From The Crypt and dozens of other alternative favourites, he stopped designing them over a decade ago after discovering many sleazy music business types were selling off his work to collectors before the bands even had a chance to see them. Now he concentrates on his fine art work, including a collection of huge canvases on display in his studio featuring his beloved devil girls in pseudo-advertisements for Hunt Magnetos (gizmos for engine ignition systems), and videogame company Atari, complete with a joystick nestled in a girl's crotch.

As our interview draws to a close, *Bizarre* gets the opportunity to hang out in Coop's studio for a few hours. There are boxes of Godzilla toys stacked against one wall, and an impressive collection of trainers to admire. It's a hard place to leave. Finally, Coop gives us a preview of his current project – an image for Japanese punk Ken Yokoyama – and then it's time to call it a day. We say our goodbyes and Coop jumps on his hot rod, honks his horn and burns off into the sunset.

GENDER BENDERS

Throwing sexuality into the blender, some of *Bizarre*'s best friends have devoted their lives to blurring the line between male and female…

AMANDA LEPORE

The transexual disco diva with a need for nude performance and a passion for

WORDS **MARK BERRY**
PHOTOS **JAMES STAFFORD**

"Would you like to see my mouse tattoo?" purrs Amanda Lepore, America's number one transsexual and owner of a fully functional fake vagina, placing her hand on *Bizarre*'s trembling knee. We look tentatively across her silicone-augmented body, but none can be seen. "Oh my!" giggles the outrageous club diva in shock, fingers covering her mouth. "My pussy must've eaten it!"

We're at a club night in Hollywood, Los Angeles, where Amanda Lepore – the transgender New York 'it' girl – is making a rare personal appearance and singing a selection of pop numbers. As the crowd waits for her to take the stage, body glitter sparkles across the dancefloor in a kaleidoscopic light show as clubbers squeal with delight to the campy sound of 1980s electric lolli-pop. →

"Talk to the hand, dahling!"

Suddenly, Amanda struts into the club – energetically bounding around the stage and pumping the air like she's performing at a stadium rock gig – as fag hags scramble for their cameras and start snapping furiously. Amanda unpeels her leopard-print outfit to flash a breast at the delighted audience, then starts to sing. And while it feels like we're eavesdropping on a glamorous, camp world where only the truly fabulous belong, *Bizarre* is still honoured and dumbstruck to be witnessing such an amazing and exclusive show.

Painted lady

Amanda Lepore resembles a surreal, early-1950s pin-up painting; a sculpted Jayne Mansfield with tumbling peroxide-blonde hair and matinée-idol eye make-up. But although she's a cosmetic caricature of womanhood – a surgically sliced, diced and re-arranged experiment – there's no denying her femininity. The nip-tuckers and collagen-implanters should be smug; the work is astounding. Amanda looks like a girl. She's a living, singing and fucking Barbie doll – even perhaps a breathing piece of pop art. Andy Warhol would've adored her.

"I just did what I thought was pretty," she explains, when *Bizarre* quizzes Amanda on her extreme quest for beauty. "But I'm surprised that sometimes people don't know I was a man. Guys still ask me if I'm on the Pill during sex. I wonder if it's because in the back of their minds they wanna believe they're really with a woman. Maybe it's a trick, or maybe it's that they just want to cum inside me."

Since the early 1990s, the disco diva's distinctive transgender-model looks have appeared in books, television commercials and international photo shoots. It's an image most famously captured by auteur photographer David LaChapelle, who pictured her squashed by a giant cheeseburger and snorting diamonds.

"David's so creative and has wild ideas," she exclaims. "He first saw me at a club and knew he had to photograph me. He thought I looked like the imaginary women he used to draw doodles of, with big breasts, cheekbones, lips and everything." →

Pouting in full pin-up mode

In bed with Amanda

The queen of clubs

Amanda is a constant fixture in the clubs and galleries of New York. She famously entertains clubbers totally naked, performing magic shows and making animals out of balloons. One would think that in draconian America this might cause a problem with the authorities, but Amanda reckons her convincing female looks keep her out of trouble.

"I think I look perfect," she pouts. "My skin, the make-up, the hair, the shoes – maybe the police don't think it's real? It's not so offensive. I don't look vulgar. I don't look like some truck whore who's prostituting or something."

"Some of my lovers don't realise that I used to be a man. They ask if I'm on the Pill when they want to cum"

But the transsexual star caused a frenzy when she was sacked as a go-go-dancer at a West Side club. Along with fellow man-to-woman Sophia Lamar, Amanda was replaced with a genetic female, causing hundreds of transsexuals and their supporters to demonstrate against 'transphobia' at the resulting court case.

By using her cartoon image and chic New Yorker style as promotional tools, Amanda is the world's first transsexual to have created a merchandising bonanza. She's released perfumes called 'Happy Hooker' and 'Lemore', and has the fastest-selling limited-edition Swatch watch, which comes emblazoned with her image. Not surprisingly, she was also the subject of a series of plastic dolls made by designer Jason Wu, which sold out instantly on release – much to the disappointment of hopeful celebrity collectors such as Pamela Anderson, Hugh Hefner and Elton John.

Blood sugar sex magik

Before her operations, New Jersey-born Amanda was known as Armand, a waif of a boy bearing a strange resemblance to Mia Farrow. The gender-challenged youth undertook his first cosmetic procedure aged just 15 (a nose job), before completing the full transition to womanhood during her last year in high school.

During the delicate sex-change operation, the tip of Armand's penis was cut and used to form a clitoris. The shaft of his member became the lining of Amanda's vagina, with the nerves remaining intact. We wonder, is it as good as the real thing?

"Oh, it definitely works," she pouts. "I like sex a lot. My clit's really sensitive and I orgasm easily. I was surprised because a guy in Germany was just fingering kind of on the outside and I came. I thought you only came through penetration. He had magic fingers." →

Feeling feline at a club performance

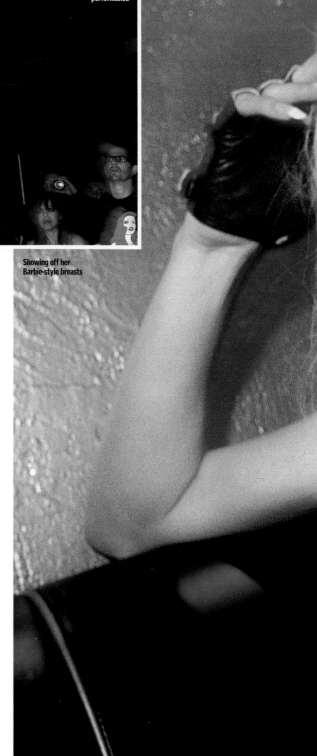

Showing off her Barbie-style breasts

"I think I look perfect. I don't look like a trucker whore"

Amanda now claims to have "pretty much finished" with surgery, using the knife just to "kind of tweak things and for maintenance". Her most recent operation, though, was a breast enlargement, plus she had her bottom rib broken and pushed in to make her waist appear smaller.

While Amanda's procedures may sound extreme to some, she could never compete with her friend Jocelyn Wildenstein, an American socialite of Brazilian ancestry who attempted to emulate the facial characteristics of a cat, and went a few surgical procedures too far.

"Jocelyn's an outsider," says Amanda. "She's just not interested in, or happy with, the way she looks. It's bizarre to a lot of people, but if she wants to look like that, then why not? I really think it's a personal thing. With someone like Jocelyn it's kind of like a sculpture. If you keep on working on something until you get it where you want, you can sometimes mess it up by tweaking it."

Amanda plays with the archetypes of the 'dumb blonde' persona, and it's difficult to tell when she's faking it and when she's being herself. But as she's prepared to take extreme measures to remain absolutely fabulous, and knows how to manipulate New York clubbers and the media, it's clear this is one outrageous blonde who knows *exactly* what she's doing. B

PICTURES: MARK BERRY

PLASTIC FANTASTIC!

A cosmetic surgeon gets under the skin of Amanda's body

Any serious performing transsexual knows you can't just flounce out on stage wearing nothing but a sequined thong and a smile. Nowadays, it takes more than a waxed crotch to earn your place among the successful chicks-with-dicks line-up who bump and grind in glitzy clubs, all vying for the same success on the circuit. She may have been under the blade more times than a knife-thrower's assistant, but what is Amanda Lepore actually made of? Consultant plastic and cosmetic surgeon John C McGregor cast an eye over our Amanda and gave his verdict on her surgical journey so far...

THE EVIDENCE

"It is, of course, not easy to say exactly what surgery Amanda has had without knowing a little about her features beforehand. The breast result looks good and realistic, and is not what could be described as unnatural or 'Jordanesque'! The overall facial appearance is, in my opinion, in keeping with what was probably desired by the surgeon or surgeons."

THE JUDGEMENT: OPERATIONS AMANDA MAY HAVE HAD

- A rhinoplasty (nose job) to feminise any masculine features, such as a dorsal bump or upward tilt.
- A face and neck lift to improve sagging, jowls, and so on, and possibly liposuction to remove fat.
- Surgery to reduce baggy lower eyelids and any excess upper-eyelid skin hoods.
- Cheekbone implants.
- A brow lift or Botox injections to reduce wrinkling.
- Collagen injections or surgical implantation of materials to enhance the volume of the lips.
- Surgical thinning of the Adam's apple.

THE VERDICT

"Overall, I consider the result of the procedures to be good and to be enhanced by make-up and hair, which may be a very well-made wig! I'm sure Amanda is delighted with the work, and it has helped her significantly in her chosen career."

Adrian was born female and had a 5-year relationship with a girl while he was at school

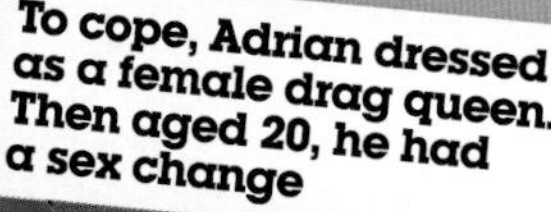

To cope, Adrian dressed as a female drag queen. Then aged 20, he had a sex change

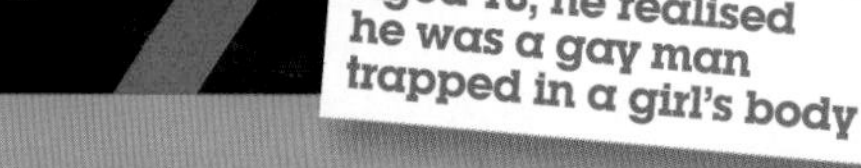

Aged 18, he realised he was a gay man trapped in a girl's body

ADRIAN

Follow him on his journey from female, to male, to drag queen – complete with his own penis

Now a man, he still performs in drag at gay club nights across London, and recently had an operation to attach a cock!

WORDS **ALIX FOX**
PHOTOS **ASHLEY/SAVAGESKIN.CO.UK**

"Pick any restaurant you like, it's on us," *Bizarre* told 30-year-old female-to-male homosexual transsexual (or 'transman') Adrian Dalton, when we first met him over dinner. He chose an all-you-can-eat vegetarian buffet in London's Soho that specialises in faux beef and pork made of soya. And so it came to pass that someone who was due to have a phalloplasty – an operation in which doctors craft a functioning penis using flesh taken from the arm and leg then graft it onto the groin – came out with the classic line, "I just love what they can do with fake meat these days!"

The pioneering surgery that gave Adrian the meat and two veg he craved marked the end of his long quest to re-sculpt his body into the masculine form he always wanted. For when he first entered the world in January 1978, Adrian had two 'X' chromosomes and a vagina. Physically, at least, he was a girl.

Hit and miss

At first, no-one noticed there was anything amiss with Adrian being a Miss. Katherine, as his parents named him, loved playing with make-up and wigs as he grew →

up in the Cotswolds, and asked for a tiara "just like Princess Di's" one Christmas. "I wasn't a particularly girly girl, but I wasn't a butch tomboy who loved Action Men and Tonka trucks either," Adrian recounts. "I was theatrical, whimsical, fey... if I'd looked like a boy I would've been called camp, but as a lass it didn't seem anything about me was unusual."

At that time Adrian couldn't put his finger on what was wrong, or why he didn't feel at home in the skin he was supposed to call his own. "As my childhood progressed, I felt increasingly odd," he says. "When I learned about puberty, I had this strange, overwhelming fear that there was something defective about me that'd stop the process happening. As I grew boobs and started my periods, I was initially relieved to be 'normal'. But then panic set in as I realised I still wasn't quite right; I'd been hoping for this magical teenage metamorphosis to not only transform my body, but also my mind. I'd hoped everything would suddenly slot into place and, hey presto, I'd feel 'right'. But I didn't."

Adrian hanging out as as Miss Lola Terry

Adrian's confusion grew when he joined an all-girl boarding school in Wiltshire, and was shunned by most of his classmates: "I remember asking the other girls what was wrong with me, and I was genuinely interested to hear their answers in case they held the key to why I felt so uncomfortable. But they just told me I was 'weird'. Hell, I already knew that!"

Barbie girl

Still unsure of who he really was, but painfully aware that his current incarnation was unpopular, Adrian decided to reinvent himself. "At that stage I wasn't interested in being true to myself – I didn't even know what the truth was," he reflects. "Instead, I consciously created a persona I thought people would find attractive." That meant dolling himself up until he looked like a pseudo-Sindy.

> "I realised I was a gay man trapped in a woman's body"

The new beautiful-but-bogus Adrian dreamed of being rich and famous so, part way through his A-Levels, he left the Cotswolds and bought a one-way ticket to the Big Smoke. "I was totally naïve," he laughs. "I didn't have a plan, but somehow I managed to blag work in London. My best fluke job was being flown to Oslo to make a kitsch, *Tarrant On TV*-style advert about trams. If only it'd been about trans..." He also had a part in a pop video and did some modelling, experiences he hoped would help him feel good about himself. But his nagging identity crisis continued.

Though a mixed-up Adrian fell in love with a girl at school and had a five-year relationship with her, he generally fancied men, not women. So to help him come to terms with his sexuality, Adrian resolved to check out London's gay scene, beginning with a now-defunct club called Dante's Inferno. And in hell, Adrian found heaven – and the enlightenment he'd been seeking for 18 years. "In this bar full of homo blokes, I finally found a crowd I identified with," he explains. "I don't have brothers, and I'd been in an all-female environment for most of my education, so I'd never had any male counterparts to compare myself to, let alone any who weren't straight. If I had, I might've realised sooner who I was – a gay man trapped in a woman's body."

Dress to express

However, there was a big problem: Adrian's body was an exceedingly womanly prison. With Coke-bottle curves on a teeny tiny frame, a pretty, feminine face and a dainty voice, he was concerned that people wouldn't believe him if he revealed his true masculinity.

"The famous FTM (female-to-male) transsexuals people had heard of were often butch tomboys before they started gender reassignment therapy, whereas I was this little, camp, blonde babydoll," he sighs. "Even if I told my friends on the gay scene I felt like one of them, they'd just think I was being cute. If I cut my hair and wore men's clothes, I'd look blatantly like a girl wearing outsized boxer shorts."

An encounter with a drag queen called Miss Jezebel inspired Adrian's short-term solution: femme drag, or being a woman dressing as a man, dressing as a woman. "I christened myself Miss Lola Terry – Miss Terry, Mystery, geddit? – and wore gigantic hairpieces and OTT →

Adrian lashes on the make-up

Life through heart-shaped glasses

"Who you calling white trash?"

evening dresses," he says. "Occasionally, someone would mistake me for a real man in drag, which was a wonderful feeling. But when I went home and took off my costume, I was still a woman underneath, which was enormously upsetting."

For the next few years, Adrian bounced back and forth between the gay and drag crowds, getting increasingly depressed and down about his situation – and attempting to use wine as a buoyancy device. By his early 20s, Adrian was a full-blown alcoholic. Eventually, after breaking down in tears at work in 2004, he went to see a doctor to ask for help to sober up – and to become a 'sir'.

Breast in show

Adrian's GP helped him get into recovery, and referred him for psychotherapy to make sure gender really was the issue at the heart of his feelings of alienation, and that there weren't any other underlying mental problems. A year later Adrian was teetotal and ready to begin his transition. "By this stage I was like, 'Get these goddamned boobs OFF me!'," he says. "I knew I was a man – an effeminate, camp, gay man, but definitely a man. I'd tried every interim measure and temporary fix to try and get by. Now it was time for my body to match my brain."

Adrian bought a chest binder from support group FTM London to squish his breasts down, but it was uncomfortable and sweaty – and, of course, when he took it off his boobs bounced back. Adrian was frustrated with NHS waiting times so, in December 2005, he paid £5,000 for a private mastectomy to replace his puppies with pecs.

The surgeon made an incision under each breast, cut away the excess skin, then repositioned the nipples. He now has a white scar underlining each pectoral muscle, and there's a tiny change in the pigmentation of his skin towards each armpit, perhaps where the weight of his old boobs stretched it a little. He's also got a chest rug.

"That's thanks to the testosterone I've been taking for three years," he says. "It's turned out wonderfully. The first dose was like taking a supplement of something I'd been deficient in; I immediately felt a sense of general wellbeing, and was calmer and more assertive. In time, my voice started breaking, and my singing became dire! After a year of hormones, I could pass as a man on the phone. I developed biceps, hairy legs, and a manly face; my jaw widened, my cheeks lost their plumpness, and now I shave every day. It was like a second puberty – the one I was meant to have first time."

> "It was like a second puberty – the one I was meant to have"

There'll also be no pole dancing until Adrian's own pole has healed; but he practises at home to keep fit, and wants to work some moves into the shows he performs at gay club nights such as London's Duckie – back in drag as a woman.

"I've resurrected Miss Lola Terry," he smiles. "I don't wear fake breasts, but I do cover myself in glitter, fabulous false eyelashes, and I have a Medusa headdress crafted out of chicken wire and paper-mâché. But this time I'm dressing up for fun, not to try and hide my gender. Lola's not a mask, but a celebration." Ⓑ

DICK, DICK, HOORAY!

Adrian's operation is a success

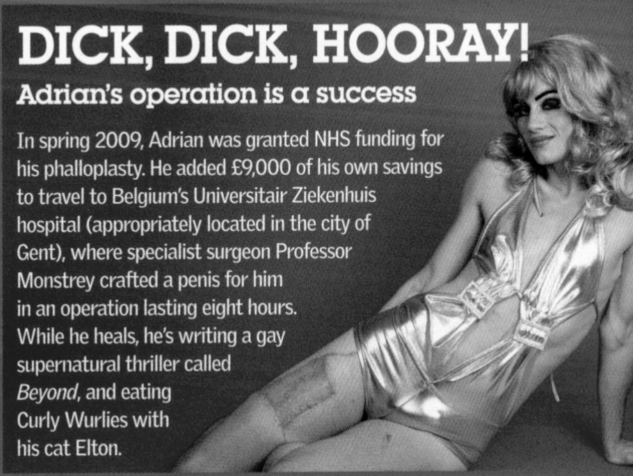

In spring 2009, Adrian was granted NHS funding for his phalloplasty. He added £9,000 of his own savings to travel to Belgium's Universitair Ziekenhuis hospital (appropriately located in the city of Gent), where specialist surgeon Professor Monstrey crafted a penis for him in an operation lasting eight hours. While he heals, he's writing a gay supernatural thriller called *Beyond*, and eating Curly Wurlies with his cat Elton.

THE GODDESS BUNNY

Star of a haunting internet tap dance video, she's now aiming for the top

PHOTOS **JAMES STAFFORD**

In October 2005, while *Bizarre* was drifting aimlessly through broken links and gruesome Mpegs in a dark corner of the internet, we clicked on something that came with a guarantee to "make us sick". Moments later, we were gawping at The Goddess Bunny and her now-infamous 'tap dance with parasol' (see above). Words can't do justice to the experience. It's creepy, sure, but so much more. It has an indefinable *something* that leaves unprepared viewers confused and mildly traumatised. Watch it and you'll see why people have compared it to *The Ring* and the work of David Lynch.

The power of the clip is summed up by Nick Bougas, who directed a documentary about Bunny in 1998. "Although it was essentially an innocent, almost quaint scene, this video has a tendency to unnerve first-time viewers," he says. "It seemed as though the sight of a horribly malformed individual attempting to do something graceful was somehow unbearably appalling to most people."

Although The Goddess Bunny has become an internet superstar, she prefers to be called Sandie Crisp. Moreover, she's actually a male drag queen rather than a transsexual. The name 'Bunny' is a remnant of her first stage name, Bunny Victoria Venice. But before Bunny or Sandie, 'she' was Johnny Edward Baima – born in January 1960, and rendered quadriplegic three months later after contracting polio. →

Divine child

"As a kid I couldn't move my hands, my arms – nothing," Sandie says, chatting to *Bizarre* in her Hollywood apartment. "I was paralysed from the neck down. Doctors said I was going to be like that forever. My mother had to carry me and my leg braces and load me in and out of my wheelchair and in and out of the car. It was hard on her. With the leg braces on, I weighed a good 70-80lb."

But it turned out the doctor's prognosis of life in a wheelchair was premature. At six, during a church service, the physical damage caused by the polio was somehow reversed. "I'd fallen asleep during the service," Sandie says. "While I slept Jesus came to me, and when I awoke I told my grandparents to take off my braces. My grandmother was hesitant, but my grandfather listened and took off my braces and it was the first time I could feel my legs.

"My mother took me into the hospital and showed the doctors. The doctors gathered round and were like, 'Why is this person walking? They're not supposed to be walking.' I was a miracle child."

"She said, 'You're very talented. When you get older, you've got to come see me'," Sandie says. "She offered me a job when I graduated high school. Well, I was six, but I remembered that all the way through elementary, through junior high and high school. When I was 18, I went to MGM studio, got in to see Mary Tyler Moore's husband and said, 'Well, your wife told me to come and I am here. Where's the job?'"

Unfortunately, what the six-year-old Sandie regarded as a solid job offer, Mary Tyler Moore had intended as morale-boosting small talk

In Marilyn Manson's 'The Dope Show'...

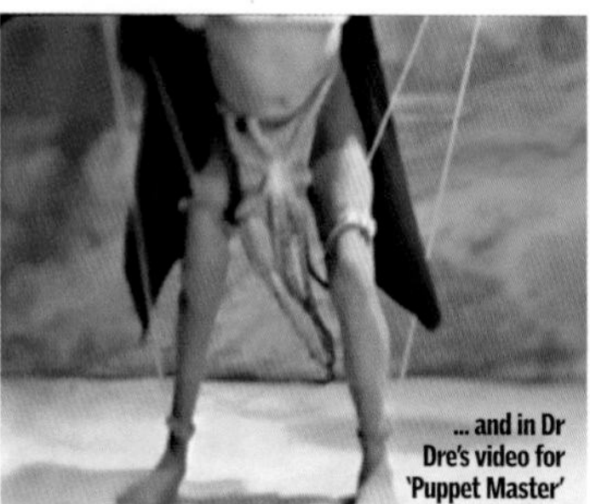

... and in Dr Dre's video for 'Puppet Master'

> "While I slept Jesus came to me and it was the first time I could feel my legs"

But the good news didn't last. Sandie's parents divorced not long after her remarkable recovery, and she was placed in a series foster homes. She says staff in a care home broke her bones, a foster sibling sexually abused her, and a foster mother forced her to swim because she thought it'd help build muscle strength.

"I'd been told to do upper-respiratory exercises and, of course, my foster mother thought swimming would the best thing," Sandie says. "She kept me in the pool for six or seven hours a day, sometimes eight, and my back eventually collapsed. I used to be able to run and do cartwheels, but I ended up back in the hospital and in traction. I had a spinal fusion operation. I was in hospital for about 10 months. Believe me, I know what medieval torture is."

The spinal-fusion operation meant a metal rod "about half-an-inch in diameter and about 18in long" was clamped to Sandie's spine. It was meant to be removed when she hit 16, but the doctor who performed the initial operation died before then. "I can feel it moving around every once in a while, but hey, what can you do?" she sighs.

Going up

The hospital that treated Sandie as a child used to invite celebrities to join the children for the Thanksgiving and Christmas celebrations. One year, when sitcom actress Mary Tyler Moore visited, Sandie impressed her with her piano playing.

for a child spending the holidays in hospital. There was no job.

"I was disappointed and upset and angry," says Sandie, "so I started wandering about the studio with my wheelchair. I came across a sound studio that was open and I rode my happy little ass in there and found a phony elevator – I pushed a button and the doors opened and then they shut behind me – and I was trapped there for an hour.

"Then the lights came on and I heard people, so I kept quiet. They'd started shooting. Ed Asner (who played Tyler Moore's boss, Lou Grant, in *The Mary Tyler Moore Show*) walked in. I said, 'Good afternoon, Mr Grant,' and he said, 'Good afternoon' back to me. They thought it was very natural and kept it in."→

Hat's life! Sandie keeps on smiling

Comfortable in her own skin

A kiss from Sandie's 'Bunny' days

"I was dressed like a puppet nun, with a live octopus wired to my crotch"

Sandie's debut movie role came about in equally unlikely circumstances eight years later. While smoking a cigarette on Hollywood Boulevard – "I was just watching traffic go by" – a woman pulled up, handed Sandie a business card and said she wanted her to be in a movie. The woman was Penelope Spheeris, who'd later direct *Wayne's World*, and the film was *Hollywood Vice Squad*, starring Carrie Fisher. It wasn't a big part, and the film wasn't exactly *Citizen Kane*, but it made casting agents aware of Sandie and helped her get more work.

Tiny dancer

In the eight years between Sandie's small-screen and big-screen debuts, she claims she had three children, but also had to endure the pain of her second marriage breaking down. And it was during this period of turmoil that the notorious tap-dancing video was created. But what many viewers don't realise is that the existence of the video and Sandie's gaunt, skeletal appearance are due to HIV. She found out she had it when she was just 20 years old.

"I was diagnosed back in 1980," she says. "They said I got it through a blood transfusion; I had lots of operations. Now I take enough pills to choke a horse. It's distressing."

The tap-dancing film was shot at the same time as a series of photographs intended to portray Sandie as an 'AIDS terrorist'. The pictures showed her covered in false lesions made using eyeliner and other make-up and holding various weapons, and copies were sent to President Reagan.

"I was very thin in the film," she says, casually understating the fact she weighed barely 5st. "I was going through a lot of →

Posing like
a Hollywood star

depression and not eating. I was thinking I was going to die anyway, so what was the point in eating? I looked like a cut-out of a Karen Carpenter doll. Now I eat and I'm healthy and I feel good about myself. I weigh somewhere between 114lb and 121lb."

Her return to health led to more work. In 1986, Sandie was approached by artist Joel-Peter Witkin who asked her to appear in a photographic reinterpretation of Leonardo da Vinci's *Leda And The Swan*. Witkin is one of the most controversial artists currently working, and has been accused of being sacrilegious, sick, and everything in between for his persistence in working with dead bodies and the physically deformed.

The shoot took place in a dance studio in Santa Monica early in the morning. After establishing that Sandie was comfortable with nudity, Witkin asked her if she could get an erection. "I said, 'Not in front of people, I just don't do that,' but he took the picture anyway," she remembers. The result is one of Witkin's most famous pieces.

At home with the Goddess

"I have a steel rod clamped to my spine. It's not meant to be there and I can feel it moving around"

Sandie also counts Marilyn Manson among her admirers: "Marilyn saw a picture of me on some internet site and he searched all over Hollywood for me," she says. "Finally, a casting director called and said, 'I have someone on the other line that would like to speak to you,' and it was Marilyn Manson. He said, 'Would you like to do a music video for 'The Dope Show'?' and I said, 'Sure.' He's the sweetest guy I've ever met. He just accepted me for me."

When Dr Dre saw Marilyn's video, he invited Sandie to appear in his 'Puppet Master' video. But it wasn't the classiest shoot ever. "I was dressed up like a marionette puppet nun with hardly anything on. They took a live octopus and wired it to my crotch," Sandie recalls ruefully.

Other career low points included a pilot of a TV movie called *Werewolf*, in which Sandie plays a hooker who gets mauled by a lycanthrope, and her appearance (wearing a zebraskin all-in-one) in the video for Gloria Estefan and Miami Sound Machine's cod-Latino cheese-fest 'Rhythm Is Gonna Get You'.

She'll be back

However, the most remarkable thing about Sandie isn't her chequered showbiz career. It's how she deals with what has been, by anyone's standards, a traumatic life.

Her first husband died in a car accident when he drove his car off Mulholland Drive. Her second was sent to prison for attacking her. A few days before *Bizarre* arrived to shoot these pictures, she was mugged. She once worked as a prostitute for two years to support her unemployed partner's drug habit, and she was raped by two men in an underground car park. The copy of *Leda And The Swan* that Witkin gave her as a present was surrendered to an ex-boyfriend simply because he loved it so much.

"I've got a big heart," Sandie sighs. "You've got to in this world. My mother says I'm too nice to everybody, but she always taught me that positive people get positive things back. That's my motto in life. If you're negative, your life goes nowhere. If you're positive, then things will go right for you."

If things are going to come good for Sandie, they're taking their time. She lives in a rented apartment and admits that once it is paid for and the bills are settled, she ends each month the same: broke. But what of the future?

"First, I want to become Empress of Los Angeles, then I want to run for city council, then I want to run for Mayor, then I want to run for Governor," Sandie proclaims. Sandie Crisp, Governor of California, might seem hard to imagine, but the route from a cult documentary, via a raft of brainless Hollywood films, has been made at least once before. Who knows? Stranger things have happened. Especially if you're Sandie Crisp. Ⓑ

CHI CHI LARUE

From small town boy to larger-than-life tranny, Chi Chi LaRue's life has never been a drag

WORDS **KATE HODGES, VICTORIA HOGG**
PHOTOS **JAMES STAFFORD**

Chi Chi LaRue is a rude, lewd, John Waters in a frock. He's the porn director with the biggest hair, the biggest belly, and the biggest attitude in the business. Formerly known as Larry Paciotti, Chi Chi made his name directing classic gay porn including *Bitter She-Males, Roll In The Hay, Wetness For The Prosecution*, and *My Sister's Husband*. In 2003 he joined the renowned Vivid Entertainment team, and directed their phenomenally successful run of straight porn flicks, whose stars included Jenna Jameson and Tera Patrick. Chi Chi now runs his own gay porn companies, Rascal and Channel 1 Releasing. →

Chi Chi grew up in the tiny town of Hibbing, Minnesota, USA, where everybody knew everybody's name – and everyone was white. "There were no ethnic people – Spanish, latin, or black – whatsoever," he says. "I remember watching TV shows with other ethnicities and going 'God, I wanna know some people like that!' I desperately wanted to get out of this 'normal' box I was in. I wanted to experience other cultural things. There wasn't even a McDonald's in Hibbing."

The self-confessed misfit always knew he was gay, even if he didn't know what 'gay' was: "All I knew was I liked to look at naked guys, so I'd steal *Playgirl* magazines from the grocery store. At school, I stuck out a little. I've always been large, a little bit feminine – probably a lot more feminine when I was younger. I was friends with the girls. I always wanted to be a cheerleader, and to go into the boys' locker room and see them naked!"

Chi Chi reaches for a truncheon

But the sassy minx avoided being bullied by using a few clever tactics. "I turned my insecurity around," he says. "I was outgoing, the class clown. I made myself popular by being talkative and funny. Back then I used to dress differently. I had giant puffy hair, and I'd wear women's stirrup pants that were tight against my legs, and a big blousy top, thinking it made me look thinner. In reality, it made me look like a giant Chupa Chup."

Porn to do it

As a teenager, Chi Chi was obsessed with porn. When he was 16 he watched *Pretty Peaches*, which was Sharon Kane's first film – and she's now one of his best friends. But he didn't settle for straight porn by choice. "I was into straight porn because I had to drive 120 miles to see *any* kind of porn," he remembers. "There was gay porn in the peep booths, but at 16 or 17 years old, it was scary to go into those places."

Chi Chi's first job was in Minnesota in the Twin Cities area, performing as one half of drag act The Weather Girls. But when he moved to California he was hired as a publicist and admin assistant at porn company Catalina, thanks to his in-depth knowledge of the industry. In 1987, he got his first directing gig, and over the past couple of decades he's helmed hundreds of gay, bisexual and straight films.

One of the reasons Chi Chi broke into the porn industry was because many directors in the late 1980s had become ill with AIDS, and he thinks he avoided the disease because he was less promiscuous than his peers due to his unconventional body size. "My fat was a saving grace for me," he says. "When you're fat, people don't look at you and they don't want to have sex with you – unless you're a fat, fabulous drag queen! The gay community can be very judgmental. I guess I should be happy about that, because if I was thin I'm sure I'd have sucked every dick and have got fucked by everyone in those booths. I wasn't, so I didn't. So I never got sick."

"If I was thin I'm sure I'd have sucked every dick and been fucked by everyone"

In an industry that often allows bareback sex without batting an eye, Chi Chi is a rare role model in his adamant promotion of safe sex. The actors in the first feature movie he ever directed – *FLEXXX*, in 1987 – wore condoms, and he's insisted on them in every movie he's directed since. Chi Chi also raises AIDS awareness with his condom-championing 'Wrap It Up' video that plays at the end of his films, which can also be seen on YouTube.

Bitch of a son

As with most people who work in the porn industry, Chi Chi had a hard time squaring his career with his parents. "I think my father, until the day he died, still thought I worked in a porn store!" he laughs. "He was an old Italian guy who never understood the concept of me doing it."

Consequently, the director would rather his family didn't see any of his work, and just think of him as a regular person. "I just want them to know I'm happy and successful, and that I'm a good person and I'm not hurting anyone. I'm sure my mom would rather she could go to her bridge club meetings and say, 'Oh, my son just discovered the cure for hepatitis'. She doesn't really want to go and say, 'Well, Larry just wrapped *Anal Maniacs*.'" →

Hello, boys!

Me-ow! Chi Chi gets his claws out

There are some perks to the job, though. Chi Chi's a cult superstar, even popping up in Madonna's 1992 'Deeper And Deeper' video – alongside former Andy Warhol superstar Holly Woodlawn. A-list director John Waters – whose kitsch, quirky films stopped Chi Chi from feeling isolated when he lived in Minnesota – has gone on record saying that Chi Chi is his favourite director, and the two catch each other's one-man stand-up shows when possible.

"He's a funny man!" says Chi Chi of John Waters, "He's like a perverted, sex-offender teacher. The best thing about being in this business is meeting people – like Debbie Harry, Cher and Marc Almond. Marc told me he was my biggest fan. We went to a strip club and stuffed dollars in girls' G-strings."

But as a porn director who dresses in drag, he wasn't always popular. "When I made my first movies, they didn't like the name Chi Chi as it was too feminine," he says. "So I changed it to Taylor Hudson. As in Rock Hudson and Elizabeth Taylor! You couldn't *be* any gayer. Then, through my stand-up act, Chi Chi LaRue became popular."

The gayest man in the village!

"I haven't woken up with my wig smelling of pee in a long time"

By contrast, other drag queens who've tried to direct porn have fallen by the wayside. "You either have it or you don't," he says. "People think if they have a camera they can direct a porn movie, but it's not that simple."

Also working under the name Lawrence David, Chi Chi admits that nothing shocks him any more: "There are things that gross me out. I'd rather die than watch a scat video! Ick. I don't think that's sexy – it makes me gag. I also hate cigarettes, but there's a huge smoking fetish. You know what? A smoking shit video would be my worst nightmare!"

But Chi Chi concedes that his 2001 video *The Missing Link*, where Carlos Morales takes a dildo with a 10in circumference up his butt, was pretty shocking. "It was huge," he laughs. "It was like a lamp! And it had a big bottom on it so we could shoot into it, like a telescope. So we were actually shooting *inside* his rectum, which was... kinda cool! It was shockingly beautiful."

Sweet transvestite

Although Chi Chi, who's also a DJ, has taken drugs and loves being in drag, he's sick of the perception that he's a raging addict who can't function without wearing a pair of falsies and six-inch stillettos. "Gaaargggh! How could I keep up my schedule *and* be a drug addict?" he says. "It's hilarious. Although, OK, when I'm in drag I *can* put away 12 dirty martinis without a blink of an eye. But I've never smoked a cigarette, never shot heroin, never done Special K."

Chi Chi now drags up only two or three times a month, depending on whether he has a show. "It gets harder as I get older," he says. "Things like shoes, earrings and corsets hurt more now. But it's definitely a security blanket. I'm more boisterous, louder and, some would say, bitchier and meaner in drag, but I'm mellowing. I've had some amazing, beautiful, crazy, wild times in drag. I haven't woken up with my wig smelling of pee in a long time, though."

But don't count on seeing Chi Chi in drag forever. As he puts it: "Nothing's more tragic than a granny tranny. I have good skin because I've never smoked, but everything may go south when I'm 50. And as I lose weight I may need a little nip'n'tuck, darling."

Chi Chi's personal life took a big hit in 1994 when his star actor, muse and close friend Joey Stefano died of an overdose, rocking the world of gay porn. But he has never slowed down creatively, and has published several books and calendars since. Is he angling for a new line in respectability? "Honey! There are rock-hard dicks in those books! That isn't respectable. It's art!" he cackles. "It's fabulous. I'll never be fully respectable. I wish I could dirty up *more* aspects of life! Anyway, we just finished the new Rascal 2010 StarFucker Calendar with Benjamin Bradley on the cover, and we'll probably make a coffee table book for my new movie *Taken: To The Lowest Level*, for everyone to enjoy."

But if you're hoping to become Chi Chi's special someone, you'll need to be *really* special. "I've never had a boyfriend," says the 49-year-old. "I don't want one. I have a small group of people I'd call my friends, who know my worst and my best. The rest is my public persona, and I don't want to be with anybody who wants that persona."

However, Chi Chi has recently become friends with Hollywood gossip king Perez Hilton: "I recently had drinks with him in West Hollywood – he's quite a character! And I'm always happy to see my dear friend Andy Bell of Erasure, when we actually get the chance to hang out."

So, all's well in camp Chi Chi, then? "It couldn't be better," he smiles. "I'm losing weight and still at the top of my game!"

BODY SHOCKERS

Join *Bizarre* as we celebrate amazing bodies, and chat to a sublime selection of the most remarkable people on Earth

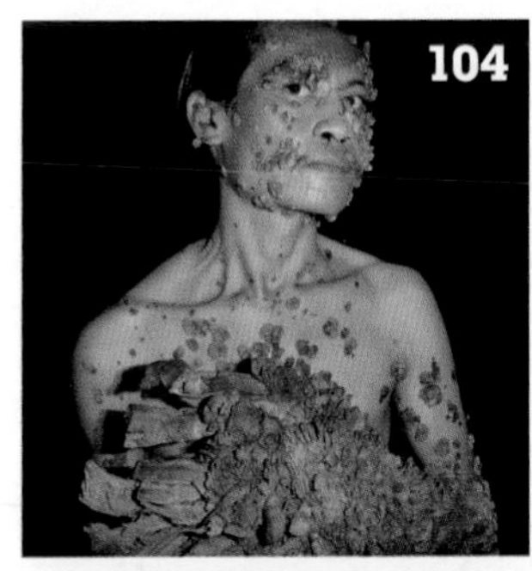
104

112

118

TREE MAN

Indonesian Dédé Koswara has a rare condition that's stumped doctors the world over. And Bizarre was the first to interview him...

WORDS **JOHN LITTLE, VICTORIA HOGG**
PHOTOS **JOHN LITTLE**

When *Bizarre* first featured Dédé – or 'Tree Man', as he's come to be known – back in March 2007, no-one expected the phenomenal storm of letters, emails and calls that followed. A huge number of readers – and indeed, documentary-makers – wanted to know more about the then-37-year-old from West Java, Indonesia.

There are some folk who just don't deserve the bad luck that's heaped upon them, and Dédé Koswara is one of those people. The pleasant, radiant and calm man has had to live with two rare and pernicious medical problems – the human papilloma virus (HPV), and an abnormally depressed immune system. The combination of these conditions has resulted in root-like warts sprouting from his body for most of his life – an affliction that's uncomfortable and deeply traumatic, and which has effectively turned this Johnny Depp lookalike into a sideshow freak, unable to dress himself, walk normally or even brush his own teeth. Add to that months of complex and painful surgery, and it's a medical nightmare that must've been unbearable. Now on the other side of the extremely complicated surgical process, is Dédé finally cured? →

Managing to hold a cigarette – but only just

Growing pains

Dédé's condition appeared in his early teens, with a small tumour on one of his knees – but it didn't bother him much. When he got married a few years later he only had a few warts. But after the birth of his second child, the part-time farmer and builder found that the condition began to take hold. "It gets itchy sometimes," he told us during his first *Bizarre* interview, when the tree-like growths on his arms and feet were at their worst, growing 5mm a month. His elbows were raw and bleeding where he'd scratched himself. "I feel sad because I can't touch my children – I just want to be cured so I can fish and earn money, so I can feed them."

One of the most unpleasant side-effects of the condition was the smell. Dédé reeked to high heaven – a staggeringly pungent, musty stench, much like rotting undergrowth. Every day, his family would take turns to clean him. "He can't get wet or he smells worse," explained his mother, "so we fill a garden spray with 70 per cent alcohol and use that. It usually takes about 20 minutes. We need to do that three times a day." When they could afford it, his family also applied drops of thick, scented Arabian oil to his arms and legs – the only thing that could cut through the clinging smell. Dédé's mum also put zips in all his clothes so he could dress more easily, though it was still near-impossible for him to do everyday tasks.

Dédé's luck grew worse. His wife ran away in 1993, leaving their son Utis and daughter Entang behind. When Dédé couldn't care for them any more, his sister brought them up. As his condition took a turn for the worse, Dédé's family sent him to hospital, where he spent a year and a half. At the time, doctors couldn't say what was wrong with him, but they cut away as many of the longer growths as possible to make him comfortable. When his family ran out of money Dédé came back home, but his condition returned with a vengeance. The only way his parents could keep it under control was to take a pair of scissors or a knife to the growths.

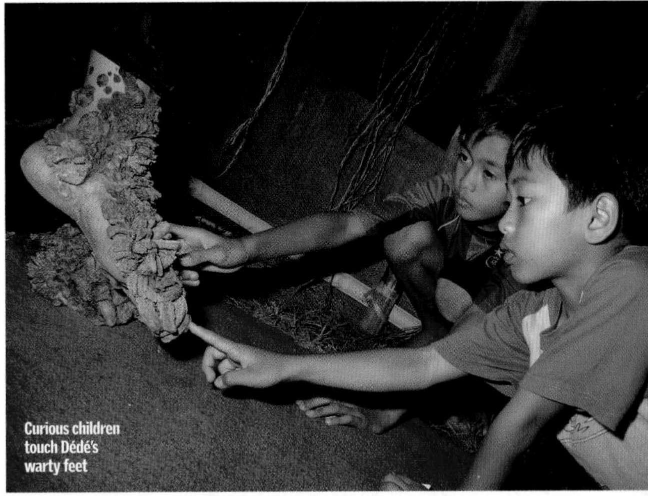

Curious children touch Dédé's warty feet

> Dédé had horns growing from his head, but his family cut them off with shears

Dédé with Wawan from The Association Of Strange People

Leaf him alone

Bizarre first met Dédé at a theme park in East Jakarta, Indonesia, where he was part of a sideshow called The Goeriank Troupe Of Padjadjaran, AKA The Association Of Strange People, where he let rich people have their photograph taken with him in a portable studio inside a tent. "I'm quite used to it," he told us with a shrug, "I don't think about anything when they look at me."

Dédé was making about £3m rupiah – or £165 – per show. He was a good draw: at one point he'd even had warty horns sticking out of his head, before his family cut them off. But as Dédé's father said at the time: "All we want is for him to come back to us safe and sound. We know he's made new friends in The Association, and that's great for him – great for his spirit – but we just worry. We don't want him to come to any harm." And being part of a freak show was never going to be an ideal career move. →

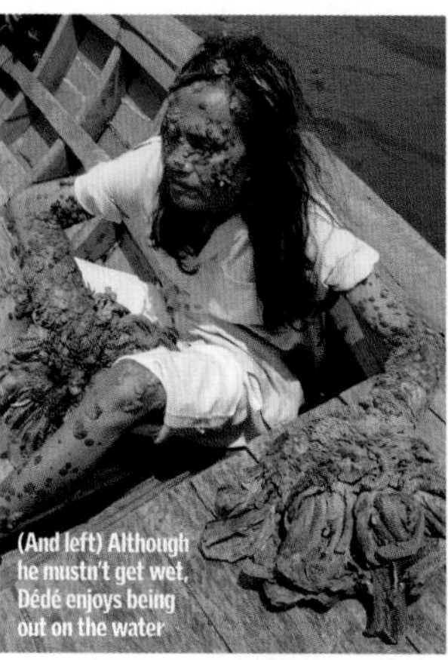

(And left) Although he mustn't get wet, Dédé enjoys being out on the water

Growths push out from his legs and feet

Dédé's huge growths give off a pungent stench, much like rotting undergrowth

Even after The Association went freelance, cutting their own hours in half and controlling their money, Dédé was still fed up. "Frankly, I just want to go walking to the corner shop again without everyone staring," he told *Bizarre* at our second meeting. His condition had deteriorated, and the smell was getting worse due to damp weather conditions and the pressures of life on the road.

Happily, help was around the corner. Not long after *Bizarre*'s second trip to Indonesia, a medical breakthrough was made. Dr Anthony Gaspari, chief of dermatology at the University Of Maryland, USA, had heard about Dédé's condition and, calling it "a unique case", decided to offer his expertise. While searching for a cure, he discovered that Dédé was suffering from human papilloma virus, or common warts, which under normal circumstances would eventually disappear. Dr Gaspari concluded that the warts were flourishing because of Dédé's poor immune system, and that a course of Vitamin A was the cure.

Tree surgeons

But, curiously, Dédé soon found himself in different hands. Despite the fact the Indonesian government had ignored him for years, officials suddenly stepped in to prove to the world that *they* were going to support Dédé in his hour of need. Without consultation, an ambulance roared into Dédé's village and bustled him off to Bandung's Hasan Sadikin Hospital, where Professor Cissy Kartasasmita, hospital director, said: "We can provide a world-class service for him right here. Dédé doesn't need to be taken overseas." Caught on camera by channel Five for its *Extraordinary People* series, Dédé's father said: "It's as if he's been snatched by an eagle. Maybe they're embarrassed because they ignored us for so long."

And thus began the next extraordinary chapter in Tree Man's life, in what looked, oddly enough, like a custody battle for his body. In the blue corner was Dr Gaspari, who advocated non-invasive treatment involving synthetic Vitamin A that promised to stimulate Dédé's immune system. But in the red corner stood the staff of Hasan Sadikin Hospital, who had hardcore surgery in mind – six months' worth in eight stages, including wart removal and skin grafts for the whole of Dédé's hands. But Dédé had already had removal treatment and the warts had grown back. "It's a never-ending cycle," said Dr Gaspari of the removal process. "It's *not* the solution."

Dédé's life became a ward-based media circus. First, *all* treatment, both invasive and non-invasive, was delayed because he was suffering from tuberculosis. Then when surgery began, 30 members of the press followed him into the theatre, filming the heavy-duty power-saw as it sliced through the warty growths on his hands. "If we cut right down to the bone, he might die," said the surgeons. "We have to trust our instincts." The seriousness of the situation was summed up by a beetle being captured on camera escaping from the inner growths, where it had been living undetected. During the first five-hour operation, a staggering 5lb of growths were removed from Dédé's hands. →

WITH SPECIAL THANKS TO FIVE'S *EXTRAORDINARY PEOPLE* PROGRAMME

In the undergrowth in Indonesia

Though his wife left, Dédé's parents stuck by him

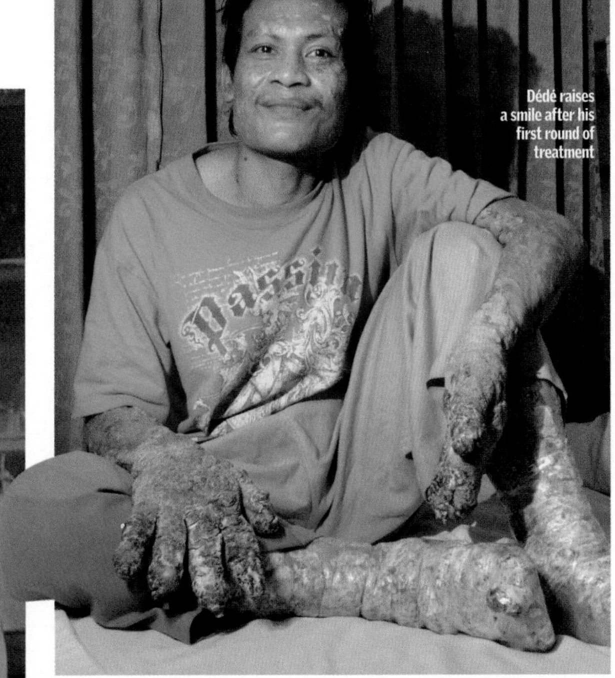

Dédé raises a smile after his first round of treatment

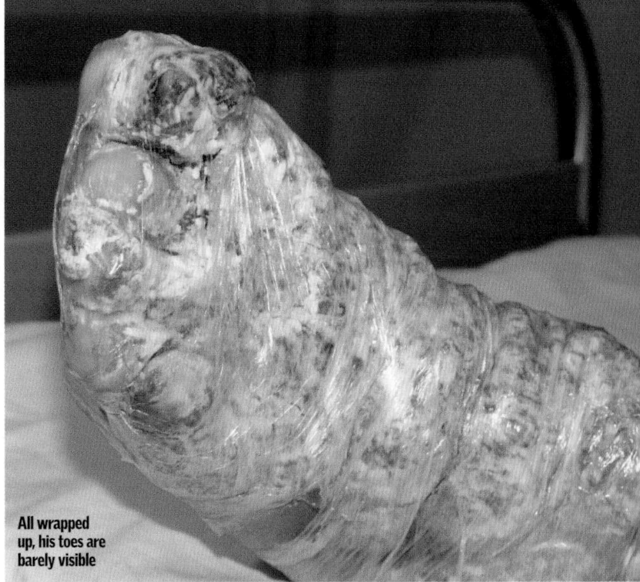

All wrapped up, his toes are barely visible

Though the doctors had tidied Dédé up and removed a particularly irritating wart that dangled over his right eye and obscured his vision, the exhausting round of operations and Vitamin A intake ground on and on, with Dr Gaspari suggesting chemotherapy infusions as an even stronger solution. In the meantime, Dédé had balloons inserted into his wart-free back to inflate the skin, thereby stretching his flesh enough to create grafts for his hands. However, Dr Gaspari's prognosis was discouraging. "Even if the grafts are successful, it's likely the wart virus infection is going to occur in that grafted tissue," he told Five.

The nightmare continued. The hospital agreed to delay hand graft surgery while they trialed the chemotherapy drug treatment, but the drugs took well over the four weeks expected for them to arrive from the US. The skin grafts went ahead, so as not to waste the skin they'd created with the stretching balloons, but this skin also now had warts growing out of it. The final blow came when the doctors told Dédé that the bones in his hands had been damaged by osteoporosis.

Finally the chemotherapy drugs arrived, and Dédé was also provided with anti-osteoporosis drugs and calcium. After a nine-month stay in hospital he was allowed to go home again, relieved to be merely an outpatient

His living chainmail gone, Dédé was the same stoical, calm figure. "It's okay if I can't feel again," he said of the loss of sensation in his hands, "the important thing is that I can work. I'm free and I'm happy to be with my family and friends." He'd even got a new girlfriend and was making serious plans for the future. "Eventually, I want to open a little grocery shop," he told us.

Press filmed the power-saw as it sliced through the warty growths on his hands

Going to seed

Sadly, at the beginning of 2009, Dédé's condition returned and the warts on his hands began to grow again, closing up the gaps between his fingers. After the surgery he could use a pen to text from his mobile phone and fill in his beloved sudoku puzzles, but now this is impossible and he can only just balance a cigarette on his fingertips. Although the disease is not life-threatening, *Bizarre*'s heart goes out to Dédé because of the unbelievable psychological and physical torment he's had to endure for so many years. We hope a cure will be found soon.

PRE-TEEN WOLF

Seven-year-old Nat Sasuphan has thick hair across her back and face. Some people call her a werewolf, but *Bizarre* reckons she's just a normal kid

PHOTOS **JEFFERY R WERNER**

In Bangkok, the capital city of Thailand, Supatra Sasuphan barely notices the taunts and stares of people on the street. And at her recent kindergarten graduation, proudly wearing her cap and gown, she was accepted by all her classmates as one of them. Strangers call her 'wolf-girl', but her friends and family lovingly call her Nat.

Seven-year-old Nat suffers from congenital hypertrichosis, a rare genetic disorder that makes fur grow over her back and face. The disease affects only one person in a billion, and just 50 individuals have been diagnosed with it since it was discovered in 1648. But Nat, whose condition used to make people believe in werewolves, doesn't allow all that fur to get her down.

PICTURES: BARCROFT MEDIA

Happy meals

Just like any kid her age, Nat loves to play, laugh and smile, and enjoys trips to the local McDonald's with her parents and sister Sukanya, 12. She also enjoys cartoons and monkeying around with her friends at school. The young girl is the second-fastest runner in her class, and gymnastics is one of her passions.

Nat's teachers say she's highly creative and intelligent, and often has her hand up →

Nat is one of the smartest kids in her class

Chicken McNuggets for tea – yum!

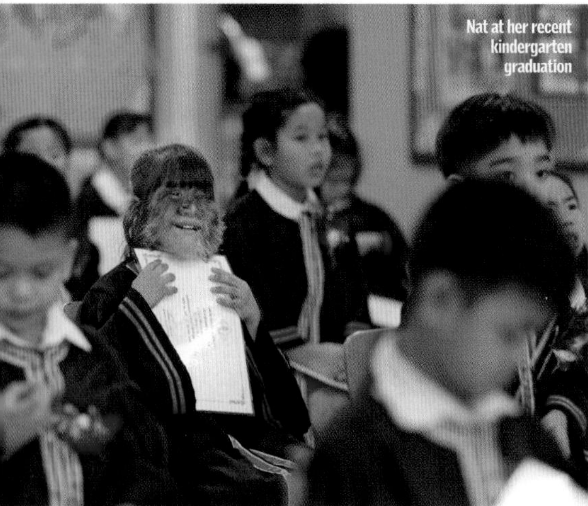
Nat at her recent kindergarten graduation

"At first, the other kids at school didn't speak to me. But when they got to know me, I soon made lots of new friends"

to answer questions before anyone else. Nat's dream is to go to college so she can train to become a college tutor.

Even though Nat's mother, Somphon, and father, Sammreung, are proud of their daughter, they admit her condition was initially overwhelming. "I had a scan when I was pregnant, and the doctor told me my little girl looked very hairy – but we thought it was normal hair," she says. "I had a Caesarean section, and when the doctor handed her to me I was really shocked. I cried at first, but then I realised that she's my baby and I accepted her as my own."

Hair today

When Nat was young, her parents took her to a doctor who tried laser treatment to remove her hair. The session worked temporarily, but left her skin itchy, green and swollen. But before long, Nat's hair grew back. →

A face in the crowd: Nat always stands out in school

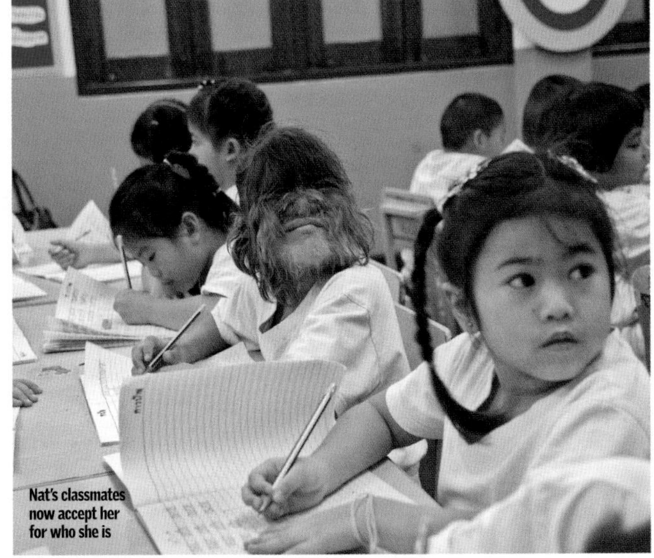

Nat's classmates now accept her for who she is

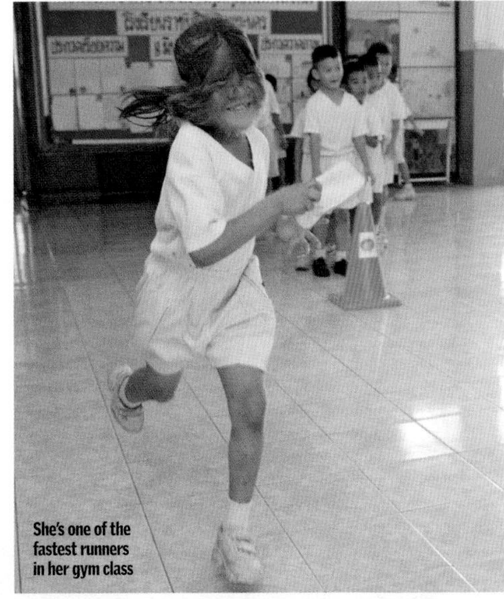

She's one of the fastest runners in her gym class

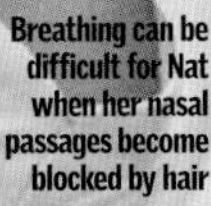

Breathing can be difficult for Nat when her nasal passages become blocked by hair

"I'm a normal girl. I may look different, but I'm just like everyone else"

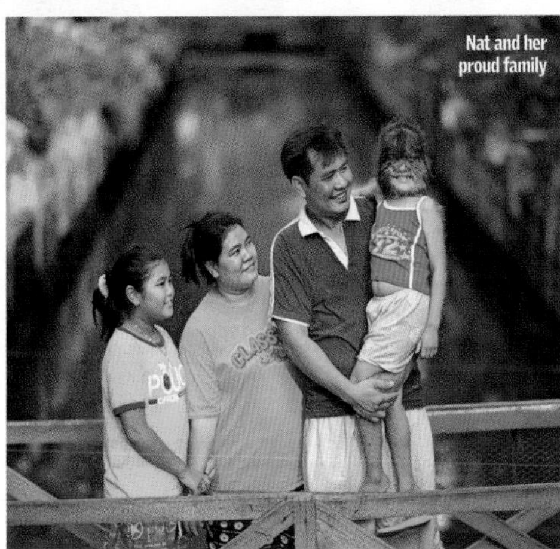

Nat and her proud family

Her father says: "The doctors have told us to try again when she's older, but we don't know if it'll work then, either." Nat's condition is so rare doctors have been unable to find a cure. When Nat's older, she'll have to decide for herself whether to remain hairy, or face a lifetime of shaving or using hair-removal creams.

Nat's condition has also left her with some real medical problems. When hair growth in her nostrils started to get so thick it made breathing difficult, she had to have an operation to cut it back.

"I don't mind my hair," Nat says, "but sometimes it grows so long it gets in the way and I start feeling too hot. So Mum cuts it down for me." Mother Somphol says: "I shave her face from time to time. But other times she doesn't mind and isn't self-conscious about it at all."

Furever friends

When her parents first brought her home from hospital, Nat was met with stares and jibes from neighbours, but eventually her cheerful disposition won them over. And although some strangers still call her 'wolf-girl' behind her back, she's totally accepted by the neighbourhood and her schoolmates.

"I love my bike and riding about with the other kids," says Nat. "We've just moved house and now I have lots of friends. At first, a few of the kids looked at me strangely and wouldn't talk to me. But then they saw me talking and laughing with the others, so they started to like me."

"She smiles all the time," beams her mum, proudly. "Everyone who knows her remembers her for her smile, not her hairy face."

Nat has the last word. "I'm just a normal girl. I may look a little different, but I'm just like everyone else. I just want to be me," she says, sitting on her grandmother's lap, combing her face and smiling broadly. Ⓑ

CYCLOPS BOY

When cyclops boy lost his eye to cancer, a sharp sense of humour and a willingness to shock made him a sideshow celebrity

WORDS **MARC HARTZMAN**
PHOTOS **BIFF YEAGER**

In the world of professional freakery, being born with a physical deformity or adorning yourself with tattoos and body modifications are the most common routes to sideshow notoriety. But Chicago's Pumpkinhead The Cyclops Boy – a former member of The Brothers Grim Sideshow, who keeps his real identity secret – began his career after surviving a devastating bout of cancer. It's now been over 20 years since the handsome husband and father was diagnosed with cancer of the sinus – an adenoid cystic carcinoma tumour, to be specific – and chose major, appearance-altering surgery over the threat of death.

The tumour followed Cyclops Boy's optic nerve endings, rendering it necessary to remove his entire eye to ensure all the cancer was gone. But not only did the young patient lose his left eye and eyelid, but he also sacrificed a portion of his left cheekbone and half of his mouth to stay alive. The procedure left a golf ball-sized hole where his eye used to be, and a large dent in his temple. Initially, a rubber prosthetic eye was developed to plug the socket in Cyclops Boy's face, but without an eyelid there was nothing to hold it in. To work, it required specially designed, outrageously large glasses to keep the fake eye from bouncing out. So rather than →

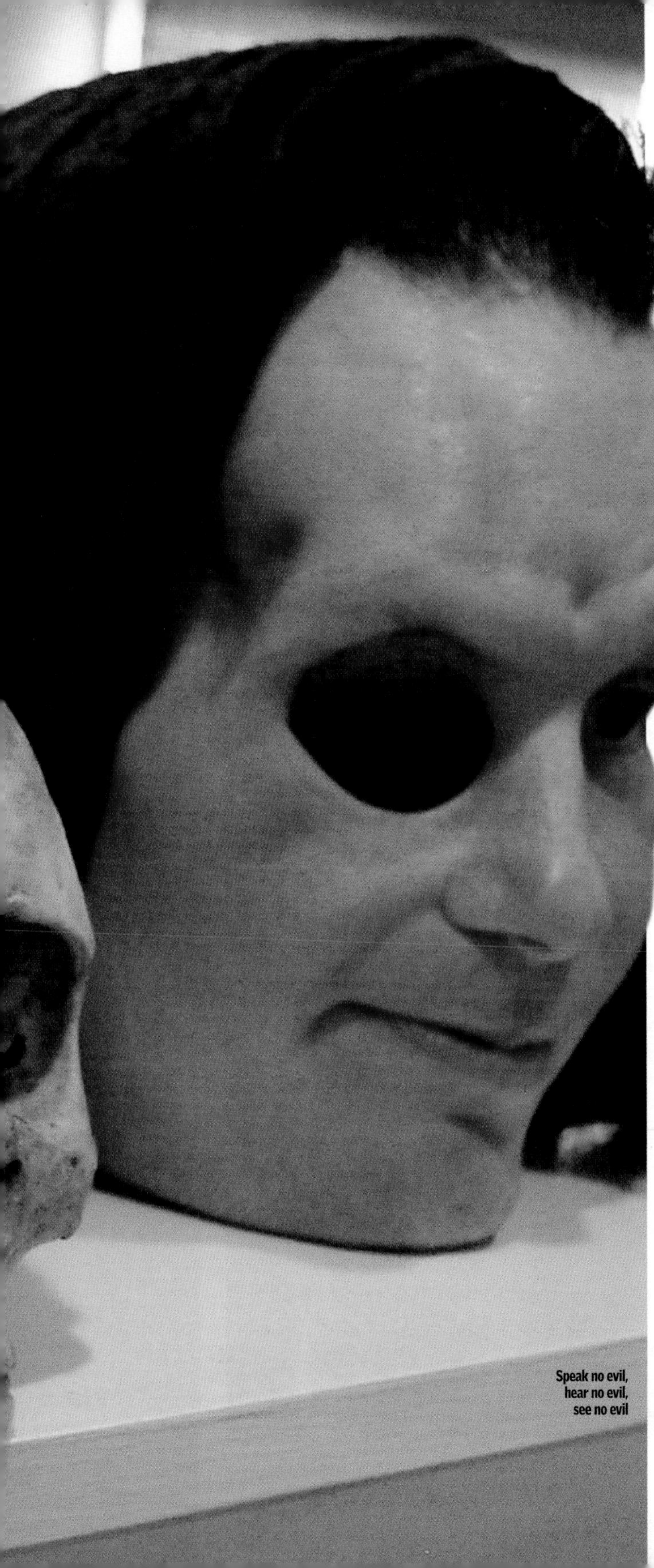

looking permanently wide-eyed or in constant shock, Cyclops Boy ditched the fake eyeball for a patch.

Head like a hole

After a few years of wearing an eye patch – and a specially designed prosthetic in his mouth and under his cheek to give his mouth a proper roof – Cyclops Boy developed a sense of humour about his condition. When driving without his patch, he'd turn towards another motorist at a traffic light, smile, and give the driver an unexpected fright. His missing peeper also came in handy at a Halloween party as part of his skeleton costume. But Cyclops Boy knew he had greater potential.

"I was having a beer and got curious," he says. "I wondered if I could drink through my eye socket, and if the liquid would go down my throat. I thought it would be a cool bar trick."

Sure enough, Cyclops Boy found he could tilt the neck of the bottle right into his socket. Soon, he discovered he could inhale a cigarette orally and exhale the smoke through his eye socket, and with his prosthetic taken out his tongue realised its →

"I enjoy being a freak. Good has come from the surgery"

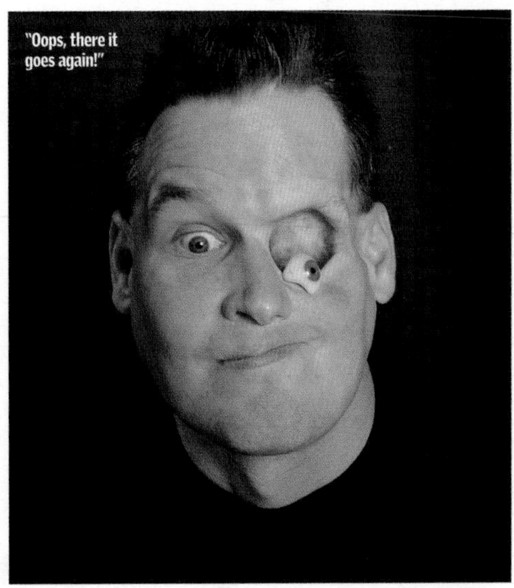

"Oops, there it goes again!"

Speak no evil, hear no evil, see no evil

true dexterity by lunging upward and wagging through the empty socket. And he earned his other stage name of Pumpkinhead with a stunt involving a torch in his mouth and a glowing eye – just like a Halloween lantern.

Stars in his eyes

Armed with his unparalleled talents, the one-eyed wonder made his first foray into the sideshow world by auditioning for a local radio show's search for freaks. The host, a DJ called Mancow, loved the act and hired him on the spot. In the first of a series of monikers, Mancow dubbed our hero T2 in honour of the Terminator, whose eye got blown away in the Schwarzenegger blockbuster. Cyclops Boy further enhanced the image by sporting a flat-top haircut and a leather jacket. Now, he was ready to shock his first big crowd.

"At my first show the crowd went nuts. I felt like a rock star"

"When I did my first big show with the radio station, the crowd went nuts and I felt like a rock star," Cyclops Boy says. The event not only launched a new part-time career, but also introduced him to several other seasoned performers, including fire manipulator William Darke and the Torture King, Tim Cridland, formerly of the Jim Rose Circus.

But despite his sudden celebrity, Cyclops Boy wasn't prepared to be a full-time freak; he'd maintained his regular 40-hour-a-week job as an electrician since his surgery and, above all, he was a family man with responsibilities. In fact, by the time he'd become a star, Cyclops Boy was Cyclops Dad to three young children – and Cyclops Coach in their youth sports club. So travelling with the sideshow became a rare event.

"Most guys who perform in freak shows for a living are just scraping by," he explains. "Me, I don't need the money. I don't like missing baseball and football with my son. The price has to be right for me." →

"To be, or not to be..."

Look, it's Mr Pumpkinhead! Spooky!

Looking smokin' hot!

Socket to 'em

After making the right connections, Cyclops Boy did the odd local show in Chicago, including opening for the Red Hot Chili Peppers. However, a promotional tour for Slim Jim beef sticks, featuring wrestling legend Randy 'Macho Man' Savage, was lucrative enough to lure him to six different cities across the United States.

During this series of shows, Cyclops Boy met The Brothers Grim Side Show impresario, Ken Harck. Ken's show – a tribute to the sideshows of yesteryear – includes sword swallowers, human blockheads, and natural-born freaks such as the Wolf Boys of Mexico. Ken befriended the one-eyed performer and later recruited him. In fact, it was Ken who gave him his current moniker. In the years that followed, the two worked together whenever possible. "He's a great attraction," Ken says. "He's certainly a show stopper."

Perhaps not surprisingly, Cyclops Boy is often a showstopper in the literal sense. He begins his performances dressed in a dark, hooded cloak and sunglasses. A narrator introduces him and offers

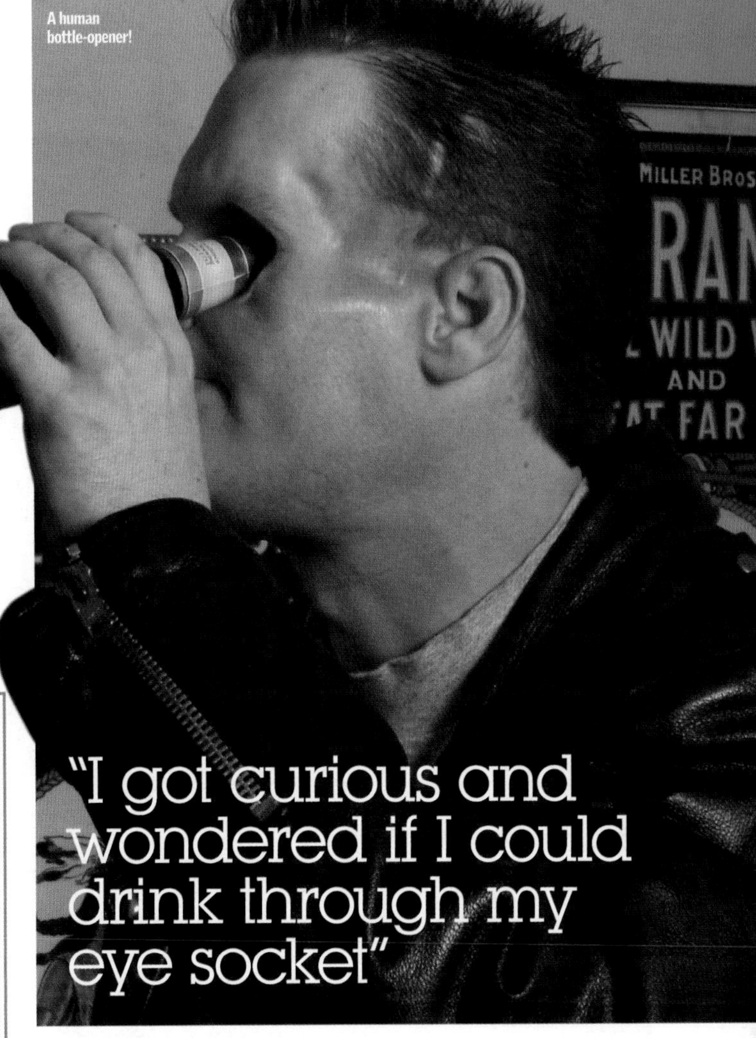

A human bottle-opener!

"I got curious and wondered if I could drink through my eye socket"

a toast, then Cyclops Boy removes his glasses, pours the beer through his eye and spits it out his mouth. After his other eye-opening tricks, he closes the set by waving goodbye with his tongue reaching through the socket. Those who haven't fainted stare in shock and awe.

Most nights, a few members of the audience vomit. But, in the end, most are sympathetic to the way in which Cyclops Boy lost his eye and applaud him for overcoming his cancer and his bizarre appearance.

"Other people have had the same surgery I've been through, but I've never heard of anyone else doing stuff like this," Cyclops Boy says. "I enjoy doing it. Something good came out of it, that's how I look at it, rather than all doom and gloom and being depressed about it." And that's a triumph even greater than defeating his cancer. Ⓑ

Eye-popping fun!

CELEBRATING *BIZARRE*'S 100TH ISSUE!

To celebrate the 100th issue of *Bizarre* back in July 2005, Cyclops Boy had a bottle of vintage champagne on us, and downed it in one gulp through his socket. "It's a real honour to be one of *Bizarre*'s favourite people," he told us. "I find it hard to put into words, but I really like the fact that people find me interesting."

GREGG VALENTINO

He claims to have the biggest biceps in the world – and he's certainly got a big mouth...

WORDS **PAUL CHEUNG, VICTORIA HOGG**
PHOTOS **GREGG VALENTINO**

Gregg Valentino is a freaky-looking guy. At only 5ft6in, but with biceps that look like a pile of human heads squeezed into shiny sausage skin, it's no surprise the native New Yorker has been a guest at Ripley's Believe It Or Not!, as well as appearing on big US programmes such as *The Tonight Show With Jay Leno* and *The Howard Stern Show*.

A body builder since the age of 13, Gregg's super-sculpted arms make him a one-man freak show. In fact, professional body builders' arms rarely exceed 24in in circumference, while Gregg's weigh in at a whopping 27in. "I guess I look retarded," he admits in his trademark gravel-shovelling, rasping shout. "It's not normal. I'm short, but my arms are ridiculous! I have small-man complex. I figured if I can't grow taller, I'm gonna get bigger. Do I think they look good? Fuck, no. They're disgusting."

Pumping more than iron

Gregg's not just outspoken about the size of his arms, but is also happy to talk about the way he got them. "Testosterone was my drug of choice," he admits. "I took a *lot* of testosterone. →

"I can take this popcorn! Bring it!"

Way more than I should've: about 3,000 milligrams a week. The human body shouldn't take more than 200 milligrams! I grew pretty easily anyway, so the minute I took steroids my body went into warp drive."

But Gregg wasn't always a testosterone abuser. "I lifted weights for 23 years without even touching a drug," he says. "When I started to take drugs, my well-trained muscle grew better than my untrained muscle. The drugs add size, plus you're taking shots: it's called 'locating', which means you're injecting it right into the area: a double whammy. My arms are solid as rock."

Gregg's behaviour has got him into hot water with both body building fans and its officials, though he remains unrepentent: "I don't think I abused it any more than any other pro," he says. "If you see other body builders backstage, you'd see they're lucky if they can get up, walk about and pose. You should see these pros when they're not on a steroid cycle. They look terrible. They're fat."

But Gregg's luck didn't last, and in 1998 his right arm became infected. "I was an idiot!" he says. "I was dropping needles on the floor and just wiping them off and sticking them in me. I was bound to get an infection."

"I have small man complex. If I can't grow taller, I'm gonna get bigger"

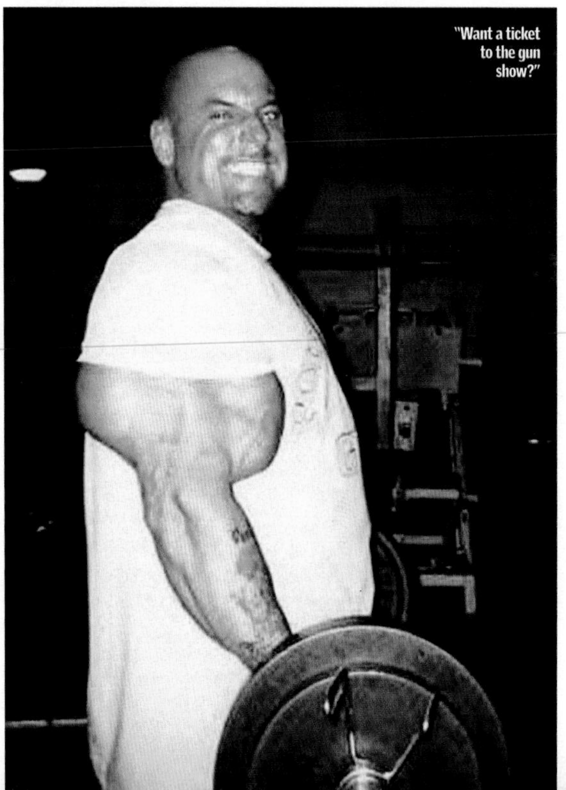

"Want a ticket to the gun show?"

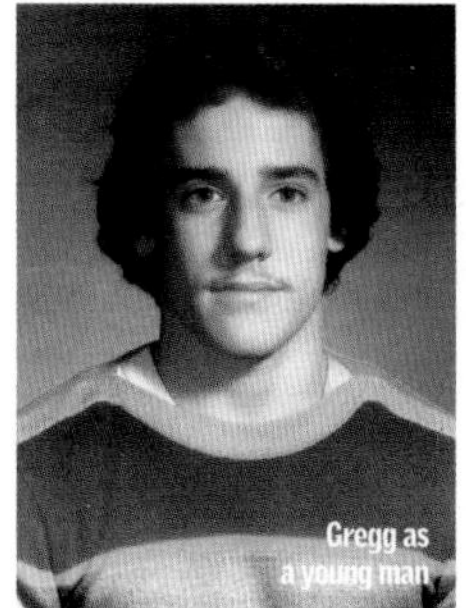

Gregg as a young man

Bulked-up and posing

His muscles are bigger than machines!

Jailhouse rock-hard

Whether or not his frankness brings the sport into disrepute, there was no escaping the law for Gregg. In April 2001, he was put on a five-year probationary period after being convicted of 'possession with intent to sell anabolic steroids and possession of two unlicensed handguns'.

"In the drug dealing business I was big," he says. "I was up there. You always hear: 'You're being watched, you gotta watch what you do,' and it happened for me at the gym one night. There was a huge banging on the door and a *swarm* of police rushed in and took me."

Police found $75,000-worth of illegal muscle-building drugs in Gregg's home and he was sent down. Despatched to Westchester County Jail in 2001, the tobacco-free teetotaller hasn't touched steroids since: "I lost *everything* – my son still won't speak to me, the cops confiscated all my money, I lost my gym, my brand-new Yukon XL SUV. My girlfriend killed herself, my mother had just died and my ex-wife took the rest of my money. But the arrest woke me up and changed my life."

But while it may sound odd that a man who's been on the cover of hundreds of magazines and was mates with the Hollywood glitteratti should turn to a life of crime, Gregg's decision to become a dealer was purely financial. After all, there's little money to be made from pumping iron. →

"Mike Quinn made the top six in Mr Olympia (body building's most prestigious contest) one year, but at the same time he was a bouncer in a bar! Most of these guys have to work other jobs. Girls make more at beauty pageants – $100,000, new cars – but the only guy who gets anything is Mr Olympia. There's a big difference between first and second. That's why body builders all own gyms, do personal training, sell videos. To be a professional athlete at the top of your sport but still have to bounce in a bar at night? Sit there and do personal training? Smell some guy's rotten breath? Forget it!"

The high-protein diet also wreaks havoc. "When you're eating that kinda food, you get monster fucking explosions coming out your ass!" Gregg laughs. "I was driving a bus full of retarded kids; they were so severely handicapped they didn't even know they were on a bus. And I had to take a really bad shit. So I parked the bus; the kids were all up front – they didn't know I existed. I ran in the back, put newspaper on the floor, and 'Boom!' blasted right on the paper like a dog. Then I threw it out the window, and pulled my pants up."

Gregg's muscles. And Gregg

"When you're on a high-protein diet, explosions come out of your ass!"

In cuffs outside the police department

Just a normal guy...

"Wonder if I'll make the next series of *Gladiators?*"

Building the future

The love life of the most hated man in body building is as complicated as his career path. Married for 10 years and with a son and a daughter ("My Gina, who's 12, is a super athlete – a basketball and lacrosse star. I would die for my kids!"), Gregg still couldn't resist living the full drug dealer lifestyle. He cheated on his wife with a Puerto Rican heroin addict and prostitute called Julissa, who'd been in prison 11 times and killed herself after an argument with Gregg ("My last words to her were 'Fuck you', he says. "It haunts me because I was very close to her."). Happily, Gregg now has a girlfriend now who he's been seeing for the last couple of years: "She's a great girl and I think she's my lifemate. She helps me be me."

The father of two is now a media-savvy mainstream figure. A mini-documentary with ESPN aired in April, and he has an autobiography coming out at the end of the year. He's also a columnist – *Muscular Development* magazine's 'Rambling Freak', who offers advice to diehard fans. Would he have done things differently, given another shot?

"Oh, yeah!" he says. "I wouldn't have got involved in drug dealing, and I'd try to be a professional baseball player. I'm still athletic to this day. I don't sit here and think, 'God, I look good.' I think I look like Uncle Fester on too much testosterone! I have regrets, but I don't sweat it. I'm not gonna bang my head on the wall – I'll just hurt my head."

"Eat spinach and you too can be like me!"

PICTURE: REX FEATURES

WILD WOMEN

Whether they're hosting porno cookery shows or struggling with their secret male genitalia, *Bizarre*'s best girls aren't your normal magazine lovelies

148

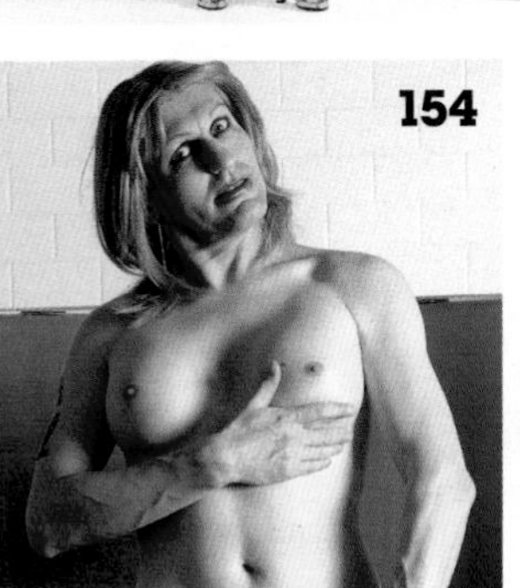
154

134

PORCELAIN TWINZ

They tease fetish fans with their lesbian antics and, yes, they're really twins...

WORDS **CHRIS NIERATKO, VICTORIA HOGG**
MAIN PHOTOS **JAMES STAFFORD**

Double trouble. Twice as nice. There are few greater turn-ons than identical twins. And there's nothing hotter than the Porcelain Twinz, who dress in outrageous rubber gear or satin skimpies, pretend to go down on each and often end a show with a strap-on session. We're sold.

Many twins try their damnedest to separate themselves from their identical sibling. Thankfully for us, Heather and Amber Langley have chosen the opposite route. They do everything together, dressing the same on stage and off, finishing each other's sentences – and, of course, perfecting their stunningly sensuous, near-illegal act.

Wrong side of the tracks

The unique USA honeys hail from "a real small, hick, hillbilly town" near Portland, the capital of Oregon – the state also known as (you couldn't make this up) the Beaver State. →

Porcelain Twinz: very naughty

PICTURE: LLOYD KINELDORF

Wednesday Adams meets burlesque

PICTURE: DAVID HINDLEY

Getting red and racy

PICTURE: LLOYD KINELDORF

"We've been dancing about in our underwear from an early age!"

The sexy siblings first strutted their Sapphic stuff back in 1997, when their three-year-long college careers as long distance runners ground to a halt, due to the twin constraints of injury and impoverishment.

But, thanks to the Beaver State's laws on beaver-flashing – and thanks to the girls' raw ambition – Amber and Heather hit pay dirt. Oregon's quirky constitution means that Portland boasts the USA's highest concentration of strip clubs, which in turn has meant the Porcelain Twinz and their USP have been guaranteed a strong following.

"We'd never had any formal dance training, but we've always been passionate about it, dancing about in our underwear from an early age," Amber says. "We caught on quickly how to move like strippers. After just a few months, people thought we'd been dancing for years."

Sex and the city

After a couple of years doing shows here and there, the Twinz landed a weekly slot at Dante's Sunday Inferno cabaret – a routine that gave them a springboard to tour across the USA. In September 2007, they moved to New York, topping the bill at the Lower East Side's super-chic vaudeville venue The Box, but they left a year later, reportedly disillusioned by the club, and have since taken out a law suit against it. It was reported in the *New York Post* that the owner "harassed" the girls into performing a show called 'Twincest', which they were uncomfortable with.

"If we hadn't changed our performance, I believe we'd have been fired," Amber reportedly said. "It was a huge compromise, but we made it very artistic so we could hold our heads high." After yet more pressure from the club owner, the girls took control and defected back home to Portland. They still live there with their teacup silky terrier called Morgan, dancing most regularly at sexy Portland strip bar the Boom Boom Room.

But it's not just about stripping – the Twinz see themselves as artists. Though they'll openly simulate sex acts, Heather and Amber (also known as Zen and Zero) don't do 'porn' – they call it erotica. "Really, it's all just performance," Heather says. "Some of our shows are really, really racy, and sometimes it's like, 'Oops, I licked your crotch, sorry!' And we'll start laughing."

Taking up the 'performance artist' mantle, Amber and Heather quickly developed →

beyond being merely a strip act – with roles in films, music and videos – not least to avoid prejudice from society. "We've had trouble when renting, getting health insurance, claiming taxes... it's a profession we've had to hide from society to avoid discrimination," says Heather.

Instead, the Twinz created their own genre – 'modern burlesque' – which combines a 'butter wouldn't melt' first impression with some outrageously raunchy antics. It's a highly erotic combination that can't be topped, given the girls' matching DNA.

Tease me, baby

What makes the Twinz unique is their approach to burlesque. While most sexy ladies on the nipple tassel scene start at merely

> "Some of our shows are really racy, and it's like, 'oops, I licked your crotch, sorry!'"

Pole dancing queens of performance art

PICTURE: DANIELLE BEDICS

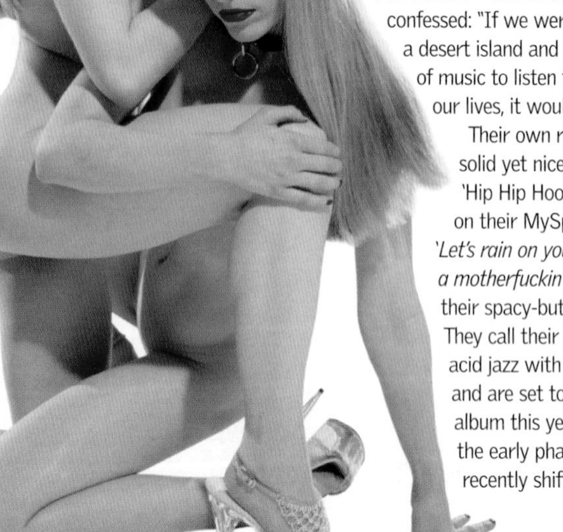

titilating, then gradually become more lewd, the Twinz worked backwards, starting from the Jalapeño-hot, strip-club end of events and creating a broader, more teasing show – with a few outrageous twists. "We choreograph all our performance art pieces or dance routines," says Heather. "We come up with a theme, which is usually inspired by the music, and it develops from there. It's a very intense process."

The Twinz's shows are a gorgeous mix of fire and fanwork, incredibly tight moves and trademark nods to hardcore. "We do love performing live," they agree. "The high we get when performing in front of a crowd that is giving to us as much as we are giving to them is nearly indescribable. It's like an out-of-body experience."

Their website states the Twinz are "filmmakers, writers, directors, producers, singers, models, dancers and actors", and it's no idle boast. They shot their first erotic art film, *The Masked Charade*, in 2006, and the box cover describes "a highly stylised, dark, decadent, and ambient film... with a foray of visual vignettes that take you through a dream-like voyeuristic fantasy". The Weimar-esque circus features original music from solely Portland-based bands, including The Dandy Warhols.

Music is high on the Twinz agenda. They're also known as the Porcelain Dollz – self-taught musicians who wrote the title track to *The Masked Charade*, a weirdly compelling, twisted, leftfield collection of ambient beats with the girls singing over the top. Their favourite artists reek of effortless cool – Goldfrapp, Ladytron, Gogol Bordello, The Streets – and a recent Twitter entry confessed: "If we were stranded on a desert island and had one choice of music to listen to for the rest of our lives, it would be Radiohead."

Their own records are rock-solid yet nicely tongue in cheek. 'Hip Hip Hooray', to be found on their MySpace page, drones: *'Let's rain on your parade / It's a motherfuckin' jolly good day'*, in their spacy-but-tuneful manner. They call their sound "trip-hop acid jazz with a carnival twist", and are set to record their first album this year: "We're still in the early phases, but we just recently shifted our focus →

PICTURE: FRANK NESSLAGE

In-flight drinks trolley: just out of shot

PICTURE: FRANK NESSLAGE

Getting it on, 1920s style

to finishing the record, and we're going to allot the time needed to do this," says Heather. In fact, the girls are already in talks with a Portland studio and several producers: "We love working on music; we want to do more, and for it to be very avant-garde – but it has to be right. It's really important when you meet people that you're on the same page creatively, that it's going to be a good experience." They even plan to tour live.

Girls on top

And so to the duo's publishing arm. Heather and Amber's book – 2005's *The Porcelain Twinz: Our Life In The Sex Industry* – is their autobiography from their birth up to 2004. There are 265 shots in a 'photo album' in the back, but no nude pics. "But we do *feel* naked, and we do bare all. It's a tell-all book," they agree.

The Twinz are already writing a second book, which will pick up where the first left off, plus a coffee table special that'll feature their favourite pictures from their photoshoots. They organise their own publishing, but are always looking at the bigger picture. "In the big scheme of things we'd love to publish other artists," they agree.

The Twinz also want to make another film. "As much as we crave the adoring audience, we do aspire to make feature films," Ambers says. "It's our biggest ambition – something we've dreamed about for many years. We want to turn our autobiography into a feature film, making it a dark musical that tells our story through a series of fetish-burlesque cabaret shows with dialogue. If you know any millionaires, send them our way – feature filmmaking is expensive!"

"Sucker!"

PICTURE: MARK BURGE

"I don't think we'd go down on each other. Strap-ons are OK, though!"

How sexy would it be, then? "We could shoot a hardcore film, but it'd be really arty, and more fetish." Would there be 'touching of parts'? "We've kinda discussed how we'd do it, and I don't think we'd actually go down on one another. But toys are OK, strap-ons, yeah. No hands. We're not really into the whole 'finger your sister' thing. Besides, there are lots of laws!"

Life partners

Last time *Bizarre* spoke to the Twinz, they were single. "The twin relationship is quite complex," explained Heather. "It's kinda like being married. I guess we're not only sisters, but also business partners and best friends – it's just non-stop. Anyone else comes second and a lot of people can't deal with that.

"We've had some fun with boys, but they can never really live up to the expectation of the whole 'twin fantasy'. They get intimidated with the pressure! They go into it thinking we're going to be all over them, but really we want them to be all over us, so it's our fantasy."

This time, Heather and Amber are keeping quiet about their love lives – "We're saving it for our next book!" But they've certainly got their hands full: music, film, documentaries, books, modelling, live shows, an adoring public and, of course, their gorgeous terrier.

"Morgan is an only child!" Amber laughs. "She's tiny, but she thinks she's really tough. We Twitter more about her than we do about ourselves!" Ⓑ

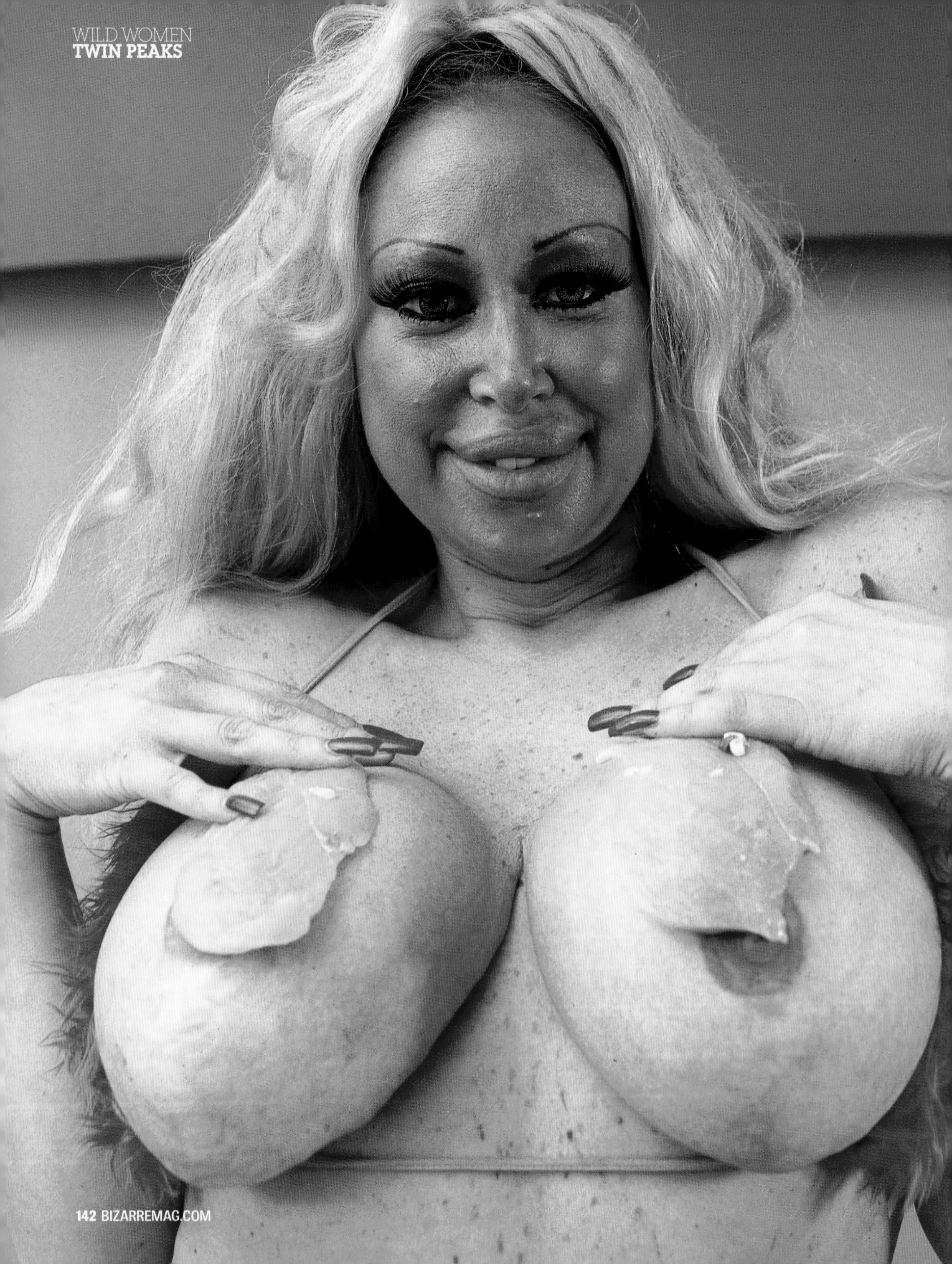

WORDS **DENISE STANBOROUGH**
PHOTOS **JAMES STAFFORD**

PAMELA PEAKS

This LA adult actress has size 50GGG breasts and plans to go even bigger. Are you a Pam fan?

At the tender age of 15, Pamela Peaks had her first breast implants, propelling the already C-cup girl down a path that would soon make her the most famous big-breasted adult star in the world. Around the same time, the Canada-born hottie started stripping, which she favoured over her previous 'normal' jobs. "I was a stripper in Canada for a couple of years, then I went into the porn industry," she says. "My family were cool if it made me happy."

Pamela kick-started her film career in 2001, and since then the busty blonde with her eye-watering 50GGG breasts has starred in literally hundreds of porn movies, becoming – as *Hustler* magazine hailed her – "one of the most versatile girls in the business".

Versatile is the word: The LA-based honey owns and runs over 250 websites and is a manager for adult and mainstream models and actors. She brokers work for men, women and transsexuals in film, print, the web, private shows, bachelor parties and feature dancing. There's also her 'porn party' sideline – she throws a big LA-based bash twice a month. She's even directed and produced four movies through Pamela Peaks Productions, with more to come, and knocks out two TV shows with long-term business partner Randy De Troit, an entrepreneur who also shoots and edits. →

"I start work at 8am, seven days a week," she says. "I'll work all day then I go to the gym at night with a personal trainer. I'm getting very toned. I'm even considering going to school to become a certified personal trainer. I get around six hours sleep if I'm lucky. I'm going non-stop! I have a ton of energy!"

Breast is best

A lot of this energy is spent on her appearance. Besides the training, Pamela has had "three, going on four" breast augmentations, with more planned. "I'm going bigger! I'm getting expander implants so they can continually be made bigger," she exclaims. "Any girl who gets breast implants and says her self-esteem doesn't go up is lying. But you have to be very careful with the doctors and do your research because some doctors only go to certain sizes. I've got some Europe inside me because my implants are from Paris."

The 5ft9in siren has also had "a nose job, liposuction, brow lifts, cheek implants, chin implants, jaw implants and my lips done". She explains, "Once you start, you get addicted. It *so* raises your self-esteem and it's instant gratification, it's like fast food. I went in and came out an hour-and-a-half later with the boobs of my dreams and I put it on a credit card."

Cooking up some X-rated stunts

Getting saucy while in the kitchen

"You get addicted to surgery. It raises your self-esteem, it's like fast food"

It's not easy living with massive boobs, though, and she had an unfortunate accident while working as a lapdancer in Canada. "I woke up one morning with one boob!" she says. "I'd let so many guys squeeze my boobs, the saline solution had actually leaked into my body. I was walking around the club with one normal-sized boob and the other one about half the size. It was so embarrassing! I worked one night like that and got on the phone with one of my doctors and said, 'You've *got* to fix me!'"

Showing off

Besides her vast library of skin flicks, Pamela crossed over into the semi-mainstream with her two cable shows. She first got into TV when she told Randy that she wanted to present a show that was "fun, positive and interesting about porn". Randy came up with the winning formula that was 2004's *Pamela Peaks In The Kitchen?!* – a bonkers comedy mix of top porn stars, chat, gourmet meals and, of course, large portions of nudity and sex.

"I'll find out if any adult stars are single, invite them on, give them drinks to loosen them up, and next thing you know, they're going at it behind me!" she exclaims. "I did a great show with →

When these photos were taken in 2005, Pamela told us she was just 23 years old...

Sticking it to the... oven

That's not Santa!

Cleaning up after one of her crazy parties

"I came out with the boobs of my dreams and put it on a credit card"

a few midgets. We put the midgets' heads in between my boobs and my friend Echo Valley's, to compare sizes."

The other show Pamela presents is *Pamela Peaks Speaks*, where she pounces on stars at adult industry parties. "I started this show because many interviewers didn't really know a lot about the actors they were speaking to, or about porn in general, which made for really boring interviews," she explains. "Also, they were often mean to the porn stars, which isn't fun or interesting to watch."

Pamela's unique insider knowledge makes her subjects feel at ease. "I was a crazy porn fanatic *before* I started doing porn, so even though I'm a porn star myself now, I'll always be that geeky fan," she says. "The actors all really like the fact that I know a lot about them; it makes them feel really comfortable. It's a total blast!"

Thinking big

Pamela's next big project is to publish a magazine, *Porn Star Entertainment*, which will be on sale by the end of the year – although its website is already taking orders. "It's a triple-X magazine with triple-X pics," she says. "I'm gonna have layouts of all your favourite big-boobed girls, as well as girls who aren't so busty. So long as they're hot, they'll get in the magazine! There'll also be hilarious interviews with both porn stars and mainstream people."

What's clear with Pamela is that comedy is close to her heart. When asked how she unwinds, Pamela says, "working out, masturbating, making people laugh and watching comedies. I love *Saturday Night Live* and all the *SNL* stars' movies, for example. The new show *Eastbound And Down* is awesome and one of my favourite movies ever is *The Brothers Solomon*. I grew up in a comedy household."

She also loves to scuba dive, play sports, go clothes shopping, and buy computers. "I have five computers so far, with more coming". Great – but tell us more about the masturbating. "Ha ha! To relax I'll masturbate with a huge dildo while watching hot male porn stars with huge dicks fuck big-tit girls – and then I'll sleep."

SELENE LUNA

This pint-sized burlesque artiste is bigger than most other stars in the world...

WORDS **DENISE STANBOROUGH, VICTORIA HOGG**
PHOTOS **SAM SCOTT-HUNTER**

It may be a cliché that the best things come in small packages, but we don't mind repeating this adage in the case of Selene Luna. There's something timeless about this pint-sized vixen's beauty and style that means she can effortlessly straddle the vintage world of burlesque and the modern movie arena, taking in satirical comedy along the way.

The 3ft10in star was born and raised in Mexico, but emmigrated illegally with her parents to the USA aged two. "That was a big challenge!" she remembers. "I don't have many fond memories from my childhood: for the most part it was dark and lonely. The best entertainment my parents could afford for us kids was cruising around Hollywood in the hope of celebrity sightings. But all I was trying to make sense of was why the two handlebar-moustached gentlemen on Santa Monica Boulevard were holding hands."

All the way to the tap

From an early age, Selene – pronounced 'Su-lenny' – knew what pushed her buttons, creatively speaking, thanks to a trip to see a double feature of *The Wizard Of Oz* and *Singing In The Rain* on her fourth birthday. "They were the most incredible images I'd ever seen!" she gushes. "Entertaining came naturally to me because my whole life I thought, 'I have to tap dance for people.' Because I'm little, people always stare at me, so I thought, 'Well, I'll give them something to look at!'"

Selene got started in showbusiness by doing improvisation in Hollywood. "I sucked really bad at it! But it gave me a real good indication of what I wanted to do," she says. "After the →

comedy circuit I worked as a magician's assistant, and that's where I started my kind-of-circus stuff. Then I fell in love with being a dancer with Velvet Hammer."

Velvet Hammer Burlesque was created in 1995, and is credited with kicking off the USA's massive burlesque revival. It boasts women of all shapes and sizes. "When they asked me to join I was over the moon," says Selene. "The troupe's not feminist by any means – it's just a bunch of gals who love making costumes and dressing up. We just thought, 'Damn it! Let's put it on a stage!'"

The recurring themes in Selene's burlesque turns are lust and humour. "Burlesque has provided a marvellous platform to express my feminine sexuality, vulnerability as an actor, and acceptance of my body," she says.

That acceptance must be paramount to a little person, though she says it took a while for her to cotton on to the fact that she was different, due to her protective parents: "My parents meant well, but they were a bit extreme in trying to provide a normal life for me. So much so that, in high school, the reality of my physical status hit me like a ton of bricks. That's when I truly realised that I was different."

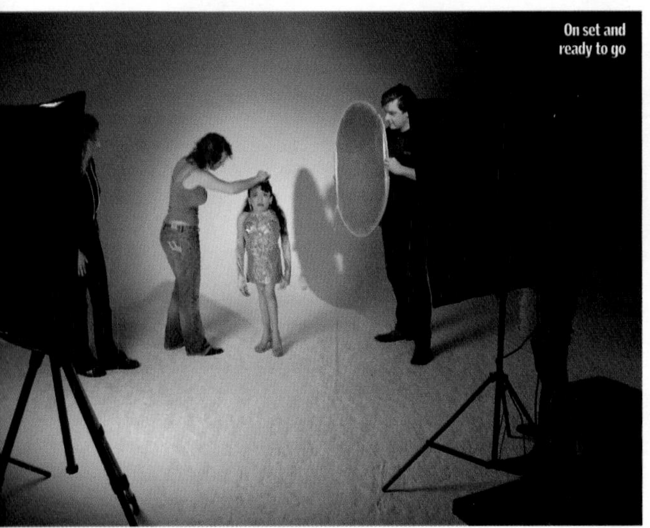

On set and ready to go

Selene always comes out swinging!

"Men feel riddled with guilt when they think about me sexually"

From small screen to big

Selene is one of only a handful of little person burlesque artists in the world, but she isn't afraid to use her other talents. She's been in music videos for bands such as the Smashing Pumpkins, Stone Temple Pilots, Madonna and Marilyn Manson.

Miss Luna's no stranger to film work, either, and she worked on 2004's *Van Helsing* in a back-breaking costume. "It was made from heavy leather and metal and I was covered from head to toe," she recalls. "It was twice my weight, I couldn't even sit down in it! I was on the set lying on the floor like a turtle for 17 hours. They were like, 'Don't get out of that costume, we might need you.'"

In 2005, Selene played Harriet in *Firecracker*, a story of a travelling circus. "Steve Balderson's script was the first one I'd ever read where I found an actual artistic relevance to having a 'freak' in the story," she explains. "Most times it's lack of creativity and freaks are just 'thrown in' for people to look at. In Steve's script it was more about my relationship with Karen Black's character."

Ask Selene if she's ever felt exploited and she's quick to reply. "Oh yeah!" she giggles. "Everyone in the film industry is limited by what they look like, so I'll get whatever generic little-person or ethnic hooker part there might be going. Little people in the industry are nothing more than physical props. The little person is always a monster or a goddamn Christmas elf! I've walked away from a lot of 'Christmas elf' jobs. I used to be bitter, but I ended up losing money because of it: if you don't want the job, there's a whole *bunch* of little people who'll do it instead. Career elves, you know?" →

Smokin' hot as a sultry biker babe

"Moi? In the spotlight? Never..."

Most recently, Selene worked on peppy gorefest *My Bloody Valentine 3D*, starring conventional Hollywood hottie Jaime King, and stars in VH1's *The Cho Show*, a reality sitcom with comedien Margaret Cho that features Selene as Cho's assistant and saw Sandra Bernhard, Michelle Rodriguez, Kat Von D and Joan Rivers all make guest appearances in the first series.

She also has a double act with comedy writer Nadya Ginsburg, which can be seen on YouTube. As *Luna And Ginsburg*, they've spoofed a US Corn Refiners Association infomercial and shot a hilarious sketch called 'Madonna And Child', with Nadya as Madonna and Selene as daughter Lourdes sporting a black beret, moustache and monobrow like those in paintings by Frida Kahlo, one of Madonna's favourite artists.

Apart from her flourishing film, TV and stage work, Selene sometimes entertains at private parties for the stars. She once performed for Demi Moore's daughter, Rumer. "In 2004, I did her sixteenth birthday party," she says. "Bruce Willis and Ashton Kutcher were there, and Demi was so sweet – she was concerned about me being cold and kept offering to go and get me a sweater."

"As long as the genitals line up, height's not an issue during sex"

Getting sexy with a sombrero

Her 1970s disco revival didn't work out

Luna-tic fringe

Far from being starstruck, though, the mini-minx is candid about her private clients: "My own friends are much more interesting! I'd rather be with them, to be honest. In fact, that I get hired to be a guest at a party at all tells you how dull some of these people are. If you're a big celebrity and you have to 'hire' the atmosphere, then there's a problem, right?"

Selene's friends are mostly bonkers artists on the fringes who offer a skewed creative view, but they've helped Selene get where she is today: "Some of my dearest friends have had a huge influence on me as an entertainer – Vaginal Davis, a walking installation piece, and Buck Angel, the first and only female-to-male transsexual porn artist."

But she has her own thoughts on getting sexual attention. "Men seem to be intrigued, as if they've discovered a new toy, and yet they're riddled with guilt for having sexual thoughts about me," she explains patiently in her even voice. "Society teaches us that disabled or physically unconventional people don't have sexual desires. I've always embraced my sensuality as a woman, and I think that's what confuses men when they meet me. Mostly, I think it's innocent fascination and men don't know where to place it."

Luckily she doesn't have any dating horror stories other than simply not connecting spiritually. "To put it bluntly, as long as the genitals line up, height's not an issue," she grins. Ⓑ

SARAH -JANE

PHOTOS
JAMES STAFFORD

From a young age, Sarah-Jane knew there was something different about her…

If there was a form to assess someone's suitability for appearing in *Bizarre* magazine, Sarah-Jane could lose a whole afternoon to box-ticking.

Have you worked as an escort and professional submissive? Tick. Are you a regular on the BDSM scene? Tick. Was your first job selling your body on the streets at the tender age of 14? Tick. Have you got 40DD implants, which you've given the pet names Molly and Polly after the twin daughters of Dr Glossop and his wife in 1980s kids' TV show *Pigeon Street*? Tick… →

Sausages for breakfast, anyone?

But as interesting as those elements of Sarah-Jane's life are, they stand in the shadow of the real reason we're talking to her. Which is that Sarah-Jane has a couple of things most people don't: an extra chromosome and, consequently, more than her fair share of genitals.

Or, to put another way, when Sarah-Jane was born in Liverpool on 28 April 1957, she was born with 'ambiguous gender, mixed gonadal tissue, and has an XXY karyotype'. As Sarah-Jane bluntly puts it: "I have unique genitalia; I've got a vagina and a penis." And, unlike most intersex people of her age, Sarah-Jane still has them.

Sarah-Jane always pees like a woman

Mum's the word

Although in the 1950s it was common practice to operate on newborn hermaphrodites and leave the child to grow as one gender or the other, there was no surgical intervention in Sarah-Jane's case.

"Because it was a provincial hospital, they didn't do anything," she says. "I don't think my mother and father knew exactly what was wrong. My father didn't want to talk about it anyway.

"I wouldn't care if I'd been born a boy or girl, but this is a joke"

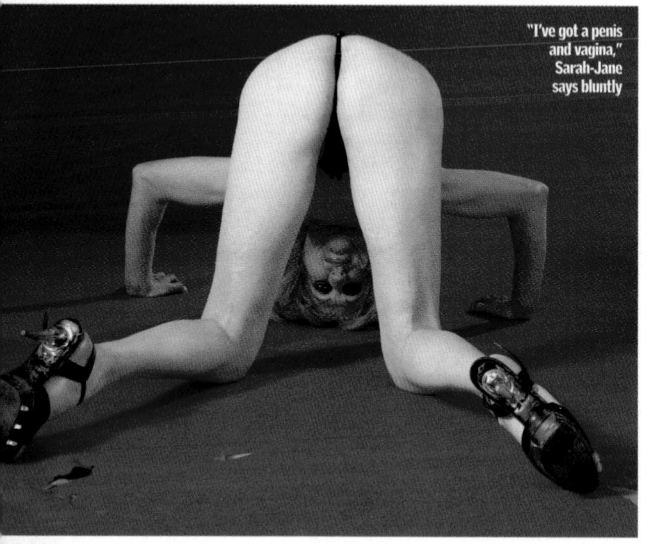

"I've got a penis and vagina," Sarah-Jane says bluntly

"Leaving me like this was wrong," she continues. "I wouldn't care if I'd been a girl or boy, but this is a joke. And the joke's on me."

Growing up, Sarah-Jane never discussed sex with her parents, and just figured out she wasn't the same as other people. "I've always known I was different," she says. "I could look at a little girl or little boy, but then I'd look down and see that I wasn't either."

Testing times

As you can imagine, not many people look down and see both male and female genitalia. The percentage of births that result in hermaphroditism isn't clear, but research by Leonard Sax in the *Journal Of Sex Research* (2002) puts it at 0.018 per cent of births.

And while there's no way to be certain why Sarah-Jane is a hermaphrodite, her father's sexual dysfunction may have been to blame. "My father had to have injections into his testicles in order to produce enough sperm to fertilise eggs in my mum and have me," she explains. "I think that's where I went wrong."

When she was younger, it was easier for Sarah-Jane to hide her condition. The teachers didn't know her secret, let alone her classmates, and only her sports teacher was made aware "in case there was a problem in the changing room". Fortunately, there never was. →

Working girl

Sarah-Jane started looking more masculine as she grew older, but still considers herself female – her passport (see p157) says she's female, and she "pees like a woman". When she began working as a prostitute at the age of 14, she earned as much money as other escorts because people assumed she was a normal girl.

But despite starting out as a traditionally female hooker, over time Sarah-Jane's hermaphrodite status has allowed her to offer a unique service, and one that's essential for repeat business in the competitive world of commercial sex. "Guys love me," she grins. "They'll be fucking me, and I'll understand as a 'man' why they enjoy it. My clients love that, it turns them on. They come and see me where they wouldn't see a transvestite or a transsexual, but visit me because I have the female chromosome and the male and female bits. They'll even pay extra for the privilege."

Being a hermaphrodite also helps Sarah-Jane give her female clients what they want. "Ladies buy me as an intersex woman, and as I'm bisexual there's no problem," she says. "Some ladies prefer to go with a woman who looks more masculine, so they can pretend they've got a boyfriend who's a girl *down there*."

"I love working on the streets as a prostitute. I thrive on danger"

Not only that, but being intersex also helps Sarah-Jane when she's working the streets – something she still does from time to time.

"I can't get enough of it!" she laughs. "I'm a nymphomaniac. Although I work most of the time as an escort or dancer, I love working the streets. I thrive on danger. That's what I've been doing since I was 14, so I'm pretty streetwise."

But while being intersex doesn't protect Sarah-Jane from the hazards of working on the streets, it does bring her relative immunity to being prosecuted for it. "I've been arrested, but I've never actually been charged because they don't know what to charge me as, a girl or a boy," she laughs. "I think the police are embarrassed as they don't understand what intersex is!"

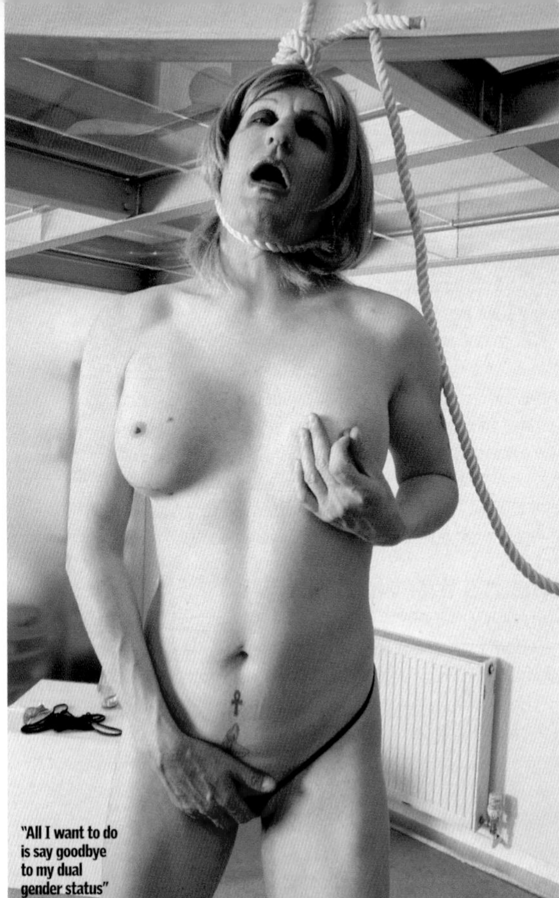

"All I want to do is say goodbye to my dual gender status"

Vagina monologues

If you think Sarah-Jane's dual gender brings her the best of both worlds, think again. It's more like the worst.

"I'm sterile," she says, clearly upset. "All hermaphrodites are sterile. We can never have children. Nature has never intended someone with both sets of genitalia to impregnate themselves." And whereas some transsexuals talk about their situation giving them the ability to empathise with both men and women, Sarah-Jane experiences something similar, but for her it's negative. "It's like I've got two brains and they don't work in unison," she says. "The male and female sides tolerate each other, but they don't like each other."

She reveals the plan for her next move: her male genitalia will be surgically removed and her vaginal canal made larger, leaving her solely female for the first time in her life. Although *Bizarre*'s time with Sarah-Jane ended soon after this disclosure – and we never saw her in the flesh again – we hope that an operation planned to remove her gender ambiguity was successful.

"All I want now is to say goodbye to my dual-gender status and be like everybody else," she told us. "You have an existence as an intersex person; you have to make a life out of it. I haven't coped; I've existed. My life might be a hell of a sob story, but it ain't a tragedy – and as long as I'm alive, I'll make sure it isn't a tragedy and never becomes one. I've had so much unhappiness in my life, I'm not going to let myself be unhappy any more. Why should I?"

As a call girl, Sarah-Jane is happy to service both male and female clients

SPIRAL
SPIRALDIRECT·COM
Viscose
Viscose
FALLEN ANGEL
Ref NAME CODE SIZES DESCRIPTION PRICE
A = FAITH DW170219 XL L M S BATWING £17.99
B = MORTIFICA AS103219 XL L M S BATWING £17.99
C = VIPER QUEEN DT168220 XL L M S RING BOATNECK £16.99
D = ARACNAFARIA AS100221 XL L M S RIBBON CAMI £14.99
E = ANGEL HEART DT169199 XL L M S 2IN1 MESH VEST £13.99
F = BLEEDING HEART TR263189 XL L M S LACEUP LS £17.99
Ref NAME CODE SIZES DESCRIPTION PRICE
G = SKULL FAIRY AS104221 XL L M S SLVLESS £12.99
H = BLACK CAT DT153221 XL L M S RIBBON CAMI £14.99
I = GOTH NIGHTS DT151227 XL L M S ONE SHOULDER £17.99
J = VIOLA & ECHO SF115170 L M S LS MESH GLOVE £13.99
K = FALLEN ANGEL DT132217 XL L M S RING HALTERNECK £14.99
FREE CATALOGUE
Ref NAME CODE SIZES DESCRIPTION PRICE
L = SHADOW VAMPIRE WM108700 XXL XL L M LONG SLEEVE £13.99
M = MIDNIGHT HOWL DW168880 XL L M S SLVLESS WORKER £19.99
N = DEMON ROCK TR266550 XL L M SLVLESS £11.99
O = DEATH RIDE TR264550 XL L M SLVLESS £11.99
Ref NAME CODE SIZES DESCRIPTION PRICE
P = SOUL DEMON DW148550 L MS SLVLESS £11.99
Q = SHADOW MASTER TR245555 L M S SLVLESS £11.99
R = KILLING EDGE DT137880 XL L M S SLVLESS WORKER £19.99
S = SHROUD OF SOULS WR120552 XL L M SLVLESS AO £16.99
Ref NAME CODE SIZES DESCRIPTION PRICE
T = PHOENIX RISING TR261700 XXL XL L M LONG SLEEVE £13.99
U = ZOMBIE DRAGON LG160600 XXL XL L M T-SHIRT £11.99
V = DEAD MANS HAND TR229840 XXL XL L M FULL ZIP HOOD £32.99
W = BONE SLASHER WR119606 XXL XL L M T-SHIRT AO £16.99
FREE PHONE
0500 000 880
Ref NAME CODE SIZES DESCRIPTION PRICE
X = BONE SLASHER TR262935 XXL XL L M S SHORTS £33.99
Y = DEATH METAL TR231800 XXL XL L M HOODIE £27.99
Z = NIGHT OF THE WOLVES DT166700 XXL XL L M LONG SLEEVE £13.99
1 = GAME OVER TR260600 XXL XL L M T-SHIRT £11.99
COMPLETE THE ORDER FORM BELOW, DETACH & POST TO US WITH YOUR CHEQUE OR POSTAL ORDER TO: SPIRAL DIRECT LTD, SPIRAL HOUSE, 29 - 35 GLADSTONE ROAD, CROYDON, SURREY, CR0 2BQ.
OR BY CREDIT CARD SIMPLY ORDER ON OUR FREEPHONE HOTLINE 0500 000 880 DURING 10AM & 8PM WEEKDAYS. WWW.SPIRALDIRECT.COM
Order Form
VISA MasterCard Maestro AMERICAN EXPRESS
BIZARRE MARCH 09
CODE PRODUCT SIZE QTY VALUE
EXAMPLE
T R 1 6 0 1 2 3 One Shoulder L 1 10.99
*PLEASE ADD 95P + £1 PER ITEM FOR POSTAGE & PACKAGING (E.G. 2 ITEMS = £2.95)
SPIRAL GUARANTEE!
FULL REFUND OR EXCHANGE WITHIN 10 DAYS OF PURCHASE IF YOU ARE NOT FULLY SATISFIED.
*P & P £ 0.95P +£1 PER ITEM
TOTAL £
PLEASE CONTINUE ORDER ON A SEPERATE SHEET IF REQUIRED
NAME TEL NO
PLEASE FILL ALL DETAILS IN CLEAR CAPITAL LETTERS
ADDRESS
POSTCODE COUNTRY
PAYMENT METHOD: *SIGNATURE *REQUIRED TO AUTHORIZE ORDER
PLEASE TICK THE APPROPRIATE BOX (MAKE ALL CHEQUES & POSTAL ORDERS (GBP) PAYABLE TO 'SPIRAL DIRECT')
CHEQUE(UK ONLY) POSTAL ORDER MASTERCARD VISA MAESTRO AMEX
CREDIT CARD NUMBER :
START DATE EXPIRY DATE ISSUE No CVV2 No.
CVV2 = THE LAST 3 DIGITS ON REVERSE OF CARD (4 DIGITS FOR AMEX)
SPEND OVER £20 & GET A QUALITY T-SHIRT FREE>>
MEN'S (BLACK) XL L M
LADIES' (BLACK) L M S